BARONESS COX

'The story of a woman of amazing energy, patent faith and commitment on a grand scale.' *Christianity*

'Manages to capture on paper the complex character of Caroline Cox.' *New Christian Herald*

'Read Baroness Cox for the descriptions of the suffering people of Nagorno Karabakh, Burma and the Sudan, and remember them each time you fill up your car with petrol.' *The Expository Times*

'Informative, balanced, lucid and fair.' *Renewal*

'Challenges complacency.' *Methodist Recorder*

Author and journalist Andrew Boyd has travelled with Baroness Cox to the Sudan to buy back slaves and expose the existence of the slave trade. He accompanied her to the beleaguered enclave of Nagorno Karabakh and to Eritrea, among the guerrilla forces of the exiled Beja Congress.

His searing eyewitness accounts have appeared in *The Sunday Telegraph*, *The Observer* and *The Guardian*, as well as Channel 4 News, BBC Radios 4 and 5 Live!, the World Service, and the international media. He has also covered conflicts in Liberia and Sierra Leone.

Andrew Boyd trained as a print journalist before moving into radio as a producer and news editor. Today he has his own video company, Crossfire Productions. He has lectured in journalism extensively and has produced the leading textbook on *Broadcast Journalism* (Focal Pres[...] *Dangerous Obsessions* (HarperCo[...] *Rumours* (HarperCollins, 1991).

Andrew Boyd has two childr[...] Hampshire.

Speak up for those who cannot speak for themselves,

for the rights of all who are destitute.

Speak up and judge fairly;

defend the rights of the poor and needy.

Proverbs 31:8–9 (NIV)

BARONESS COX

A Voice for the Voiceless

ANDREW BOYD

A LION BOOK

POLAND

It was an eight-hour journey from Wroclaw to Warsaw. It was made even longer by the fact that Caroline was forced to sit knee to knee with a secret policeman in the confines of a crowded railway carriage. 'Black Satchel', short and sullen with a sallow complexion, was giving her the eye. Caroline, in turn, presented him squarely with the book jacket of Daphne du Maurier's *Don't Look Now* and flicked through the pages as nonchalantly as possible. Difficult when your rucksack contains a bundle of banned Solidarity badges and you are travelling across Poland without a ticket...

ERITREA

The haul across the mountain was a roller-coaster ride over rocks as sharp as dragon's teeth. The Russian-made military truck grunted and wheezed like a soon-to-be extinct dinosaur of the desert, its olive drab all too visible against the sand-blasted boulders. It was a sitting target for a single soldier with a rocket-propelled grenade and an intimate knowledge of the terrain. Caroline opts to ride it out standing in the open back with the Beja Congress guerrillas. It means several hours of riding the truck like a surfboard as it sways and plunges over the mountain, ducking and diving to avoid the thorn trees, as their vicious two-inch spikes scree along the sides. Quite a pastime for a 59-year-old grandmother of six. She disembarks in Eritrea, dusty and bloodstained from a close encounter with a thorn bush. She sucks her bleeding fingers, grinning...

RUSSIA

The psychiatric hospital in Leningrad was brick-built and bare, looming over a courtyard of raw, exposed concrete... The small group of visitors was led inside the secure adolescent wing, along a bare corridor and into a dingy ward with grey walls devoid of decoration. Beside the few beds were piles of soiled brown mattresses. Igor was about 14, but small for his age. His thin, white face looked listlessly up at them from beneath a shock of brown hair. He was shabbily dressed and obviously drugged... he had tried to run away from the bullies at the orphanage, so they had locked him up in the psychiatric ward. His admission notes read: 'nothing abnormal detected'. Yet, scrawled in ball-point beneath was a single word: '*schizophrenia*'. Igor's face was pale and pointed. His eyes were dark and bruised. He looked at Caroline, and pleaded, 'Please will you find me a mother, I want to get out of here.' Caroline went out into the courtyard and wept...

NAGORNO KARABAKH

The pounding of artillery started up again. It took a moment or two to realise their jeep was the target. Anti-tank rounds were falling all around. The mountain road was a slash of ice and snow. The Armenian driver put his foot down, skidding and slewing frantically. The shells kept coming, and the gunner was getting their range. One exploded close enough to lift the back of the vehicle clear off the ground. Caroline was sitting on the left – the gun side. 'Just can't think why I volunteered to be on this side going back,' she said...

BURMA

Evidence was emerging of biological warfare. Many of the Karen people had gone down with a form of cholera, which they believed was linked with the use of plague-carrying weather balloons dropped into Karen territory. Soon afterwards, disease spread out in a pattern that could be traced along the watercourses from where the balloons and their attached devices had fallen. Caroline was shown one of these devices. It was a polystyrene box, some 18" by 8", with a depth of three to four inches. It had a battery and an electric contrivance inside but the name of the maker and an identification strip had been ripped off. 'Interesting. One for the scientists back home.' She promptly stuffed it into her rucksack and had it brought back on the plane as hand luggage...

SUDAN

Nothing could prepare her for what she found in Nyamlell... No sooner had their Cessna Caravan touched down, kicking up plumes of dust, than people emerged from all directions, relief written large on their faces. 'Thank God you've come,' said the Commissioner. 'We thought the world had completely forgotten us'... In the blackened ruins of their tukuls, remaining townsfolk line up to bear witness. 'We were armed with spears and they were armed with Kalashnikovs,' says Garang Amok Mou. 'My brothers were killed because they were [trying] to rescue their family'... When the 2,000 Arab militia swept in on horseback, they killed 82, mainly men; and left the old for dead. They put houses to the torch, stripped the village of personal possessions and rounded up the cattle. And herded behind the horses went 282 women and children – taken across the border and into slavery. Blind Abuk Marou Keer's children are among them. 'If I live,' she cries, 'I hope God will bring them back to me'...

Copyright © 1998 Andrew Boyd

The author asserts the moral right
to be identified as the author of this work

Published by
Lion Publishing plc
Sandy Lane West, Oxford, England
ISBN 0 7459 3735 7

Hardback edition 1998
Paperback edition 1999
10 9 8 7 6 5 4 3 2 1 0

A catalogue record for this book is available
from the British Library

Printed and bound in Great Britain by
Caledonian International Book Manufacturing, Glasgow

Contents

Preface

This revised and updated edition of *Baroness Cox: A Voice for the Voiceless* contains significant new evidence of modern-day slavery in Sudan. It also exposes a large-scale massacre carried out by Government forces. The slaughter of civilians – in the name of *jihad* – was undertaken in the mistaken belief that it could be kept from the eyes of the world. But in barring outside observers from the area, the Government of Sudan had not reckoned on Baroness Cox. Her eye-witness account of the aftermath of massacre makes harrowing reading.

This edition also reveals the collaboration between Sudan and Saddam Hussein in the production of weapons of mass destruction. Iraq is aiding its ally in the manufacture of mustard gas for use in Sudan's long-running civil war against the South.

This is the story of a remarkable woman. But as will already be clear, it is more than that. The story of Caroline Cox is interwoven with the stories of Sudan, Nagorno Karabakh and Burma. Her story and their stories make this a tale of nations in turmoil, a turmoil caused in part by the collapse of the British empire.

At the close of the Second World War, Britain withdrew from its colonies to lick its wounds. To offer independence was right and inevitable – over time. But Britain withdrew in haste. More than 50 years later, war still rages in Burma and Sudan because of that hasty abandonment. For these things Britain should apologize.

Today history is set to repeat itself. Oil has outlived empires to become a new colonialism. Oil plays a role in Sudan, as does gas in Burma, in stimulating foreign powers to favour tomorrow's rich trading partners over yesterday's impoverished allies. But there is another colonialism recorded here also – an aberration of Islam engaged in a holy war against humanity. It is the colonialism of the *jihad*, which is exposed here in all its naked brutality.

This book can be read on several levels. It is the collected adventures of a great English eccentric, an indefatigable reformer from the same mould as Wilberforce, with a wicked sense of humour, who risks her all in foreign lands. The geopolitical sweep against which her human rights campaigning is set gives this story an epic dimension. And for serious researchers, there are extensive and detailed footnotes.

Inevitably, politics plays a role, as does faith, and here I declare an interest. I share the Christian convictions of Baroness Cox, though our denominations are at opposite ends of the spectrum. Our political positions also differ.

But there is no intention to force on anyone either politics or religion. The political career of Lady Cox has been relegated to the appendix – at her insistence – so the voices of those who really matter, the oppressed and dispossessed, should not be drowned out in the din of controversy.

This is above all their story: the story of forgotten people in forgotten places, whose names are recorded here for us to remember. It is the story of ordinary, extraordinary, transcendent humanity caught up in, but not crushed by, these new colonialisms. This book is intended to make you weep and to make you rage – and to fill you with hope. It is *my* hope that it also stirs you to prayer and to action.

Christian Solidarity Worldwide can be contacted at PO Box 99, New Malden, Surrey, KT3 3YF. Tel: (0181) 942 8810.

My thanks to the many who have made this work possible; at Lion to Maurice Lyon and my editor Angela Handley; to Jenny Taylor and to my researchers: my wife and constant source of encouragement, Seren, and my friend Hazel Southam. Thanks to human rights campaigners John Eibner, Martin Panter, Stuart Windsor, Mervyn Thomas; to Alan Parra of the UN; to Christian Solidarity International and Christian Solidarity Worldwide; to Amnesty International; the US State Department; Human Rights Watch; Anti-Slavery International and Medical Aid for Poland. Thanks to John Marks; Jana Pearson; Congressman Frank Wolf; David Atkinson MP; Christopher Besse; Roger Scruton; Bernard Levin; Vanya Kewley; Myriam Guame; David Moller; Olivier Roy; Nick Banatvala; Bishop Maurice Wood; Richard Wilkins; Harald Lipman; Katherine Adler; Lidia Bialek and Peter Tatchell. In Karabakh and Armenia thanks to: Archbishop Torkom Manoogian; Bishop Parkev Martirosian; Zori Balayan; Robert Kocharian; Vazguen Sarkissian; Movses Poghossian; Gersyk Gabrialian; Galia Saoukhanin; Rouben Mangasarian and Vardan Hovnahessian. In Sudan and Eritrea, thanks to: Abuk Marou Keer; Aleu Akechak Jok; Adut Wol Ngor; Gino Aguer; Colin Nelson; Noon Anguon Mauyual; Deng Deng Gong; Akuil Garang; Bol and Mohammed Kuol; Aluat Majok; Chok Dut; Seedi Mohammed Hadal; 'Malachi'; Tewelde Tesfay; Thomas Cirillo; Mustapha Issa Omer; Omer Musa; Taha Ahmed Taha; Clement Deng; Simon Mayuat Bol; Omer Nur el-Dayem; Yemane Ghebreab; Jacob; Ali, and Andrew Allam. In the House of Lords, thanks to: Lord Pearson; Lord Longford and the late, lamented Lord Tonypandy. Grateful thanks also to Caroline's family: Robin, Pippa and Jonathan, and to the Battling Baroness herself, Lady Caroline Cox, without whom, for many, this world would be a lonelier place.

Andrew Boyd

Foreword

LORD TONYPANDY (former Labour MP, speaker of the House of Commons and latterly a crossbencher in the House of Lords):

I regard Caroline Cox as one of the great women of our generation – a 20th-century prophet. She has awakened the conscience of the House of Lords to the terrible challenges that face Christians in other lands. In Sudan, Christians have been crucified – unbelievable as it sounds in the 20th century – yet it has only caused concern amongst a handful, and they are the handful set on fire by Lady Cox.

I look with affectionate respect at one who I know suffers physical hardship in order to bring love and care to the hungry and the needy in other lands. Our Lord could do almost anything, but there is one thing he couldn't do: he couldn't walk past a suffering person who cried out. He had to stop. She is like that: trying to walk in the steps of our Lord and master. None of us does it exactly, but she does it to a degree which inspires me. She takes the gospel message into dark and dangerous places at great risk to her personal safety but with complete trust in the protection of the Lord. She has the courage of a lion.

She is everything one would hope to be oneself, but we are not – she is. That is why both sides of the House regard her as one of the most cherished members in this place. The roundness of her witness has ensured that what she does will endure. She is a remarkable woman making a remarkable contribution and I believe she is going to leave a mark in history.

(Lord Tonypandy died in September 1997.)

FRANK R. WOLF (US Congressman):

I've known Baroness Caroline Cox for a number of years. She's normally found in remote locations around the globe bringing hope to disconsolate people living in fear and despair. She is as likely to be seen in Sudan or Nagorno Karabakh as she is in London. As a former nurse, she has brought medical care to people living in the painful aftermath of battle and tiny children with only a flimsy grip on life.

Baroness Cox is a passionate and articulate spokesperson for those caught in the hell-holes of political and military struggle. She has testified before the US Congress, thereby sensitising Americans as well as those in her native England to the pain and suffering being endured by so many around the world.

Baroness Caroline Cox has dedicated her life to helping those that much of the world seems to have forgotten. She is the voice of those who are not being heard. She is the champion of men, women and children who have few others who even know of their travail. She is, indeed, on a lifetime mission of mercy, and I am proud to call her my friend.

PROFESSOR HRATCH ZADOYAN (from the citation for the Spirit of Armenia award):

From her very first perilous trip to Karabakh, Lady Cox gave voice to the voiceless, carried their story to the world and in doing so, and in returning time and again at great personal risk, she has given our people in Artsakh, as in Armenia, the hope and the determination to persist. If hope and faith and commitment are central to the struggle of Karabakh, and indeed to our nation's struggle, Lady Cox is our symbol of hope and our model of faith.

They sit with infinite patience, unnaturally still in the shade of the spreading mango tree, conserving every ounce of energy in the stupefying heat. They neither stretch, nor yawn, nor engage in conversation.

Their dark eyes betray a mixture of resignation and anxiety. The huddle of boys, young women and children have the eyes of the hunted, the look of prey. And they have learned the silence of fear: that survival depends upon remaining still, small and unnoticed.

Huddled around the twisted green trunk, glad of its strength and shelter, the slaves of Southern Sudan simply watch and wait for their redeemer.

Around the market in Manyiel, in rebel-held Bahr el-Ghazal, Arab traders peddle their tea, salt and gaudy clothing; a picture of sultry normality.

But one trader is conspicuous by his absence. His stock is here, beneath this tree, but the one known as Ibrahim is camera-shy. The one who trades in slaves is unwilling to show his face.

Instead, he sends his middleman to collect a million Sudanese pounds – cash in advance for 22 Dinka slaves. Ibrahim steals them to order from their Islamic captors in the North and sells them back to their families in the Christian and animist South.

A stinging rivulet of sweat slops from a saturated eyebrow and plops into my eye. I am here to observe the transaction, the handing over of a straining carrier bag filled with cash, donated by the human rights organization, Christian Solidarity International. It is acknowledged as a desperate measure to expose a desperate trade and return some women and children to their villages.

I clamber uncomfortably to my feet, blistered from our three-hour trek through the bush, and hobble for a closer look at the man who has been sent to clinch this deal in human livestock.

Rolling a milky white eye, our slave trader is gaunt and grinning in his white *djellaba* and skull cap. 'I am delighted to free slaves,' he beams, 'because these people are my brothers.' Even slavers, it seems, are schooled in the sound-bite.

But the instant altruism evaporates in the steaming Sudanese heat when I inquire about his plans for his share of the money: 'I will go with it and eat and drink from it,' he grins.

Beneath the tree, 13-year-old Bol Kuol squats on his haunches. His studied indifference cannot conceal the well of sadness in his eyes. His little brother Mohammed, who apes his posture, was born in captivity. Relatives scratched together the five cows demanded for their return, but could not afford to free Bol's mother. She remains in slavery. His father is dead – killed by the Arab raiders who captured them.

Aluat Majok was 12 when the men on horseback swept across the border for her and the other children. 'There were so many,' she says. Those who resisted were killed. Her master took her north into government territory and set her to work pounding grain. 'And when the wife went somewhere to market, the master call me to his room and I conceive this child.'

Bikit Osman, eight months old and naked save for a thread of beads around his waist, roots again for his mother's breast.

Hostilities between Arab and Dinka have been fought out by spear for centuries. But the Kalashnikov is a sinister innovation. Civil Commissioner Aleu Akechak Jok claims the government of Sudan had been handing out AK47s by the armful to his Arab neighbours and encouraging them to fight their 40-year-old civil war by proxy. The spoils are theirs for the taking: possessions, cattle – and human beings.

Eight miles from the market lies what remains of the village where the Commissioner is based, Nyamlell. Overlooking a bend in the River Lol, a tributary of the White Nile where fishermen wade to cast their nets, is a killing field.

'On 25 March, militia – Arabs – came in large numbers,' says Akechak Jok. 'They raided the village, looted all the properties, burned it down. Then they took children, women and girls towards the North.'

The Commissioner helped bury 30 of the dead in a deep latrine. Those who remain tend their wounded and wait for the Arabs to return. 'We are waiting under these trees to die,' says Adut Wol Ngor. When I ask how many militia came, she shrugs: 'The one who want to save his life cannot count all the horses.

'The children who refused to go with them, they kill them, and the children they accept, they tie them with rope and pull them behind their horses like cattle.'

Akuil Garang was stabbed with a spear, then caught in the side by a round from an AK47 for good measure. Two of her children were burned to death in their hut. Her third, six-year-old Atong, was taken into slavery.

Her eyes light up: 'The one who is dealing said the boy is alive. He said to prepare money to redeem this child. I will get money,' she tells me.

'Do you have any money?' I inquire.

'I have nothing,' she replies.

14

All are slaves. Those who were taken and those who remain. They have to begin again to get cattle to survive and then more cattle to pay off the slavers.

Christian Solidarity has agonized about handing over the money to the dealers in human flesh. 'We have no other option,' shrugs John Eibner, who flew out from CSI's headquarters in Zurich.

Representing CSI UK was Baroness Caroline Cox, a deputy speaker of the House of Lords. 'What would you do,' she flips the question back at me, 'if your child had been taken into slavery? Would you let them stay in slavery, or would you pay a price and buy back their freedom?'

Hands are shaken and the slaver stalks off with his ransom. One by one, those who are redeemed depart with their redeemers.

Adapted from an article by Andrew Boyd, 12 November 1995

Illustrations

MAPS

PLATES

The plate section can be found between pages 224 and 225.

*Photos are reproduced courtesy of the author, Andrew Boyd,
CSW and Baroness Cox.*

Part One

The Scarlet Pimpernel

'Every time it made my blood run cold. The first time we came was at night. It was floodlit. Every 100 yards there were gun turrets, with soldiers with their guns facing inwards. You felt you were entering a vast prison. Waiting to get through, you felt the atmosphere of intimidation and callous brutality begin to envelop you.'

Baroness Cox

ONE

Dodging the Doodlebugs

England, 1940

The little girl looked up from her tricycle and shielded her eyes against the summer sunlight. The bright blue sky over Plymouth was dotted with pretty puffballs, but the child was too young to be afraid, or suspect the significance of these signs in the sky. Britain was at war and the anti-aircraft gunners were at work. The three-year-old had been evacuated to the West country. Now war had followed her here in a game of join-the-dots across the sky.

Caroline Cox was born on 6 July 1937, into a small but contented upper-middle-class family in Highgate, north London. Early childhood was shared with brother Michael, three years her senior, and a succession of full-time nannies. As befitted a household with domestic staff, meals were enjoyed in splendid isolation in the nursery. Eating with parents was reserved for special occasions. Yet affection flowed and, despite the war that raged around them, theirs was a happy and sheltered upbringing.

Her father, Robert John McNeill Love, was an eminent surgeon and co-author of the standard text, *A Short Practice of Surgery*, by Bailey and Love. Early in the mornings, he would rise to prepare the latest edition of his book in his study, dressed with the formality of the period, in suit, waistcoat and tie. Wreathed in smoke from his pipe he would sit at the table in his large leather armchair, drawing inspiration through the substantial sash windows from the garden beyond. And when inspiration was absent, he would open the right-hand drawer of his desk and sneak out the length of salami he kept hidden from his wife and cut himself a slice.

Dorothy Ida, née Borland, was a gentle Scot with raven hair and striking good looks, who disapproved of her husband's eating habit which she was convinced would make him ill. The eminent surgeon paid lip-service to her wifely concerns and ate the salami nonetheless, though under conditions of strictest secrecy.

Dorothy was a product of her class and age: the intelligent woman whose professional career is quietly sidelined to pursue that of full-time wife and mother. She declined a place at Oxford, in preference for a teaching qualification from the Froebel Institute in Roehampton. She was later to lay that to one side, too. Gifted and creative, her inner frustration would eventually turn to intermittent depression.

With the onset of the Blitz, the McNeill Loves sought refuge, naturally enough, in south Devon. Both parents hailed from Devonport and had a family home in Newton Ferrers. Caroline's grandmother lived there, too, in a fisherman's cottage. The ensemble arrived just in time for the Blitz of Plymouth. They weathered that, then headed back to London right on cue to greet the first wave of doodlebugs. Enough was enough. Keeping the family together was seen as a personal challenge from Hitler. If they were going to die, they would die together, but there would be no further disruption of childhood.

Father was appointed a civil surgeon at Barnet General Hospital and bought an unremarkable pebble-dashed house in Potters Bar. When Caroline was five, she awoke one night to find her mother praying by the bed. A doodlebug was almost scraping the roof of the house. As her mother prayed, it passed over to fall and explode about a mile away.

Prayer was an unremarkable occurrence for this Christian household and so were flying bombs. The latter became a way of life, a commonplace hazard to be treated with a certain respect. 'There was a sort of intense interest as to when the doodlebugs might cut out,' recalls Caroline, 'but no panic.' She remembers a V1 sputtering into silence above them on the ridgeway towards Cuffley. Her father calmly slammed on the brakes of the Austin 7, hauled her out and threw her into a ditch.

A surgeon's stories

Robert McNeill Love saw service in the First World War, salvaging the victims of trench warfare serving in Mesopotamia and Gallipoli. The accounts of his adventures pervaded Caroline's childhood. Most vivid was his description of undertaking 40 amputations in a single night on board a hospital ship without a trace of anaesthetic. Mercifully, for his patients, he got it down to a fine art.

When the fighting shifted from that theatre of war many of his compatriots frittered away their time playing cards and drinking gin. But McNeill Love set himself to learn Arabic and passed an exam in it. The Army promptly employed him on goodwill missions to places few

Europeans had been before. He would roam Mesopotamia like a medical Lawrence of Arabia, undertaking such health care as he could. When word got out of his arrival villagers brought out their lame and their halt for healing. For this deeply religious man, the experience was bitter-sweet, as there were many he was ill-equipped to help.

One tale held a particular fascination for Caroline. Her father had been assessing the situation in a township and preparing to undertake what treatments he could when he awoke one morning to find himself surrounded by dying rats. He was in the middle of an outbreak of bubonic plague. Turning up the collar of his trench coat and tucking his trousers into his boots he did what he could to alleviate suffering and prevent the spread of infection. He isolated the township with himself inside it. To his surprise, he survived.

Towards the end of the epidemic he had an urgent message from the sheikh, saying his favourite wife had gone down with the plague, and could he please come and save her. According to local custom, if you wanted to go to heaven, you had to be sure that you died in your coffin. By the time he arrived, the favourite wife was already prostrate in her elaborate wooden box. McNeill Love examined her and found she did indeed have the plague, but only in its mildest form. There was no reason why she should die.

Summoning his best Arabic he tried to persuade her out of her coffin, but she was far too concerned about her place in Paradise to abandon it. McNeill Love sought an alternative solution. He surveyed his dwindling supply of drugs and his eyes alighted on just the thing. To the sheikh's favourite wife he administered a colossal dose of Epsom Salts. She was out of the coffin in ten minutes and never looked back.

The sheikh was so delighted that he presented McNeill Love with a set of carved silver cruets engraved with perfect copies of the doctor's signature, and an Arab stallion. The grey ran like the wind. He had never ridden a horse like it before and never would again. Too bad he had to leave it behind.

In another township he had been carrying out operations on cataracts. The chances of success were slimmer in those days, so McNeill Love carefully explained to all his patients that he could give no guarantees. An operation on an elderly man was not one of his success stories. That night, as he slept in a hut, some sixth sense woke him. As his eyes adjusted to the dark he saw the handle of the door turning slowly and a figure creep stealthily in. It was the man whose sight McNeill Love had been unable to save, and in his hand was an enormous knife.

Determined to take his revenge, he began to feel his way towards the bed. There was no room for McNeill Love to make his escape, so, as silently as he could, he rolled himself over against the wall and under the side of the bed. From his new vantage point he could see the man's legs, and above him could hear the pat, pat, pat of the blankets as the would-be assailant felt for a body to stab. Taking a firm grip of his ankles, McNeill Love brought him down and removed the knife. He disarmed him further by apologizing again for failing to save his sight, and then gave him back the knife. The man was so moved that McNeill Love had spared him that they became good friends.

Caroline was riveted by his stories: 'You could feel the fear as he described how this poor old blind man had been feeling on the bed to stab him to death.'

McNeill Love was a powerfully built man of above average height; an accomplished athlete of great stamina who represented the London Hospital in a variety of sports at first-team level. Above his expressive grey-green eyes was a full head of Brylcremed hair, parted on the left, which he retained until he died in his mid-80s. When Caroline's fiancé, Murray, was due to meet him for the first time she told him he would recognize her father by his green hair. Caroline's own hair, which she wears in a long bob secured by an Alice band, has traces of his ash-green hue, and it was from him that she inherited her remarkable stamina.

'Father had a good sense of humour and a taste for fun,' she recalls, 'but he could be very serious. He was a man who did not like pomp and circumstance but who had a great respect for the deep values [a phrase she uses often]. He would respect legitimate authority and courtesy, and render respect where it was due, but he wasn't one to embrace it for its own sake. He was Conservative with a large and a small "c". He could be warm and tender when people were vulnerable, but also very tough. He had a lot of courage. A man of great principle. Churchillian – that sums him up.'

But there was one principle against which Caroline was to later rebel: that of separate meals and separate circles for the children. For all the storytelling and geniality that pervaded her childhood home, there was a lack of intimacy and an occasional feeling of remoteness. And she has worked hard to swing the balance the other way with her own family. 'My parents were much more distant than I ever wanted to be from my own children,' she says. They reflected the middle-class lifestyle of their time.

The best times were during seaside holidays in Devon. Caroline has fond memories of fishing in Kelpie, their rowing boat, picnics, walks across Dartmoor, and assaults on Sheep's Tor. Some way up the southern side of this granite outcrop is a feature known to the locals as Pixies' Cave. During the Civil War a fleeing Royalist managed to conceal himself for days while Roundhead troops searched for him in vain. McNeill Love used to clamber up Sheep's Tor ahead of his children and sneak into Pixies' Cave through the hidden entrance. He would call out, while Caroline and her brother, Michael, scrambled round the rocks trying to find him. 'We could hear him teasing us,' she says, 'but could never find the entrance.' Trips to Pixies' Cave became one family tradition which Caroline did pass on to her own children.

Her mother Dorothy had a talent for mimicry and entertained the children by imitating broad Devon and Scottish accents. Both sides of the family had migrated from Scotland. The Loves were of the clan Mackinnon – Caroline was told her paternal great-grandfather had been Provost of Perth – while Dorothy's side came from Kirkudbright. She passed on her Celtic good looks to Michael, much to the envy of Caroline, who took after her father. 'Mike had that same lovely black hair and fresh complexion. I got landed with my father's nose and colour scheme.'

Her mother is remembered as gracious and warm, clad in tweeds or plaids, twin sets and pearls, her black hair turning grey with the onset of the years. Dorothy was brought up in Plymouth and went to Plymouth High School for girls. Caroline still treasures the books her mother won as prizes. Her creativity was encouraged by her Froebel teacher-training and she would set about pieces of plywood with a fretsaw to produce Beatrix Potter characters for the children.

Take courage – that's an order

Life in Potters Bar was an interlude before moving back to Highgate, to a substantial house in Stormont Road, near Hampstead Heath, close to the area known as Millionaire's Avenue. It was an idyllic home for a seven-year-old, hidden behind a high privet hedge, with an orchard at the back and a swing, tennis court, hen run and summer house. Inside was a playroom which metamorphosed to incorporate table-tennis, then billiards, as the children grew.

But being a younger sister had its drawbacks. Both parents were strict and Caroline always felt she got the blame for her brother's misdemeanours. He walked free, leaving her to take the flak. But the petty injustices of childhood never managed to dent the affection between brother and sister.

Between them, they saved up and bought a pony, a strawberry roan called Trixie. Later, Mike was to own a racehorse, a beautiful but temperamental creature by the name of Corn Lore, which he took steeplechasing. Being the elder brother, it was always Mike who got to ride Trixie in gymkhanas while Caroline was relegated to outings when Trixie wasn't already booked. The highlight of the year was when they could each hire a pony and go riding with their father in Devon along the Membland Drives. Built as a carriageway, this coastal ride near Newton Ferrers followed the edge of the estuary and cut through the woods before emerging onto the spectacular open cliffs.

There were more significant tensions in the home than sibling rivalry. Both parents had potentially volatile tempers and Dorothy's lack of fulfilment became more apparent as Caroline grew older.

The house was maintained by a plethora of servants. Apart from the nanny there was the cook, housekeeper, handyman and gardener, and the Austin 7 eventually made way for a chauffeur-driven Rover. Although he could have afforded better, McNeill Love had a distaste for all things flashy and pretentious. Running the household was the expected role for a woman of her station and Dorothy managed her task with quiet efficiency, although one suspected her heart was never fully in it. Marriage, too, ran along conventional lines. 'It was a compartmentalized relationship,' Caroline recalls. 'The woman's place was in the home.' Father was a member of the local shoot, and that occupied most Saturdays. His work and his play were kept separate from the world prescribed for Dorothy. There was happiness for her in the one day a week set aside for each other, but their rigid existence fostered a growing sense of loneliness.

Caroline's schooldays were happily spent at Channing School with other children of similar social standing. But at the girl guides it was different. Here she mixed with a much wider range of children, and found them to her liking. She took pleasure in the camping, hiking and other outdoor pursuits, and followed in the family tradition to take up first aid. The guide company patrols were named after flowers. One was called the Scarlet Pimpernel. Their motto sticks in the mind: 'Do good by stealth.'

Both Caroline's parents were Anglicans, turning from Presbyterian non-conformity before she was born because of an appreciation for the beauty of the liturgy and the sacraments; loves passed on to their daughter. Churchgoing was central to family life. Mother taught in the Sunday School and father was a District Commissioner in the Scouts, which was more overtly Christian in those days. He knew Baden-Powell and took many scouting awards. But family prayers were confined to corporate acts of worship in church.

Caroline's personal faith grew throughout her childhood – a process of evolution, rather than revelation. She took her prayers seriously, and recalls kneeling on the floor, once on the brown linoleum of the breakfast room and again on the cold white tiles of the kitchen, to give her life to God.

The biblical story of Samuel, familiar from Sunday School, captured her imagination. At first Samuel failed to recognize God's calling. He was told to go back and listen. Caroline made a conscious effort to hear God. She prayed to be open to his will. 'If God was calling me, I hoped I would be responsive.' Her prayer was, 'If you want, send me – where you want.'

Her confirmation at the age of 11 remains significant. It was a clear decision; a choice, rather than a yielding to any family expectations. She possesses her confirmation text to this day and still draws comfort from it, 'especially when I am about to go into one of the more hairy situations, when I have my fit of faithless, fearful dread'. The text is Joshua 1:9 (KJV):

Have not I commanded thee? Be strong and of a good courage; be not afraid, neither be thou dismayed: for the Lord thy God is with thee whithersoever thou goest.

'I used to latch on to the second half,' she says, 'but when I get really terrified before some of the missions I remember the first bit: "Have I not commanded you?" It is not just a comfort, it is actually a requirement. It's an order.'

During her early teens Caroline believed she had a calling to the mission field, which came while she was praying in her bedroom. She describes it as a calling into her, rather than a calling out from her. It was not something she had wanted and was seeking God for, but a desire that seemed to be planted inside her. Alongside this grew the idea of a career in nursing. She kept her missionary aspirations to herself, but her vocationally oriented family warmed to the vision of Caroline as a nurse. Meanwhile her school had other ideas. Caroline had attained a distinction in S-level English and Channing was steering her towards a scholarship at Cambridge. But she describes her parents as 'allergic to blue-stockings', and the pressure was effectively counterbalanced at home.

The decision to opt out of academic life went down extremely badly at Channing. Caroline was now head girl and the expectations of the school were upon her. 'They looked on me with absolute horror,' she recalls. 'I became the black sheep of the school.' The headmistress, Elizabeth Haigh, was held in great affection by Caroline. 'She was mortified that I was going into nursing. I was told that one of the last things she said before she retired was, "For goodness sake, make sure that Caroline McNeill Love goes to university."'

That she was ever chosen as head girl came as a surprise to Caroline, not least because of what she describes as her pathological shyness, a trait inherited from her mother. A highly effective coping mechanism kept it from others, and still does. She was made to take diction at Channing, and diction meant public speaking. From her earliest schooldays she recalls being made to stand up and give speeches in front of the whole school. 'I remember the sheer agony of it. I was absolutely terrified. I still am. Nothing changes.' The feeling of apprehension remains whenever she addresses the House of Lords or is called upon to speak in public. 'I dread it,' she says. 'It is like a cloud on my horizon for days ahead and I feel physically sick.' Her pulse rises and she occasionally suffers from palpitations.

The Prankster

The other factor she felt would disqualify her in the head girl stakes was her reputation as a prankster: 'I was always playing practical jokes and being sent out of the classroom,' she says. She once found a bird skull in the playground with a wicked beak that resembled a bird of prey. The lower fifth was divided into two classrooms in the afternoon: one half repaired downstairs to the arts studio; the rest wrestled with Latin in the room directly above. Caroline usually took a seat by the window to relieve the tedium. That day, she threaded a length of string through the skull and surreptitiously lowered it out of the window, until it appeared in full view of the class below. The only person not privy to the sight was the arts master, Mr Wallace, who taught with his back to the window. The moment gales of laughter floated up from below, she whisked the skull up and away, so when Wallace whirled round, he was greeted by serene normality. As soon as he regained his stride, she repeated the performance. Caroline stifled her mirth about the imagined scene below, and only later let on that she was its author. That and similar stunts contributed to her popularity at school and did nothing to diminish her standing among the staff.

Her career as a practical joker continued unabated into nursing, which she took up at the age of 18, following in her father's footsteps to the London Hospital. The regime was strict. Student nurses were drilled with military precision in an atmosphere of stern formality. It was a challenge to the most dedicated mischief-maker.

Caroline was in residence at Tredegar House, the preliminary training school at the London Hospital of Nursing, when she decided to stage a stunt using an anatomical model, affectionately known to the student nurses as

Annie Brown. The obliging Mrs Brown could be pulled apart for nursing practice. Her abdomen would unscrew to permit the bloodless removal by would-be surgeons of various bodily parts. Caroline thought it was high time Mrs Brown had the experience of pregnancy, so she sneaked down one evening to hide a doll inside her, anticipating the expression of the nurse who would make the discovery at some later date.

But the next morning, to her horror, the Head of the Training School announced at breakfast that the matron of St Thomas' Hospital, their rival institution, was coming to watch the class at work to compare their practices. The Head of the Training School was the ultra-strict Miss Peggy Daly, who inspired terror and respect. Worst of all, the demonstration was to take place that morning in the practical room where the baby doll had been neatly installed in the abdomen of Mrs Brown. There was no opportunity to steal in there and remove it. The nurses were informed in no uncertain terms that they were representing their hospital and were expected to turn out in clean, starched aprons with shiny shoes to provide an unrivalled demonstration of meticulous nursing.

Miss Daly strode into the practical room with the matron of St Thomas' beside her. Two student nurses were selected to sit Mrs Brown in the proper position of a patient recovering from a mastectomy. The bed was perfectly made and, by the book, the nurses addressed Mrs Brown and began to move her with clinical precision. Then, suddenly, emerging from the depths, came a muffled cry. Perplexed looks were exchanged. Once again the nurses carefully resumed their textbook manoeuvres. Again came the cry, muffled but unmistakable; a thin wail; a single distinguishable word: 'Mama!' And each time Mrs Brown was shifted her stomach repeated its cry.

The astonishment on Miss Daly's face turned to thunder. Caroline didn't know where to hide. Several more plaintive calls cut through the demonstration. Blushing furiously, Caroline stepped forward and apologized, saying, 'I think I can explain this', before performing a Caesarean section in front of the assembly to retrieve the offending offspring from deep within Mrs Brown. 'I thought I would be expelled from nursing for ever,' she grins. Instead, the nurses elected her set leader, much to Miss Daly's chagrin. 'I was always getting into trouble, yet for some reason found myself in positions of responsibility.'

An unbearable loss

By now, Mike was 21, a graduate in agriculture of Magdalene College, Cambridge; an easy-going, athletic six-footer, with a sense of fun –

straightforward, decent and kind. He was a regular at cross-country events on Corn Lore, a formidable beast which Caroline, in the last of her school days, had had to exercise in his absence. Mike and his father both loved the land, and when McNeill Love senior retired as a surgeon he bought a farm in Hertfordshire for Mike to take over and run. Not that McNeill Love was ready for his dotage. Despite the services of a full-time farm manager and farm-hand he retained an active involvement. He named each of his cows individually after shops with double-barrelled names. One was Dickens; another was Jones. Mike had already started a pig farm around the back and fought their quarter furiously against the ignorant who failed to take them for the clean, intelligent, affectionate creatures they are. Mike was a Cambridge half-blue in royal tennis. He was still playing when he graduated; which made his death months later all the more of a shock.

It was a kind of Hodgkin's disease which turned into leukaemia. Caroline was 19 and Mike had just undergone a course of radiotherapy and was getting plenty of rest. Going back to see him at all had been difficult, as student nurses were usually only entitled to a single day off per week. Caroline was sitting in the drawing room of their William and Mary farmhouse at Brickendon, near Hertford, when she was surprised to hear Mike coming down the polished wooden stairs. It was too much for him and he fell. His bones, weakened by his treatment, could not take the fall, and both femurs shattered.

Caroline was grief-stricken. Her parents had gone to Canterbury for the day, leaving her to look after her brother. 'It was grim they came back to that.' Mike died soon afterwards, at the age of 22. He was buried in a country churchyard in Newton Ferrers. 'We were very good friends and very close,' says Caroline. 'I still miss him.' Her loss is self-evident from her face. 'There is one word which sums him up well, which is: valiant. He was incredibly brave. He knew he was dying but would never admit it to his parents, because he thought it would make it worse for them. He was a huge loss to the family.'

It is difficult to imagine how things could have been much worse. When Mike died, the farm became a broken dream. And for Dorothy his death came as an unbearable loss. The depression she had struggled with since the children left home deepened. It would reveal itself in mood swings and sudden flashes of anger, which Caroline found disturbing. She felt it incumbent to go home to visit her mother whenever she had a day off. But when she said goodbye she knew she was leaving a vacuum. 'When Mike died, her life emptied.'

Watching the progress of her mother's depression left its mark on

Caroline. It hurt all the more because there was nothing she could do about it. After Mike's death when she returned to the farm, she would sometimes find her mother weeping. Within three years, Dorothy, too, was dead.

There had been nothing for her to fall back upon. Her teaching career had been nipped in the bud. 'She would have made a wonderful teacher,' says Caroline, 'she had so much potential. I'm personally very thankful that I come from a generation where women are much freer and encouraged to develop their own interests.' Her mother died at the age of 61.

Poetry in the rhubarb patch

Caroline met Murray Cox while she was still a student nurse at the London Hospital's Brentwood annexe in Essex. She had just turned 19 and was facing her first night duty on the TB ward with some apprehension. Tasked with covering for casualty she was responsible for phoning for the house surgeon to deal with patients as they were brought in. Her very first case left her speechless with embarrassment. It was a little boy who had a stricture of the penis.

Caroline had to phone the house officers in their mess, and was well aware of their reputation for rowdiness. 'This is student nurse McNeill Love speaking, could you come down to casualty?' Not unreasonably, the house officer inquired why. Caroline struggled to recall the technical term but it eluded her. All she could blurt out was, 'There's a boy here who has trouble with his penis.'

Back down the phone came gales of laughter as the house officer relayed her embarrassed call to his colleagues. But what aroused his curiosity was her name, McNeill Love. Here was the daughter of the author of every young surgeon's set text. When he hurried over to see her, Caroline had to remind him firmly that there was a baby boy in some discomfort who had a prior call on his attentions. From that moment, Murray went out of his way to be around her. Suddenly, the rarefied presence of a neuro-surgeon on the TB ward became less of an oddity. Murray was six-foot tall, possessed of a shock of wavy hair, brown eyes and classical good looks, and, needless to say, was the object of no little gossip on the wards. The handful of eligible young men at the annexe drew the attention of student nurses like wasps to a jam-jar.

'I couldn't believe it was happening,' says Caroline. While romance was the staple of most conversations, the sheer imbalance of women to men made turning words into deeds virtually impossible. Besides, anything more than talk would be strictly frowned upon. Marriage was out of the question.

To cap it all, Murray was six years her senior. His younger brother Alister had recently become engaged to someone older than Caroline, and his parents had been dismayed that she was too young. It looked like a hiding to nothing.

But romance knows no bounds. When they were both on night duty, Murray stayed up to join her for her lunch break between 1 and 2 a.m. and they would meet in the moonlight – and to blazes with the scandal. 'Nobody would believe it,' says Caroline, 'but we used to read poetry to each other in the rhubarb patch.'

The weight of official disapproval began to bear down after Murray was discovered – once again – apparently at a loose end in the women's TB ward. The night sister raised her eyebrows and, with not a neuro-surgical patient in sight, inquired as to what Mr Cox was doing on the ward.

Their nocturnal trysts continued, only with rather more caution. Fortunately, the night sister timed her rounds with clockwork precision between 10 and 11 and again at the end of the night shift. Murray agreed that discretion was the better part of valour and would make himself scarce before 10. The annexe had its own early-warning system – an echoing concrete corridor, known as 'the Hard', with a prefabricated wall adjoining. One night, the two were sipping their hot chocolate surrounded by sleeping TB patients when unmistakable footsteps began to reverberate down the Hard. With indecent haste, Caroline bundled Murray into a convenient cupboard.

No sooner had the door shut behind him than the ward sister strode into the room to make her inspection. Caroline's face was a picture of deferential innocence. Then, suddenly, from the cupboard came an enormous crash. Stumbling in the dark, Murray had sent 28 food trays and 28 sets of assorted metal cutlery cascading to the floor.

Ward sister and nurse started in unison. 'What on earth is that, student nurse McNeill Love?'

'I think it's that cat, sister,' offered Caroline.

Whether the ward sister believed her or not, she sagely decided to leave the cupboard – and its contents – to Caroline.

On another occasion, the sister had completed her round and Caroline was expecting her usual house call from Murray. She filled a substantial bladder syringe with water and set up an ambush behind the door of the sterilizing cupboard. Soon there were footsteps, and as the figure appeared she blasted a syringe-full of ice-cold water straight in the ear. While the figure was reeling damply in a state of total disorientation, Caroline realized it was a case of mistaken identity. She had assaulted the night sister, whose starched lace cap was limp and dripping. Caroline used the cover of her confusion to beat a hasty retreat, hurrying off to tend a patient before the sister could gather her senses and formally identify her assailant.

Together, those incidents could have brought an end to a promising career, but fortunately for Caroline, the professionally strict sister possessed a sense of humour and a streak of pure humanity. Nothing was ever said about the ambush.

The sexual chemistry was fizzing, their souls were satisfied with a mutual love of Browning and Housman, and they were able to share in matters of the spirit as well. Both were committed Christians, for whom faith was at the forefront of life. Murray was the son of a Methodist minister and graduate of St Catharine's College, Cambridge, where he developed a love for Evensong in the English choral tradition. From this sprang a warmth and an openness towards the Anglican liturgy. Although he was becoming a Methodist lay reader, Murray took confirmation so they could share the sacraments together, an act of generosity for which Caroline remains grateful. They were engaged within four months of their first meeting. But marriage would have to wait until Caroline finished her training. She bade her final farewell to out-patients on a Thursday afternoon and they were married the following Saturday, on 10 January 1959, at St Giles-in-the-fields, London. The church was packed.

TWO

Baptism of Fire

'The coronary on the left'

The wind whistled up the filthy open staircase of the concrete tenement in Whitechapel. The young woman in the nurse's uniform was pleased to get out of the draft and into the corridor. Her footsteps echoed off the stained concrete floor. Behind each door she passed was a family. And at the end, to serve them all, was a single, heavily soiled toilet with a makeshift door that made a mockery of privacy. Adjacent stood a single cracked washbasin with a single cold tap. Water was running down the wall.

Caroline tapped at one of the doors. It was opened, and she was beckoned inside. Beside a large bed was a table with a newspaper for a cloth. There was little else to speak of. The family of five lived in that one room.

The East End of London was where Caroline's father had trained, in the same hospital as Sir Frederick Treves, the doctor who tended the Elephant Man. McNeill Love later combined his NHS work with a private consultancy, but often waived his fees for patients who could not afford them. As a District Commissioner of Scouts, he took slumland boys out of the city for their first experience of the countryside. Life in leafy Highgate was acknowledged to be a privileged existence. McNeill Love had a saying: 'In bearing the burden of others, your own are less hard to bear.' The ethos sustained him during the illness and death of his son. Caroline grew up to make the Protestant work ethic her own.

Overarching this was a continuing sense of calling which she believed would lead overseas to the mission field. But for the moment, it drew her to the decrepit social housing of Whitechapel. 'It was bleak and it was dirty,' she recalls, 'yet, when the kids went to school they looked smarter and more respectable than my children ever did. Such dignity amid such poverty really did hit me.'

Almost overnight her politics swung towards socialism. She was neither an activist nor a party member, but her allegiance shifted decisively. 'You

31

can't nurse in the East End and read sociology and be anything but a Labour voter,' she later told *The Sunday Times*.[1] 'Father was not amused.' He had seen the same sights and felt similarly compelled to respond, but his politics, as his outlook, remained staunchly Conservative. It was not something he talked about; it was something he was. He would have approved of the saying that if you are not a Socialist at the age of 20 you haven't a heart; if you are not a Conservative by the time you are 30, you haven't a brain. Rather than face a family rift, Caroline decided to keep her burgeoning passion for equality and social justice to herself.

Caroline and Murray decided to start their family immediately, and Robin came along 11 months later. Within 18 months of the wedding, Caroline was diagnosed as having tuberculosis, possibly as a result of caring for TB patients during her training. She was confined to Edgware General Hospital and remembers looking around the ward and thinking, 'Am I really going to see nothing else for six months?'

Trying to find carers to look after Robin proved to be a nightmare. But what Caroline feared most was that Robin would have forgotten her entirely by the time she came out of hospital. She left a baby in a pram and returned home to find a toddler. To her delight Robin stepped straight up to her, took her hand and walked her up the path of their home at 146 Stag Lane, Kingsbury.

It was their second married home, and quite a contrast to their first, a small rented flat above a fish shop in a Hampstead garden suburb. Their fortunes changed when Murray took up partnership in a general practice in Kingsbury. The family home now boasted four bedrooms and a GP's surgery at one end.

Caroline held on to her expectation of going to the mission field. Murray was sympathetic and a husband and wife pairing looked probable. But the tuberculosis put paid to that. At the end of six months she was left with a cavity in her kidney, which effectively ruled out spending any length of time in a hot country. Under dehydration, kidney stones can form in cavities and lead to acutely painful renal colic. A country like Sudan would provide the perfect hot-house for such a condition to flourish. Murray and Caroline were forced to accept that missionary life was not perhaps, after all, God's will.

In 1962, three years after the birth of Robin, came Jonathan. Pippa followed in August 1965. Robin was given the middle name Michael, after Caroline's brother. He later adopted by deed poll his mother's maiden name, which would otherwise have died out with her father. The business of raising a family ruled out nursing, so Caroline ploughed her energies into education instead.

She became a London University external student at Regent Street Polytechnic reading sociology, which she somehow managed to shoehorn into her evenings. When she took her Part One she was so heavily pregnant she could only hope the chair would not be fixed to the desk in the examinination hall, otherwise she would never be able to squeeze in. Six years on, she emerged with three children and a degree. Caroline had shown early academic promise, taking two A and S levels with two further As at Channing. Her tendencies as a polymath were revealed in the combination of arts and science, along with classics and modern language.

It was the shortcomings of her nursing training that drew her towards sociology. In her experience, patients were often referred to as objects, rather than subjects: Mrs Smith became 'the coronary in the fourth bed on the left'. Psychology had been skipped through in the curriculum and sociology was conspicuous by its absence. No attempt was made to understand the social and cultural context of the patient, even if it had a bearing on their problems and their willingness to seek care. 'There was a big gap,' says Caroline. 'It meant we couldn't respond to the totality of the patient's needs.' To help fill that gap she went on to write the textbook *Sociology: An Introduction for Nurses, Midwives and Health Visitors*.[2]

The book was an attempt to relate sociology directly to clinical practice. It aimed to help nurses establish a better rapport with their patients, by understanding more clearly who they were and where they were coming from. It also encouraged carers to reach out into the community to help those who, by culture and background, might avoid medical care. *Sociology* went through many reprints and was eventually translated into Swedish.

Caroline graduated in 1968 with a first-class honours degree, which she described as 'unreal – a bombshell'. One of the external examiners tipped her the wink that she might do well, but she could scarcely believe the outcome. She was hanging out nappies on the line and thinking, 'If I have got a first, I can't believe it! But I want to offer it to you, God, for your service.' Then the phone rang and it was the Polytechnic, congratulating her on being one of only three out of more than 800 to get top honours. With the bit between her teeth she went on to take a Masters degree in economics. It took a further two years, the same way, studying part-time in the evening after working full-time as a mother.

Like every parent, she wanted to pass on the best of her childhood memories to her offspring. One family tradition she maintained was that of the seaside holiday in Devon, complete with their own small sailing boat. Robin well remembers one incident which she would probably prefer him to have forgotten. Caroline was wading out to the rowing boat in Newton

Ferrers and had seriously underestimated the sheer muddiness of the operation. 'She was up to her waist in slime and mud,' recalls Robin. It was dark and the path was seldom used and secluded. To clean herself up, she peeled off all her clothes apart from her top, and then sent the children up to get some fresh things from the hotel. 'Mum was standing in the bushes with nothing on from the waist downwards when the inevitable happened,' says Robin. 'I think the passer-by must have thought she was a sailor's friend from three centuries ago. He was quite surprised.'

Into the cauldron

The constraints of family life and all this education conspired to turn Caroline from a nurse into an academic. She took her first lecturing post at North Western Polytechnic, blissfully unaware of the trouble in store. In 1971, after a merger with Northern Polytechnic it was renamed the Polytechnic of North London, boasting 7,000 students and an academic staff of 550.

After a year she was promoted to senior lecturer, which she describes with hindsight as an attempt to bring her into line. At the time it wasn't evident, but from the beginning she found much about the place which puzzled and disturbed her.

During a sociology seminar several students openly stated that they had come to the college to 'create a Marxist cell' and protested at being taught anything but Marxism. Another student in her third year, when asked to consider a variety of sociological perspectives, complained bitterly, 'We have already been taught the truth [i.e. Marxism]. If you criticize it, what *do* we believe?'

One afternoon, shortly after taking up her post, Caroline was sitting in her office when a first-year student rushed through the door in floods of tears. She explained that she was due to give a seminar paper at two o'clock that afternoon. She had just been to the canteen and had watched the lecturer and other students in her seminar group reading her essay and roaring with laughter. As she looked on they tore it to shreds. She couldn't face them. Caroline wondered what on earth she could have written. It turned out to be a straightforward and unremarkable piece about the family. What her tutor had been angling for was a devastating critique on family values. Her essay had called down the ridicule and scorn of the Marxists.

Another student was already living on her nerves because she had recently watched her husband shot dead on the streets of New York. She submitted a seminar paper which also received the full hard-left treatment. She was labelled a bourgeois bag for failing to rubbish the family and family values.

A little later, when Caroline was in the cloakroom, a student came in, caught her eye, and glanced over her shoulder to make sure no-one was listening. Once she was sure she was out of earshot she unburdened herself. 'I must come to see you,' she blurted. 'I'm having real difficulty maintaining my Christian faith while studying sociology.' Caroline said the student was welcome to see her any time. 'But I daren't be seen entering your office,' the student replied. 'All the other staff will get at me and say, "Why are you going to see that fascist pig?"'

'I was slightly surprised,' says Caroline, 'because at the time I was voting Labour.' In the end she had to escort the student off the premises because the student was so terrified of what the other staff would do to her for talking things over with Caroline. 'I began to feel this was not what Higher Education was about.'

What higher education *is* about, she believes, is the freedom to pursue the truth while remaining self-critical and open to new ideas – and then being able to test those ideas against all available evidence. 'What I saw going on around me was real intimidation,' she says, 'academic blackmail and the use of brutal tactics against students who were not conforming to the prevailing orthodoxy.'

'Racist... fascist...'

Before long, the college was swept by a series of student occupations. The battle lines were drawn over the impending appointment of a new director, Terence Miller, who like a red rag to a bull, had been Principal of University College, Rhodesia, during the days of Ian Smith. His opposition to Smith's policies resulted in his near-dismissal. Yet the same man was described in the Student Union Handbook as 'an incompetent, reactionary, authoritarian buffoon'.

Mr Miller was forced to make his first formal entrance to the Polytechnic through a window. It was the only way to circumvent the human barrier of student demonstrators in the corridor. And when the governors finally called a meeting to appoint him, militant students climbed the fire escape outside and let loose a barrage of fire extinguishers through the air vents. The governors were forced to retreat in disarray.

That was just the beginning. The designation ceremony of the new director was in November 1972. It was to become known in student circles as the denigration ceremony. The event at the Queen Elizabeth Hall turned into an angry, noisy eruption of student power. Trouble loomed from the start. Police were in evidence outside, but there were none in the building. Students from the hard-left poured in to outnumber all others. Soon after the start they were on their feet, ripping up their programmes and flinging them into the air. Speeches were to be made by the Chairman of the Court of Governors Brian Roberts, the Under-Secretary of State for Education Norman St John Stevas, the impending director Terence Miller, and the President of the Students Union Terry Povey. What happened is recorded in *Rape of Reason*:

> Students shouted abuse as the main speakers arrived. There was ugly heckling of the speech by Brian Roberts, but his words could be heard. During Norman St John Stevas' speech the shouting from the student phalanx in the audience (about 200) grew deafening, completely drowning out his words... Terry Povey claimed the designation should not take place, and was ushered off the platform by the director. The sound now rose to a stupendous volume – the students screaming, chanting, throwing paper, clapping, stamping their feet, kicking the metal backs of the chairs. During the succeeding speech by the director, Terence Miller, the hall resounded to the roar of the slogans, '*Racist... fascist... racist... fascist...*' making it impossible to hear anything else at all.[3]

Most of the hall joined in. In vain, the governors cranked up the loud-speakers, but it was an unequal battle. Having worked up a hunger, the demonstrators surged as a pack to the room where tea was laid out and devoured the lot. When the official guests eventually made their dazed appearance they were greeted by debris.

Student vigilantes

In October 1972 the students occupied Ladbroke House, a converted factory close to Arsenal Football Club. It housed two radical departments: sociology and social work, and two conservative ones: law and accountancy. The occupation was mobilized by a collective which included members of staff. They took over everything from the telephone exchange to the library. The collective met to decree what could and could not be taught during the occupation. A blackboard was erected in the foyer of Ladbroke House, slating the programme of alternative education for the day that had been approved by the collective. The menu included France 1968, Permanent Revolution, Perspectives for the British Class Struggle, and the Greenham Common Women.

The target of the occupation was, as ever, the new director Terence Miller, who had been cast as a racist and fascist by the student body. Miscast, in Caroline's view: 'He had been nearly kicked out of Ian Smith's Rhodesia for helping black students, so in no way was he a racist. He fought in the battle of Arnhem and saw many friends slaughtered around him. He risked his life to fight fascism. The occupation was utterly built on lies.'

As the uprising gathered momentum, Caroline met her students early in the day. She asked them whether they wanted to go ahead with the class. It could mean confrontation with student vigilantes, who were breaking up classes not deemed to be 'alternative education'. Exams were looming and a number of mature students who had made sacrifices to be there were impatient to continue. The class and Caroline made their way to the seminar room, and she placed her chair squarely in front of the door.

After about 30 minutes a band of vigilantes turned up and hammered on the woodwork, demanding to know what was going on. Caroline opened the door the merest crack and informed them it was a BSc in Sociology, and not alternative education. 'It's what I'm here to teach,' she said, 'and what I'm determined to teach. This is my responsibility and I will continue to do so, and if you want to stop me, you are going to have to knock me off my chair. If I get hurt in the process I will see that you are personally liable.'

At that, she banged the door as convincingly as she could, given a mere quarter of an inch of leverage. She resumed her teaching about the latest theories of deviance, which, as she remarked to the class, seemed appropriate at the time, to muffled cries of, 'We'll be back, dearie.'

The next 15 minutes were tense and concentration was difficult. The period was almost completely over before enough students could be marshalled to break up the class. Caroline was perched on the chair, trying to hold the door shut, when about 14 of them burst in, knocking her over. She took a light bruising, but her main concern was for her students. 'They subjected that group of decent, hard-working, conscientious students to about half-an-hour of vitriolic verbal abuse.'

The student magazine *Fuse* described a similar operation to break up a law lecture:

Law students barricaded the door to the lecture room and wouldn't let occupying students in to discuss the broken agreement. The occupiers eventually forced their way in, but the offending students still wouldn't listen and the lecturer continued. Banging on the metal lockers outside the lecture room had no effect so it was decided that it was about time the Rolling Stones should intervene at full blast. The lecture ceased, with one female student running out in hysterics.[4]

One of Caroline's sociology students was the young Peter Tatchell, who went on to run unsuccessfully for Parliament in 1983 and become a key figure in OutRage!, the militant gay organization which names homosexuals to force them to go public.

Tatchell describes the mood among the students as 'verging on insurrectionary', and the atmosphere at the Polytechnic as 'exhilarating'. Though not involved in student politics, he joined in a number of campaigns. He describes Caroline as a professional, but lacking the warmth and friendliness of most of the other staff. He formed the firm impression that she didn't like students.

'I can't remember a single occasion when we agreed about anything,' he says. 'She was always very civil to me, but not easily approachable. Never impolite, but always rather correct and cold.

'Caroline was fairly fixed in her ideas. She drew the battle lines very sharply and didn't seem willing to allow give or take. She never came across as having much understanding of the grievances of the students. There were some staff who were also quite right-wing, but seemed much more willing to engage in serious dialogue. There was a good rapport, but that didn't exist with Caroline.

'Her attitudes and demeanour hardened over time. Progressively she fell out of favour and lost respect because of her political stance.'

But Caroline sees things differently. At the beginning of the next academic year there was a curious reversal. The student who led the assault on Caroline's classroom during the occupation came to her office and asked if she would be his third-year tutor. Tony was a tough character – a merchant seaman who had seen life. Caroline replied: 'I'd be delighted – I like living dangerously.' Tony later confessed that many of the third years would have liked to have had her as a tutor, but didn't dare, because of the official line against her.

At 2.30 p.m., 18 November 1974, the governors were due to meet in the board room at Holloway Road to try to whittle back student representation on the academic board. They wanted it cut from 36 to 21 per cent. The students had other ideas. That morning, leaflets were handed out specifying where to meet to begin the disruption. By 2 p.m., 60 students were in place to block the corridor. The director and governors had to abandon their attempts to get into the board room and were forced to file past hissing, clapping students into the staff common room. Then, for safety, the 20 or so locked themselves inside a small, airless, inner sanctum. Many had to stand or sit on the floor.

Soon after the meeting began there were sounds of a commotion: the students had discovered the meeting place and had broken through the feeble outer defences and into the large common room. There were noises outside: a heavy thud and the crack of splintering wood, as a student hurled himself against the door. Another one like that would have completed the job. Gradually, the noise built up: stamping, chanting, banging on the wall, the metal chairs, the big cauldron and salvers in the kitchen. It settled to a steady, growing, cacophonous roar as the hysteria developed.

Inside the room, the Chairman had to raise his voice. He had not been long on the Court [of Governors] and this was his first experience of a full-scale performance. He was clearly shocked: his face was grey and his cheekbones stood out. A few of the governors were calm, but most were worried. This was not what they expected when they took the job. The noise mounted quickly. By now the Chairman was literally shouting to make himself heard: 'Item number four: Report of the General Purposes Committee...'. All crowded in close; the range of hearing was no more than three feet... A group of students tore out two of the louvres [from a side window] and thrust their power hailers into the room. The repetition of hate-filled obscenities came through at tremendous volume: 'Get out, you c**ts, motherf*****s... Get out of this Polytechnic. Get out... we don't want you. Get out of this Poly...'. The Chairman had developed a tic. He was visibly wilting. Finally he gave up. The door was unlocked, and the governors, once more defeated and degraded, slowly filed out through the ranks of the jubilant disrupters.[5]

NOTES

1. 19 March 1989.
2. Butterworth Heinemann, 1983. Ironically, Caroline now feels the pendulum has swung too far. She believes today's nursing training emphasizes social and behavioural context at the expense of sound clinical practice.
3. K. Jacka, C. Cox and J. Marks, *Rape of Reason*, Churchill Press, 1975, p. 70.
4. *Fuse*, 22 October 1972.

5. *Rape of Reason*, pp. 75f. Terry Povey, the Student Union sabbatical officer for four years, declared his credo in a signed article in December 1973: 'No institution can be won away from the system by means other than the destruction of the system itself. For us, therefore, representation is a tactic, not a solution.'

Caroline had consistently fought against giving authority to the General Assembly with its 50/50 mix of students and staff. She was accused by the SU vice-president, Peter Polish, of having 'consistently used the concept of academic standards in the sociology department to undermine the processes of democracy'.

SU meetings themselves were often inquorate, yet passed sweeping constitutional changes. In 1971 the General Meeting pledged full support for the IRA in its fight against British imperialism. Four years later, Caroline asserted, 'Two students who were elected to represent the whole student body received nine votes each from a total electorate of nearly 4,000.' When the student admissions policy came up for discussion, staff who suggested educational qualifications might be checked were openly accused of being fascists. As one of the beleaguered minority said, 'We might just as well recruit 50 people from the nearest bus queue.' And at examiners' meetings members of staff claimed they were being pressured to upgrade the marks of students who were likely to fail.

THREE

Lightning Conductor

Caroline believed she could chart the process of subversion among students at the Polytechnic. Degree by degree, many were taking on what she describes as the physiognomy of hatred. 'Students would come with open eyes, open minds and freshness in their demeanour. But for some, when you could see them becoming ideologically converted, they would lose that openness. You'd see the kind of unfeeling, granite-like expression I later observed so often in Iron Curtain countries; what I call the glass-eye phenomenon. You'd lose any human responsiveness in visual contact. You would see this at staff meetings, too – they were utterly unresponsive.'

She believed she was witnessing the embracing of an ideology so all-encompassing that it denied its converts any openness to ideas or individuals who might pose a challenge. It was an imposition, an oppression, a mask of fanaticism which was being etched on people's faces.

On 27 March 1974 Caroline was appointed Head of Sociology, which set her up as a punching-bag for the far-left. Under the headline 'Crisis in the Sociology Department', the student magazine *Fuse* declared, 'That this is... a disaster for the Department is accepted by most staff and students.'

Vote of no-confidence

Before long, Caroline found herself facing the inevitable vote of no-confidence. Decision-making in the department had been partially delegated to a General Assembly of staff and students. It felt like an arena of hatred. Students sympathetic to her sidled up and discreetly apologized for not turning up to vote. They were against the proposals, they explained, but didn't dare make their feelings known in public, as they feared some academic staff might fail them in their exams. The vote of no-confidence was proposed and the General Assembly voted unanimously to support it. Students who would have opposed the motion were conspicuous by their absence.

The vote had no practical effect, other than the considerable power to embarrass and humiliate. After Caroline had finished welcoming the incoming cohort of undergraduates, she called for questions. One of the members of staff got in first and invited her to make her response to the unanimous expression of no confidence in her by the staff and students.

'Immediately,' she recalls, 'the students' faces fell. From looking reassured, they were suddenly perplexed and worried.' She chose her reply carefully: 'I hope you realize you are embarking on a course of higher education, and higher education is all about the freedom to pursue the truth and weigh all the evidence in a balanced way before coming to any conclusions. I hope you will do precisely that.'

Caroline began to understand what it must feel like to be a lightning conductor. 'That was exactly the sensation,' she says. 'I was attracting an enormous amount of hatred and attack, and I was trying to earth it, trying not to spread the viciousness, by taking it to myself, grounding it and finishing it.'

It took its toll. 'By the end of every week I would feel disintegrated, physically and psychologically. I used to cry every Sunday night at the thought of having to go in on Monday. I felt my internal gyroscope was haywire.'[1] She found herself constantly testing her own attitudes and actions against the fundamental values of her faith. 'Love and truth are two of those,' she says, 'and what I saw going on around me was their antithesis: the deliberate use of hatred to intimidate, to try to destroy those who didn't conform to the prevailing ideology.'

But after weeks of sustained conflict, even her own values started to feel shaky. Her own voice became added to those questioning and challenging her essential assumptions. It was a time of disorientation. Biblical texts, like the calling of Joshua, given for her confirmation, were one source of comfort. Another was St Patrick's Breastplate,[2] which she used to recite each day with fervour, either in the car going to work, or in the office:

I bind unto myself today
The strong name of the Trinity,
By invocation of the same,
The Three-in-One and One-in-Three.

I bind unto myself today
The virtues of the starlit heaven,
The glorious sun's life-giving ray,
The whiteness of the moon at even,

The flashing of the lightning free,
The whirling wind's tempestuous shocks,
The stable earth, the deep salt sea,
Around the old, eternal rocks.

I bind unto myself today
The power of God to hold and lead,
His eye to watch, his might to stay,
His ear to hearken to my need.
The wisdom of my God to teach,
His hand to guide, his shield to ward;
The word of God to give me speech,
His heavenly host to be my guard.

I bind unto myself the name,
The strong name of the Trinity;
By invocation of the same,
The Three-in-One and One-in-Three,
Of whom all nature hath creation,
Eternal Father, Spirit, Word:
Praise to the Lord of my salvation,
Salvation is of Christ the Lord.

It was a method of mental and spiritual preparation: 'You never knew when you were going to face an attack; to be set up for something,' she explains, 'and need wisdom and quick judgment. Everything I stood for was under challenge. Each day people were out to discredit not only me, but what I stood for. And I thought that if people discredited me then they would discredit the philosophy which underpinned my work, which was the basic liberal, democratic tradition of freedom to pursue the truth.'

The Sunday morning eucharist was an opportunity to touch base. It was a moment for the bones to be knitted together again; a time of strengthening and enabling. Yet away from the intimacy of communion, she describes her personal spiritual exercises in terms that are almost dispassionate, as though a distant observer of an act of co-operation between mind and will. The conscious reiteration of texts, the deliberate choosing to hang on to their truths. To hear her speak, there is little sense of inner soothing by the presence of God.

'I don't think I was necessarily conscious of a tremendous calm and peace,' she says. 'If I look back, I'm more conscious of stress and anxiety and endurance. In the sacraments there was a peace, but it was always tempered by dread – dread of going back to work, dread of what was going to happen next.' Where there was a transaction with God, it was the receiving of strength, the enabling to continue.

Caroline's way of renewing her stamina was to take up squash. She took to it with a passion and played in the Middlesex League, where she was 'fiercely competitive and far too good for her age', according to one partner. 'When you are playing it, you can't think of anything else,' she says. 'It's fast; it's intense; you use every muscle in your body and it's a game of wits. It's fun.' It was a passion that endured. More than two decades later, in her 60th year she remained unbeaten in all her team matches. But her competitiveness did nothing to dent her popularity. A surprise party was thrown to celebrate her birthday and her team captain observed: 'She's such a nice person, even her opponents become her friends.' But back at the Polytechnic, that was not the way things were panning out.

By the end of each week Caroline was shattered, and home became her haven. Walking and talking with Murray and the children was a good means of unwinding. Caroline kept the conflict from her family as best she could, but inevitably, some of the stress showed through. 'On Sunday, she would be crying in the kitchen,' remembers Robin. 'But she felt it was her mission to go through the picket lines, to stand up for what she believed was right.' Pippa was still a child, but she could feel the tension. 'I know she was very stressed, and sometimes I could hear her crying. I think then she started to realize that either you shut up or lie low or take a stand and take the consequences.'

What also helped enormously was the shared experience of writing a book about events at the Polytechnic. She stumbled upon a publisher for *Rape of Reason* during lunch following the memorial service for her father, who died in October 1974.

Robert McNeill Love had kept on the William and Mary farmhouse at Brickendon after Mike's death. It was a gracious home of classical proportions, three storeys high and surmounted by a cupola, set back from the road in a large garden with lime trees. Over the barn in wrought iron, he had crafted the sign: 'Think and thank'. It was to become Caroline's family motto. Even in retirement he combined managing the farm with serving as an examining surgeon and supervising successive editions of his magnum opus, *A Short Practice of Surgery*.

During the last 48 hours of his life, when both he and Caroline knew he was dying, she joined him at the farm. He asked her to help him. In his hand was a piece of paper which he was cutting into strips and putting in envelopes. With a twinkle in his eye he said, 'Girl,' which is what he always used to call her, 'all my friends who used to get copies of Bailey and Love with my personal inscription will think the next time it comes out it won't have a message from me. I'm going to give them a surprise.'

He had written personal messages to all his colleagues who usually received signed copies of his book. 'Help me cut these up, will you?' he asked. And each signed message was placed in its own envelope to be sent to the publishers to be stuck to the flyleaf of the new edition. 'That'll give them a shock,' he said.

Rape of reason

McNeill Love would have approved of *Rape of Reason: The Corruption of the Polytechnic of North London*. He would have been pleased, too, that it was published by the Churchill Press, whose titles included *Right Turn: A Symposium on the Need to End the 'Progressive' Consensus in British Thinking and Policy*. Most of all, he would have been glad that his one-time Labour voting daughter was taking something of a turn to the right herself.

Though what he would have made of her book's co-authors is another matter. On the face of it, Keith Jacka would seem a strange choice as collaborator, describing himself as a Melbourne University drop-out and bohemian. Later he became a researcher in mathematics and medicine at Melbourne and Harvard, before joining the Polytechnic to teach maths. He is described as being 'inoculated early against totalitarianism, and toughened by the PNL to become an unrelenting opponent of everything totalitarian'. John Marks emerged from a working-class background to study physics at Cambridge and become a PhD. After lecturing in Sweden he joined the Polytechnic in 1966. He was a member of the Labour Party at the time of writing the book.

The three were described in vitriolic terms in the Student Union Handbook. Of Caroline, it was written: 'Her name is linked with the extreme-right... be they private armies or the Nazi-based National Front'. John Marks was billed as: 'the most dislikeable man in the Polytechnic'. Of Keith Jacka, they wrote: 'Wouldn't he look superb in a Nazi uniform?'

The collaborators came together to try to find a way to withstand the onslaught of the far-left. This much they had in common. Marks and Jacka had rejected Christianity. In fact, Keith described himself as an atheist, but coming through the fire at the Polytechnic helped them both to find faith. 'John and Keith were my human anchors,' says Caroline. 'It was very helpful to be able to talk through these things with them.'

Their partnership extended beyond the book. 'We did our intellectual homework very thoroughly,' recalls John Marks. 'When Caroline had to go into those awful course committee meetings, when it was her against the multitude, she went in very well prepared. We rehearsed for them. She used to go through all the awkward questions that might arise before a meeting and we would collectively prepare ourselves for what would be the worst question or tactic we could face. Caroline was excellent at formulating all the awkward questions the opposition would ask. She had a real talent for it.' It was a talent that would stand her in good stead in her later careers in politics and human rights.

Through *Rape of Reason* the triumvirate of Cox, Marks and Jacka were able to declare to whoever would listen that: 'Propaganda – hate-filled, sneering, vilifying to an astonishing degree' had become the constant background noise at the PNL. They went on publicly to accuse the authorities at the Polytechnic of 'a failure of nerve' and to criticize 'the ostrich mentality' of others who sat by while the far-left came to power. The Marxists had subverted the basic liberal values of the college, using liberal members of staff as their inadvertent allies.

The book was more than an exercise in pique, an airing of the PNL's dirty laundry in public. Caroline and the others suspected that events at the PNL were part of a much wider onslaught on the values and fabric of Western liberal democracy.

Such a notion seems almost quaint in today's post-Iron Curtain climate. But similar upheavals were also being reported in West Germany.[3] A year before *Rape of Reason*, Lord Annan had published his report on the disturbances at the University of Essex. He later described affairs at the PNL as 'a public scandal', adding, 'many members of staff have been terrorized'.

Well before the Berlin Wall came down Caroline had begun to visit Eastern Europe, and what she saw of Communism in practice alarmed her. What the Tory MP Dr Rhodes Boyson saw happening at the Poly alarmed him, too. Speaking at the press launch of *Rape of Reason*, he called for the PNL to be closed for a year and the entire staff to be sacked and re-appointed.[4] Of Caroline he said: 'She looked into the abyss, the awful pit, and in horror she recoiled.'[5] The Polytechnic said the document concerned events that were in the past and a battle that had since been won.[6] Caroline and her co-authors begged to differ.

So did Bernard Levin in *The Times*. He made a feature of their volume in three successive columns. His first: 'In all its brutality, the making of an intellectual concentration camp', described *Rape of Reason* as 'one of the most serious books I have had in my hands for a good many years...'

Rape of Reason is no Ranter's Handbook, nor a selection of *Daily Telegraph* reader's letters... *Rape of Reason* tells, with an astonishing degree of judicious calm, of the planned destruction of an institution of higher education, with the use by the destroyers of physical and psychological intimidation, of totally unscrupulous dishonesty, of violence, theft and vandalism, of obscenity and defamation and of a wide range of literally criminal actions. It tells also of something worse: that is, the resignation and retreat, in the face of this campaign, by those whose undoubted task it was to resist and combat the corruption. And it tells, finally, of something worse still: of the way in which the assault was actively aided by some of those who had the duty of defending free inquiry, intellectual tolerance and integrity of thought, but who instead connived at the assault on all three and frequently helped to instigate it.[7]

Writing the book was a cathartic experience. It also helped Caroline to find her bearings and strengthen her inner convictions. 'I had to think through everything,' she explains, 'my political and intellectual position, my philosophy and epistemology. It was a very therapeutic learning process.'

Against the background of chaos and disruption at the PNL they set out their core philosophy of education. They drew inspiration from Karl Jaspers, professor at Heidelberg until suspended by the Nazis in 1937. Jaspers wrote:

The university is a community of scholars and students engaged in the task of seeking truth... in defiance of all internal or external attempts to curtail it.

When Caroline realized she would never be able to change anything at the Polytechnic, and by remaining was only giving her endorsement to the continuing mayhem, she decided to look around for another job. A Nursing Education Research Unit was being set up at Chelsea College. The post of director was available. At heart, Caroline considered herself first and foremost a nurse and lamented being out of touch with clinical practice. The new post would combine her career strands of nursing and education. She left the PNL in 1977.

The Research Unit began with three different projects. One was midwifery training. Another was a study to examine how well ward sisters and charge nurses were prepared for the demanding responsibilities of their post. The third was to follow three cohorts of student nurses from training school to the time they qualified, and look at their clinical experience. It involved watching them on the wards and it took Caroline right back to being with the patients.

It was like coming home. At the first patient she encountered she did what every good nurse does instinctively – she smiled. 'And I suddenly thought what a joy this is. I can actually smile with my whole being; just a totally spontaneous, wholehearted, unreserved smile.' At last, she could smile naturally and with integrity, without worrying about its implications or its hidden meanings. 'I wondered what kind of existence I had been living at the Polytechnic that I couldn't even smile without worrying how it might be interpreted. It was a great relief suddenly to go back to being myself.'

Life was changing, and for the better. Work was satisfying, but not all-consuming. There was time for the family. Time to relax. Plenty of time to smile. But not for long. 'I suddenly got this bolt from the blue which changed my life.'

NOTES

1. *The Independent*, 8 September 1988.
2. Translated by C.F. Williams, copyright 1928 OUP.
3. In West Germany, Rudolf Leonhardt, deputy editor of the liberal weekly, *Die Zeit*, was reporting: 'Students had demanded and won a voice in academic affairs. Radical leftist groups had taken power almost everywhere... the students then used their position in the academic appointments committees to usher Marxists into permanent berths; in this way they could take care of their own and build a bridgehead of ultra-leftists into the professors' camp. Where the radical leftists cannot get their own way they do not stop at terror; they disrupt and boycott courses and examinations. The goal of these students is to gain firm control of the universities and then bring down the parliamentary system from there', cited in *Rape of Reason*, p. 130.
4. *The Times*, 29 September 1975.
5. *The Times*, 5 May 1988.
6. *The Observer*, 5 October 1975.
7. *The Times*, 30 September 1975; and 1 and 3 October 1975.

FOUR

Elevated to the Peerage

It was a dark and drizzly Friday afternoon in mid-December. Caroline cut and thrust her battered Ford Anglia past the Palace of Westminster with her usual spirited, take-no-prisoners technique reserved for London traffic. Glancing up at the Houses of Parliament, she thought, 'What a pity there aren't more nurses in there.' In her firm opinion, too much was being spent on high-technology health care, at the expense of bread-and-butter nursing that was never going to grab the headlines. It made her angry.

Care of the elderly and dying, the chronically sick and mentally handicapped was being whittled away by under-resourcing. And nurses' pay was pathetically inadequate. She had expressed her views forcibly and clearly in writing to her MP. Cutbacks in nursing meant patients would suffer. As the House of Lords receded in her rear-view mirror she reflected sadly that there was only one nursing peer and it was unlikely there would be another.

That weekend she was preoccupied with putting the finishing touches to her textbook, *Sociology for Nurses*. On Monday morning she dropped off the manuscript at Butterworth's, with a satisfying sense of finality, and returned to the bosom of her family. Now she had finished her book, she was going to 'cut out all the extras and just enjoy my job, my family, and the simple life'. It was bliss. At Chelsea the next day she felt completely relaxed. She fairly skipped home to an evening of shopping, cooking and domesticity. With energy to spare, she flicked through her telephone message book to see if she was wanted for a squash match or to ring bells at a wedding. She was a bell-ringer at St Mary's, Monken Hadley, a 14th-century church in north London. What she loved was the 'concept of timelessness; the reminder of the transcendental'. Another joy was a cathedral organ in full flight: 'It zooms the spirits – exhilaration and adrenaline!' It was then that she caught sight of the note: 'Please ring 10 Downing Street.'

The simple life was great while it lasted. All of 22 hours.

Downing Street

Caroline was puzzled by the request, but grateful the caller had left the phone number as it wasn't one she was likely to find in her address book. 'I had no idea what it was about,' she says. She dialled the number, to be greeted by a well-modulated female voice which intoned, 'Thank you for calling back. The Prime Minister wonders if you could possibly spare the time to call in and see her over the next few days.'

Caroline nearly fell off her chair. When she recovered her senses, she managed to mutter, 'Of course.' The voice inquired, '4.45 tomorrow afternoon?' Floundering for a lifeline, Caroline asked for some idea of what it was about. With the formidable presence of Margaret Thatcher looming large in her imagination, she added, 'I don't mind coming with an open mind, but I'd rather not come with an empty mind.' The refusal was polite, but emphatic, 'I'm sorry, we can't. We'll see you at 4.45 tomorrow afternoon.' She was left with a headful of questions and the dialling tone.

Her first thought was, 'Aha! Democracy works.' Maybe her ferocious letter to her MP about nurses' pay had been pushed to the top of the pile. She was also chairing the education study group at the Centre for Policy Studies and wondered if perhaps the PM wanted to talk about that.

The following day, 8 December 1982, her middle son, Jonathan, volunteered to drive her down in their ancient Anglia. Perhaps with Mrs Thatcher in mind, they stopped to say a prayer. It was already dark. As they were about to turn into Downing Street, they were halted by a policeman, who had sized up their geriatric Ford and was poised to pounce: 'Aye, aye... you're breaking the law. You haven't got your lights on.' Jonathan apologized and explained he had turned them off when they stopped.

Undeterred, the apparition in blue demanded in a tone that was vaguely menacing: 'What are you doing here?' Caroline smiled sweetly and replied, 'I've got an appointment with the Prime Minister at 4.45.' The policeman cast an incredulous glance over their rustwork. Suspicions aroused, he muttered darkly into his walkie-talkie. The box squawked back and, with an incredulous smile, he bade her enter.

Caroline dabbed apprehensively at the bell-push on the black-panelled door with the brass number ten. Her heart was pounding and she was desperately trying to remember the salary scale of a ward sister. Inside, she paced around a waiting room, occupying herself with the paintings until the double doors swung open and a gentleman in formal attire with polished vowels informed her, 'The Prime Minister wants to see you now.'

Taking a breath, she made her way through the portal and into the presence. Margaret Thatcher thanked her for coming, and said: 'Please sit down. I'll come straight to the point, because I believe in coming straight to the point.' That figures, thought Caroline. The Prime Minister continued, 'I've read some of your books on education and I'm preparing a list of names to give to Her Majesty the Queen for recommendations for life peerages. May I put your name on that list?'

'I nearly fell over backwards.'

Caroline had no inkling this could be the purpose of their meeting. Not even in her dreams. She had no active involvement in politics, and was not even a member of the Conservative Party.

While she was getting her breath back, Mrs Thatcher said, with a twinkle, 'I hope you'll support us on education. I know you don't always support us on health, but you have always got freedom to speak and vote according to conscience.'

There was no room for equivocation: 'I was bowled over.' The Prime Minister asked her to treat the issue in confidence because the Queen had to ratify the list and it could not be pre-empted. A press release would follow within a week. Caroline's complete secrecy would be required until then, 'Except of course,' continued the PM, 'you can tell your husband. Spouses are different.' She paused. 'I suppose everyone knows you've come to Downing Street?' Too right, they do, thought Caroline.

Mrs Thatcher continued, 'Well, we'll have to think of something to tell them, won't we?' Caroline's thoughts went to the kitchen back home which was seething with curious kids, friends and neighbours. The Prime Minister offered, 'Why don't you say you've just come to have a little chat about education?' Caroline swallowed hard. Tell that to the Marines, she thought, before being ushered out of the presence. 'Somehow I wafted out of the room and floated down the stairs in a complete daze.'

No sooner had she stepped through the door at Stag Lane, than she was bombarded with questions. She tried a deflection, 'Well, the inside of Downing Street is much bigger than it looks from the outside.' The Inquisition continued unabated. Pippa, taking a leaf from Mrs Thatcher's book, got straight to the point, 'What did she want, Mum?' Caroline replied exactly as prompted, 'Oh, just a little talk about education... and that is all you're going to get out of me.' Eventually the ravening pack retired and Caroline slipped out with Murray to what had been his surgery and was now his office. When he had recovered sufficiently from the shock, she asked him, 'Do you think it means I am going to be a Baroness?'

Curiosity got the better of her and she scrabbled around for a book which would reveal all. The best she could come up with was a children's encyclopaedia. When nobody was watching, she went up to Jonathan's bedroom and looked up 'P' for 'Peers of the Realm'. Tucking it under her arm she went back to the study to read the entry in peace. It was the *Children's Britannica* that informed her she was, indeed, going to be a Baroness.

The myth that she had gone to No. 10 for a little chat about education became increasingly difficult to sustain. Two days later, she got back from college, and there in the phone book was, 'Phone Garter King-of-Arms'. Similar messages appeared almost daily. Eyebrows were raised and quizzical looks exchanged among the family.

Queensbury rules

The one thing she did know about the fate awaiting her was that you had to have a name. She chose Queensbury. During the tough years at the Polytechnic the church that had helped knit her bones together again was All Saints, Queensbury. 'It was very much my spiritual anchor during those difficult years,' she says. Secondly, although they lived in Kingsbury, which was adjacent to Queensbury, the latter sounded more feminine. And her third reason? 'If anybody decided to tease me about the Queensberry rules I would say, "I believe in getting up and fighting for what I believe, but fighting fairly."'

She went down to Garter King-of-Arms, armed with her name and arrived at the ancient and impressive College of Heralds. She was greeted at the door by a venerable figure who informed her, 'Good morning. I'm Garter and my office is 800 years old.' Caroline eased herself down in a chair that could have been there from the beginning, and was asked if she had thought of a name. 'Queensbury,' she replied, with a smile.

With a flicker of annoyance, Garter demanded, 'But is it a *name*?'

Puzzled, Caroline replied, 'Well, I live near there.'

'Is it a *name*?' Caroline's eyes flicked round for an escape route. 'It's got a parish church,' she offered, lamely. 'That's why I chose it.'

Wrong answer. 'Is it a *name*?'

With an edge of desperation, Caroline said, 'Well, it's got a London transport underground station.'

'Is it a *name*?'

She tried to conjure up a single observation that would cut some ice in an office that was 800 years old. She hazarded, 'Well, I think it's mentioned in the Domesday Book.' Was it? She had no idea. At that Garter levered himself out of his creaky leather chair and reached for his book of names.

Mercifully, Queensbury was a name that was acceptable to Garter. It became her name: Baroness Cox of Queensbury.

She kept the secret from her family and finally broke it to them obliquely, suggesting they look at the headlines of *The Times* the following day. 'I was in a total state of shock,' says Robin, 'then thought, "Brilliant, Mrs Thatcher, on your choice of life peer."'

Robin accompanied her to the Lords to hear one of her first major speeches. Shortly before she was about to rise, a liveried messenger handed her a sealed House of Lords envelope. She received it formally and opened it up. Inside was a folded page of official notepaper, bearing the red lion and unicorn crest of the House. Inside that was a piece of stiff card. It was a photograph. The subject was Caroline at a party, wearing a giant pair of comic pig's ears. A momentary, and highly informal, grin flew across her face, before she recovered her composure and began her speech, watched over by Robin, grinning from ear to ear in the Gallery.

As far as Pippa was concerned, Mum was still Mum, and made light of her peerage. Caroline tried to combine her various roles for a while, but found being a member of the House of Lords too much like a full-time occupation. Motherhood was a fixture, so it was the job that had to go. She resigned from Chelsea College in 1983 and, even today, says she still hasn't recovered from the shock of her peerage, which she puts down to her contribution to *Rape of Reason*.

John Marks believes there was more to it than that: 'A more important factor was a book called *The Right to Learn*, which we edited, and which was published by the Education Study Group of the Centre for Policy Studies (CPS).' Caroline chaired the Education Group when it was first set up, and spoke at CPS annual meetings, which were attended by Mrs Thatcher. According to John Marks, Caroline's presentations were highly effective.

The Prime Minister had read *Rape of Reason*, and three months before awarding the peerage she was given a copy of *The Right to Learn*. The book made a radical call for more diversity in education, including centres for excellence and the introduction of vouchers. It also questioned the right of teachers to a job for life.

After her peerage, Caroline took the Tory whip, but, despite press reports to the contrary, never got round to joining the Conservative party.

FIVE

Showing Solidarity

It was an eight-hour journey from Wroclaw, the old German town of Breslau, to Warsaw. It was made even longer by the fact that Caroline was forced to sit knee to knee with a secret policeman in the confines of a crowded railway carriage. 'Black Satchel', short and sullen with a sallow complexion, was giving her the eye. Caroline, in turn, presented him squarely with the book jacket of Daphne du Maurier's *Don't Look Now* and flicked through the pages as nonchalantly as possible. Difficult when your rucksack contains a bundle of banned Solidarity badges and you are travelling across Poland without a ticket. Hidden behind her novel, Caroline had plenty of time to reflect on her journey and her reasons for coming to Poland.

It all began in 1983, the eventful year of her peerage, when she was asked to become the patron of the Medical Aid for Poland Fund. The charity was sending out trucks laden with medical supplies to a country whose main accident and emergency hospitals were hard pressed to scrape together a few syringes.

Not content to be a name on a letterhead, Caroline was determined to travel with the trucks wherever possible. 'I believe in the principle of accountability,' she says. 'I wanted to make sure the aid got through and wasn't siphoned off by pilfering. I wanted to assess the situation to see what the priorities were. Then to be able to come back and say, "I've been, I've seen, and this is how it really is."' Not long afterwards she found herself clambering into the cab of a 32-tonne truck.

Her journey began one Sunday morning at a large warehouse in Hayes, near Heathrow airport. Caroline joined a band of dedicated volunteers – scouts, church groups and others – who spent the next six hours piling equipment and supplies onto the vehicle.

Their cargo was a reflection of the situation in Poland. Solidarity leader Lech Walesa had sent out an SOS when martial law was declared. Another urgent appeal had just arrived from the University Hospital in Warsaw, saying they had run out of bandages. These were included, along with needles, syringes, catheters and cotton wool, clothes and gluten-free flour for people with coeliac disease. Caroline was requested to carry one box in the cab with her and to take special care of it: the precious cargo was gluten-free communion wafers.

The truck was despatched to Dover in the early afternoon. They crossed on the truckers' ferry to Zebrugge and set off on the long haul across Europe through the well-kept countryside of Belgium, the Netherlands and West Germany. And then they reached the Iron Curtain.

Every time it made my blood run cold. It was always spine-chilling: just stretching from horizon to horizon. The first time we came was at night. It was floodlit. Every hundred yards there were gun turrets, with soldiers with their guns facing inwards. Behind a huge electrified fence was a swathe of sand, which was heavily mined. Behind that was another fence. Then there were the tanks and the sniffer dogs, who would sniff not for drugs but for humans. You felt you were entering a vast prison. Waiting to get through that Iron Curtain you felt the atmosphere of intimidation and callous brutality begin to envelope you.

Part of that process was the nine-hour wait at the East German border, often in the bitter cold. After an age, the truck would be taken up into a tunnel lined with inspection bays, where guards would strip it down to the floorboards. They ripped open the boxes containing sterile operating equipment, and scrabbled through them with their dirty hands. Then they stabbed the boxes of gluten-free flour with knives until the precious powder was blown away on the wind. Finally, the trucks would have to be painstakingly reloaded by their weary drivers.

The first time Caroline ran the gauntlet was in June. The hardest times were in the winter, when temperatures were below freezing. She found it soul-destroying to see the deliberate savaging of supplies, which were like gold-dust in Poland.

Sometimes the only way to prevent the trucks from being completely dismantled was to bribe the guards with coffee and cigarettes. They were lucky to get away with that. Many drivers who have made that run will know the lubricating effect of a duty-free box of Marlboros or a few dollars discreetly folded into the manifest.

Once across the border, the smooth autobahns of the West would give way immediately to the bumpy roads of East Germany which took them around the Berlin ring road. Ahead were yet more delays at the Polish border. The goods were treated with more respect, but sometimes the Poles would strip the lorry down, saying apologetically that the East Germans were watching and if they failed to put on a good show they would be in trouble.

Dangerous paper

Caroline's first visit was to Warsaw. She lived the life of a trucker, eating and sleeping on the move and cleaning up at truck stops. 'When we stopped at Aachen in Germany,' she told a newspaper, 'there was just a hawthorn bank shared by 300 drivers for a loo. But they really are the gentlemen of the road.' Their brace of 32-tonners had been on the road since Sunday and arrived at dawn the following Wednesday. Their destination was the church of Father Jerzy Popieluszko, an outspoken opponent of the Communist regime who was later assassinated by the secret police in 1984.

'You could feel the fear in the air,' she recalls. An arrangement had been made for schoolchildren to help unload the trucks by forming a human chain. The work continued until lunch time. The offloads were always surrounded by customs officials and secret police. Normally, Caroline would take pictures, but the atmosphere was so tense she kept her camera to herself. 'People were so vulnerable.'

Next stop was Kielce, an industrial town 150 miles south east of Warsaw, where they were greeted by the parish priest, Father Alexander Chycki. With him was a group of medical students and seminarians waiting to unload the truck. Despite the presence of the ubiquitous officials, people seemed more relaxed and Caroline asked if it would be all right to use her camera. Father Alexander replied, 'Take whatever photos you like. These are brave men. They have either been in prison or soon will be. They have nothing to lose.'

After they had finished unloading, they sat down to a meal prepared by their hosts. For non-party members, food was a scarce commodity. 'For all the years I went I hardly ever saw good quality fresh fruit available for ordinary people,' Caroline recalls. 'It was in the party shops, but nowhere else. I remember seeing only one fresh lemon. It was on a market stall in Warsaw. We worked out the price at £12 sterling.'

One of the church members grew strawberries on a small allotment. His entire annual harvest of this exotic fruit was liberally distributed among the British drivers. 'The people around were almost salivating at the sight of them,' says Caroline. 'I felt really bad about eating them, and wanted to refuse, but it was their dignity and their pride to give you their best.'

As they prepared to move on the people embraced them and handed out

Solidarity badges, little tin emblems of defiance in the days of martial law and General Wojciech Jaruzelski.

Caroline's driver was Tony, a cockney; a big man with a big heart and a thatch of brown hair, who was never to be seen without his gold earring and bracelet. He told Caroline that when he went to Communist countries, the locals could not believe the jewellery was his. They thought the gold was given to him in order to impress the Communists that British truck drivers were so well-paid. They were convinced he had to give it all back when he returned.

Caroline busied herself with the almost constant task of clearing the cab of the truck, which was home for the rest of the journey. She stretched her hand under the seat and felt the crinkle of paper beneath her fingers. She pulled out a brown paper bag and quizzically peered within. It was the rest of the strawberries, which had been secretly placed there by their hosts. Shaking her head, she said to Tony, 'When you get back to Britain, how do you ever begin to describe what it's like out here? How can you ever make people understand the poverty, and yet the incredible generosity?' Visibly moved, Tony replied, 'All I ever say is, "They've got nuffink, and they give you everyfink."'

Their journey took them on to Wroclaw, where they arrived around midnight. They pulled up in the square by the cathedral and collapsed for some well-earned sleep. Almost immediately, it seemed, their rest was shattered by the peal of bells for six o'clock Mass. Caroline was a keen bell-ringer herself, but this was pushing a point. They abandoned all thoughts of sleep, and decided to go to Mass. Although it was an ordinary weekday morning, the church was full to capacity for the sung service.

When they returned, it was time to start offloading the truck. Distribution took place under the auspices of the church, which had proved itself trustworthy and was well aware of the needs of the local people. As usual, there was the corridor of secret police and customs agents, along which they had to pass to take the goods into the seminary. It was their final destination and the lorry was almost empty. Caroline returned for another load to find the usually good-natured Tony swearing vigorously. It was the first time she had seen him lose his cool in the week they had been together.

She asked him what on earth was the matter. He replied, 'Look at **** this!'

She looked, but all she could see were two boxes of blank computer paper. Puzzled, she said, 'So what, Tony? Two boxes of paper.'

He flashed her an angry glance and said, 'Don't you **** realize we could be imprisoned for this?'

Caroline checked the secret police were out of earshot. They were – just. 'I didn't, Tony,' she replied, 'but if that's true, you'd better shut up.'

Calmer now, Tony said, 'What do we do? We can't leave it here, they'll come and find it.'

Still puzzled, Caroline responded to his sense of urgency and realized they had to act quickly. As a concession, they had been allowed to take in a large consignment of the *British Medical Journal*. Anything less subversive than the BMJ was hard to imagine, but often the authorities even drew the line at those.

Caroline arranged a camouflage cover of BMJs and set off to brazen it out past the secret police. She passed through without a problem, and came back for more.

That night she stayed with a Polish paediatrician, and still perplexed about the incident, picked her moment carefully and asked, 'I just don't understand. Could we have been sent to prison for bringing in two boxes of blank paper?'

'Of course! Don't you realize that in a totalitarian state, blank paper is dangerous?'

Caroline looked as blank as the paper in question, so her host spelled it out for her, 'You can write ideas on it.'

In that moment, says Caroline, she understood the full meaning of totalitarianism and the value of freedom.

Knee to knee with a secret policeman

After the incident with the paper, Caroline and Tony separated. He was to return on the truck, while she remained in Poland to gather information about priorities and health needs. It meant going back to Warsaw by train, a substantial journey. The priest explained to Caroline that she would probably be followed by the secret police, as they would have tapped the phone and known she was travelling. Duly warned, she headed off with a friend, Maria, an attractive, fair-haired Pole, to get a ticket from the station.

The queue was interminable. It would have meant lining up for several hours, by which time the train would have gone. They walked together to the head of the queue to see if anyone could be persuaded to let her in. Nobody could. Maria said, 'You'll have to travel without a ticket.'

'Thanks a million,' said Caroline. Her Polish was about as effectual as her Serbo-Croat, and travelling on a train without a ticket felt like a one-way trip to the nearest jail. She asked Maria to come down the platform and help pacify the guard.

To talk about *the* guard was an understatement. Every door leading on to the endless grey-green carriages seemed to be blocked by men in uniform. Eventually they sized up one who looked relatively human and Maria put on her best pleading. The guard proved amenable,'Get on and stand just there, and when the train starts to move I'll come and sell you a ticket. Don't move.'

Caroline obeyed, embarked, waved goodbye to Maria, and thought, 'As long as I don't lose contact with this guard, I'm OK.'

She had been told to stand in the corridor, near the door. The train was filling up rapidly. After several days roughing it in a truck, all Caroline wanted to do was to snatch some sleep. But the remaining seats were being taken by the second and bodies were spilling out into the corridors. Someone had even staked out a claim to the lavatory seat. As yet more people pushed on Caroline struggled to keep her position in the doorway and her eye on the guard, who was her lifeline.

As she was standing there, surrounded by an ever-growing crowd, she suddenly noticed a man on the platform with a black satchel who was staring at her. She told herself not to be so paranoid; it was only a coincidence.

Time passed and still the train refused to budge from the platform. More and more passengers piled on until it felt like the tube in the rush-hour. 'Black Satchel' was still there, staring, and she thought, 'OK, Caroline Cox, you're not that attractive, maybe it is the secret police. If so, so what? There's nothing to be ashamed of or to worry about.'

Minutes dragged on into half an hour, when a stranger tapped her on the shoulder and asked if she was going to Warsaw. She said, 'Yes', and he promptly grabbed her rucksack and pushed her off the train. After a brief tug of war for her bag, which she lost, he led her along the platform to the front of the train, explaining in pigeon English, 'The train divides. This part goes to Warsaw. This part does not. You here.' He threw her rucksack into the carriage, shoved her aboard and disappeared.

To Caroline's surprise, it was half empty. Her initial reaction was, 'Good, at least there's some seats.' Her next thought was that she had lost touch with the only person who understood why she was on the train without a ticket – the guard. She decided to carve her way back through the crowds to where she had come from.

At that moment, Black Satchel reappeared in the corridor next to her. He was a weaselly, cadaverous-looking figure, clad in a leather jacket, and standing too close for comfort. He resumed his attempt to stare her out. Caroline reasoned that as Black Satchel had attached himself to her there was little point in going back. She decided to stay and ride it out.

Then her imagination kicked into gear. Maria had known she wanted to go to Warsaw. So had the guard. And they had both knowingly placed her in a part of the train that some stranger had said was not going to Warsaw. Whom should she believe? And where was the stranger now? Perhaps this part of the train was going to divert to the middle of Poland where nobody would know where she was. She consoled herself with the thought that she was on a humanitarian aid mission and had done nothing to compromise her position.

Suddenly, she remembered her growing collection of Solidarity badges and broke out into a cold sweat. The little red and white metal enamel badges had been showered on her at the various places she had visited. Each bore the crest of the local organization, which would both chart her visit and incriminate those she had met. She swallowed hard and composed herself, trying to maintain her sang-froid for the sake of Black Satchel.

Under casual observance her illegal collection ought to have been safe enough. She had pinned them inside the collar of her dirtiest shirt and wrapped that around with a pair of trousers that had become mud-stained and sodden after she had taken a tumble in a river. Those in turn, were wrapped around with other unsavoury items of well-used laundry. It would have taken a very committed Communist to have found them. Black Satchel looked just the man.

She decided it was best not to get herself arrested and wondered what she could do about the badges. She toyed with the idea of eating them, but abandoned that when she remembered their crude little safety pins. She would prefer to be in a Polish prison than a Polish hospital with a perforated gut. Then she wondered whether to go to the toilet and dispose of them, but thought, 'No, they're used to that game.'

By this time Black Satchel was standing shoulder to shoulder with her. If she began to unpack her rucksack everything would be in plain view. The train had been standing at the platform for almost an hour and still showed no sign of moving, so she thought maybe the time had come to cut short her abortive exercise and rejoin Tony and the truck in the market square. He wasn't planning to go till evening, so there was still time.

Just as she was about to step off the train, it jolted forward and began to gather momentum. The prospect of flinging herself from a moving carriage was less than appealing. As she was now committed to the journey she thought she might as well sit down. Taking her leave from Black Satchel she made her way into a compartment with four other passengers, one in each corner. That left two brown plastic-covered seats on either side in the centre. Caroline and her rucksack took one; while the secret policeman and his sinister black satchel took another. He parked himself down bang opposite, knee-to-knee, still staring.

His secret service credentials were ratified immediately by the reaction of the other passengers. They all studiously avoided Caroline's eye, which was out of character for the Poles, who normally enjoy chatting to strangers. Black Satchel seemed bent on continuing his staring game, so Caroline became equally determined to make the most of her journey – wherever it would take her.

She extricated a fat novel from her rucksack and started to read it. She always carried a thick book on truck journeys, to while away the inevitable hours in the company of officialdom, and to help her unwind at night and get to sleep. Her favourite read was Daphne du Maurier, whose stories of the West Country reminded Caroline of childhood holidays. She placed the book squarely under Black Satchel's nose and snapped it open. The title was *Don't Look Now*, and she only hoped he could read English.

After some three hours with Black Satchel staring at her book cover, and she staring equally hard at the pages, the ticket collector came round and allowed her to pay her fare. At last, she was travelling legally. When the train pulled up at the next station Black Satchel got off. Caroline presumed the train had reached the end of his jurisdiction. She realized Black Satchel would not have invested so much in following her that far, without having someone else to take his place.

She scrutinized the oncoming passengers to try to pinpoint her new minder. It wasn't difficult. He marched straight into the compartment. He was conspicuous by his clothing, which was well beyond the pocket of ordinary Polish people. To double-check, Caroline stepped out of the carriage and into the corridor. Immediately he followed her, placed himself right next to her, and started talking to her in English. She thought, 'Thank you for making it so obvious.'

The rest of the journey became a battle of wits. He would fire questions at her to try to trap her into saying something inappropriate that would get her into trouble. His opening gambit was to ask for her views on Communism. What he lacked in subtlety, he made up for in persistence. She would evade his questions and try to trap him into divulging who he really was. It was as good a game as any to while away the journey.

Glancing at his feet, she said, 'That's an extremely smart pair of shoes you're wearing.' Only party members and upwards could afford solid leather hand-stitched shoes in Poland. He did a double-take at his expensive brown Oxfords, and parried, 'They were a present from an aunt in Germany.' The verbal skirmishing continued in much the same vein all the way to Warsaw.

When they got off the train, Caroline searched for ways to shake off her unwanted chaperone. Black Satchel had looked unfit and easy to outrun. This one was younger, leaner and an altogether more difficult proposition. Caroline did her fair share of ducking and weaving and back-tracking to try to throw him off the scent. Moving as quickly as she could, she melded with the crowds on the platform until she could no longer see him. Realizing that didn't mean he could no longer see her, she took a number of detours up and down flights of stairs. She was to be met at the station and was eager to shrug him off before he could catch sight of her contact. Though with that degree of surveillance his employers were probably well aware of where she was staying and with whom. As she was to find out.

Every step you take...

The Polish secret police had ways of letting Caroline and her contacts know they were still around. Caroline used to go out with the aid trucks to Kielce, a major industrial city bypassed by many of the convoys in favour of easier destinations closer to the border. Each time she went, Caroline would stay with Lidia Bialek, an English teacher and niece of Father Chycki. Her husband was to become the first editor of *Gazeta Lokalna*, the first independent regional newspaper in Poland under democracy.

Whenever Caroline wrote to Lidia in advance to tell her she was coming none of her letters was acknowledged. Usually, when she arrived at the flat, it came as a complete surprise. Then Lidia would receive her mail in full the following morning, when all the missing letters would arrive through her post-box. 'It was their way of saying, "We know you're here." They were just the silly, harassing little gestures of a police state, which were very intimidating to the people who lived there.'

Often, within half an hour of her arrival at various different addresses, there would be a loud knock at the door and men would burst in, claiming to be from the electricity board. They would make a great show of explaining there were problems with the light bulbs and insist on changing the bulb. 'They were obviously putting in bugs,' says Caroline. 'At least they were blatant about it. It just made me wonder what they were doing that was not so obvious.'

If it wasn't the light bulbs, it was the phone. They would turn up uncalled for and unwanted and proceed to 'repair' the handset. When Caroline and her contacts were speaking, they would never mention names. Names would always be written down on a piece of paper and passed over. Then the paper would be destroyed. Lidia's flat was uncomfortably close to the secret police headquarters. She was aware they could pick up conversations by aiming high-powered microphones at the window. Conversations in the flat were always stilted.

Once, in the middle of winter, they braved temperatures of between minus 10 and 20 to go to the park, to talk away from prying ears. 'We were in the middle of the park, out of earshot of anybody, and within a few minutes this guy came running towards us, and just stood there taking photographs, before disappearing again. It was all a message: "You're being watched, we know exactly where you are."' Her greatest worry was whether the people she was with would pay a price for her being there.

Empty baskets, empty shops

If word did get through to Lidia that Caroline would be coming, she would save up her old newspapers for weeks and take them to a recycling station to trade them for a single roll of toilet paper for Caroline.

One Saturday, Caroline asked to go shopping with Lidia, to get a feel for what it would be like to be a Polish housewife buying provisions for Sunday lunch. They wrapped up warm against the sub-zero chill and made their way to a butcher's. Or, more accurately, they made their way to the end of the queue of 40 which wound its way into the butcher's. After an eternity of foot-stamping amid a fog of freezing breath, the queue was no further forward. Caroline excused herself and followed the line up and into the shop. The counters were completely bare. There was not an ounce of meat to be seen. Caroline looked at the counter, looked at the queue, shook her head in disbelief and made her way back to Lidia. She said, 'What are they all queuing for? There's nothing here.'

It was ten o'clock in the morning. Lidia replied, 'They've been told there might be some meat coming in at midday.'

There was no guarantee that even if rations did arrive, they would stretch to the end of the queue. A shipbuilder from Gdansk told her how they would sometimes begin queuing at five in the morning, often in freezing rain.

They left the stoical carnivores to their fate and moved on to a greengrocer's. This time there was food on the counters, though the term seemed hardly appropriate for the mouldy potatoes and shrivelled greens. There were a few nuts, which were prohibitively expensive, and some brown and bruised apples that were fit for the pig bin. That was all. 'It was typical,' she says. 'And yet when you ate with them you would never know the sacrifices they had made to give you that meal. There would never be any indication that you had probably eaten all their winter supplies. The meal was given with such generosity and hospitality. It was very humbling.'

Queuing for food could stretch right into the evening. Grandparents and elderly relatives would stand in line for the rest of family while they were out at work. Occasionally, some old folks would die of the cold as they stood there. They fought the adversity with humour. A joke doing the rounds was the one about the elderly woman who was going shopping. She was halfway between her home and the shops. She looked in her basket, saw it was empty, and said to herself, 'Am I on my way to the shops, or am I on my way home again?'

There were many visits to Lidia, who describes Caroline as her mentor and friend. She impressed Lidia with the way she took pains to understand the situation, to learn about the everyday life of the Polish people. 'Journalists used to come just to write their piece,' says Lidia, 'but she really cared. She listened, she learnt and she understood, so she could report accurately about the real Poland. Caroline was very sympathetic, very open. She was wonderful and we admired her – we developed a black humour to deal with the everyday hardships.'

Agonizing choice

The courage of the Poles was also apparent in the children's hospital in the historic city of Krakow. What was once a dignified building was a run-down structure of bleak staircases and bare concrete floors. At least it was clean, which Caroline noted was no mean achievement, given the shortage of soaps and detergents.

On one ward were children with malignant diseases. Many had the kind of leukaemia which would be treatable in the UK. The doctors and nurses were well aware that it could be cured, but they had only a fraction of the resources necessary to treat it. So they faced the agonizing decision of choosing which child to treat, and which to leave. Those who were left had little hope. Those who were treated faced an ordeal. The treatment involved intravenous injections at four-hourly intervals. Paediatric-sized needles were a rarity, so nursing staff would have to use large-bore items intended for adults. 'It might take hours, literally, to try to get one of these big needles into these little children's veins.'

Caroline talked to some parents about the courage of the children she saw in those wards. They told her the story of a 12-year-old boy in the Warsaw uprising. The fighting was at its height, tanks were approaching, they were under constant bombardment and people were dying all around. With his own death imminent, the boy wrote these words on a wall:

I believe in the sun, even when I cannot see it.
I believe in love, even when I cannot feel it.

It moved Caroline immensely. 'For a 12-year-old boy to write those words in the middle of the horror going on around, is typical of the spirit of the people of Poland.'

At another hospital, providing accident and emergency cover for a radius of some 50 miles, Caroline went into the intensive care unit and was shocked by what she saw. It was almost empty. The unit, which would take all major emergencies and acute cases, had a single ventilator which was kept going by cannibalizing all the others. The drug cupboard was bare, save for some vitamin C, a handful of British syringes and a few needles from Scotland. There was nothing to put in them. 'The Poles called themselves, with good cause, the Fourth World.'

The situation was the same at Kielce. The maternity unit for the whole of the city was devoid of standard incubation equipment for premature babies. Undersized infants would have to be rushed 50 miles to the nearest incubators, by which time they could be dead. The hospital had no incontinence pads or soap and detergent to keep the linen clean. It was enough to bring a shudder across the countenance of staff nurse Cox: 'The very thought of trying to look after incontinent people without incontinence pads, soap or detergent!'

On the wards was an incontinent adolescent boy in a deep coma following a road accident. Caroline noted with approval that there was not even a sign of a pressure sore. 'The quality of nursing was superb – better than you get in many Western hospitals.' She congratulated the medical director, who explained, 'My staff achieve this by giving of themselves to compensate for what we haven't got.'

'It was heartbreaking,' says Caroline. 'You were with people who knew what they could do and what they should be doing, but who just didn't have the basic resources.'

They were heading into Katowice, in southern Poland, with another run of basic, essential medical supplies. The Roman Catholic Bishop Domin would be there to greet them. As they approached their meeting place, a hall, Caroline felt a growing discomfort. 'Here was this bishop, a dignified, cultured, educated man, having to wait with empty hands for whatever motley collection of things we happened to be able to put on this truck. How awful it must be. How much easier for us, from the affluent West, to bring out the truck and to give.' She thought, 'I couldn't bear it if he says thank you.'

When they arrived, before the bishop could utter his thanks, she apologized for sounding rude, but begged him to stop. 'This isn't altruism,' she explained. 'If you look at this in a long-term perspective, this is our own self-interest, because as we in the West become more cynical, more secular and more materialistic, I believe we shall find our spiritual salvation from the suffering church. So please don't thank us. It is we who ought to be thanking you.

'I believe to this day that we receive so much more from the persecuted than we can ever give them. They are a living witness, an inspiration, and it is a privilege to be with them.'

SIX

Death in the Desert

It was Caroline's intention to accompany the hundredth truck out to
Poland, but by now she had become a junior whip and was categorically
barred from going. She was told, 'We really couldn't have a junior minister
bouncing around on a truck, crossing the Iron Curtain.' It was ruled
completely out of court.

Caroline set her jaw and bided her time. At the end of the summer
session, as Parliament went into recess, she handed in her resignation. To
have done so any sooner or any later would have been interpreted as a
political statement. She had been in the post just five months. Friends and
allies warned she was committing political suicide. 'I probably was,' she
admits. 'A lot of people still think I did the wrong thing.'[1] But what it did
was buy her freedom.

It was with relief that she returned to the back-benches. 'The kind of
things I had done, which led me to the Lords in the first place, would be
better served by being a back-bencher, with its independence, rather than
being in government.' It meant she could speak her mind, and she could go
back on the trucks. It also left her free to get lost – several times – in the
deserts of Sudan.

It was Christmas 1985. The card arrived, postmarked Sudan. Eagerly,
Caroline opened the envelope. As expected, it was from her son, Jonathan.
The tall 23-year-old had excelled at school and toyed with the idea of
following his elder brother, Robin, into the Royal Navy. But instead, he felt
God's call to work in the Third World and decided to become a nurse,
qualifying at the London Hospital. Now he was working as a missionary for
Emmanuel International, known in Sudan as the Fellowship for African
Relief (FAR). His card contained a welcome letter, chatting about his work
and bemoaning that some of their projects were in danger of collapse
because of an acute shortage of nurses. Caroline read it through again and
wondered. *Acute shortage of nurses.* The words sank in and stuck there. She
sent back a card by return, breezily saying she regarded it as a personal
challenge and was willing to consider coming out the following summer.

'What a concept!' came the reply from Jonathan. Caroline prayed about it and talked it over with Jonathan's girlfriend, Tessa, a dark-haired Gibraltarian, with striking Mediterranean looks. Both of them decided to put in an application to Emmanuel International, and almost before they knew it, they had arrived in Khartoum.

'Followed to Sudan by my mother and my girlfriend!' said Jonathan. 'I took a lot of stick for that.'

But if Jonathan feared he was about to be inundated by over-attentive women, he got off lightly. Tessa was assigned to the FAR HQ in the Sudanese capital, while Jonathan continued his work with Eritrean refugees at Damazin. Caroline, meanwhile, was packed off to the desert. 'The organizers must have thought that either I was dispensable or a tough old bird because they sent me to work in what was generally recognized as their toughest project, a health education programme in north Kordofan.' She was assigned to Hamrat-el-Wiz, whose name, she recalls, translated approximately as 'the little red town of the wild geese'.

First came the preparatory work and the rote learning of survival Arabic, including such all-important phrases as 'is there water in the wadi?' Just as well. She would need them. To get permission to carry out the health programme in that part of Kordofan would involve a lengthy journey to El-Obeid. Caroline and her companion, Katherine Weins, a Canadian nurse, took an internal flight to El-Obeid on a Sudanese domestic airliner. It was all that remained of a fleet of two – the other had been shot down. The trouble set in when that one surviving plane was later blown over in a desert storm. By then, Caroline and Katherine had successfully presented their case for the health programme and needed to return to Khartoum. The only way back was to hitch a lift from another non-governmental organization.

UNICEF came up trumps, with a driver and a vehicle, although the transport left something to be desired. The terrain would have been punishing for most vehicles; a vast, uninhabited desert with jagged mountains and axle-breaking ridges, but this was a road car which was being returned to Khartoum because of a persistent problem with overheating that had defied the combined skills of all the El-Obeid mechanics.

By midday two calamities had overtaken them. They were lost. And, true to form, the engine's temperature gauge was straining at its endstop. The sun was straight overhead when the road petered out and they found themselves meandering round and round in circles. There was no means of taking a bearing. No other vehicles were in sight. Curls of steam were sizzling from the bonnet and the only way to keep the ailing motor from bursting was to drive for ten minutes and rest for twenty, though cooling down was an impossibility under the blazing sun. To make matters worse, their road tyres were beset by punctures, and because the journey was taking so long their water was running low, forcing them to eke out every remaining drop.

Eventually, and with great relief, they struck a track and followed it down to a village. Sudan had been hit by both drought and famine. The villagers had little enough water for themselves, but with true desert hospitality, they generously stocked up the strangers with enough to drink, and filled their equally thirsty jalopy. Then they pointed them back in the direction of Khartoum. Half an hour passed and they had their fifteenth puncture. The journey was stifling, wearying and slow, and the succession of stops to fix tyres just seemed to be taunting them. Somehow, they avoided turning ratty and kept their spirits high. While their driver was spinning the tyre levers, Caroline slumped down on another old tyre which a previous unfortunate had abandoned in the desert, and settled down to watch the proceedings. Katherine's yell broke the stillness. It was directed at Caroline: 'Get up – there's a scorpion in there!' She didn't stay around long enough to investigate.

It was getting on for midnight when puncture No. 16 made its presence felt. By now they were a dab hand at dealing with these unwelcome intrusions, but this one presented a particular problem. They were completely out of puncture repair outfits. Not that it made any difference, because about the same time the engine uttered its final death rattle and gave up the ghost. They were tired and thirsty, but no-one was admitting to depression. There seemed to be an unspoken agreement to keep their grumbles to themselves. Inwardly, Caroline was worried. She prayed silently and privately, trying to resign herself to the situation and praying God's will be done, whatever that would mean. There was nothing else for it, but to bed down on the sand beside the hunk of useless metal and see what the next day would bring.

The pitch dark was pinpricked with stars, and as Caroline was about to slip into sleep, her eye caught the shape of a silhouette along the skyline. In the starlight the hair appeared white and the teeth were parted in a smile. It was the most welcome face in the world. The Arab had heard them from his compound, which was shielded from their view by a ridge. Although it was almost two in the morning, the villagers immediately got up and offered the visitors their wooden and goat thong beds. Hot, sweet, Sudanese tea was produced from nowhere, which tasted like nectar. They gulped it down, suddenly acutely aware of how dehydrated they had become. The beds were moved out under the stars, in readiness for sleep, when, suddenly, a man came running round the corner of the compound. He had a message. At 2 a.m., in this obscure patch of Sudanese sand, miles from anywhere, a taxi had appeared.

'Getting a cab in Khartoum was tough enough,' says Caroline, 'but this was as though the Archangel Gabriel had arrived.' Their journey had already taken 22 hours. No-one could summon the energy to ask the cab driver why he was there. They just piled into his taxi and fell into a deep sleep. By dawn they were back in Khartoum.

A self-basting turkey

From Khartoum, they left to make their way to Hamrat-el-Wiz. A British team was creating a tree belt there to try to hold back the Sahara, which, unopposed, would eventually smother the village and their embryonic health centre. Transport was a truck bearing an enormous black and white chequered water tank. The road out of Khartoum was good by desert standards, and the pace was relatively swift. But gradually, the track began to give way to sand. The going was softer than they had grown used to. The journey was still punctuated by frequent stops, but instead of attending to punctures, they had to dig the truck out of the sand. It was thirsty work. Their final contact with humanity came at a scrubby township called Jebrat el-Sheikh, and was celebrated in style with a Coke. Not that Caroline enjoyed the hot and sticky, fizzy liquid – she never touched it at home – it was just the final symbol of anything that seemed familiar.

Beyond Jebrat el-Sheikh, they found themselves in a vast, uninhabited wilderness of stone and sand. The route was never clear. Their maps just showed a desert, and points of reference for a compass bearing were few and far between. Navigation was by a combination of stopping and interrogating anyone they saw on a camel, and guidance by the oldest of all methods – the stars. Somehow it worked. They got there.

Throughout the journey and beyond, Caroline had one persistent worry. There was no way of contacting their parent organization. 'If you got into trouble you got yourself out of it, or you died in the desert.' After what they had already gone through, the prospect of having an accident was cause for concern. But what troubled her more was the possibility of going down with renal colic. The TB she had contracted as a nurse had kept her away from the mission field, because kidney damage, plus dehydration, meant a high probability of developing kidney stones. Passing one of those was not for the faint-hearted. The strongest pain-killers in their medicine chest were Anadin.

Renal colic kept at bay. But for much of her time she was suffering from giardia – a bug that produces diarrhoea. The symptoms were particularly unpleasant during the feast of Ide, at the end of Ramadan. The philosophy of their organization, FAR, was to live among the local people and build up friendship and trust. So it was with some trepidation that she felt compelled to accept an invitation to join some villagers for a meal in their hut.

Normally, the temperature inside the circular, mud-walled tukul with its thatched roof would be around 40 degrees centigrade. But with a fire burning, it felt like stepping into a furnace. Suspended on the wall of the hut, staring back at her with its dead, black eyes, was the head of a sheep. In an enamel bowl over the fire were its intestines, green and glistening in the cooking oil. That was to be their feast. It would have been a severe breach of protocol to have made her excuses and left, and worse still to be sick, so Caroline braced herself for what had to be. Her genial hosts handed round the bowl to each of the guests in turn. Mercifully, when it reached her, there was a little bit of intestine hanging over the side which was darker and crispier than the rest. She broke it off and ate it as quickly as possible. According to custom, once you have partaken of the feast, your obligation to eat is discharged, so the next time she could pass the bowl with impunity.

Their compound at Hamrat was good, as these things go. There was a mud hut, which served as a kitchen, and a straw shelter. Their team-mates were two men, a Briton and a Filipino. Electricity was unheard of, but water was delivered each day by donkey, and the large grey plastic containers were left out in the sun to steam. The shower room was a couple of mud walls adjoining the compound. The idea was to ladle scalding water over yourself with a cup. Caroline understood how it must feel to be a self-basting turkey. Keeping the liquid in the shade seemed to make little difference. Even the drinking water was hot enough to strip the skin off your lips. At its coolest, the mud hut was almost halfway to boiling point. They decided to use it as a store for their belongings, and to sleep out in the open. That was the best part of the day: when the sun went down at six and the air began to cool. Nightfall in the desert never failed to be stunning, with the sky ablaze with stars and the planets so clear you could almost touch them. Without electricity they had little option but to crash out and go to sleep, to rise again before the sun.

For a time, Caroline and Katherine tried reading in their beds by the light of a hurricane lamp perched between them. The glow was a magnet for every conceivable variety of flying insect, which flitted and fluttered and buzzed and bumped around the lamp. They learned to put up with it. Until one night, when a large flying beetle decided to dive-bomb deep into Caroline's right ear. 'It really was excruciatingly painful. It couldn't go into reverse, so it was trying to go forward and it was biting and clawing and scratching at my ear drum.' Caroline gathered her thoughts and with a nurse's logic concluded that if it perforated her ear drum and wedged itself in her middle ear, the torture would be indescribable. Sitting up, she remarked to Katherine, with as much composure as she could muster, 'I've a beetle in my ear. Do you think you could possibly get it out?'

Katherine responded to the hint of urgency in her voice, by having an exploratory peer into the peer's ear. It was pitch dark and there was nothing to be seen, so she went off in search of a pair of forceps. It seemed an eternity before she returned and started rummaging around for the flying object. Finally, she managed to extricate it before it had burrowed in too deeply. The little brute had some blood on its claws, but Caroline's eardrum was still in working order. 'As nurses we should have known better,' she says. 'We should have poured in oil and floated it out.' Still, the story was filed away to be brought out at school speech days, where it always went down well. 'You never know when you might be walking on the Pennines and the same thing could happen. It's a useful lesson.'

Their work in Hamrat was to lay the foundations for immunization programmes and health education. They set up a mobile medical clinic, dispensing vitamin A for night blindness and other medicines in short supply. And having established their base in Hamrat they were asked to take the work to even more remote villages, still deeper into the desert.

Stranded in the sand

Caroline and Katherine set off in a jeep to visit the village of Um Surra, on the horizon towards a distant mountain. There were no roads, tracks or maps. Finding the right direction was a matter of following one's nose and spotting someone to ask. After two and a half hours, while the mountains seemed as far away as ever, their jeep suddenly ground to a halt. It was nothing dramatic. Just an absence of useful activity in the engine department. Nothing could prompt it to fire up again. Right then, a radio would have come in useful. The sun was directly overhead. It was a rule of the desert that if you had a vehicle, you should never leave it. But while that would make sense if you were in a convoy or on a marked road, it made no sense at all to stay in that out of the way spot and fry. The only other vehicle known to use that route (not that they could be sure they were *on* that route), was a souk lorry which went to the market once a week. Their remaining option was to walk the rest of the way. They arranged the slings from their first aid boxes across their heads to try to stave off the heat-stroke and took their water-bottles. Caroline's was made of metal and was almost too hot to handle.

Together they began trudging in the direction of the distant mountain, their feet baking in the sand. One hour gave way to two. There was still no sign of habitation. Not for the first time that trip, Caroline thought her end had probably come. And again, not for the first time, they stumbled upon a rescuer. To their amazement, they came across an Arab boy tending goats in a wadi. The ten-year-old led them back to his settlement, where they were warmly welcomed by the locals. One minute there was a little baby goat licking their hands, and the next it was hanging upside down being skinned. Ten minutes later they were enjoying the freshest barbecued goat ribs possible.

After they had eaten, the tell-tale signs of a haze on the horizon gave way to a sandstorm that seemed to blast and burn into everything. They ran for shelter in a tukul, but already the sand had seared through their clothes, clawed at their eyes and caked in their eyebrows. After the storm had passed, the local women helped them out of their clothes and offered them long robes that wound around them, before washing their sand-smothered clothes and shaking them dry in the open air.

It was too late to try to return to Hamrat, so they spent the night in the tukul, puzzling how to get back. In the morning, summoning her best survival Arabic, Caroline asked in her perfect English accent if they would be able to hitch a lift on a local camel. The message was understood and passed round, and an owner was found. Judging by the animal he produced, he might have been pleased to see the back of it. The beast was prancing all over the place and refusing to come to heel. It was a far cry from the tame camels the child Caroline had been fascinated by in the zoo. The instant dislike was mutual. It opened its mouth and spat green cud all over her. Wiping herself down, Caroline wondered how she would manage to stay on the beast for more than two minutes. 'The thought of having a broken back in the middle of the desert with only a pack of Anadin, was not my idea of a fun Tuesday morning.'

She asked the camel owner, hardly daring to hear the answer, how long it would take to get back to Hamrat. He glanced at these two ridiculous foreigners, who didn't seem to realize that no self-respecting Sudanese woman would be seen dead riding a camel, then peered at the sun, which was low on the horizon at dawn. He said, 'When the sun is like that...' making an arc of nearly 180 degrees with his hand, 'you *may* make it back to Hamrat, *insha-Allah.*' He proceeded to construct a makeshift double saddle that would accommodate the women in tandem, and with Caroline perched precariously on the front and Katherine clinging grimly to the rear, he led them back into the desert on foot.

After about an hour they had got the hang of the camel's swaying motion, and passed the next two hours chatting happily. By the beginning of the fourth, they were hot, dehydrated and made sorely aware with every jarring step that thin cotton skirts were not the most appropriate garb for a camel ride. Another hour passed, and a small voice somewhere behind Caroline's left ear inquired, weakly, 'Caroline, I'm feeling rather faint. I think I'm going to fall off. Do you think you could tell me a story?'

There was still no sign of Hamrat on the horizon. If Katherine fainted or fell they would never get back. Caroline unstuck her tongue from the roof of her mouth and performed a creditable impression of Scheherazade. The storytelling continued for an hour, until a peculiar glint on the horizon caught her eye. It was the sun gleaming from the corrugated iron roofs of Hamrat.

Caroline realized the sight of these two *khawaja* women perched atop a camel would be a major source of merriment for the good people of Hamrat. She quickly devised a new logic to life, 'If you are going to make a fool of yourself, look as though you are enjoying it. Laugh and the world laughs with you.'

They braced themselves. As their camel entered the village, the children were the first to come up and fall about in fits of hysterical laughter, then it was the turn of the adults to rally round and share the joke. It was the funniest thing they had seen in years. Caroline and Katherine grinned and waved as though they had been planning the carnival all their lives. The camel was too disdainful to acknowledge the humiliation. It immersed its head in a bucket of water and drank it down without coming up for breath. As for Caroline, she found herself stuck with a new nickname: camel legs.

'*Tuwaaaali!*'

Towards the end of their stay in Sudan, work beckoned them towards one of the furthest villages in their area, called Mahabis. They set off in an aged Landrover, with Sami, a male interpreter, at the wheel. Sami was an Arab in his forties, with handsome chiselled features. After an hour and a half of spirited driving they reached the nearest village and asked the local sheikh how much further they had to go. The Arabs have a word to convey distance: *tuwali.* The further the distance, the longer the word is made to sound. 'I never heard such a long *tuwaaaaali*,' says Caroline. The sheikh began an elaborate description of the various mountain ranges they would have to cross, and there was soon too much detail to remember. So the sheikh sent one of the village elders to accompany them in the Landrover.

It was a first for the guide, who clearly had expert, intimate knowledge of routes taken by camels, but made no concessions for their inferior mechanical equivalent. They went straight down and straight up every wadi they came to. The revs were high and the gears were low, and the four-wheel drive was fighting for all it was worth. At their fifth wadi the passengers were feeling the strain and fearing for the Landrover. Caroline asked the guide how much further. The *tuwaaali* was still too long for comfort and there was at least one more mountain range to go. Then the Landrover lurched over the top of the ridge and emerged onto open flatland. Sami set his jaw, put his foot down and made like a Paris–Dakar rally driver.

Caroline scrabbled for a hand-hold, and clung tight, looking increasingly dubious. Then, without warning, the flatland dived into a wadi, which sprouted boulders and rocks, and the Landrover piled straight into a large one at full speed. The impact turned over everything inside the vehicle, including its passengers, but the Landrover, mercifully, remained on its wheels. Caroline shook her head and cleared her vision, felt her bruises and checked her bones. What had broken, however, was their water container. The Landrover was awash. Realizing that to go any further would be impossible, they decided to turn around and head back to Hamrat with all due haste, boulders permitting.

The stalled engine fired up immediately, but the vehicle was going nowhere. The wheels wouldn't turn. The impact had dislocated the clutch plate. Nightfall put paid to any chance of carrying out emergency repairs. They braced themselves for an uncomfortable few hours without any water.

Then, almost on cue, a silhouette appeared, an Arab on a camel. Caroline asked him if there was water in the wadi. There was, but they would have to dig for it. He showed them where, and melted away. Eventually, to everyone's relief, a pool of filthy water appeared. To boil it, they lit a fire of scrub wood, and after drinking their fill, settled down without mosquito nets to spend the night in the desert.

At daybreak, they divided their labour. Some worked on the Landrover, while Caroline set to boiling yet more water in a billy-can. She had her prayerbook of daily readings which were a mixture of Psalms, prayers and poems. She opened up the reading for the day. The poetry was an extract of the chorus from T.S. Eliot's *Murder in the Cathedral*. Halfway down the page, her eye alighted on the phrase, 'the death in the desert'. Even in that temperature, a cold shudder went down her back. She thought, 'Are you trying to tell me something, up there, God?' She kept her concerns to herself and carried on praying as she boiled up the water.

After a while the Landrover was back together and the engine was running, but still nothing would persuade the wheels to turn. Caroline thought, 'We're in for a long stay.' She prayed some more and kept on boiling the water. About ten minutes later, the Landrover was moving. Sami had decided to try it in a different ratio. It worked, but it meant they would have to make the rest of the journey in high gear. If they tried to cross the wadis there was every chance they would get stuck. And there was no guarantee, if they did, of finding water again. If they stayed where they were, at least they could be sure of water, but that was all. By the time anyone realized they were missing and sent out a rescue vehicle, their tyre marks would have been obliterated. And because they had been taking a camel track, the route was not the way any other driver would knowingly choose. Not for the first time, Caroline longed for a radio. 'We decided to say our prayers and try to make it back.'

Each time they reached one of the wadis, which had almost defeated them on the way out, their prayers became more fervent. Gravity-assisted descents were one thing, but somehow they made it up again. 'It was an amazing sensation,' Caroline recalls, 'almost as if an invisible hand had plucked the Landrover out of these wadis. We almost floated across them.'

With Hamrat almost in their sights, Caroline suddenly remembered that she had arranged a meeting with the leading sheikh, and many other local sheikhs. It was a crucial meeting to discuss the continuation of their programme. Understandably, it had gone clean out of her mind in the desert. The meeting had been arranged for midday. They made it back to Hamrat at precisely ten to twelve. She splashed down, applied a double dose of Anaïs Anaïs, threw on some clean clothes, and on the hour found herself addressing the august meeting of the sheikhs. She felt like the captain of the 'poor condemned English' in Shakespeare's *Henry V*:

> Nor doth he dedicate one jot of colour
> Unto the weary and ill-watched night,
> But freshly looks and over-bears attaint
> With cheerful semblance and sweet majesty.

As for that other quotation, the one about death in the desert, 'I put it down to God's sense of humour.'

NOTES

1. She told *The Times*, 'I wish to give more time to other activities in the field of education, and I need the freedom of the back-benches to do that', 3 August 1985. She was supported in the decision by her family. 'There are very few politicians who would resign a ministerial post and a potentially glittering career in politics so they had the freedom to speak on the back-benches. That was a tribute to my mother,' says her eldest son, Robin.

SEVEN

Share the Darkness

Caroline's work in Poland was beginning to take on a more subversive complexion. Not everything she did was concerned with relief aid. Some of her actions behind the scenes were more overtly political. It all began with a simple insight into the way traditional values were being maintained even under Communism.

It was the heat of the summer, some years before democracy, in Kielce. All the medical and seminary students were on vacation. It meant there was no-one around to unload the truck, which was marooned in the yard. They went in search of helpers and found some Scouts – boys and girls – who were camping nearby. Immediately they volunteered to help. They worked solidly in the heat for the next five hours. At the end, to say thank you, she tried to give them some money for a drink or an ice cream. With dignity beyond their years, the 13-year-olds declined and said, 'If we have been able to help some people who are less fortunate than we are, then that is reward enough.' They shook hands and left.

Caroline wanted to thank the Scout leader, so the following day she tracked them down to a camp in the middle of the forest. The leader chided her gently. 'You shouldn't be impressed,' he said, 'It was no more than they should do.' They chatted on and she explained that her father had known Baden-Powell and she had one of his thumbsticks as a family heirloom. Then out of curiosity, Caroline asked how the Scouts' promise to do their duty to God held out in Communist Poland. The Scout leader drew her discreetly to one side and showed her the printed version of their promise. God had been deleted and the obligation of duty was now to Socialism. He said with a wink, 'When it really comes to it, we always put God back in the promise.'

She made up her mind to do whatever she could to help strengthen Poland's traditional and academic values. She got together with a group which included right-wing philosopher Roger Scruton and Jessica Douglas Home, who had been married to the nephew of the former Prime Minister, Charles Douglas Home, an editor of *The Times*. Their aim was to provide a different kind of aid for Poland, and to throw out a spiritual and cultural lifeline to a number of Communist countries.

Caroline was aware of the danger of compromising the Medical Aid for Poland Fund with her activities, so she went to check things out with an interpreter, Maciej Pomian-Srzednicki, her researcher on education. Her intention was to find scholars who had been driven underground because their work had become politically unacceptable, and to help publish their writings in the West.

The trust they were planning would offer financial support to scholars who had been stripped of their salaries. It would also make available publications forbidden in Poland, such as the works of Solzhenitsyn and other 'unacceptable' writers. 'We wanted to keep freedom alive, particularly the freedom of ideas.'

Caroline and Maciej went to the Jagiellonian University in Krakow, one of the oldest in the country and the broad equivalent of Oxford or Cambridge. It was in the days before democracy, and martial law was still in force. It meant going through the usual dreary routine to make sure they weren't being followed. They walked round and round the building some six times in the dark, coming at it from different angles, before suddenly diving in the door.

Her contact was a professor of history, a leading Polish academic. She explained, 'I really don't want to make life more difficult for you. If you don't want this conversation to take place, I will go immediately. If you are prepared to meet us, we would like to put an idea to you and would value your comments.'

'Of course we would like your help,' the professor replied. 'If we don't continue to use the limited freedom which we still have, we are already lost.'

It seemed to say it all. On the strength of that, Caroline returned to Britain and helped set up the Jagiellonian Trust.[1] It was modelled on the Jan Hus Trust, an organization already established for Czechoslovakia, named after the Bohemian founder of the Moravian Church. Jan Hus was put to death as a heretic for opposing the burning of books and the abuse of authority among the clergy.

The Jagiellonian Trust was to be an underground relief organization offering support to groups and individuals concerned with maintaining free inquiry, intellectual debate and the traditions of learning and religion in Poland. There were further visits to scholars and students. Many works were published which would not have seen the light of day in Poland. 'It gradually created the sense that the Communist authorities were a paper tiger,' says Roger Scruton, 'and that underneath, the real life of society proceeded without them.' The trust was wound up in 1996, when its services, mercifully, were no longer required.

Although the medical situation improved, the legacy of acute shortages and lack of resources meant there was still much to be done by the Medical Aid for Poland Fund and Caroline continued to travel with the trucks. She had one basic rule, which was never to mix agendas. The one occasion she broke it, she almost came unstuck.

Caroline was accompanied by a young Polish driver who had taught himself English by listening to the BBC on the long runs from Poland to England. He was keen to try out his conversation so they talked about everything and anything. They became friends, and he decided to treat her to breakfast in a Polish café. He changed some money at the border, but as soon as they were in Poland, the customs took the truck apart. The cab was ripped open, the upholstery savaged and all but destroyed. He explained that the East Germans had seen him changing money and were getting their revenge. They had telephoned through to the customs people at the next control point, and they had set about their task with gusto.

Caroline felt sorry for him, and a little concerned for herself. Although the trip was with Medical Aid for Poland, she had combined it with running an errand for the Jagiellonian Trust. The academics desperately needed computer software. In her hold-all were some floppy disks which were not on the list for customs. 'It was the only time that I had ever mixed two agendas,' she says. 'I was sitting there cursing myself for putting Medical Aid for Poland at risk.'

The customs officers were working their way through the truck progressively. Her rucksack on the bunk was the last remaining inviolate item. They had torn apart the driver's hold-all until there was virtually nothing left of it. Hers was next. Caroline shot up a prayer and was just waiting for them to set about her bag, when a message came through and the customs officer was called away. Her rucksack was left untouched, while the rest of the truck was vandalized.

Caroline felt a mixture of anger, relief and regret. 'It was an example of totalitarian control,' she said. 'The driver had paid the price, just because he had wanted to give me some Polish hospitality.'

The middle of nowhere

It was her last trip out before democracy came to Poland. The truck driver had taken a particularly circuitous route and ground to a halt in the middle of a forest in the small hours of the morning. Whether or not they had broken down, Caroline couldn't say, because the driver was Polish and the limits of conversation were prescribed by their mutual ability to mime, which in his case, wasn't great. The driver had gone off for purposes of his own and Caroline was left alone. It was pitch dark.

Driven by her normal, frantic schedule Caroline often found it difficult to make time to stop and meditate on her faith, although she appreciated moments when she could 'be still and know that I am God'. Now she was sitting in a cramped, uncomfortable truck, in the middle of the night, in the middle of a Polish forest in the middle of nowhere. And she thought, I have no reason whatsoever not to use this time to meditate. Trying to still her anxiety, she committed the time to God and asked him to help her listen to his word and respond. It took a while to calm her thoughts. 'Then the words just came into my mind,' she says, 'and they have stayed with me to this day. They were: "Share the darkness."' On her own, in the black of the forest the words came as an affirmation.

The next truck she travelled on went out in the summer of 1989. In the meantime, that June, Poland had emerged from totalitarianism to become a fledgling democracy. It was her first journey into free Poland, and she was looking forward to it immensely. She had received an invitation to go the Parliament buildings in Warsaw to attend a combined meeting of the Solidarity members of the Sejm, the lower house, and the Senate. After all she had seen the Poles go through, she stepped into the heart of their new democracy in high spirits. 'It was a joy to be in their parliament chamber,' she says, 'and see so many people of great integrity, democratically elected to their own Parliament, who had paid such a high price to achieve their democratic rights.' They thanked her for the help that Medical Aid to Poland had given during their dark days and then thanked her personally for sharing their darkness. The phrase made her catch her breath. She was subsequently awarded the Commander Cross of the Order of Merit of the Republic of Poland.

Caroline went to Poland about a dozen times, fought their corner in Parliament and did whatever she could to raise funds and awareness. Medical Aid for Poland described her as 'Dedicated and involved; not just a patron, not just a name on paper. She is charming, full of vitality, and once she decides to do something she actively supports it.'

Caroline looks back on her life as a trucker with affection and enduring admiration for the Polish people. Her contribution to Poland was summed up by Father Alexander Chycki, who told the *Reader's Digest*, 'Theologians sometimes get it wrong – Good Samaritans, never.'[2]

NOTES

1. Named after one of the early Polish kings.
2. David Moller, 'A Baroness Goes Into Battle', *Reader's Digest*, October 1992.

EIGHT

Close Encounter with the KGB

Moscow, 1988

It was the era of *glasnost* and *perestroika*. Many of the Soviet Union's senior dissidents had been freed from the prison camps of the infamous *gulag*. But KGB pressure was mounting; there was renewed harassment, and fears that the iron hand of totalitarianism was about to clamp down again. Caroline found herself addressing a subversive conference of leading Soviet dissidents in a flat in Moscow known to be bugged by the KGB. She had calculated the risk of arrest and decided to chance it.

A message had been smuggled out to the West asking for a parliamentarian to help stage a press conference to raise the dissidents' profile. Any attempt to break it up would be certain to reach the West, and the Gorbachev government was already showing signs of embarrassment over its record on human rights.

The plan was to hold the press conference in the apartment of one of the leading dissidents, Valery Senderov. A deeply committed Christian of the Russian Orthodox persuasion and a brilliant mathematician, Senderov had spent many years in the *gulag* and solitary confinement.

Back in England, a video had been passed to Caroline in which Senderov put in a plea for Western Christians to support dissidents and believers in Russia. He urged, 'In the Bible we are exhorted to visit those in prison. We are in this huge prison, please will you come and visit us.'

'It was not an invitation I could say no to,' says Caroline. But saying yes would involve some hard thinking. Technically, holding such a conference could be classified as subversion under the Soviet constitution. There was an edge of risk to the venture. The feeling was that if they held the press conference and got out immediately, they should be safe. Any decision to arrest a British parliamentarian would have to be passed all the way to the top of the Politburo and down again. By the time the Soviet bureaucracy had made up its mind to arrest them, they would be out of the country.

Caroline went into Russia on a Thomas Cook tour. Joining her on the long weekend package holiday was Malcolm Pearson, later Lord Pearson of Rannoch, who agreed to accompany her. They had met during her polytechnic years, when he had become honorary treasurer of the Council for National Academic Awards. He had shared her qualms about the far left in higher education.

After their first meeting he became an active supporter of her work. 'Malcolm had this strong commitment to resist what he perceived as evil,' she says, 'and he always saw Soviet Communism as one of the great evils in the contemporary world.' Lord Pearson had been raising money for the dissident networks, and Aleksandr Solzhenitsyn had stayed in his Scottish home when he came to collect the Templeton Award for his contribution to religion.

Bugged

Despite *glasnost* – or because of it – the KGB was still very active. Caroline and Malcolm would need to take elaborate precautions over meeting their contacts. They checked into their hotel, a vast Stalinist edifice, devoid of both soul and bath plugs, and met their contact and interpreter, Vera, as prearranged. Their rooms were dark and grubby and in all probability bugged, so they kept their conversation to trivialities, or communicated by notes or in the bathroom with the shower turned on full blast.

On the first morning they broke loose from their package-deal party and tried to get to a telephone. The phone in the hotel was probably a hot-line to the KGB. Outside, it was bitterly cold and the pavements were solid sheets of ice. Walking was impossible. They hailed a taxi, a large black Volga, similar to a Vauxhall from the late sixties. That was when they had their first open encounter with the KGB.

An enormous man tried to squeeze into the Volga with Caroline. 'He was a typical caricature of a KGB thug: large, raincoat, fur hat.' The Baroness wasn't having it. She shoved him in the stomach and caught him off-balance. Malcolm Pearson added impetus by squeezing in beside Caroline and shoving her along until 'Fur Hat' was forced out the door and into the road. As they drove off, their would-be travelling companion immediately boarded the cab behind and set off in hot pursuit.

They had been well briefed by insiders, before they went, on the different techniques that would be used to follow them. First was the high-profile approach: the man on your tail you were supposed to know about and be intimidated by. Next came the more subtle surveillance, which was designed to leave you guessing. Lastly, there was the discreet tail you would never know about. Fur Hat fell squarely into the first category.

Caroline had two items on her agenda: to get to a phone, and to find a worshipping church. They broke it to the cabby gently. First they asked him about the church. Then Malcolm casually said he could do with having a word with his business back in Europe, and would he mind taking them to a telephone. The taxi driver froze. 'It was as if every word we were saying could be heard in the car behind.' The driver didn't answer. Malcolm and Caroline exchanged glances and, not wanting to compromise their driver, changed the subject. A look through the rear window confirmed Fur Hat was still on their tail.

They had been driving for about ten minutes when the Volga swerved to the right without warning, and the taxi driver said, very loudly, 'I've decided not to take you to that church; I'm going to take you to another church.' He veered off down a side street, while the taxi with Fur Hat bowled on ahead. The cabby waited till it was out of view, then cautiously pointed below the level of the windscreen and across the road. There was a church, and opposite that, a telephone.

Later, back at the hotel, they conspicuously made their arrangements for the press conference. Using the hotel phone, they rang around the dissidents and invited the British Ambassador to the conference. He not only accepted, but offered to send his car for Malcolm and Caroline. *The Times* Moscow bureau was also put in the picture. It was their way of telling the KGB: we know you know, but break this up and you'll have a diplomatic incident on your hands.

High-risk game

They made contact with Valery Senderov, who had been given the word on the underground network to expect them. Since his release from the *gulag*, the mathematician had been working as a night porter in a factory. They arranged to hold the press conference in his apartment the following day. Among the invited guests were representatives of the independent journal, *Glasnost*, and the *Expres Chronika*, one of the main *samizdat* newspapers.

The newspaper was produced on an ancient typewriter with lines huddled together to save space. Every millimetre was precious. Getting at a photocopier was out of the question, so they had to rely on carbon copies. By the twelfth carbon the image was really faint. Caroline was given a top copy to take back to the West.

The various underground luminaries turned up at the appointed time and jammed into Senderov's flat. His mother looked terrified. Things had been bad enough when her son was in the *gulag*. The telephone had been cut off by the KGB. Straddling the dead phone in a gesture of defiance was a notice bearing a single word, '*Glasnost*'. The flat, of course, was bugged.

The theme of the press conference was democracy and the rule of law. Policies were discussed for reform and democratization and for transforming agriculture and the economy. The KGB would have heard plenty to interest them. 'It was very subversive,' says Caroline. 'They were playing a high-risk game.' All of them knew the risks and were prepared to be sent back to the *gulags*. But they were worried that younger and lesser-known dissidents were being targeted, and if the high-profile names were silenced, there would be nobody to speak for the next generation of activists. Having a British parliamentarian in to talk about a democratic future would ensure a level of publicity which could make the KGB think twice about sending them back to the *gulag*.

Besides, Geoffrey Howe, the Foreign Secretary, was due to be in Moscow the following week. Malcolm Pearson quipped that although they might languish in jail for a couple of days, Geoffrey would get them out for a price. Caroline had her doubts. By that time, she had already been causing the Conservative government a certain amount of trouble with amendments to Bills. Her riposte was, 'Geoffrey Howe will probably pay them to keep me in.'

Twenty people crowded into a small apartment room, which had been stripped of furniture to make way for a huddle of chairs, leaving just a table strewn with copies of the *Expres Chronika*. The delegates were well aware they were being bugged by the KGB, yet were determined to talk openly about their hopes for a free, democratic Russia and in detail about their programmes to develop economic and agricultural life. In Soviet terms, the whole exercise was deeply – and openly – subversive.

Caroline and Malcolm's flight from Moscow was booked for the following day. To celebrate a successful conference, they planned to take Valery Senderov out for a meal. At the first two hotels, the moment the doormen clapped eyes on Senderov they banged the door in his face. At the third restaurant, Caroline changed her tactics. She insisted on walking in first. As the doorman made way for a wealthy Westerner, she ushered in Valery, with Malcolm following on behind.

Over a meat supper, Senderov talked about his time in the *gulags*, where he had spent a considerable period in solitary confinement. He was thin-faced, pale and still almost skeletal. It had been so cold in the winter that a veneer of ice formed on the inside of the cell. When food was given, on alternate days, it was cold water and mouldy bread. He used to keep his sanity by working out advanced and complex mathematical equations. Senderov thanked God for the period in the prison camps, because it made him a better Christian. When Caroline asked him to explain, he said, 'Through all that suffering, although I learnt to hate the system, I praise God that I never, ever, hated my jailers.'

Senderov believed the soil of Russian consciousness was fertile and spoke optimistically of the future. Spirituality had survived the dark years like mushroom spores and when the light came up again, it would respond and grow. Religion had not been stamped out by 70 years of Communism, but was alive and quiescent, and would flourish again. 'He kept this incredible tranquillity and equanimity,' recalls Caroline. 'His face was almost translucent with spirituality. I have a huge respect and admiration for him.'

The meal passed off without incident and they were able to leave the following day without difficulty. For those who remained behind there were no reprisals, although Caroline was later informed the Soviet Union had acted to cancel certain weekend tourist breaks to Moscow.

The following week she went on a lecture tour in the USA with the Foundation Endowment to debate the politicization of education and freedom of speech on campus. She had two hours to spare on her first morning in New York and went with a colleague to see the Statue of Liberty. As their pleasure boat headed back to the quay, she caught a sight which set her chuckling. A character was looking down a telescope at their launch. 'He was exactly like a prototypical KGB agent, with a mackintosh and fur hat.' She and her colleague enjoyed the joke and it vanished from her mind.

An hour later she went jogging in Central Park to find the same man staring at her ostentatiously and taking notes with a pencil and pad. When she returned, an hour later, sure enough, he was there again. Once at the Statue of Liberty and twice in Central Park was too much of a coincidence. 'It was fascinating. The message was, "We know what you're doing."' Aware of the KGB's reputation for causing 'accidents' to those who ignored its warnings, she reported the incident to the FBI. The rest of her visit passed off uneventfully.

NINE

Sent to Siberia

Caroline's work in Russia and Poland began to come together. In 1989, while she was still delivering aid, Caroline was invited by some of the newly elected Solidarity leaders to help establish an independent human rights conference to be held in what was still the Soviet Union. It was a provocative gesture.

The Soviet Union had just embarked on the road to democracy by holding local government elections. But the Politburo was still very much in control of the Soviet central system. Leningrad had held its first elections to the Len-Soviet. The Poles flew out to meet its newly elected leaders, who agreed to host the human rights conference in their city. The Soviets had little choice in the matter. To have denied visas to Leningrad would have been seen by the world as a vindication that there was indeed a human rights issue to address.

Caroline was invited onto the central co-ordinating committee and asked to chair the group looking at human rights and the environment. She had pushed hard to include the environment on the agenda. Evidence was beginning to emerge of catastrophic pollution throughout the Soviet Union.

She flew out with her colleague, John Marks. At the airport they were greeted by a welcoming party, and John remarked pleasantly that it was good to be in Leningrad. Their host, a student, drew himself up to his full height and informed them: 'I am a citizen of St Petersburg.'

'You had the feeling something was happening,' said John.

They stayed with a family in the heart of Leningrad, as close to the conference as possible. Home for the duration was a run-down apartment block. The pre-Soviet building was substantial, by Communist standards, with two living rooms, a kitchen, a bathroom and high ceilings that made keeping the place warm a nightmare. It was shared by the husband and wife, son and two grandparents. Olga, their hostess, was an academic at the Leningrad Academy of Arts. Her husband, Viktor, was a lecturer in engineering at the Polytechnic Institute. Olga was initially shy about speaking English, but as the week wore on, she pulled out her dictionary and became more confident.

On the evening of the fourth day they ate meat for the first time. Only after her chicken supper did it occur to Caroline that the rest of the family had not eaten with them. To her horror it suddenly occurred to her that they had eaten the family's entire allocation of meat. The following morning, as they rushed out to the conference, Caroline said, 'Olga, when we come in tonight, please, don't feel you have to cook for us. We'll get something to eat at the conference. Please, just some tea and some cheese when we come in. Bread and cheese would be marvellous.'

It failed to produce the desired effect. Olga's face dropped a mile. She said before she could check herself, 'I don't have any cheese, and I don't know where I am going to get any.'

Caroline could have kicked herself for being a crass Westerner and tried to offer some reassurance, 'Don't worry about the cheese, Olga, just some tea would be lovely.' But it was too late. By the time they returned that night, sure enough there was cheese. 'I am sure she spent all day and a fortune getting it,' says Caroline. Later, when she looked for cheese in the shops, she never saw any. 'So where Olga got it from, or the price she paid, I shudder to think. When naïve people come back and say, "We never had any shortages; the tables were always full," I think they probably don't realize the sacrifice that goes into those full tables.'

On Sunday morning they all got up together at 5.30 to worship at one of the remaining churches and attend their liturgy. By the last night of the conference all awkwardness had disappeared and they were chattering like old friends. They spent most of the night in conversation. Olga and her family played their Russian liturgical music, which Caroline loved, and handed round photographs of old churches in Leningrad. They produced a map covered in red and blue dots. The red dots represented churches destroyed by Stalin. The blue ones were those still standing, though most were now warehouses or museums. Tearfully, Olga showed them pictures of churches that had been destroyed.

They went to bed to snatch an hour's sleep before breakfast. The entire family crammed into the tiny kitchen and huddled around the table for their *kassa* – Russian porridge. When they all sat down together they were wedged so tightly it was difficult to stand. The painted walls were decorated with the occasional ikon. The little space was shared by a bulky gas cooker of antique design, and a tiny work surface by the sink. There was scarcely any room to turn round.

Unexpectedly, Olga squeezed to her feet, and said, with obvious embarrassment, 'Please, if you do not mind, I would like to make a speech.' It was quite a turnaround for the woman who, days before, had been too shy to utter a single word of English. Clearly, she had been working on what she intended to say. When she started to speak, it was Caroline's turn to feel embarrassed.

Olga began: 'I just want to thank you because you have given us a vision of a world where people can smile. We in this country can never smile. When we go to work, we never know who we can trust. But you have shown us a vision of a world where people can smile, and you have given us hope that one day we might have a world like that, too.'

It struck a chord with Caroline, and as Olga sat down, she rose to her feet to respond, 'We in the West have our freedom and our food. We ought to smile. I'm sure when God looks down from heaven you make him much happier than we do, because you have kept the light in times of great darkness, and you have kept the faith in times of persecution. Thank you for giving us that vision to take back to the West, which is far greater than anything we have been able to give you.' It was a sacramental moment.

Speech-making, often accompanied by protracted bouts of ritual toasting, was to punctuate the many trips that followed to Russia and Armenia. Sentimental speeches are part of the Russian tradition. They may seem overcoloured to English sensibilities, but Caroline was to develop a gift for producing sincere and impromptu speeches of her own in the grandiloquent Russian fashion.

Years later, she reflected on Olga's words. It was true. People didn't smile in the Soviet Union. 'In those days, wherever you went, you saw what I used to call the glass-eye phenomenon – an inhumanity in some people's faces, especially officials. Looking in their eyes was like looking at marbles. There was no light in them. You'd go through the Metro, and any official you saw would give you this glass eye. It was the same as at the Polytechnic of North London, when people would look over their shoulders to make sure no-one was in earshot before saying anything. So I really knew what Olga meant.'

TB or not TB?

Caroline's involvement with Russia continued to deepen. In 1993 she was approached to help set up a British equivalent of Médecins Sans Frontières (MSF) by a team which included Christopher Besse, a former member of MSF. But the French organization made it plain they had no intention of establishing an operational branch in the UK.

On reflection, Besse felt Britain had more to offer than a pool of recruits for foreign networks. To tap into the country's high level of medical training and tradition of overseas and voluntary work what was needed was a British operation. With MSF out of the picture, the project developed into MERLIN: Medical Emergency Relief International, and Caroline became a founder trustee.

That same year, she received a letter out of the blue from the Siberian town of Tomsk. It was an invitation from the Siberian Medical University to become an honorary professor and member of the board of trustees. Caroline was keen to develop whatever links she could with the newly democratized Russia. She accepted, but could find neither the time nor the resources to go to the formalities.

Then, during a game of squash with Christopher Besse, she asked him where he was going for his travels. 'Siberia' came the reply. Caroline told him about her invitation to Tomsk. Besse told her not to be so ridiculous. It was too much of a coincidence. MERLIN had been asked to set up a programme to fight tuberculosis based in, of all places, Tomsk. The region was in the grip of an epidemic and the disease was developing a resistance to antibiotics. The doctors were keen to get their hands on MERLIN's medicine and microscopes, but were less willing to review their practices. Under Communism, Tomsk had been designated a scientific area – a closed city. For all but the past two years it had been cut off from the rest of the world. Medical practice was in a time-warp.

The doctors were getting results, but at a price. The Russian system involved the screening of every citizen once a year and extensive periods of quarantine for anyone found to be carrying TB. 'They were using the same treatments we were in the 1950s,' says MERLIN's medical advisor Dr Nick Banatvala.

Meanwhile the World Health Organization had developed an effective programme to combat TB at around one-twentieth of the cost. The question was how to persuade the Russians to modernize their methods – a process certain to involve cuts in manpower. Christopher Besse knew MERLIN lacked the clout to impel the senior doctors to review their practices. 'They didn't know us from a piece of soap,' he says, 'but they kept going on about this wonderful Lady Cox.'

So Caroline went to Tomsk. After receiving her honorary degree she sat down with the senior medical staff and congratulated them on all they were achieving. Cautious as ever to avoid the impression that West is Best, she tiptoed tactfully round to the central issue. 'You obviously have such unparalleled experience of treatment of TB,' she said, 'and such fascinating clinical manifestations. With your reputation for scientific rigour, wouldn't it be a good idea to set up some randomized control trials, to combine treatments which are well established with the World Health Organization protocols? You could produce a scientific assessment of the efficacy of the different kinds of treatment.'

The trials were duly conducted and the appropriate – and correct – conclusions drawn. The Russian scientists recognized the need for change by themselves, and the TB programme in Tomsk is now highly successful.

'It was a happy coincidence,' says Caroline, 'that of the whole of the Russian Federation spanning seven time zones, the one place that offered me an honorary degree was where MERLIN happened to be running their TB programme. The good Lord provides in a remarkable way.'

MERLIN went on to operate in other bases in Siberia and to work with Caroline on projects in Sudan and Eritrea. 'She gave a great boost to our programme,' says Besse. 'I don't think MERLIN would have been set up without her and her larger-than-life enthusiasm.'

Caroline's larger-than-life energy also became evident to the Russian authorities. Once, when Besse was with her in Russia, she insisted on cramming on her running shoes and taking to the streets. The authorities had assigned two security men to watch over her, both former top athletes. But if they imagined the British baroness would be a soft assignment, they had another think coming. Says Besse: 'They were two ex-Olympic runners who were pickled on vodka and into their middle age. They ended up having to follow her round in a Russian Lada, because they couldn't keep up with her on foot.'

Tushinskaya

As the Iron Curtain parted and the drive for reform gained momentum, Russia opened itself up to international expertise. The quality of care in children's hospitals came under scrutiny. Tushinskaya Paediatric Hospital is one of Moscow's few new, purpose-built hospitals, and displays its progressive credentials by bearing a name instead of a number. Convinced of the need to reform nursing practice, Dr Harald Lipman and his wife, Nahid, from Hampstead, set up the Tushinskaya Children's Hospital Trust and in 1993 invited Caroline to be its President. There were two main areas for concern.

The first was to provide family-centred care that would enable parents to spend time with their children while they were in hospital. In Russia, the practice was to kiss your children goodbye until the hospital saw fit to discharge them. Some establishments in Britain did the same, not so long ago. The reasoning was that parental visits were all well and good, but children got upset when Mum and Dad had to go home. Today, the pendulum has swung towards encouraging maximum parental contact, which can create different kinds of tensions. 'It's a difficult balance to get right,' says Caroline.

The second problem, which had shades of Tomsk, was infection control. The hospital was new enough to boast architectural barriers against infectious diseases. The outside world would have to pass through several layers to reach a child who had been placed in a cubicle. So far so good, but the doctors and nurses were passing from one cubicle to the next without changing their clothing or washing their hands, with predictable consequences. Any change would have to begin with the nurses and work its way upwards.

The Tushinskaya Trust devised an exchange programme involving Russian paediatric nurses and British tutors. Many of the nurses from the Moscow hospital visited Great Ormond Street and Queen Elizabeth Hospital in Hackney. In return, British nurse tutors went back to Moscow to try to introduce whatever changes might be appropriate within the Russian context. The patron of the Trust was Princess Diana. Caroline accompanied her during a high-profile visit in 1995, to open the hospital's school of paediatric nursing. She described the Princess as, 'very good with the children', while the Trust described Caroline as 'extremely supportive at all times'.

Caroline's work with Russian children neither began, nor ended there. Earlier, on the brink of the human rights conference in Leningrad, a newly elected deputy on the city council sent an urgent plea for help to the Solidarity Human Rights Commission in Warsaw. Alexander Rodin claimed many orphans and abandoned children were being wrongly diagnosed as mentally handicapped.

They were sent to special institutions, where they were subjected to drug abuse, denied an education and pressed into forced labour. He called for international experts to assess the situation. They were to uncover a system of widespread abuse and degradation, and to point to the use of orphan soldiers trained in the art of atrocity. It was to lead Caroline to become involved in an extensive programme of reform with the potential to transform child care throughout the Russian Federation.

TEN

Suffer the Children

The psychiatric hospital in Leningrad was brick-built and bare, looming over a courtyard of raw, exposed concrete. It was one of the city's main institutions for the so-called mentally ill. The small group of visitors was led inside the secure adolescent wing, along a bare corridor and into a dingy locked ward with grey walls devoid of decoration. Beside the few beds were piles of soiled brown mattresses. Apart from that, nothing. Only the boys, some ten on each side.

Igor was about 14, but small for his age. His thin, white face looked listlessly up at them from beneath a mop of brown hair. He was shabbily dressed and obviously drugged.

Igor was in the secure psychiatric ward because he had tried to run away from an orphanage when he was bullied. Others were there for the same reason. Neither he nor the boy with him appeared mentally ill to the Western professionals who had suddenly descended upon their ward. Their admission notes were divided under different headings. Under Physical Assessment, it read: 'nothing abnormal detected'. Under Psychological Assessment: 'nothing abnormal detected'. Yet, scrawled in biro beneath was a single word: 'schizophrenia'.

Igor's face was pale and pointed. His eyes were dark and bruised. He looked at Caroline, and pleaded, 'Please will you find me a mother, I want to get out of here.' Caroline went out into the courtyard and wept.

She had taken time out from the human rights conference in Leningrad to respond to the request of two of the city's newly elected deputies. They claimed orphans were being wrongly diagnosed as mentally handicapped, stripped of their rights and subjected to abuse.

A fortnight before, she was staying in Scotland with Lord Pearson, who had accompanied her on their visit to the Russian dissidents. With her was Irina Alberti, the editor of a respected independent journal. A fax arrived from the Solidarity Human Rights Commission in Warsaw. It was from Alexander (Sasha) Rodin, a deputy of the Len-Soviet. His position gave unprecedented access to institutions that previously had been sealed off to the public.

Rodin, young, fair-haired and sensitive, had visited several orphanages for oligophrenics. The word comes from the Greek; it means a person with a small brain. What he saw disturbed him deeply. He was convinced many of the children were perfectly normal and had been falsely diagnosed. Once diagnosis had taken place they were deprived of all their human rights. Many were physically and sexually abused. He was asking the West to send a team of experts to find out the truth. The conference was imminent. There was little time to respond.

Caroline handed the fax to Irina and asked, 'Do I take this seriously?'

Irina's eyes flicked down the text, then looked pointedly at Caroline. She said, 'You certainly do. Whoever wrote that must be a very brave man.'

With time at a premium, Caroline managed to find a consultant paediatrician with an interest in the Soviet Union who had worked with *refuseniks*. It was hardly a full-blown team, but it was a start. Accompanying Caroline to Leningrad was Katherine Adler, from Birch Hill Hospital in Rochdale.

Katherine's first shock was the sight of Caroline in her running gear in Moscow: 'She'd done a quick canter before breakfast.' Her second was what awaited her at the orphanage.

Too sane for their own good

Sasha Rodin arranged to visit an institution for oligophrenics. It was in a well-established house, set in grounds. They arrived in the hall to be greeted by two large posters. One was a quotation from Marx, the other from Lenin, on the value of work. Conditions were drab and dismal, but otherwise tolerable. There was no evidence of the extreme deprivation found in orphanages in Rumania or China.

The children were well-dressed, bright, lively and eager to talk. Yet they were described to their faces as oligophrenic and totally incapable of ever doing a normal job.

Caroline went into the recreation room and joined in with a game of table tennis. The 'oligophrenics' had her on the run. It was telling. Mental handicap is normally associated with some loss of physical co-ordination. 'But if their prowess at ping-pong was anything to go by, there was no problem there.' Nor did they appear intellectually impaired. Some were playing chess. 'They seemed to have been socialized into accepting the definition of themselves as oligophrenic. They probably didn't realize what that would mean when they left the orphanage, what trajectories of despair lay ahead.'

The *Oxford English Dictionary* defines oligophrenia as 'feeble-mindedness'. R.J. Campbell's *Psychiatric Dictionary* refers to it as an alternative term for mental retardation.[1] But Moscow psychiatrist Vladimir Kozyrev, director of Kashchenko Psychiatric Hospital, put a different spin on it. He said, 'In Russia, to become orphaned or abandoned is virtually synonymous with becoming an oligophrenic.'[2]

Soviet psychiatry identified three kinds of oligophrenics: idiots, imbeciles and debiles. 'Idiots' were the profoundly retarded, devoid of intellect, purposeless, incapable of speech, and able to express only raw emotions. 'Imbeciles' were incapable of abstract thought and of being taught in school. A few might manage primitive reading and writing. 'Debile' patients suffered from moderate mental retardation or learning difficulty. They could just about cope with the primary school syllabus – under favourable conditions. Their behaviour could be random and driven by emotions. Debiles were incapable of subtle intellectual feelings, which Soviet psychiatry defined as duty, comradeship and satisfaction.

The director of Moscow Children's Psychiatric Hospital No. 6 was asked to estimate where the children under her care fitted into those categories. She put debiles at 50 to 70 per cent; imbeciles at 20 to 50 per cent and gave the rest as idiots.[3]

The 'idiots, imbeciles and debiles' of the institution visited by Caroline and Katherine were so excited by these strangers they insisted on conversing with them about a wide range of subjects, including international politics, and then accompanying them back to the Metro so they wouldn't get lost. 'They were out and about in the streets, capable of handling Leningrad traffic,' says Caroline. 'They were not, on the face of it, oligophrenic, or mentally handicapped in any way.'[4]

She left feeling dismayed and perplexed by what she had seen, and said to Sasha Rodin, 'I can't understand what's happening here.'

He replied, 'What's happening is these children are being identified as oligophrenic, therefore they're not given a proper education; they're not qualified for jobs of their choosing, and not able to realize their potential.' He paused. 'The Soviet Union needs unthinking, unskilled, manual workers, and that is all that these young people will be fit for.'

The next day they absconded from the conference to visit the psychiatric hospital. 'It was heartbreaking,' recalls Caroline. 'The diagnosis of schizophrenia appeared completely arbitrary and unwarranted. And the drug regimes disturbed us profoundly.' Alongside drugs prescribed for schizophrenia were others, like injections of magnesium sulphate. 'It's not an injection you would generally use in the West. It would give you intense headaches.'

Some of the children were on sulphazine, a drug with a track record in psychiatric torture, which induces fever and cramps. Injected, it can drive the temperature up to 40 degrees and render every movement painful. Its use had been reported in Dnepropetrovsk Psychiatric Hospital in the 1970s as a punishment for misbehaviour.

As Caroline and Katherine were leaving the ward in some distress, a middle-aged man in a white coat put in an appearance. He was the hospital's medical director. He demanded to know why they were there. Sasha Rodin cut in and explained that he had exercised his right of entry to the hospital, as a deputy. 'The medical director wasn't best pleased,' recalls Caroline.

'I asked him why these boys were on injections of magnesium sulphate.' He tried to fend her off, muttering that magnesium was used for all sorts of things, including constipation.

Caroline cut him short, 'I know that perfectly well – I'm a nurse – but this is not how we would give it in Britain.'

The director replied, 'You had better ask the doctor on the ward, he's responsible.'

'I have,' said Caroline. 'And he said he didn't know, because he was new and these drugs were already prescribed before he got here. So I would like to ask you, because you are the medical director responsible for the whole hospital.'

At that the director took off, with Caroline in hot pursuit, running across the courtyard after him, saying, 'Sorry, sir, I didn't quite hear your answer to my question.' He scuttled through a doorway and disappeared.

'Caroline was firm,' said Katherine Adler, 'but I never saw her lose her temper. She was lovely with the children; very kind, and able to draw them out.' They left the building with Igor's plea to find him a mother ringing in their ears.

Igor had been caught in a trap that was precisely the opposite of Joseph Heller's Catch-22, where if you tried to get away by pleading insanity you were obviously sane. When Igor had done what any sane person would do and tried to get away from his wretched institution he had been pronounced insane. 'He was too sane for his own good,' says Caroline.

She later found out that 70 per cent of the boys who were admitted to orphanages for oligophrenics were sent to psychiatric hospital at least once, perhaps many times, during their adolescent years. Sometimes they were sent for being too independent-minded. Instead of going to summer camp in the country, children who were too assertive would be locked up on a psychiatric ward.

Orphan soldiers

Caroline's head was reeling. 'What I saw at the orphanage was bad enough,' she told Sasha. 'This is really horrific. I just don't understand the dynamics. I can see the need to produce unskilled manual workers, but what's going on here?'

Sasha replied ominously, 'It was reported that the soldiers who carried out the atrocities at Tbilisi were orphans.'

In April 1989, troops beat 16 protesters to death with shovels in Tbilisi. According to reports, the soldiers responsible belonged to an orphans' brigade. Further unconfirmed reports said troops involved in killings in Riga that year also had orphans in their ranks.

Sasha explained that because the orphans were vulnerable, and had never known family life or normal relationships, they could be manipulated to perform tasks that ordinary people would never do.

His words followed Caroline back to the UK. She sounded out a number of people, one a seasoned radio commentator on the Soviet Union with a particular interest in military affairs. She told him about the orphan soldiers. He made a gesture of recognition and said, 'That explains something I never understood before.' While he was being shown round a barracks near Moscow he noticed a separate unit. He asked why the unit was on its own, and was told it was where they kept orphan soldiers. They were always kept separate. He asked why, and was told, 'Because where there are men who have never had anything they can call their own, they can be trained to do things that other people could never do.'

She tried out the idea on a psychiatrist friend and asked him if it made sense. He replied, 'Of course it does. There's a whole literature on this from the time of the Ottoman empire. This is well-known.' And he wondered out loud whether it was perhaps no coincidence that the Rumanian dictator Ceausescu had chosen for his bodyguard the most brutal members of the Securitate – all reputedly orphans.

Inquiries to a human rights organization produced support for the claim. Many orphan boys went into the army after leaving their orphanages. Their emotional deprivation made them more susceptible to obey orders to carry out brutalities. Their vulnerability and lack of resistance meant orphan soldiers could be turned into useful instruments of war.

'There was an abyss in front of me,' says Caroline. 'Abandoned children and orphans, many completely normal and lively, could be systematically deprived of their rights and education. Those who ran away, or were too independent, were sent to psychiatric hospital. Some were taken into the army and manipulated into carrying out atrocities. It seemed almost too horrible to believe. It was an enormous burden.'

The Soviet definition of an orphan was broader than that used by other nations. It included children removed from parents who were addicts, alcoholics, criminals, or would have been regarded as religious 'fanatics'. Cramped living conditions, poverty and a shortage of food made it hard for parents to maintain their children. Some gave up the fight and handed them over to institutions. Once deprived of their parental rights, there could be no further contact with their children.

In the whole of Russia there were some 750,000 abandoned children. In St Petersburg alone, 19,000 were living in special institutions in 1990 and a further 10,000 were homeless. Only 6 per cent of children in institutions were fully orphaned, without either parent. The rest had been abandoned.[5] Alexander Rodin asked Caroline to help. But first she needed an organization behind her.

At the airport returning from the Leningrad conference she had told the story of the Russian orphans to one of the delegates, a bearded, scholarly American by the name of John Eibner, who was working in Switzerland. 'She spoke from the heart,' he said, and moved by her account, Eibner carried her concern back to Switzerland. It was not the last he would see of Caroline Cox.

Christian solidarity

In the autumn of 1990, Caroline received an invitation to become a board member of an organization she had never heard of. Few in the UK had heard of Christian Solidarity International (CSI). She was already highly committed to a host of different projects, and the last thing she was looking for was more to do. But she follows a principle, that 'if God opens a door in front of you, you go through it in faith and see what's on the other side. Unless you do, you may miss the opportunity God has given you.'

Caroline had been buttonholed in the House of Lords' tea room by CSI's Chairman, Mervyn Thomas, a lively man with sparkling eyes and the zeal and determination to make things happen. Mervyn had taken the chair of the UK branch of the Swiss-based human rights charity. CSI aimed to focus on the cases everyone else overlooked. 'Remembering the forgotten peoples' was one of its slogans; being a 'voice for the voiceless' was another.

CSI was founded in 1977 and established a base in the UK three years later. As the name implied, it was interested in showing solidarity with persecuted Christians, but it had a heart for others in trouble, too. The more obscure, the more inaccessible, the better. If the oppressed people had never been seen on TV, if no-one within a thousand miles had ever heard of their plight, then CSI intended to be there, showing solidarity.

Mervyn got to hear about Caroline in a roundabout way, through Bob Dunn, a junior minister in the Department of Education, whose wife was on the CSI board. Bob said to Mervyn, 'She's right up your street: she drives trucks into Poland.'

The minister fixed up an interview at the House of Lords. Mervyn's immediate target was to persuade her to add her name to the letterhead. Then he would try to get her on to the Board. But gently did it.

They sipped tea in the genteel gilded surroundings of the Lords and something clicked. 'After talking to her for about 30 minutes,' says Mervyn, 'I realized she was a special lady and I was impressed.' At the end of the interview, Caroline asked: 'Well, what do you want me to do for you?' Mervyn blinked twice and decided to go for it. He asked her there and then to join the Board and she agreed.

Caroline still had a get-out clause. She would go to a meeting, weigh it up, and see if there was anything she could contribute. They would take it from there. But after losing her way around London's backstreets in the pouring rain, she was beginning to regret the hasty agreement made in the comfort of the Lords' leather armchair. It was already dark, and none of the road names she peered at seemed to match. Each time she stopped to check the A to Z, someone behind would hoot, flash their lights and force her to move on. She was going to be late – as usual – and was getting steadily 'more fraught, frantic and frenetic'.

Most Board meetings are held in Board rooms. Not so CSI's. It was early days for CSI UK, and the budget could only run to a room in a terrace on the south bank of the Thames. Wet and anxious, and at least 30 minutes late, she climbed a rickety set of stairs in a ramshackle house, with a growing conviction this was going to be her one and only meeting.

When she stepped inside, what greeted her seemed more like a church gathering than a Board meeting. Her mood lifted almost immediately. There was a sense of spirituality, integrity and sincerity. She was struck by their obvious lack of pretentiousness and was relieved to note that this cheerful coterie of men in suits didn't look like liberation theologians or closet Marxists. As they talked, they seemed to share many of the values she was committed to. Mervyn Thomas sensed the immediate resonance. 'She came in and felt an instant affinity with the kind of things we were saying.' Almost despite herself, she was deeply impressed. She grew as determined to become involved as Mervyn was to involve her. 'Little did I think what it could lead to,' she chuckles. 'CSI opened up opportunities I could never have foreseen for some of the most rewarding experiences of my life.'

CSI's mission statement loses something in its translation from the German: 'CSI is an interdenominational human rights organization for religious liberty, helping persecuted Christians and others suffering from repression, victimized children and victims of disaster.'

As her involvement grew, Caroline made up her mind to give more of her time to the work, even though it meant shedding other responsibilities, eventually taking over the UK presidency from David Atkinson, MP.[6] Several years down the line, CSI UK would branch out from its Swiss parent to pursue an independent stance. Like all divisions, it would be painful. CSI UK would change its name to Christian Solidarity Worldwide, with Caroline as its UK president.[7] But all that was ahead. Right now, the pressing question was how to help the 'victimized children' of the Soviet Union.

Caroline went on a weekend retreat with CSI in Sussex. The problem was churning round in her mind. Hans Stückelburger, CSI's founder and international president, had flown over from Zurich. His colleague, John Eibner, had already briefed him about Caroline Cox and the Russian orphans. He listened now with furrowed brows and said, 'Yes, we must take this seriously.' They agreed to carry out a pilot study to gauge the extent of the problem.

Caroline returned to the Soviet Union in 1991 with the wiry American, John Eibner, and journalist Felix Corley, who acted as their interpreter. To try to broaden the picture, they went to different institutions in Latvia and Moscow. If they were hoping for a different picture, they were disappointed. Caroline discovered that a British doctor, Anita Kalns-Timans, had been pursuing a similar line of investigation and had come up with much the same findings.

Dr Kalns-Timans discovered that Latvian psychiatry was heavily influenced by Moscow. The cult of the perfect Soviet citizen had led to the marginalization of anyone with any defect. To make matters worse, the psychiatrists were administering tests for which they had never received any training. Few of the staff were willing to challenge the system. Their attitude seemed to be: it is easier to do nothing than to do something, as if you do nothing, you won't be blamed.

Dr Kalns-Timans wrote:

At the first children's home I was told, 'They don't have emotions' and therefore it wasn't necessary to celebrate birthdays... Meal times and bath times were described in the same language one might use to describe feeding and slopping out farm-yard animals... Classrooms and bedrooms were bare with no drawings... the children had no personal possessions; even the clothes in which they played both inside and outside being shabby pyjamas. There was an obvious shortage of shoes and socks. Few toys were visible anywhere. I was told that any put out would be stolen. A child with behavioural problems and learning difficulties... had his hands tied behind his back.[8]

Caroline's heart sank when she read the report. She had hoped the Baltic states would be the least contaminated by the Soviet system. They were the most Western and supposedly the most progressive. The concerns raised went way beyond those being widely expressed about orphanages in Rumania. 'This was much subtler, much deeper and immensely sinister,' she says. 'This was deliberate manipulation for ulterior motives. The cold, calculating use by the system of vulnerable children made my blood run cold. Now it was corroborated in Latvia and Moscow. And as everyone said to us, the further east you go the worse it will get.'

NOTES

1. According to a textbook of the Leningrad Paediatric Medical Institute, oligophrenia is a 'state of general mental retardation... general mental backwardness... manifest in difficulty in social adaptation', cited in *Trajectories of Despair: Misdiagnosis and Maltreatment of Soviet Orphans*, CSI, 1991, p. 17.
2. *Trajectories of Despair*, p. 8.
3. *Trajectories of Despair*, p. 17.
4. Caroline's empathy with the orphans impressed John Eibner, who said: 'I was deeply moved by the warmth Caroline had for these suffering children. It was remarkable to see the smiles she put on their faces.'
5. According to the Department of Social Security and the Family, cited in *Trajectories of Despair*, p. 8.
6. In 1996.
7. As most of this book concerns the period before the split took place, late in 1997, to avoid confusion, CSI UK and its employees are referred to throughout by their titles at the time, rather than by their subsequent designations. Interviews for this book are presented in the present tense, but as they were conducted before the name change in 1998, interviewees are referred to by their designations at the time.
8. Dr Anita Kalns-Timans, *The Latvian Experience*, cited in *Trajectories of Despair*, Appendix 2.

ELEVEN

'Here Come the Half-wits'

In September 1991, Caroline returned to Russia with a full team. Accompanying her were educational psychologist, Martin Turner, clinical psychologist, Valerie Muter, paediatrician Katherine Adler, Soviet expert Felix Corley, and to record their findings, cameraman Vaughan Smith of Frontline News. Leningrad had by now reverted to its original name, St Petersburg. They met Sasha Rodin and visited 15 orphanages for so-called oligophrenics both there and in Moscow.

'With few exceptions, there was little attempt to make the children feel this was their own "home",' she says. 'Their rooms contained rows of beds, and little else. There were no pictures, curtains, lockers or cupboards for any personal possessions. There were no possessions at all – not even teddy bears or dolls. It seemed that many of the children possessed nothing apart from the uniform they stood up in.'[1]

The team carried out assessments on 171 children. After running extensive tests they found some two-thirds of the orphans were of average or above-average ability. 'There were notably very few who would have found themselves in institutions of any kind in the West.' To make matters worse they discovered that only one in a thousand would ever be reassessed. The label oligophrenic would be theirs for life.

The lifelong label meant lifelong stigma. Valery Fadeyev, a member of the Permanent Commission for Freedom of Conscience in Moscow, told CSI, 'Because someone on a high level once decided that all these orphans are handicapped for their whole lives and can't be changed, it is not thought necessary to care for them or to do anything about them. And the only thing they can do for society is work – cheap labour.'[2]

At one institution, in the name of work therapy, children sat for hours on end folding egg boxes or sticking price labels on perfume bottles. Their need for education took second place to the demand for their unpaid labour.

Viktor, a composed adolescent, was asked on camera what he would ideally like to do as a job. He thought for a moment then articulated clearly,

'I want to study chemistry and learn a foreign language, as they do in normal schools. Then I want to go on to further education and to take up shipbuilding and marine architecture.'

'You have an icicle's chance in hell,' thought Caroline. It was more than she could do to hold back the tears. Viktor complained that the schoolwork demanded of him was 'weak'. Martin Turner, the educational psychologist, conducted an extended interview and concluded that Viktor was intelligent, and with a realistic appraisal of his own potential – should he ever be allowed to achieve it.

It turned out Caroline's assessment of Viktor's prospects was, happily, mistaken. Vaughan Smith's film for Channel 4 was also shown in the USA. An American family saw it and came to Russia to adopt Viktor. He is now living a normal life with all the opportunities available to him that the USA can provide.

But for most of the orphans, the story was different. After leaving their homes, they were sent to hostels attached to factories. Vaughan Smith took his camera to one and found himself in a slum. He got footage of children working on antique equipment in the shoe factory for oligophrenics. The conditions were described as Dickensian.

One of the children whose face was pale and peaky explained, 'We were forcibly sent to "work school" and then to work here... either you go to "work school" or you are sent to psychiatric hospital. We have to carry a certificate from the psychiatric clinic with us. This is now the second year that I can't get into evening classes... At the home we were all diagnosed. I don't know what the diagnosis was; it was always kept secret. They called us half-wit schizophrenics, although we're all perfectly healthy.'

A second child chipped in: 'When I go past the commandant, she says, "Here come the half-wits." When we started working at the factory here, they knew we were from children's homes and they treated us very badly. Some of them behaved brutally.'

By the children's own reckoning half of them were normal and healthy. 'As for checking up whether the diagnosis is correct,' said one, 'nobody bothers.'

Three children appealed to get their diagnosis changed. 'Nothing happened,' one explained. 'Some teacher went to them and told lots of tales about us. I don't believe in anyone,' he added. 'None of the lads believe in anyone at all. Whatever changes may take place, it always stays the same for us. People should have more human rights.'[3]

There was an alternative: life on the streets and possibly prison. Vaughan Smith took his camera to the so-called 'House of Peace', a St Petersburg squat, where runaway orphans mixed with tramps and drop-outs. Caroline's report recorded, 'Here, children from the age of seven live a *Lord of the Flies* existence in appalling conditions of destitution and despair.'[4] It was one of four refuges in the city, tolerated, but unsupported by the authorities. The children kept together in their groups, the older girls looking after the others. Whatever food or clothing they had was either stolen or a hand-out from a Western charity.

In one room there were two rats in a cage. It seemed to sum it up. A runaway said, 'At first I wanted to work in a zoo, but I couldn't bear it, as the animals sit there like we did in the children's home. The animals in the zoo have better lives.'[5] In homes where there were pets, the children would shower them with affection, competing to stroke and hold them constantly.

The runaways at the House of Peace were free to speak more openly about life in the children's homes. They described being kept in check by the kind of drugs regime that was used against dissidents. One child explained, 'In the home they gave us injections of Aminazine, Tizerzin and magnesium every day. If you don't turn up or if you're late for classes they put you in the isolation cell. If you run away they send you to psychiatric hospital. There they give you endless injections.'[6]

Caroline visited the head psychiatrist for the district of Moscow in his hospital. He stated on camera that becoming an orphan in the Soviet Union was virtually synonymous with becoming oligophrenic. The same was said at three other psychiatric hospitals. The same drugs were being used. They quizzed a medical director about the use of sulphazine and she denied giving sulphazine injections without parental permission. Caroline frowned, 'But by definition, these children don't have parents.'

'Then we obtain permission from the director of the orphanage.'

'But that's the person who sent them here in the first place.' No wonder they ran away.

But with runaways forced to steal food and clothing, the House of Peace, and others like it, were often halfway houses to jail. Prison was to be the destination of some 80 per cent of orphans who had passed through the institutions.[7] In St Petersburg, the team visited a juvenile detention prison to find out where the majority would end up. Up to a third of the inmates awaiting trial were orphans. Some were there for stealing a handful of food or a jacket.

The detention centre was a crude, brick-built monstrosity. It was old and soiled, and boys in their mid-teens were crammed up to 15 to a cell designed for three, where they would share a single, open toilet. Exercise in a fenced yard three metres by five was supposed to last an hour a day, but seldom did. The boys were supposed to shower once a week, but usually had to wait a fortnight. It was a relief, really. Getting to the shower meant running the gauntlet of rubber truncheons. Medical treatment appeared to be given only as a matter of life or death.

Katherine Adler examined one boy who was limping. There was an abscess on his foot. Another had a throat infection and a liver complaint. A third looked gaunt and depressed. None had received any treatment. As one boy put it, 'This is not life. This is survival.' All of this was before they had been found guilty of any offence. They could remain in prison for a year or more awaiting trial.

Katherine was moved to tears. 'It reminded me of a concentration camp: the overcrowding and neglect of those young boys. It was obvious they were being abused.'

Despite the harrowing circumstances, Katherine was impressed with the way Caroline was able to enthuse the team and keep up morale. In one of the psychiatric workshops, where the orphans were making necklaces, Caroline bought one for each person with her, men and women alike. The consultant thanked her gravely for supporting their industry. Katherine Adler still wears her necklace today. 'It was such a sweet gesture,' she said. 'Caroline is the most unpompous of titled people. There is absolutely no side to her. She is also very much a catalyst.'

So was the report which emerged from their visit. It heralded far-reaching change that neither Caroline nor Katherine would have believed possible. The title of the report echoed an earlier phrase of Caroline's, *Trajectories of Despair*. It observed,

> Virtually all would be doomed to institutional care in special orphanages for the 'mentally handicapped' where the maximum education they would receive would be to fourth grade, instead of the eighth grade for normal children. They would subsequently be directed to work in the most unskilled manual jobs and required to reside in special single-sex hostels without the opportunity to develop normal family life. As 'oligophrenics' they will be denied basic rights, such as the right to vote or to drive a car. And the spectre of psychiatric treatment looms over them if they run away or misbehave.[8]

Even before the report came out, the system's shortcomings were slowly beginning to emerge. Yet, from an outsider's perspective, it is hard to imagine how these professionals could ever have concluded that the children were abnormal. 'Many of the people we met in the orphanages were very caring,' says Caroline. 'They would do the best they could for the kids, but on the given understanding that they were dealing with oligophrenics. We were faced with a closed society, a totalitarian system, and with people who accepted what they were told and did what they were told. Even so, many were doing what they could within the system, in spite of the system.'

As the research team's findings were processed they would report back as a matter of courtesy to the director of each orphanage. One, a middle-aged woman, almost exploded with frustration and rage. She swore, and said, 'I always *knew* those kids were normal, but now it's too late to help them.'

The root of the problem, believed Valery Borshcov, Chairman of the Mos-Soviet Permanent Commission for Freedom of Conscience, lay in the attitude towards people which had existed in Russian society for the last 70 years. He described it as a lack of respect for any individual, whether healthy or ill.

The mental blindness was explained even more succinctly by Soviet-educated psychiatrist, Dr Anatoly Koryagin, who lamented, 'Man, in the Soviet view, is valuable only to the extent that he is of advantage to society... He is a means, not an end.'[9] Dr Koryagin had been jailed for 12 years in 1981 for campaigning against the abuse of psychiatry as a means of social control.

There had already been signs of change in the air. The director of one, more enlightened orphanage told CSI:

> In this establishment, most of our staff do not believe that oligophrenia is genetic. We teachers tell the boys, 'Forget your labels and read as much as you can.' We take them on outings to other towns and museums... They feel and behave much better as a result. In the first year, there used to be many fights leading to bloodshed, but in the past year, none at all. They are also much kinder to each other. We can take them anywhere and people do not believe that our children are from a special school.

At another orphanage, further education was being arranged, and one child had been assisted to gain entry to the Moscow Conservatory of Music.

Shockwaves

The report took a constructive approach, but was inevitably hard-hitting. 'One of the things I admire about the way the Russians received it,' says

Caroline, 'is that it was critical of the system, but they still responded by wanting us to help them change.'

The report observed, 'The problems are so extensive that it is difficult to know where to begin.' It made a number of urgent recommendations. It called for staff to be properly trained in assessment, to prevent misdiagnosis. Normal children should be transferred to ordinary schools and given remedial teaching to make up for the wasted years. A complete revolution in the teaching of the mentally retarded was required, to help them achieve their potential. Drugs should only be used as appropriate and no longer as an instrument of punishment. More children should be fostered and adopted, and the ban on adopting the mentally retarded should be lifted. New family-style homes should be established for abandoned children. International experts should be called in to advise on modern child care practices. A system of social services should be developed to support parents and discourage them from abandoning their children. The law should be changed to protect the rights of vulnerable children, especially those who are orphaned or abandoned. It concluded, 'Without change of fundamental policies, such as the misdiagnosis of children and punitive use of psychiatry, countless children will continue to suffer.'[10]

But how had they come to be misdiagnosed in the first place? It was a question Caroline asked again and again. And the answer was, 'usually perfunctorily and very arbitrarily. Maybe someone would phone the authorities and say, "I know an alcoholic family and a child who is at risk." They would send officials to question the child, who, not unnaturally, would be intimidated and tongue-tied, and so immediately identified as oligophrenic and taken to an institution. Others would be diagnosed in the car, on their way from the home.' Oligophrenia was a bureaucratic classification, and not the systematic psychological diagnosis it purported to be.

The system was self-perpetuating. Psychiatric practice had to conform to Soviet ideology. Scientific findings which failed to fit were ignored, suppressed or ridiculed; especially those from overseas. Soviet psychiatry had become hermetically sealed. The ideas of Freud were heavily suppressed. And in a system which glorified manual labour, psychiatrists were rewarded with less than a third of the wage of a bus driver.

Another factor was that staff in some children's homes were paid up to 40 per cent more if they had children with a psychiatric complaint. It was an incentive to label them as mentally ill. It all added up to a bias towards misdiagnosis.

Oligophrenia was widely believed to be an incurable hereditary illness, so instead of treating it, steps were taken to contain it. As the director of one orphanage put it, 'Oligophrenia is incurable. Normal children don't enter this house. If the diagnosis were wrong, we would recognize this on the first day.'

CSI's report caused shockwaves throughout the system. At the Moscow press launch of the Russian edition in 1993 Caroline was braced for criticism, but found herself surprised by the warmth of her reception and the openness of those who were there. Several directors of orphanages were present. A number announced they had already reclassified their children. One dignified woman with grey hair, said she had demanded reassessment for 80 of her so-called oligophrenics. Each one had been reclassified as normal.

One Soviet politician privately described the report as an excellent description of totalitarianism. 'You don't have independent ideas and opinions. You are part of the system and if you don't want to end up in a *gulag*, you work within it.' The report articulated what they intuitively knew was happening, said the director of an orphanage, but what they could not objectively identify from within the system. 'But now you have given us the evidence,' he continued, 'we have the ammunition to change the system from within.' It was as though they had been given permission to see.

A few of the old-school turned up to argue, but were challenged by their colleagues. 'I have great respect for their generosity of spirit,' says Caroline. The battle was fought internally – and won. But the process of reform would be far-reaching – and costly.

Transformation

Caroline set up an appeal to try to raise money. With possibly hundreds of thousands of children trapped within the system, thinking big was essential. What was needed was nothing less than radical change throughout the whole of the Russian Federation.

She was invited to meet the Vice Minister of Education for the Russian Federation in the office once used by Lenin's wife. The furniture had been kept exactly as it was and the portrait of Nadezhda Krupskaya glowered down at the proceedings. Sitting behind her leather-topped table, the minister asked CSI to help them push through a complete reform of their child care policy. She wanted a decisive shift from institutionalization to foster care, which had been unknown in Russia for 70 years, and an end to oligophrenia. Then she asked Caroline if she would act as patron, and if CSI would be the lead organization helping to change the child care system throughout the Russian Federation. Caroline was amazed. Agreements were signed there and then and sealed with a kiss, three times on each cheek. 'It was an awesome responsibility.'

At about the same time, the Moscow government asked CSI if they would help set up foster care in the capital. They wanted to establish family foster homes in the heart of the city. They would provide alternative care for children who would otherwise be institutionalized and would become a training resource and model for the whole of Russia.

The first family foster home was opened in Moscow in 1990 in a pair of flats knocked together to occupy the entire floor of one of the capital's anonymous tower blocks. Serge and Irina Buchtoyarova filled the rooms with 11 children and somehow managed to keep the secret from their neighbours, who they feared would never understand.

When Katya came to them at the age of 16 she could read but had never been taught to count. 'She could not add one and one,' Irina explained to a visiting Western journalist. 'She knew nothing about everyday life. She didn't even know what the words river, lake or forest meant.' Within four months she could count to 1,000 and had been moved up two forms at school.

'The most important thing,' added Irina, 'is to give them respect as human beings. They have never been respected before. The second most important thing is love.'[11]

Christian Solidarity is now running the two parallel projects, for the Russian Federation and Moscow City Council. There have been exchanges between lawyers, policy-makers and professionals from Moscow, Perm, Omsk, Karelia and St Petersburg. The approach is the usual well-tried combination of diplomacy and psychology. When groups come over from Russia, care is taken never to preach at them or insist they do things a certain way. Accepted international practices are offered as a pattern, to be adapted and interpreted by the Russians to suit their situation. Change results from a journey of discovery. The key was to be positive and offer strategies for reform and improvement. The approach paid off.

Adoption was a rarity in Soviet society. It ran counter to the ethos of the State catering for all eventualities. It smacked of individualism. The handicapped were regarded with distaste, to the extent that it was illegal to adopt abnormal children. The tiny allowances given for adopted children would never begin to cover the costs. Furthermore, adoptive parents had the right to taste and try. They could hand back any child that failed to suit them by claiming the child was not 100 per cent healthy. A substantial change of ideas was needed. At the suggestion and invitation of the Russians, two experts were dispatched to advise on adoption and fostering.

In December 1995 the Russian Parliament, the Duma, introduced new measures to develop fostering and family care. And the following month, CSI opened the first foster family unit in Moscow, with no fewer than 100 applications in a fortnight to become the 'social parents' who would live and work there.

In May 1996, CSI co-hosted a conference with the Russian Federation Department of Education to introduce fostering as a policy across the whole of Russia. Seventeen regions immediately latched on to the idea. A group of directors toured the 'Our Family' orphanage in Moscow and met the foster parents. They returned determined to push through change in their own regions. 'It's mind-blowing,' says Caroline. 'More than we could ever dare hope for. When I came out of that psychiatric hospital in Leningrad and met those doctors, I never thought such a thing would be possible. It is a triumph of the human spirit.'

It was the time of the Russian Easter, and Irina Voladina, the chief child abuse inspector for the Ministry of Education put it thus: 'Easter is about bringing new hope and light in the darkness. We are here to try to bring a new hope and a new light in the darkness for Russian children.'

Reform has spread in a way that neither Caroline nor CSI could have imagined. At the time of publication, 15 children were being looked after in Moscow and 60 had been placed with foster families. The family units were run by married couples, assisted by staff trained in child care.

Yet it was a tough time to invest in Russia. The collapse of the rouble wiped out the savings of carers and many foster parents lost their jobs. Christian Solidarity's contact in Moscow warned: 'If salaries continue to drop and there is no regular payment of allowances then people will not have money to buy food.' After a disastrous grain and potato harvest came reports that conscript soldiers had starved to death in Siberia. Fears grew in the West – and in Russia itself – of civil unrest and the possible collapse of the government.

Christian Solidarity's representative in Moscow reported: 'Any further changes in the government or in the Presidency could put the country on the brink of a civil war, or could clear the way to fascism.'

It was a storm that had to be weathered, not only by Russia, but by Christian Solidarity, which somehow had to pay for the family orphanages. 'It is a nightmare working out where to get the money from,' says Caroline. 'We are living entirely by faith.' Eventually, the running of the homes will be turned over to the Russians – when the Russians can afford to run them. 'In the meantime, it is a responsibility which we have got to honour.'

Fortunately, the scheme attracted the attention of UNICEF which, after a vigorous evaluation, stepped in to provide $60,000 for training. It was a much needed boost. And despite all the apocalyptic rumblings within Russia, child care reform continues to go from strength to strength in Moscow and other regions. In 1999, a second centre in a former warehouse was due for completion and other areas of the Russian Federation were poised to adopt the programme. At the same time, new services were being set up by Christian Solidarity[12] to help prevent family breakdown and provide clinical treatment for neglected and abused children.

The child of the dream

All the children have been saved from a world of acute deprivation and emotional trauma. Two brothers, aged 9 and 14, had been left to fend for themselves for six months after their father died and their mother walked out on them to live with a new man. Eventually, the brothers made their way to Our Family, begging for help. Both were quickly placed with foster parents.

A five-year-old girl had been scavenging the streets since the age of three to collect cigarette ends for her mother. They lived together in a single room, where the girl shared a bed with her mother and her various men friends. The five-year-old was taken to hospital with multiple fractures after falling from the fourth floor. There were grounds for suspicion that she was thrown. Her mother never visited her in hospital, and on the single occasion her father turned up he was so drunk he had to be barred from entering the building.

The Our Family project gives a future and a hope to these children, and is a lifeline to foster parents. All her life, Ludmilla had wanted to have a child. She had visited orphanages but had been intimidated by the staff. Ludmilla was made welcome at Our Family and she and her husband Maxim adopted nine-year-old Sasha.

Another foster parent, Igor, believes he was given a dream by God. In it, he saw himself and his wife, Natasha, standing beneath the stars. As they looked upwards, they saw two boys falling from the sky. Both were smiling. The smaller of the two was trying to tell them something, but was unable to speak.

A year passed and the Our Family project had been established and was advertising for foster parents. Igor and Natasha were in church when they saw the advert. They applied, were selected and went through the training until they were ready to adopt their first children.

In the meantime, the children who were ready for care had been taken by the Our Family staff to the Black Sea. While they were there, a boy was found abandoned by a dustbin and was handed to the police. Little Dima had been fed on bread and water and was so malnourished that he had to be sent to a special hospital for blood diseases. When he was ready to be discharged, the police were reluctant to send him to an institution for oligophrenics, so they contacted the Our Family project.

Igor and Natasha were asked if they would come to see the boy with a view to taking him into their family. The moment Igor set eyes on him, he recognized the child instantly as the smaller of the two boys in his dream. Blond-haired Dima was four years old, the child of alcoholic parents. His mother seldom spoken to him, so he had never learned to talk. All he could do was mumble like a drunkard.

Igor and Natasha accepted him into their family and Dima quickly learned to speak. Soon he was able to tell them about an older brother he had never seen, but had heard his mother talk about. One of the Our Family social workers set about tracing the brother and found him at an orphanage for oligophrenics. Sasha was 11. When Igor went to see him at the orphanage he was in no doubt that he was looking at the second boy of his dream.

All the children in Sasha's class were well-behaved, bright and alert, and Igor was convinced Sasha was perfectly normal. It took just two weeks to arrange all the paperwork. When Igor went to collect Sasha, the child called him Papa and refused to let go of his hand, as if he were afraid he would disappear. Dima had been with them for six months and now he and his brother were united. Igor and Natasha were overwhelmed. They already had two sons and a daughter. With four sons, joked Igor, he could finally get round to fixing up the country cottage.

'It was an amazing sequence of events,' says Caroline. 'The child in the dream symbolizes the miracles on which Christian Solidarity relies.'

On a flight to Moscow that year, Caroline and Stuart Windsor, CSI's national director, were joking on the plane, letting off steam as usual. Stuart is a jovial man with a shock of white hair who is larger than life in every respect. She insulted his girth, while he criticized her for dropping three bottles of wine intended for CSI staff. Caroline had cut it fine for the flight, as ever, and had been in such a rush at the check-in that the bottles went flying. On the plane, the steward came over and jokingly threatened to separate them if they didn't behave. The next time he saw them, they were praying together in their seats. When he returned again, she had gone to pray with another member of their team, Lord Powys. The steward overheard the story of the broken wine bottles and asked them what they did for a living. When they got off the aircraft they were presented with 16 mini-bottles of champagne and 15 little duffel bags for the children at the orphanage.

Stuart and Caroline make an unlikely combination. He is an Assemblies of God minister – very non-Conformist, very low church – and teases Caroline mercilessly for praying in her high Anglican fashion. The first time she prayed down the phone, as she finished, he intoned, '"We do not presume to come to this thy table, O Lord..." I had a bit of fun with her and she laughed.

'We have this rapport wherever we go, even with high-level people. She introduces me as her boss, and I retort by saying, "No, I'm her servant." She's always full of fun.'

NOTES

1. *Trajectories of Despair*, p. 24.
2. *Trajectories of Despair*, p. 8.
3. *Trajectories of Despair*, pp. 26, 27.
4. *Trajectories of Despair*, p 6.
5. *Trajectories of Despair*, pp. 24, 25.
6. *Trajectories of Despair*, p. 21.
7. According to the Psychological Institute of the Russian Academy of Education, cited in *Development of Russian Foster Care Model*, CSI.
8. *Trajectories of Despair*, p. 5.
9. *Trajectories of Despair*, p. 11.
10. *Trajectories of Despair*, pp. 32–34.
11. Ann Leslie, 'Once they were treated as though they didn't exist, but at last there is hope for Russia's "lost" orphans'.
12. CSI-UK eventually split from CSI in Zurich to become Christian Solidarity Worldwide. The reasons for that division can be found on p. 387. By agreement, CSW took over the running of the Russian child care project. Its partners are UNICEF, the Bridge Child Care Consultancy Service, McIntyre Care and Oxfordshire County Council Child Care Services.

Part Two

Nagorno Karabakh

'For Azerbaijan the issue of Karabakh is a matter of ambition. For the Armenians of Karabakh, it is a matter of life and death.'

Andrei Sakharov

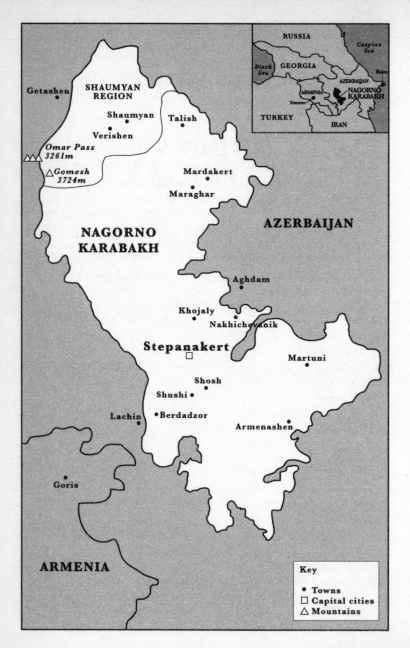

Key
- ● Towns
- □ Capital cities
- △ Mountains

ONE

A Matter of Life and Death

Gersyk Gabrialian stepped out from behind the blue striped cotton sheet intended to keep the elements from the one tiny room that still had a roof. In a few months the temperature would plummet to minus 40 degrees. Wringing her hands and smudging away the tears she described how the missile had buried members of her family alive in the capital, Stepanakert, how the missiles had kept on coming, and how the same missiles had been turned on her village, Agbulag. 'All night they were bombing us,' she told Caroline. 'We left everything. We left our casualties. We couldn't even manage to wear a nice dress for running. The Azeris came. They burned houses, destroyed houses. They attacked this village twice.'

Caroline stood close by, smiling gently, her eyes reflecting the other woman's grief, her hand resting lightly on hers. 'They killed my brother,' said the Armenian woman in the red cotton dress, dark shadows circling her eyes. 'They killed the children of my brother.' Their bodies had been shown on TV.

Armenians and Azeris lived together in Gersyk's village before the war. 'We were getting along well,' she said, 'like brother and sister. We were sharing bread with them, and when it started, these people with whom we were living, they betrayed us and said, "Look, it's our territory, you have to leave." They turned their face to the Azeris trying to attack the village.'

Under the late summer sun, on a pair of tables within the ruined stone walls of what had once been her living room, damsons were spread out and drying. The fruit from her tree was all the woman had for the winter. When her words ran out she wrapped some plums in a brown paper bag and gave them to Caroline.

It was Caroline's twenty-first visit to Nagorno Karabakh. She had learnt that to refuse a gift made sacrificially, however unnecessary, however wasteful, however pointless, would be to insult the woman's dignity. The gift accepted, more damsons were placed in bags pulled out of her room made crowded by a wooden bed and a red plastic bowl, and handed to the reporters who had already consumed her words. 'Thank you for not forgetting,' she said. 'I am sorry I can't offer you more hospitality.'

The determined delegate

The First International Andrei Sakharov Memorial Congress in Moscow was to be a posthumous commemoration of the 70th birthday of the Soviet nuclear physicist, developer of the hydrogen bomb, and latter-day dissident, internal exile, human rights campaigner and winner of the Nobel Peace Prize.

Caroline was invited by his widow, Elena Bonner Sakharov, to join the international co-ordinating party preparing for the Congress. It was a high-profile event that could not be ignored by the establishment, much to the chagrin of Gorbachev and Yeltsin, who were duly present at the opening ceremony on 21 May 1991.

There was a sense of urgency and an air of weighty responsibility about the whole proceedings; a sense that things could now be discussed upon which the lid had been firmly kept for a very long time. Caroline was chairing one of many working parties, concerned with *refuseniks* and psychiatric abuse in the Soviet Union. It was a struggle to keep the meeting on track. Groups were turning up unannounced to press issues that were off the agenda, that they were desperate to have included.

Some 20 experts were gathered around a long central table to consider human rights and injustice. Throughout it all, one delegate kept trying to catch Caroline's eye. He was a big man, with Slavic features, dark hair, a grizzled moustache and eyes like gleaming coals. He occupied a commanding position at the centre of the table and was hard to ignore. Caroline's time was as short as her agenda was long, so she studiously avoided his eye. But as the conference drew to a close, his persistence and something about his sheer presence prevailed, until eventually she felt compelled to let him say his piece.

Zori Balayan spoke slowly, with authority and eloquence about events unfolding in a place she had never heard of: Nagorno Karabakh. He described in poignant detail the systematic deportations by Azerbaijan of entire Armenian villages. He spoke with great sadness, as though each act of atrocity was a violation of his own family. And he concluded by saying: 'I am talking about what happened last week – what is happening to my people right now. Instead of sitting around tables, it would be better to stand up and go to Karabakh with me.' Although the conference was over and all were exhausted, they took him at his word. Caroline arranged at zero notice to send a delegation to the capital of Armenia, Yerevan.

TWO

The Cauldron of the Caucasus

But where was this place, and why had these events failed to impact on the news media? Size and accessibility were part of the answer. Nagorno Karabakh is a mountainous scrap of Transcaucasia, little bigger than the English county of Hampshire, but with one-tenth the population. It was hardly a major player. Karabakh is tucked inside Azerbaijan – itself little larger than Scotland – and suspended between Georgia and Turkey, with Iran just 15 miles to the south. The population of Karabakh is some 170,000. That of Azerbaijan is 7 million.

Nagorno Karabakh has been described as a cross between Switzerland and Vietnam. Its name, a hybrid of Russian, Turkish and Persian, means mountainous black garden. Oak, hornbeam and beech give way to birch and alpine meadows as the terrain grows more rugged in its climb towards Mount Gyamysh. The valleys are graced with vineyards, orchards and mulberry groves. Its inhabitants are dark-eyed Armenians whose peasants seem as weather-beaten as their hills, where searing summers and bitter winters conspire to produce an average annual temperature coincident with that of the freezing point of water.

The boundaries of Karabakh were defined 2,000 years ago by the Greek historian Strabo. The region formed part of Armenia until the seventh century, when it was occupied by Arab warriors, advancing in the name of Islam. The national, ethnic and cultural identity of Karabakh remains intertwined with that of neighbouring Armenia. Less than five miles separate them at their closest point.

History has made for a fragmented Armenia, a substantial diaspora and a good deal of cartographical confusion. Its reputation rests on four things: being at the foot of Mount Ararat, the landing place of Noah's Ark; becoming the first Christian nation in AD301; the deaths of more than a million people during the Turkish genocide of 1915, and the devastating earthquake of 1988. Its history is awash with suffering. The Armenians are the Jews of Christendom.

Their place on the map has rendered Armenia and Karabakh a tramping ground for major and minor powers, and they have been a stick in the jaws of pan-Turkic and Islamic aspirations for almost a thousand years.[1]

At the close of the 19th century, Armenia was carved up between Russia and Turkey. Two great powers had proclaimed themselves the protectors of Armenian Christendom, the Russians and the British. For a century, the Russians nurtured Armenia and Georgia as Christian vassal states, buffers against Islam.

As the Ottoman empire slid into decline, Armenian nationalism began to emerge. Matters came to a head in the 1890s when the Turks suspected the Armenians of subversion. The brutality of their reprisals shocked the world. During a single pogrom, 3,000 Armenians were doused in kerosene and burned by Turkish troops in the cathedral at Urfa.[2] By the time the massacres across the country subsided, the death toll was between 100,000 and 300,000. Their British protectors were nowhere to be seen.

For their part, the Russians were forbidding Armenians to speak their own language or run their own schools and churches, and were sending nationalist leaders to Siberia.

At the same time, the Russian empire's Turkic population were developing nationalistic pretensions of their own. The standard Russian tactic to quell ethnic unrest was to set one ethnic group against another. Clashes between Armenians and Azeris erupted in 1905 and continued for the next two years.[3] But there was a bigger conflict on the horizon.

On the eve of the First World War, Turkish Minister of War Nazim Bey declared, 'Our state must be purely Turkish... we must Turkify non-Turkish nationalities by force.'[4] Ethnic violence erupted again in 1915, when the 'Young Turks' launched their programme to systematically rid the country of all Armenians. It was carried out with a savagery that prefigured the holocaust. Armenians were burned alive, hanged and even crucified. Women and children were sent on death marches across the desert and suffocated in makeshift gas chambers. When it was over, three-quarters of Turkey's 2 million Armenians had been slaughtered.

During the First World War, Armenia became the battleground for Turkey and Russia. When revolution at home recalled Russia from the war effort in 1917, Turkish troops began rolling across Russian Armenia and Azerbaijan.[5] Armenians in Baku, the capital of Azerbaijan, rallied to the support of the Baku Soviet against the approaching Azeri-Turks. Rioting erupted and thousands of Muslims in the city were slaughtered. Thousands more fled.

Retribution followed. When the city fell to the Turks in September 1918, some 9,000 Armenians were massacred. The Treaty of Batum reduced a defeated Armenia to a shadow of its former self and swallowed up much of its territory inside Turkey. That left Nagorno Karabakh.[6] The enclave would have been overrun, but for two events: stiff resistance by the Karabakhtsis aided by their intimate knowledge of the mountainous terrain; and Turkish capitulation in the First World War.

As the Turks pulled out of Transcaucasia, the victorious British moved in. Hopes were raised for reunification with Karabakh, then quickly dashed. Oil in Baku and the Russian menace beyond the Caucasus meant Azerbaijan was wooed as an ally and potential buffer state. Karabakh was handed over like a posy. Karabakh did not yield willingly.

In 1919, an economic blockade was thrown around the enclave, with Britain's blessing, and Kurdish irregulars were let loose on the Armenians. After several months of bloodshed Karabakh surrendered on guarantee of territorial autonomy. That guarantee was broken within a year. When British troops pulled out, the provisional governor, a man with pan-Turkic aspirations, moved to incorporate Karabakh into Azerbaijan. The subsequent rebellion was crushed with characteristic brutality. The heads of the bishop and leading Karabakhtsis were paraded on pikes.

In 1920, violence broke out between Armenians and Azeris in the town of Shusha. Of the 45,000 killed, two-thirds were Armenian. But the subjugation of Karabakh and the continuing inter-ethnic conflict were put on hold by the intervention that year of the Red Army. While Azerbaijan was concentrating its forces in Karabakh, Soviet troops seized the chance to march into Baku. Pan-Turkic aspirations were subjugated by Bolshevik ambition, and Azerbaijan, Karabakh and much of Armenia were swallowed up into the emergent USSR.

On 3 June 1921, the Transcaucasia Bureau of the Communist Party settled the Karabakh issue. They decided that Karabakh belonged to Armenia. One month and one day later, in the presence of the Commissar for Nationalities, one Joseph Stalin, the Bureau rescinded its decision without debate. Karabakh was to belong to Azerbaijan, along with the four-mile Lachin corridor that had been its lifeline to Armenia. The small mountainous region that had proved so hard to conquer, was to become a Soviet stronghold in Azerbaijan.[7]

It was the ancient strategy of divide and rule which the Soviets had learned from the Romans, to place vassal states in contention so they would exhaust one another rather than rail against central authority. Placing the Armenians of Karabakh at risk and dependent on Soviet protection assured the quiescence of Armenia proper. And creating a Soviet bastion in quarrelsome Azerbaijan had its obvious uses. Baku's response was to adjust the population by shifting Armenians to Baku, where they would be in a minority, and moving Azeri settlers into Karabakh. To enforce cultural assimilation, Armenian churches, newspapers and schools were closed down. Armenians seeking higher education were made to study outside Karabakh, and then not permitted to take up employment in the enclave once they had qualified.[8]

Stalin's meddling with national identity wound up the existing stress-points and held them in perpetual tension, with the addition of new and artificial strains. Seventy years later, as soon as the lid was lifted, out flew the jack-in-the-box. The Soviet Union didn't just fall apart, it sprang apart. And where its bureaucratic enmeshment proved intractable, it tore itself apart.

Glasnost saw the first straining at the seams. In 1987, Latvia, Lithuania, Estonia and Armenia pressed Moscow to overturn the settlements forced upon them by Stalin. In February the following year, the Supreme Soviet of Nagorno Karabakh called for the transfer of the enclave from Azerbaijan to Armenia. By July it had voted to secede. Demonstrations in favour of unification took place in Karabakh and Armenia. In a counter-demonstration, two Azeris were killed in Stepanakert.

A wave of anti-Armenian violence broke out in Azerbaijan. Armenians were massacred in the industrial town of Sumgait. Before long, the tide of refugees rose to 350,000.[9] In the USA, Andrei Sakharov warned, 'The Armenian people are again facing the threat of genocide.'

Armenia retaliated in kind, with the mass deportation of Azeri-Turks from its borders, accompanied by what the United Nations High Commission for Refugees (UNHCR) described as 'major violations of human rights'.[10]

In December 1988, an earthquake struck claiming 25,000 lives and rendering up to half a million homeless.[11] The epicentre of the quake hit a resettlement area for Armenian refugees. The disaster was celebrated on the streets of Azerbaijan. Telegrams offering 'congratulations on your earthquake' were dispatched to Armenia. A traumatized and distraught population vented its anger on the Azeris. Within 18 months, virtually all the Azeri-Turks in Armenia had been deported – some 185,000 people.[12]

Meanwhile, in Karabakh and Azerbaijan, the deportations continued unabated, until almost all the 400,000 ethnic Armenians had fled. 330,000 went to Armenia, others escaped to Russia. Only a few remained in Azerbaijan. A meeting was called between Armenian representatives, including Dr Zori Balayan of the Artsakh Committee (Artsakh is the ancient name for Karabakh), and the newly elected President of the Soviet Union, a reformist by the name of Mikhail Gorbachev. He was planning a restructuring programme called *perestroika*, and made vague and unspecified pledges to bring in greater personal freedom. It fell to Gorbachev's right-hand man, Alexander Yakolev, to spell out the *realpolitik*:

> The national structure of the state can't be changed in any respect. Any revision would create a dangerous precedent; there are too many flash points where ethnic passions could explode. And besides, the particular case of Nagorno Karabakh is incredibly complex. The... Armenians living in Azerbaijan are, to all intents and purposes, hostages. The Caucasus is flooded with arms, they're being brought across the border in great quantities. One match would be sufficient to ignite a firestorm.[13]

Within two days, the Presidium of the Supreme Soviet of the USSR had rejected the transfer of Karabakh to Armenia. The decision ignited Yakolev's firestorm. It gave Azerbaijan the mandate to bring Karabakh to heel, and the mechanism to do it: Soviet might. Gorbachev acted to suspend the Supreme Soviet of Nagorno Karabakh and place the enclave under Kremlin rule, before restoring power to the Azeris, and rekindling an ancient dream.

During the period of Soviet rule, the dream of Turan, or greater Turkey, stretching from the Balkans to the Great Wall of China, continued to be cherished. The man who would go on to become the President of Azerbaijan, Abulfuz Elchibey, had made that dream his own. Elchibey served time under the Soviets for pan-Turkic activity. With the Soviet Union disintegrating before his eyes, Turkey's Prime Minister, Suleyman Demirel declared: 'The Turkic world, which... stretches from the Adriatic Sea to China, has now emerged as a concrete reality. This is the realization of our 100-year-old dream.'[14] Standing in the way of the dream were the Karabakhtsis, who set up their own rival national council. In January 1990, its members were rounded up and arrested.

Azerbaijan sent in its heavyweights, in every sense of the word. By reputation, the rotund Viktor Polianitchku, KGB officer and second secretary of the Azerbaijani Communist Party, had supervised the destruction of villages in Afghanistan. No sooner had he arrived in Karabakh, than he shut down the press and arrested the Armenian leadership. Within a month, Soviet Interior Ministry troops backed by Azeri special forces, the OMON black berets, launched an attack against Armenian villages to the north of Karabakh. Villagers were given an ultimatum to leave, for their homes to be turned over to Azeri refugees. Azeri troops moved in to the capital, Stepanakert.

By the end of 1990, the New York-based Helsinki Watch recorded, 'water is systematically poisoned... roads to the villages – the food lifeline to the capital – are cut off... Soviet troops and the Azeri militia are working together... the depopulation programme is systematically going on.'[15] In Azerbaijan proper, Moscow Radio reported 'looting and pogroms' against Armenian homes. One Armenian refugee told *Tass*: 'In one day, we have lost our home and belongings. [Azerbaijanis] stormed into our home and told us to leave. They said that they would live in our flat from now on.'[16] It was only a prelude.

The arrival of Spring 1991 was the cue to begin Operation Ring, a noose which was to tighten around Karabakh. It saw the programmed deportation of Armenians from villages in and around the enclave, by the combined 23rd division of the Soviet Fourth Army and forces of the Azerbaijani Ministry of the Interior, the OMON.

Galia Saoukhanin, a 29-year-old mother, lived in the village of Nakhichevanik. She was forced to flee with her two small children when the Azeri troops moved in. 'It was awful,' she explained. 'They killed the population here: all who couldn't escape, the elderly people who couldn't run. My brother was killed. My brother-in-law was killed. It changed my destiny and my soul. For months my children were crying without stopping. I have a terrible fear inside me. I dream every night how I am going to escape and where I am going to keep my children.'

No-one could have been prepared for the savagery of the onslaught. Medical worker, Movses Poghossian, had to trail the conflict picking up the pieces from the front – literally: 'There are bodies without eyes, without ears... they are cutting crosses, they cut hands.'

It was against such a backdrop that the Sakharov Memorial Congress was taking place in Moscow.

Into Armenia

Caroline's working party took note of the Karabakh delegate's impassioned plea. He had challenged them to get to their feet and go to Karabakh with him. The plight of the Armenians was reported back to the main Congress, where it was received with concern. Caroline was asked to lead an independent international delegation to the area, with immediate effect.

The task of setting it up fell to the delegate who had been so persistent in catching his Chairman's eye. He was Zori Balayan, an elected member for Karabakh on the Supreme Soviet and mover and shaker extraordinaire. Permission was required for internal travel, so a message was sent to the

Kremlin asking Mikhail Gorbachev to make the necessary authorization. Two days passed and the visas were still not forthcoming. The end of the Congress was imminent. Elena Bonner sent off another fax to Gorbachev warning that unless visas were presented forthwith the world's press would be informed that permission had been withheld. Their timing could not have been better. Gorbachev was in London pressing the G7 nations for emergency aid. The necessary authorization arrived within the hour, with the caveat there could be no guarantee of their security.

Zori Balayan made the necessary arrangements to take the 15-strong group, including delegates from the USA, Britain, Norway and Japan, to Yerevan. Caroline was still none the wiser about where she was going. She would have been hard-pressed to say for certain where Armenia was. She made a mental note to check the route map on the way down. It had escaped her mind that she would be flying by Aeroflot.

There was no time to waste. On the plane she pulled her delegation together; sounding out each of the members, discovering their backgrounds and finding out how they felt they should go about the task. When they arrived in Armenia, within sight of Mount Ararat, they immediately set out for Goris to meet some of the earlier deportees.

These were mainly peasant farmers, who had been driven out of Berdadzor in the South. Still in a state of bewilderment, they described being rounded up, and having their belongings looted by a combination of Azeri OMON and the Soviet Fourth Army. The operation involved helicopters, armoured personnel carriers and tanks. Troops had surrounded the villages and rounded up the civilians. 'We saw the marks on their bodies where they had been beaten, maltreated and tortured,' says Caroline. One elderly woman had been with her paralysed husband when the Azeris came. 'They told him to leave his home and get up and go. He couldn't. So they just shot him in the legs, leaving him to die. Then they dragged his wife away. That was the last she saw of her husband: wounded and in pain.'

Another woman described being forced at gunpoint to stand in a barrel. The soldiers beat her about the head and threatened her with decapitation until she told them where her savings were. Troops beat up a pregnant woman. When her husband tried to defend her, the soldiers shot him repeatedly in the throat before her eyes. Two Armenian doctors who had gone out to administer first aid were caught and beaten. Their backs were covered with blue bruising. An 80-year-old man was burnt in his home when troops set fire to it with gasoline.

One stocky elderly man, in a shabby jacket and open-necked shirt looked wistfully across from Goris into Karabakh. In the distance he could just make out his village. His hair was grey and stubbly, and tears were pouring down his face. He said, 'All I want in my life is to go back to my home.'

Official reports later corroborated that local officials and representatives of the KGB and militia had been present at the deportations. Villagers had been forced to sign statements of 'voluntary departure' under threat of torture or death. Colonel Zhukov, the Soviet Military Commandant of Nagorno Karabakh, said there was nothing he could do about it.

White flag

The evidence was appalling, but one-sided. The party agreed they needed the Azeri point of view. Phone contact was made with the Russian and Azeri command in Stepanakert, the capital of Karabakh. They explained that they wanted to come and hear the Azeri side of the story. The response was as swift as it was unhelpful. Permission was refused to fly in from Yerevan, in Armenia, and, as if to underline the point, the air traffic control tower was shot up and shut down forthwith.

Caroline was undeterred. The Azeri version of the story was essential for balance and credibility. If they couldn't fly in, they would walk in. There was a place in the north near Voskepar where it was possible to walk from a village in Armenia to another on the border inside Azerbaijan. Their Armenian hosts exchanged glances. They warned it would be dangerous; there had been shooting across the border and more was expected that night. No villager had walked that road for a month. For the second time in a week they were told there could be no guarantee of their safety. Those of a nervous disposition were invited to stay behind. Some did. Arrangements were made to fly out a reduced group of six by helicopter.

Caroline felt the need to go to church before they left. With her went Caroline Croft, a human rights worker from New York. They found a church in Yerevan, up on the ravine, and went in to say their prayers. Both were scared. In the timeless atmosphere of the church a man was singing the Armenian liturgy. 'It was absolutely beautiful. I remember feeling that even if we do have to die this afternoon, this is a real benediction.' They walked out of the church with a reassuring sense of peace.

They arrived in Voskepar to find there had been heavy fighting. On 6 May, 11 Armenian militia men had been killed and wounded within their border by shots fired from a helicopter. Further gunfire was expected. The locals did their best to dissuade them from crossing the border. A member of their party had taken a table cloth from the hotel to use as a white flag.

With great reluctance, an elderly villager broke a branch of an ash tree to use as a makeshift flagpole. He handed it to Caroline, his cheeks stained and wet. 'Please don't go,' he said. 'The last person who walked across the border with a white flag was shot.'

The clouds were grey and low, and there was drizzle in the air. Local Armenians drove them some of the way, explaining, 'If you get into trouble, there is nothing we can do to help.' They were in a state of anxiety. Caroline assured them they understood and were doing this entirely of their own volition. The group got out, and their drivers turned and hurried back towards Armenia. Caroline checked the location of Azeri OMON headquarters through a pair of binoculars. It was a house with a balcony in a curious shade of blue. The remaining mile of road into Azeri territory was littered with shell cases. It would take them down into a valley and up the other side, then over the crest of a hill and into the full view of the Azeri troops.

Caroline's walking companion was Professor Richard Wilson, an atomic physics expert from Harvard, who had been responsible for the nuclear energy side of the Sakharov Congress. Wilson was adamant about the need to cross the border. Caroline turned to him and said, 'Of all the crazy ways that I've ever spent a Tuesday afternoon, this is the craziest. What do you think we do if they start firing when we get over the top? Do we go forward, or do we go back?'

'We felt we had to do it,' said John Marks. 'We had to get the Azeri viewpoint. But if we had stopped to think about it, we never would have gone.'

As they breasted the hill they could make out through their field glasses the OMON forces looking back at them through theirs. They held aloft their makeshift white flag while Caroline brandished her British passport, in the hope the Azeris would realize they were foreigners. As they got closer, the numbers gathering to observe them from the balcony of their headquarters grew from two to about ten. The party held their breath, and the troops held their fire.

The border was marked by a burnt-out church. As soon as they reached it, they paused and waved at the ranks of field-glasses to signal their intention to come and talk to them. The Japanese member of their party was by now extremely out of breath. Half expecting to be surrounded by black berets, they approached the two-storey house that served as military headquarters. Their progress was watched, but no-one troubled to greet them. They asked to see the officer, a stone-faced man in his 40s, dressed in battle fatigues. Caroline explained they had come from the Sakharov

Congress. 'We are here as human rights workers. We have heard the Armenian point of view, and we want to hear the Azeri point of view, please.' Glacially, the commander replied, 'I would have preferred you to have come via Baku.' His words were nervously relayed via Sasha Goldin, a Russian-speaking interpreter with the Sakharov Foundation.

Caroline evaded the point about getting authorization from the Azeri capital and explained that permission to fly into Stepanakert had not been granted. 'So we were forced to come via this rather unorthodox route.'

As she persisted, reiterating their commitment to hearing both points of view, the commander began to thaw. He took them by bus to visit the bombed-out buildings and show them the damage they had received at the hands of the Armenians. Some, but not all of it, rang true. The commander pointed out several marks which he described as shell damage. They were below window level, which would make for a pretty unorthodox trajectory. Several claims of atrocities were made. The commander said Azeris had been set alight by the Armenians, but offered no supporting evidence. The battleground tour completed, they were free to walk back to Armenian lines.

The euphoria of their welcome suggested the Armenians had never expected to see them again. Safely back, the group caught their breath, gathered their thoughts and compiled their report. Following in the footsteps of Sakharov, most of the delegates shared his commitment to stand on the side of the victim. Several had been involved in sending aid to Azeri refugees. Now they had to consider where they stood about what was happening to the Armenians. Clearly, there had been fighting in both directions. There was visible damage to the Azeri village. But they concluded that there had been a massive asymmetry in what had taken place. Armenian claims of maltreatment had been supported by consistent testimony and photographs. The Karabakhtsis had defended themselves and had inflicted damage on the Azeri population. 'But,' says Caroline, 'the conflict was instigated by the Azeris. They were the primary aggressors.'

Inside the Kremlin

The group travelled on to Moscow, where a meeting was arranged in the Kremlin with Anatoli Lukyanov, Chairman of the Supreme Soviet of the Soviet Union. With Caroline was John Marks who had joined her in battle earlier against the far left at the Polytechnic of North London. Now they were at the centre of what Ronald Reagan had called the evil empire, a description with which Caroline would concur. It seemed unreal.

The building was palatial, with huge halls and chandeliers, and corridors lined with plush red carpets. Caroline's delegation entered an echoing room by one door and Lukyanov and his officials entered by the other. They met briefly in the middle, before taking sides across a long and highly-polished table. Lukyanov was well-built, articulate, and very much in control, though his expression was careworn. The atmosphere was formal and reserved.

Over the next 40 minutes the Chairman listened politely to their findings, but gave nothing away. John Marks was taking copious notes. 'To begin with Lukyanov was going through the motions, but then he realized we had accurate information. He didn't exactly deny it, but said the situation was more complex than you people could understand; that we only had half the story. He said similar things were going on elsewhere in the Soviet Union, and this was just a minor matter.' As the meeting went on, Lukyanov grew increasingly concerned to find out exactly what the delegation knew so he could bring diplomatic damage limitation to bear later. He had one thing on his agenda. He was adamant: 'I do not want you to internationalize this issue.'

From there they went to the marble edifice of the Ministry of Defence, a study in stark, brutalist modernism, to meet the Defence Minister. The stocky and medal-encrusted Marshal Dmitri Yazov seemed almost a caricature of a Marshal of the Red Army. 'He was much less plausible and articulate than Lukyanov,' recalled John Marks, 'and kept calling on his uniformed aides to answer for him. The atmosphere was intimidating. I couldn't help wondering if we were going to get out again.'

Caroline presented the taciturn Marshal with detailed notes and pictures of civilian deportees who showed obvious signs of abuse and maltreatment. He pushed them aside without a glance and said: 'I have got more examples than I ever want to know about. It is not a matter of concern.'

There may have been other things on Yazov's mind. The Second World War veteran had made public expressions of dismay that under *glasnost* civilians were apparently now permitted to criticize the army. Lukyanov, President Gorbachev's former friend and law-school classmate, had been using delaying tactics to stem the tide of liberal legislation. Within four months, Yazov and Lukyanov would be arrested for playing key roles in the abortive coup attempt against the President. Yazov is said to have begun plotting as early as December 1990. But it was Lukyanov who would be implicated as the probable mastermind behind the putsch.[17]

Caroline and her colleagues came away from their meetings at the Kremlin and Ministry of Defence with renewed determination to pursue the issue of Karabakh. What was taking place had to be exposed. They had been into

Armenia and briefly onto Azeri soil. Now they wanted to return as quickly as possible to Azerbaijan proper to hear their official version of events and to, somehow, get in to Karabakh.

Caroline tried a more direct approach. The group asked the Azeri authorities for permission to enter their country. Eventually, Caroline was grudgingly informed by fax that she could go on her own as the personal guest of Chairman Lukyanov. She didn't take the bait. She reasoned that either they were trying to neutralize her or, by reducing the size of the team, they were trying to diminish the international impact. She wrote back insisting that she should be accompanied by her full international delegation. If the Soviet Union could not find the wherewithal or resources to host the other delegates, they would, of course, be self-financing. The Soviet Union buckled under the pressure and agreed to send the group – at their own expense.

NOTES

1. Armenian national identity dates back to 521BC, when the name appeared on an inscription by Darius I, King of Persia. Persia ceded to Macedonia, ceded to Rome, ceded to the Mongols, ceded to Turkey, which ceded to Russia. In between were periods of precarious independence and subjugation by warlords bent on Turkification and Islamization. What passes for Armenia today is a fraction of what it was at its zenith. It was, for a time, the strongest state in the Roman East.

2. In Constantinople, over a two-day period in 1896, 10,000 Armenians were murdered and twice as many were forcibly deported.

3. George Bournoutian, *A History of Qarabakh*.

4. C.W. Hostler, *Turkism and the Soviets*, p. 99.

5. Azerbaijan, with Georgia, formed the short-lived Confederation of Transcaucasia in a desperate attempt to halt the Turkish advance.

6. First, the Armenians were driven out of the strip separating Karabakh and Armenia. Then the strategically important town of Shushi fell on 3 November.

7. In 1922, Russian Armenia was subsumed into the Transcaucasian Soviet Federated Socialist Republic. In 1936, Armenia was made a separate constituent republic of the Soviet Union: *Compton's Encyclopedia*.

8. Felix Corley, 'Ground to a standstill', *Index on Censorship*, 4, 1993.

9. 'The Humanitarian Situation of the Refugees and Displaced Persons in Armenia and Azerbaijan', Council of Europe Report, 14 February 1995, p. 11.

10. 'Background Paper on Refugees and Asylum Seekers from Armenia', UNHCR Centre for Documentation and Research, August 1995.

11. The earthquake caused devastation over an 80 kilometre radius. Estimates of the death toll vary between 25,000 and 55,000.

12. US Department of Defense figure: Armenia Country Report on Human Rights Practices, 1996. Some sources put the number as high as a third of a million. *Russia Briefing*, 25 February 1994, estimates 160,000.

13. Andrei Sakharov, *Moscow and Beyond: 1986–1989*, 1990, p. 49.

14. Turkish TV, cited C. Cox and J. Eibner, *Ethnic Cleansing in Progress – War in Nagorno Karabakh*, Institute for Religious Minorities in the Islamic World, 1993, p. 19. At a political rally in Baku in November 1992, Interior Minister, Iskanador Gamidov, reportedly called for the creation of a pan-Turkic state and threatened Armenia with a nuclear strike.

15. *Nagorno Karabakh and Soviet Nationalities – Conflicts: Human Rights*, Balain, Hrair, 1991, p. 55.

16. *The Independent*, 19 January 1990.

17. 'The Coup Plotters', *Time*, 6 January 1992; 'Power Vacuum', *Time*, 9 September 1991; George J. Church.

THREE

To See for Themselves

In July 1991, delegates from the Andrei Sakharov Memorial Congress flew from Moscow to Baku where they were given the red-carpet treatment. The moment they arrived at the airport they were invited to meet President Ayaz Mutalibov. Limousines were standing by to take them to his summer residence for lunch. Caroline was ready for them. The last group that had tried to get into Karabakh had found itself sidelined with endless meetings in Azerbaijan. She had insisted as a precondition that they would go into Karabakh. She explained again that they had not come to Baku on a diplomatic mission, but one of human rights. She would be happy to accept the President's kind invitation to lunch, but only if the plane was kept waiting for them on the tarmac to take them to Stepanakert in the afternoon, and only if it was guaranteed that they would be back at the airport by two o'clock. As she was a personal guest of Chairman Lukyanov, it was difficult to refuse.

When pressed about the deportations, the President justified them as a means 'to clear the area of bases used by Armenian paramilitary troops'. The intention, he said, was to dissuade Armenia from incorporating Karabakh. Further deportations could not be ruled out. The delegates later concluded in their report: 'No official with whom we met denied the possibility that Azerbaijani OMON forces are engaged in atrocities, including killing, looting and banditry, and brutality and violence directed against women, children and the elderly.'

Much as expected, the flamboyant lunch at the presidential palace looked set to drag on interminably, so Caroline insisted that they cut it short in order to get to the airport. As usual, she got her way. The plane left on time, complete with the Deputy Prime Minister of Azerbaijan.

From low in the sky, the few roads ran like scratches across Karabakh's dusty red mountains. A single railway track stretched to the capital like a telephone cable stapled to the hillside. From lower still, clusters of devastated stone houses were scattered around like so many discarded egg boxes. Their plane touched down in Stepanakert to be greeted by a floral tribute and another full-scale welcoming party; this time the serried ranks of Soviet blue berets and OMON forces. Caroline was impatient to get on with the business and asked to be shown around. With her was Malcolm Pearson, now Lord Pearson of Rannoch.

First stop in Stepanakert was the Soviet headquarters, a substantial building surrounded by spirals of barbed wire and tanks. The city had the feel of a Soviet-occupied town under military rule. While the top brass were busily explaining how they were attempting to keep order and prevent ethnic conflict, word came through that in the adjoining building, which would later become the Parliament of Karabakh, deportees were gathering, anxious to meet the human rights delegation. Meeting the disgruntled and displaced was not on the agenda, especially as President Mutalibov had continued to describe the deportations as 'voluntary departures'. Every request to see them was blocked. In the end, Caroline called a premature halt to the meeting, and walked out of the building with her delegation, who picked their way through the loops of barbed wire. Her hosts were not best pleased.

Caroline marched into the Parliament building, and found upwards of 150 Armenians packed into a single room. Many had suffered deportation, and pressed round to give their testimonies. A young mother with dark curly hair clutching a 14-month-old child began to speak. She described how Azeri and Russian troops surrounded her village on 13 May. They bound the hands of her husband and brother-in-law and threw them onto a bus. Then they made her sign a document saying she was ready to leave the village voluntarily. She continued, looking pale and still in shock, 'They grabbed my little child by the hair and said, "He's an Armenian, he doesn't deserve to speak." They threatened to rip out his tongue. I did all I could to protect him.' The woman glanced away, embarrassed. The interpreter asked her gently if she had been raped. She could not bring herself to reply. Several around her asked her to admit it, because the delegation needed to know. She said the soldier had raped her, but had left the baby alone. Her husband and brother-in-law were still in jail.

Another elderly man described being seized, beaten and taken onto a bus. 'They beat the young men so they can no longer have children,' he said, covering his genitals.

'His face was so dignified,' says Caroline. 'There was no way we could do justice to their stories in the time we had available.'

It was typical of what they had already heard. Soviet troops moved in on a village claiming to be carrying out an exercise in passport control. They rounded up the people, leaving the Azeri OMON to do the dirty work. Then

Azeri civilians in pick-up trucks would move in, loot the village and drive off with their belongings. The deportees would be either driven to the border and dumped there, or forced to flee to the capital, Stepanakert. More than 20 villages were depopulated in this way before the war began in earnest.

Spitting with hatred

The meeting was cut short by their hosts and the group was taken back to the airstrip at Khojaly. The Azeris wanted to fly them straight back to Baku. Caroline refused and demanded to see some of the villages where deportations had occurred.

It was not possible, she was told. No helicopters were available. Caroline looked incredulously at the helicopters standing idle on the airstrip. She was told politely, but firmly, that they were not free. She replied, 'That's funny, the Armenians always make helicopters available for us.'

With great reluctance the Deputy Prime Minister agreed to put a single machine at her disposal. Caroline came back, 'The Armenians make three available if we need them.'

They settled on two. Lord Pearson and half the delegation went in one, while Caroline and the rest took the other.

Caroline's helicopter took her into Karabakh, to an Armenian village. It was a picture of harmony, with Armenians and Azeris living together, in a state of blissful cohabitation. First they took tea with an Azeri household, then the exercise was to be repeated with Armenians. The event was stage-managed, Soviet style. In between house-calls, Caroline asked one of the Armenians, 'Are there any people here who have suffered deportations? Will you get the message out – we would like to meet them.'

As they were emerging from their second genteel afternoon tea a woman came running towards them. She was an attractive dark-haired Armenian in a red dress. She asked if they were the human rights delegation. They nodded. She said, 'What are you doing here? There are people who have been deported. You ought to be speaking to us, not to these people. You ought to visit my village. My village has been deported. That's where you ought to be, not here, this is a show village.'

'I know it is,' Caroline replied. 'We're trying to get there. Perhaps you would like to tell our host, the Deputy Prime Minister, that is where we have been asking to get to ever since I came here.'

The woman, whose name was Anna, boldly relayed the message to the Deputy Prime Minister, who replied there was no time to go there. Caroline cut in, 'Excuse me, but I'm not leaving Karabakh until I have.'

He shrugged, 'I don't know where it is.'

Without a moment's hesitation, Anna said, 'I will come with you. I will direct you.'

Caroline immediately took her up on her offer and the browbeating began forthwith. The Azeri Deputy Prime Minister loomed over Anna. Others in the escort party jostled round. 'I think they threatened her with everything. Our interpreter was eating his handkerchief, poor guy. He was petrified.'

Caroline told Anna it could be dangerous and asked if she really wanted to go.

She said, 'I'm coming. The truth of what is happening to our people has got to come out. I want you to come to my village.'

Anna climbed into the helicopter without even going back for her handbag or a change of clothing. There was acute consternation on board. Efforts were made to get her off. Caroline rallied to her defence, 'I'm not going unless we go to this lady's village.'

Back came the usual reply, 'We haven't got time.'

'I don't mind about time,' said Caroline firmly, 'I don't have to go back to Baku today. We'll spend the night in Stepanakert if needs be. I want to see this village.'

They changed their tactics. Anna was told, 'If we do try to find your village, we can't bring you back here. You may have to go back to Stepanakert. Or even Baku.' The first option was uncomfortable, as she would have had no way of getting back. The second was dangerous. Her dark eyes flashed, 'I don't mind. I'll go to Baku if I have to. I want the truth to be told.'

Impasse. They turned off the rotor blades. Then, all subtlety abandoned, they started shouting at Anna in Russian. A news cameraman accompanying Caroline decided to capture the moment on videotape. They relented.

The helicopter took off. Anna, who was ill-equipped for the flight, soon began to feel the cold through her summer dress. Caroline lent her her cardigan. The pilots scoured the mountainous countryside in what appeared to be a genuine effort to locate her village, to the continuing consternation of the Azeri Deputy Prime Minister. 'You could have cut the atmosphere in that helicopter with a knife,' says Caroline. Despite Anna's best efforts, they failed to find her village, but they did manage to locate another, Donalar, where her husband grew up.

The helicopter came down in a flurry of dust in a field on the edge of the village. It was well-to-do by Karabakh standards. At the centre of the single main street of small stone buildings was a war memorial, to those who had fallen in an earlier conflict. The church had recently been destroyed. Anna pointed out her husband's school and former home. The village, which had once been owned by Armenians, was now fully occupied by Azeri families. Caroline spoke to several. Some admitted feeling uncomfortable because they knew Armenians had been living in those homes just six weeks earlier. Others were histrionic. As they walked up the street towards the end of their visit, a woman ran up to them, spitting with hatred. She had a little child with her and stuck his legs out in front of Caroline. She screamed, 'Look; the Armenians burnt him. These are burns.' The child was about three years old. Caroline subjected his legs to a nurse's inspection. 'It looks more like psoriasis to me,' she replied.

Caroline was unable to find out whether the Azeris had volunteered to take over the village after the troops had pulled out, or whether they had been made to do so. But on the whole, she reflected, they had been given a good deal. The homes were sound, the land was fertile and they seemed well settled.

She had all the evidence she required. They climbed back into the helicopter and, despite the earlier threats by the Azeri leaders, the pilot landed Anna back at her home.

Lord Pearson's delegation, meanwhile, had three villages on its list. At the first two, they spoke to Azeris and Armenians whose leaders told the same story. They couldn't understand why the other villagers had started shooting at them. Their communities were integrated; they even went to one another's weddings. 'It became clear what happened,' says Lord Pearson. 'The Soviets created the conflict by sending in their Spetznatz special troops and firing both ways.' The presence on the ground of so many highly trained blue berets was telling. 'That they were there in such high numbers pointed to the direct involvement of the Kremlin and Gorbachev himself. The wretched people who were being rounded up reported helicopters arriving at their villages with loudspeakers blaring that it was all being done in the name of Gorbachev – "Mr Gorbachev wants you to leave".'

Gorbachev himself was in London at the time for G7 talks, seeking funds to shore up what remained of the Soviet system. 'It was only because he was in Britain that we were able to get into Karabakh,' says Lord Pearson.

Having seen two villages, he asked to go to the third, where troops were currently rounding up and removing the occupants. The skies were blue and clear, save for a few wispy puffballs of cloud. Their pilot flew straight up into the one smudge of cloud he could find, said it was too hazardous to continue the mission, and landed straight back on the tarmac. Lord Pearson was livid and spent the next two hours haranguing the Azeris.

Next stop was Stepanakert, and a plane back to Baku. Throughout the flight, the Deputy Prime Minister sat in a cold, apprehensive silence.

'I insist on going...'

Caroline found herself wedged next to Polianitchku, whom she describes as 'coarse, surly and particularly obnoxious'. Having shoe-horned herself in beside him, she set about persuading him to fulfil the remaining part of their brief. She explained that on their previous mission they had made a point of going to Azeri territory to obtain a balanced view. Now they were guests of Azerbaijan, she would like, please, to go to Armenia. Polianitchku demurred. It would not be possible. There were special meetings in Parliament tomorrow. He would be unable to accompany them. More special meetings had been arranged for Caroline and her colleagues in Baku.

Caroline declined his thoughtful offer. 'Rather than entertain us and look after us, it would be helpful if you could fly us to Armenia. We needn't be a nuisance to you.'

'It's not possible to fly to Armenia.'

'Chairman Lukyanov agreed that we should combine this visit to Azerbaijan with a visit to Armenia,' she said. 'I *insist* on going to Armenia.'

'You know there are no flights from Yerevan to Baku.'

'Perhaps you can arrange it somehow.'

Polianitchku played his trump card, 'If *you* can get a plane to fly from Yerevan to Baku I will guarantee its safe landing and provision for refuelling. But it's up to you to make the arrangements.'

There had been no flights from Yerevan to Baku for three years. There was a cold war between Armenia and Azerbaijan and a blockade had been in force since 1989. When they returned to the hotel the telephone lines had been cut off. Even if they could find a phone, there would be no way of getting through to Yerevan.

If she could contact Zori Balayan, who had first raised the plight of Karabakh at the conference, then it might just be possible. If anyone could do it, it would be Balayan: a representative of Karabakh on the Supreme Soviet; mountain climber, white-water rafter, snow marathon runner, weight-lifter, physician, journalist, author and illustrator whom Caroline describes as 'the Lion of Karabakh... the people's leader'.

But how to get through to Zori? They spent half the night trying to reach Moscow on public telephone, dialling and redialling, hoping for a connection. Eventually, in the small hours of the morning, they managed to get through to Elena Bonner, explain the situation and ask her to get Zori Balayan to arrange the flight. It seemed like asking the impossible.

By dawn, Balayan had convened a meeting in Yerevan of pilots of twin-engined Yak 40 civilian passenger planes and called for volunteers. He didn't have to ask twice. Permission was sought from the incredulous Azeris to land and refuel at Baku. To turn the request down would have meant a loss of face. A pointed reminder that Caroline and her colleagues were guests of Chairman Lukyanov clinched the deal.

The Yak 40 bounced onto the tarmac at Baku at 2.30 p.m. It was brimming with grim-faced Armenian soldiers. The Azeris allowed her to fly out on the understanding that she would return to Baku and go on to Moscow from there. The move cut her available time down to 24 hours.

Back in Yerevan, no sooner had they finished taxiing on the tarmac than they were given news of a massacre. Inside Armenia, close to where they had walked over to Azeri lines, a bus-load of Armenian militia had been ambushed. By now it was early evening. Caroline and her party were driven across country to northern Armenia, where they spent the night meeting survivors. They also interviewed a number of militia who had been captured and tortured and had just been released. Several were badly cut-up and one had a broken arm.

By the time their bus managed to lurch back across the mountains it was 6 a.m. They snatched an hour's sleep before their scheduled civilian flight back into Stepanakert. The authorities had not been informed of the flight they would be arriving on. This time there would be no stage-managed reception.

Many of the civilians on board were apprehensive about the treatment they would receive at the hands of the OMON forces in the capital. A beating and the theft of belongings were becoming standard. As soon as the plane slowed to a halt OMON officials clambered aboard and began pushing and shoving the passengers. The cameraman took his cue and started filming. When the OMON saw him, they grabbed the camera and began to manhandle him. Caroline intervened, explaining who they were. They let the cameraman go, and backed off from intimidating the passengers. Five civilians were arrested. Caroline tried to go with them, but was herded with her party in a different direction. It made quite a contrast to the flowers and smiles of the earlier official delegation.

They were steered aboard a flight to Baku and returned to find themselves caught up in a crude propaganda exercise. Interviews were laid on for Azeri radio. Whenever they tried to say anything critical, the interviewer grabbed the microphone and drowned them out in Azeri.

While they had been away, the remainder of their party had been trying to track down Armenian prisoners held in Baku. They had lists of names, but no addresses, and were being stone-walled by the Azeris. At first, officials denied having any prisoners in Baku, but production of the lists forced a reluctant admission. That was as far as they would go. They refused to let them see them. The Congress representatives explained that it would look bad if access was denied to a human rights delegation. Besides, it was against the rules of international convention. Grudgingly, the group were allowed to interview the prisoners, but only in the presence of their interrogators.

One, who looked much the worse for wear, was led in with fresh blood seeping through his T-shirt. The delegation asked him what had happened. Glancing apprehensively at the guard, he shrugged and falteringly explained that he had fallen off a horse. They saw ten other prisoners, all bruised from daily beatings. Several said they were deprived of water and their food was smothered with salt to make them thirsty.

Towards the end of their whirlwind tour, many of the group were also feeling a little worse for wear under the withering pace drummed out by Caroline. The first night they had just four hours sleep, and to accommodate all they had to do Caroline decided that the next night they would have to get by on even less. 'She rations her sleep like Margaret Thatcher,' said Lord Pearson. 'So we all went on strike and demanded at least five and a quarter hours, which she gave way to.'

When Caroline and Lord Pearson returned to London, Mr Gorbachev was at the House of Lords having tea on the terraces. The Congress delegation's report was handed to the British Ambassador who flew back with Mr Gorbachev to Moscow and made sure the Soviet Premier read it. It was scathing. Caroline wrote, 'Here were Christians fighting, not only for life, but for their families, for the right to live in their historic land, and also for their Christian heritage – and their struggle was largely unknown to the rest of Christendom.'[1] But she was not prepared to let it rest at that. In October, she invited Christian Solidarity International into the arena. It was to result in an active and continuing commitment. More than 30 visits to Nagorno Karabakh and Armenia followed.

NOTES

1. CSI Conference Keynote Speech, 17 October 1992.

FOUR

Under Bombardment

It was a summer of change. Gorbachev was out and Yeltsin was in. Soviet–Azeri combined operations ceased. The official policy of deportations was overturned. Politically, things looked brighter. In a conciliatory move, Karabakh said it would be prepared to drop its plea for reunification with Armenia and accept autonomous status within Azerbaijan. In September, the Zheleznovodsk agreement called for a cease-fire, an end to the blockade and an exchange of hostages. Armenia and Azerbaijan were co-signatories.

It wasn't worth the ink. Within weeks, Azerbaijan announced its intention to annul Karabakh's status as an autonomous oblast. Stepanakert, the capital, was to be given a new name. A Turkish name: Xankändi. The Armenians of Karabakh saw it as the beginning of the end.

Karabakh called a referendum, with a view to declaring independence. It was boycotted by the Azeri-Turks who made up around a quarter of the population. Nine out of ten who did vote backed the call for independence. The area in question included Shaumyan, an ethnically and historically Armenian region to the north of Karabakh and in Azerbaijan proper. A general election was held to establish a parliament, which was once again boycotted by ethnic Azeris. Parliament opened in January 1992. Temperatures plummeted and the cold war plunged inevitably into open conflict.

As Soviet forces were withdrawn by Yeltsin, OMON troops and soldiers of the Azeri army took over their positions and their weapons. In May, an agreement was signed transferring former Soviet military equipment in the region to the three Transcaucasus republics. The lion's share went to Azerbaijan, including 53 Grad missile launchers.[1] The military and economic stranglehold on Karabakh tightened, cutting off water, food, medicine and power.

Caroline returned to Stepanakert in January with John Eibner, the bespectacled, softly spoken American, based at CSI in Zurich. She was appalled by the speed and the extent of the deterioration. Families were living in cellars under constant bombardment from Alazan rockets, fired from the mountainous fortress town of Shushi, only three miles away. The

Alazans had originally been designed for cloud dispersal. The Azeris had switched their payload of iodine for high explosives. An Armenian member of parliament got a direct hit. Caroline saw his dead body in the hospital mortuary.

It was minus 20 degrees. In most of the basements, there was no light, no heat and no sanitation. The only illumination was the sporadic flash from Caroline's camera. Where the inhabitants had access to an Azeri gas pipe they contrived to tap off a jet providing a flame like a Bunsen burner. The basements were either an unlit huddle of freezing people, or a stifling and claustrophobic mass, illuminated by an oxygen-consuming flame. Breathing difficulties were rife. Above ground, the night sky was a pyrotechnic display of rockets and explosions. 'Caroline's presence in those cellars while the missiles rained down really helped raise the spirits of the people,' recalls John Eibner.

The people almost lost their bishop to those missiles. Bishop Parkev Martirosian was the first priest to return to Karabakh after the clergy were murdered or driven out by Stalin in the 1930s. He is a man whose gentle demeanour and musical voice belie a patriarchal beard and eyes that would credit a bird of prey. In 1805, when Karabakh was part of the Russian empire, there were 1,311 churches and monasteries. Ten years after its handover to Azerbaijan, all were closed and some 1,500 priests had been killed or sent to Siberia. Bishop Martirosian, an erstwhile pacifist, stepped back into a war zone and set about trying to reopen the churches.

The bombing had begun in the early hours of the morning. As the Alazan rockets came pounding in, the bishop rose immediately to pray. Within minutes, his house took a direct hit. He was shaken, but unhurt. He went to inspect the damage and found, in the middle of his bed where he had been sleeping moments before, a huge slab of concrete. His life was literally saved by prayer. Forty minutes later, a shell exploded in the doorway of a block of flats, blowing eight people to pieces. When Caroline arrived, children were collecting the bits of their fathers for burial.

Bishop Martirosian later wrote an open letter to the UN and all people of good will.

It is not only the perpetrators of crime and evil who commit sin, but also those who stand by – seeing and knowing – and who do not condemn it or try to avert it. Blessed are the peacemakers, for they will be called sons of God. We do not hate; we believe in God. If we want God's victory, we must love. Even if there are demonic forces at work, we must still love.

The bishop's affirmation of Christian endurance, and the call to engagement and action, struck a chord deep within Caroline, 'That triumphant proclamation of the priority of love, even in suffering unleashed by terrible forces, is one of the greatest witnesses to the Christian messages I have ever come across. It is written from the heart of darkness.'

Burning books

Things were to get darker yet. The water supply had been totally dependent on electricity. The loss of power left the 82,000 civilians of Stepanakert reliant upon the eight spring wells in the city. The queues, in the bitter cold, were measured not in people but in hours. It took five hours to fill a pair of buckets under fire from aerial bombardment and snipers. Caroline was with a family in a basement when two young boys returned with their buckets. They were smothered from head to toe in everything their parents could find: balaclavas, coats and gloves. The strips of face that were visible were blue from the cold. As one of them made his way down the ice-covered steps, he slipped and fell, cascading the precious water all round him. 'I would have sat down and howled,' says Caroline. 'But with incredible grace he just made a joke and went off again, to face another five hours under bombardment.'

Troops had moved into the surrounding villages and refugees were flooding into the capital. In Stepanakert the children went hungry. Rations were 30 grams of flour per adult per day and a quarter of a kilo of sugar per month. Dairy products were unobtainable. The children were found to be more chronically malnourished than those in Bosnia. Young babies were developing rickets. Things were little better in Yerevan. Under blockade from Turkey a candle cost 40 roubles, and petrol – if you could find any – would set you back around 2,000 roubles per gallon, a month's salary.[2]

The Armenian news agency, Snark, reported that people had begun burning books to keep warm, 'Special preference is given to the complete works of the classics of Marxist-Leninism which, because of their hard covers, burn longer and give off more warmth.'[3] The continuing blockade may yet backfire against Turkey. Starved of power, Armenia was later forced to reopen its ancient Metsamor nuclear power station, which was deemed a nuclear hazard and closed in 1989. The primitive pressurized water reactor is on a geological faultline 30 miles from the epicentre of the 1988 Armenian earthquake and close to the Turkish frontier. The Metsamor plant is uncontained. Should anything happen, the fall-out would be worse than Chernobyl. 'You cannot let people go indefinitely without light and electricity,' explained one official. 'Our people are cold,' shrugged another. 'They just want to be warm.'[4]

Azerbaijan had other fears about the nuclear power plant. Claiming Armenia would try to build nuclear weapons from the remains of its reactors, the Azeri interior minister threatened pre-emptive nuclear strikes against Karabakh and Armenia[5] – despite Azerbaijan being a signatory to the nuclear non-proliferation treaty.

Journalist Stephen Brook, writing for *The Sunday Times*, joined Caroline on one visit. As he was about to get into the helicopter to leave he saw a group of children. They were pale and thin and six in number. He remembered his six remaining chocolate bars and handed them to the oldest boy to share around. Suddenly, a seventh youngster appeared. All the reporter could do was watch from a distance. The boy who had distributed the chocolate promptly gave his own bar away, unaware that the eyes of the journalist were still on him.

Nothing moves Caroline more than dignity in the midst of suffering. Episodes such as these take centre-stage in her recollections. They motivate her to act, and her heady, pulpit rhetoric motivates others to respond. The neatly turned out schoolchildren under siege in Karabakh fire her compassion, much as the smartly dressed schoolchildren in the slums of the East End shifted her political convictions. She becomes as protective as a lioness whose cubs are in danger.

In common with many, she finds meaning in suffering by affording it a mythical dimension. Of the boy in Karabakh who gave up his sweets, she says, 'He may have lost his chocolate bar, but he gained a place in history, because he speaks for the graciousness, generosity, deep gentleness and strength of the children of Karabakh.'

There was nothing mythical about the suffering Caroline found in the hospital in Stepanakert. It was overflowing with casualties with glass in their eyes, burns and lost limbs. The anaesthetics and pain-killers were used up long ago. All that remained was vodka. Surgery was performed on makeshift operating tables constructed of wooden planks. Surgical instruments were sterilized over wood-burning stoves, which provided the only form of heating in the hospital, wreathing the wards in a pungent fog of smoke. Sheets and stretcher covers were boiled in buckets and bowls and beaten with sticks to remove the blood stains.

Patients were being treated for injuries sustained in an Azeri helicopter attack. A husband and wife were gunned down as they worked in the fields. The wounded were undergoing surgery for injuries to the diaphragm and lungs, thorax and neck – all without anaesthetic. An old woman who had just lost members of her family now lost both her legs to the surgeon's knife. Caroline went up to her, touched her and held her hand. Speech was beyond them, because Caroline had neither Armenian nor Russian. All she could share was her suffering. 'She shed tears in silence with this woman who had lost so much,' recalls John Eibner. When Caroline returned to Britain it was some time before she was able to sleep again at night. She felt compelled to do something, but what?

International drugs runner

The Karabakh authorities had given her a list of their most urgent priorities: hard drugs like morphine, and cocaine powder for eye injuries. She made a call to Switzerland, to Hans Stückelburger, the International President of CSI. After hearing her out, he authorized her to buy whatever was needed. She became, in her own words, 'an international drugs carrier'.

The Home Office gave her a licence to purchase and export restricted drugs. They were acquired and packed in two substantial plywood crates, marked 'Fragile, Handle with Care'. The only route out was from Heathrow to Paris, from Paris to Yerevan, and then on to Stepanakert by whatever means possible. Accompanying Caroline was Soviet expert and journalist Felix Corley.

British Airways gave permission to transport the crates to Paris free of charge, without batting an eyelid. But at Charles de Gaulle airport things were different. The standard trolleys were too small for the crates, and the lifts were too small for the crates and trolleys combined. The porter's lifts could only be operated by punching in a combination. Caroline tried to prise the necessary code out of the suspicious airport staff but they refused even to tell her how she could find out. They were stranded in the arrivals hall and their flight was due to depart.

If the airport officials could be so unhelpful over a simple matter of service lifts, they were hardly likely to be flexible over the unorthodox contents of the crates. All she had by way of paperwork was her licence to export. There had been no time to pursue any form of authorization to import anything into France, let alone such an unusual cargo. She had visions of being stranded at Charles de Gaulle with the urgently needed medical supplies.

The only thing for it was to go through the green channel. Together they heaved their oversized trolleys with their cargo plastered with warning stickers towards the Nothing to Declare. Felix was lanky and unshaven and casual to the point of sloppiness. Caroline was clad in her winter travelling rough outfit of anorak and windproof ski trousers, with merely an Alice-band hinting towards her aristocracy. They made an unlikely looking twosome. With an outward display of nonchalance, they got away with it. It was then a matter of coolly wheeling their trolleys down the ramps and through the customs. They made it. 'It was one of our more audacious and mischievous exploits – but it was in a good cause.'

Aeroflot brought them into Yerevan on a cold, crisp day, where they and their illicit cargo were transferred to military helicopter. Joining them was a medical team and a worried-looking Zori Balayan. The Azeris had escalated the conflict significantly by the use of Grad (BM21) missiles, which had been used to devastating and indiscriminate effect in Afghanistan and had been banned by international convention. Literally translated, the name means hail. Grads were fired in multiples of 40. If they exploded outside they would shred a building. If they penetrated the wall, an entire block would be shattered from within by a whirlwind of shrapnel. Their target had been Shaumyan, to the north of Karabakh. Two schools had been pulverized. Their party diverted to Shaumyan to offload some of their morphine and pain-killing drugs.

By now there were only a few remaining helicopters in Karabakh. Going on to Stepanakert, the cloud cover was thick and visibility so poor that the pilot announced he would have to put down before they flew into a mountain. Eventually, he located a break in the clouds and landed at Horatar. They found themselves stranded in Azeri-held territory, with elderly doctors and nurses in the middle of a snow-clad forest. The only way out was to walk. The roads were too hazardous, so they would have to keep to the trees.

One of Caroline's hobbies is hill walking, but playing hide and seek with Azeri snipers does not feature high on her list of pastimes. It was with mixed feelings that she contemplated the 12-kilometre trek ahead of them to the nearest village. She maintains a rigorous keep-fit regime for just such an eventuality, but was concerned for the elderly medical staff who were having to tramp through the snow. Nevertheless, the scenery was breathtaking and the walk exhilarating. She felt a twinge of guilt for beginning to enjoy herself.

Before long, they stumbled upon a farmer with a tractor and trailer, who was able to carry them and their cargo part of the way. There was room for only a few, so Caroline and several others opted to trudge on foot. It was slow going in the thick snow. Night fell and it became pitch dark. The sound of the tractor would not seem out of place in the forest, but the rest of them kept their voices down. They slithered around in semi-silence. When one fell, the other helped him up. Eventually, they were able to make out a village ahead of them. It was Armenian. The villagers invited them into their homes to eat, drink and thaw out around their log fires. A stone was later set up to commemorate the walk, which the locals called the Cox Way.

The following day, they all piled into an open cart to complete the journey to Stepanakert to deliver the rest of the medicines. Conditions at the hospital were even worse than before. It had been shelled again at the end of December. Alazan rockets and artillery shells had struck even as surgeons were performing an operation. On New Year's Day the separate maternity hospital also took a direct hit. Mothers and babies were transferred to the basement, where they were being cared for in cold, damp conditions that created a risk of hypothermia. A number of mothers had given birth prematurely. The drugs and medical supplies were seized upon. Caroline had delivered them within 12 days of witnessing the devastation at the hospital. After that, no further deaths were reported from the pain-induced shock of an operation without anaesthetic.

It was four months before the Red Cross was able to follow in her footsteps and enter Karabakh. Médecins Sans Frontières, which had managed to get in, added the Karabakhtsis to its list of peoples threatened with extinction.

NOTES

1. According to the Georgian newspaper *Gurandi*, had the weaponry been shared out evenly, as per the agreement, it would have bequeathed Georgia, Armenia and Azerbaijan each 100 fighter-bombers, 50 assault helicopters, 220 tanks, 220 armoured vehicles and 285 artillery pieces. Georgia and Armenia received less than half their allocation. *Gurandi* was cited by Lord Avebury in the House of Lords, 15 December 1992, during a debate initiated by Baroness Cox. Lord Avebury went on to call for Western pressure to stem the flow of arms to the Commonwealth of Independent States by the former Soviet Union, even to the extent of setting up a UN fund to buy up and destroy former Soviet weaponry.
2. Even after the cease-fire, three years later, a half-kilo of butter cost a month's wages and a kilo of meat two months', and the economy was acknowledged to have come under a strong mafia influence: 'The Humanitarian Situation of the Refugees and Displaced Persons in Armenia and Azerbaijan', Council of Europe Report, 14 February 1995, p. 9.
3. *The Guardian*, 29 January 1993.
4. Andrew Higgins, 'Energy-Starved Armenians Risk a New Chernobyl', *The Independent*, 7 June 1995.
5. Cited by the Earl of Shannon in *Hansard*, column 532, 15 December 1992.

FIVE

Into the Abyss

The civilians of Stepanakert would need all the resilience they could muster. Caroline was in the city when the Azeri commander in Shushi radioed to say they were going to use Grads against the civilians. It was intimidation and it succeeded. She saw real fear on the faces of the Karabakh leadership. They were well aware of the effect of Grads on Shaumyan and knew the Azeris were prepared to use them on civilians. It was not an empty threat.

When CSI returned the following month, the bombardment was underway. Stepanakert was being transformed into Gruyere cheese. Housing blocks were pockmarked with shrapnel, or left shattered and askew, reduced to life-size piles of Lego, dotted around with curtains, mattresses and the remnants of belongings. Everyone slept in basements. They would awake in the morning to the tremendous hammering of the Grads. Caroline daily counted 400 Grad attacks on the city and neighbouring villages. The head of Karabakh's Parliament, Artur Mkrtchyan, described the onslaught succinctly, 'It is not the art of war that is being displayed here, but war's ability to kill as many civilians as possible.'[1]

Economist and jazz musician Vladimir Astsaturian was one of the basement dwellers. His home, his dog and his Stradivarius violin were destroyed by the shell-fire. He described his plight to *The Sunday Times*:

It's pitch dark. We hear the terrible thunder from the Grads. Children cry piteously. [At] times I wake in horror when rats crawl over me. Sometimes babies are bitten. After waking, I immediately think, where can I find firewood, water, food – anything – for the family? This is 'white genocide' by Azerbaijan. No need for bullets. They just eliminate us by starvation. I used to weigh 96 kilos; now I'm down to 50. Stepanakert used to be a gay city. Lots of restaurants – we Karabakhtsis like to eat well. We feasted, laughed, sang and danced till early morning. Now it's like a bad joke because the stomach remembers everything. The juices still run and at night the stomach seems to stick to your spine.[2]

One 12-year-old boy was seen crossing the road with an armful of books as the Grads were thundering down. An adult dragged him to safety and demanded to know what on earth he was doing walking around during a missile strike. The child replied, 'This war could go on for ten years. Do you think I'm going to remain uneducated for the rest of my life? I'm going to school.'

Caroline later relayed that story at a Baptist church in Streatham, South London. After hearing her speak, the minister set up a link between his primary school and a school in Karabakh. His class of 11-year-olds prepared a package of Christmas gifts, individual letters, a photograph of the class and a prospectus of the school.

When Caroline returned to Stepanakert, the Ministry of Education suggested she took her gifts to the school named after Andrei Sakharov. It was a blackened, burnt out shell without glass in the windows and only part of a roof. It had no heating, lighting or electricity. It was January, and teaching was continuing in temperatures of minus ten degrees, to classes of 12-year-olds swathed in coats and mufflers.

The parcels were received with wide-eyed excitement. Then the children sat down and, unaided by their teacher, each composed a letter to one of the children in Streatham. One wrote, 'Our capital city, Stepanakert, used to be a beautiful city, but has been spoilt by bombing. However, I don't want to write about sad things, I want to write about happy things.'

Armenian and Russian have different scripts. The children could read and write both. English was their third language and their third script. And – Caroline, the educationalist, took note – their spelling was better than many British 12-year-olds.

Firing blindly

Meanwhile, in Mardakert, three miles into north-east Karabakh, the Karabakhtsis were staging a counter-attack. Their aim was to recapture the supply route from Stepanakert, via Aghdam in Azerbaijan. At the fog-bound front line the enemy could be heard, but not seen. Bullets were fired blindly into the grey murk, zipping over the iron-hard trenches like amplified mosquitoes. At the height of battle, a man would fall to the frozen ground every ten minutes, caught by a grenade or a shot fired at random by an unseen enemy. And when those who remained were air-lifted back by helicopter, after a fortnight of fear, death and clamour, their faces wore the glassy-eyed unblinking stares of shock and exhaustion – 'the look of people who have lost their hope to stay alive', said documentary cameraman

Vardan Hovnahessian. 'It's impossible to sleep. The *mujahedin* kill you with a knife if you sleep. They are very professional.'

Human rights groups protested that defeated soldiers were killed rather than captured; that enemy wounded were denied medical attention. It was true, but the truth was a little more complex. Soldiers on both sides were convinced they would be beaten and mutilated should they fall into enemy hands. Rather than face capture, the dying wounded would turn themselves into living booby traps, lying on ready primed grenades, which would guarantee a swift end to themselves and their abusers should anyone attempt to interfere with them. Rather than take the risk, both sides would shoot the wounded out of hand. But as one man who had served in the trenches explained, when your friends are dying around you and you go berserk with the noise and lack of sleep, when you see the enemy, you don't hesitate. You just kill him.

For some who were taken prisoner, death would have seemed infinitely preferable.

An Azeri reconnaissance unit overwhelmed a front-line position held by 32-year-old Basian Beniky and his colleagues. One Armenian was cut to pieces. Another had his head severed and his eyes gouged out by a sword. The Azeris would have cut off Basian's head, as well, but he moved and escaped the stroke.

He was transported to a military post near Levinavan, while his captors decided what to do with him. 'The two Azeri soldiers wanted to cut out my nose and ears,' he told Caroline, 'but there were Russians and Ukrainians present who did not allow this.'

Basian was transferred to Baku and thrown into cell number 5, Gobustan military prison. The policy was to beat every Armenian POW from 2 to 6 a.m. each morning until he lost consciousness. In the evening he was taken to a room with five or six Azeris. They would ask him where he was from. 'When I said, "from Stepanakert" they would beat me on the head.' Once he was put in a room with up to 40 Azeri deserters. 'The chief told each of the soldiers to kick me once. Some felt pity and hit me really weakly. However, the chief would order me to be hit ten times more if he noticed this.'

There was worse to come. 'The soldiers heated an iron skewer until it was red hot,' said Basian, 'and then thrust it into my legs and feet. When the Azeris thrust skewers into my legs, one said to another, "Why are you doing that? You make it dirty because it has touched a Christian." The Azeri threw the skewer away.'

Another pastime for their guards was to take the Armenians outside, burn them with cigarettes and force them to eat excrement. Those who refused were severely beaten. Those who complied were beaten anyway.

Food, when it came, was left-overs from the prison officers. 'The guards would spit in the food and put cigarette butts in it,' said Basian. 'I thought for several hours what to do, but I was very hungry, so I ate it.'

Twice during his 80-day confinement, Basian tried to slash his wrists. 'I do not know why I am still alive,' he said. 'Once I asked Ashot [another prisoner] to kill me. Ashot said, "What do you think of me?" I cried only once, when I cut my veins. But I remembered my daughter and saw her telling me to come back.' Another prisoner, Artur, was a committed Christian. 'He was a different kind of Christian, a believer,' said Basian. 'He was always lying on the ground and praying to God for our daily bread and for our release.'

That release was heralded by a visit from the Red Cross. When a representative came and handed out cigarettes, one of the prisoners put a cigarette into his mouth and began chewing. When asked what he was doing, the prisoner explained that he was eating a sweet. He had been driven insane by the torture. Among the others pronounced insane was 17-year-old Irina Tarnikian, whose mind was shattered by multiple rape.

Basian and the others were released by the Red Cross and flown to Yerevan. His kidneys were enlarged from the beating. A bone in his chest was broken. A closed knife wound was festering inside. His toenails were rotting from being made to stand barefoot in a cold, wet cell. He will bear the scars of his ordeal for the rest of his life. The most conspicuous is the sign of the cross which was burned into his back with cigarettes.

Other former inmates of Gobustan spoke of electric shock torture and of having salt rubbed in their wounds. Another says he was ordered to sexually abuse Armenian women hostages for the entertainment of the guards. 'We refused,' said 20-year-old Minos Karapeti Vardanian, who had been captured on sentry duty. 'They were our Armenian sisters.'

'What did they do to you when you refused?'

'They beat us harshly and kept beating us.'

'How did you get the willpower or strength to make yourselves refuse?'

'Our souls did it for us.'[3]

NOTES

1. *The Daily Telegraph*, 19 March 1992.
2. Vanya Kewley, 'A life in the day of'.
3. 'Humanitarian Aid Mission to Armenia and Nagorno Karabakh', Appendix to CSI Report, 27 May –

3 June 1997. Soldiers were still being captured at the front line well after the declaration of the cease-fire in 1994. Another released from Gobustan was 39-year-old Larissa Kiragosian, who had gone to Turkey as a tourist. She claims she was captured by Azeris there and taken to Azerbaijan where she, too, was raped repeatedly. Other Armenians were allegedly being abducted from Georgia to be used as hostages to force the exchange of Azeri soldiers in Armenia. CSI called on the governments of Turkey and Georgia to investigate the reports and condemn those responsible for the kidnappings.

Christian Solidarity's evidence on hostage taking was borne out after the conflict in 1998 by an independent report from *Physicians for Human Rights*. They travelled to Karabakh and examined 67 former hostages – many of whom were civilians. Some had been abducted after the cease-fire. One woman was seized in Turkey. All had been tortured. The youngest were children of one and three. Even their doctors were among the torturers. The report concluded: 'Many were convinced their religious faith and strong belief in family values was the reason for their survival.'

SIX

Golgotha

Caroline made other trips into Karabakh that winter, often flying in to Armenia from Kent on a Russian cargo plane laden with aid, sporting a cracked windscreen and tyres that were down to the canvas. As one photographer wryly observed, 'It would never pass its MOT.' During one visit, she helped put out a fire in a warehouse which had received a direct hit from a Grad. It was their last reservoir of supplies. People ran in under flaming ceilings with burning wood cascading around them, to try to rescue children's clothes and boxes of Biros.

In April, the Azeris overran the village of Maraghar, in north-eastern Karabakh, and according to survivors, committed a massacre. The attack had commenced at 7 a.m. with an artillery bombardment. Then up to 20 tanks and armoured personnel carriers had come, and behind them the infantry. Behind the troops were civilians with pick-up trucks to loot the village. According to witnesses, 45 villagers were massacred in cold blood, and a hundred women and children were taken hostage. After the bones of the village had been picked clean, what remained of it was set alight.

Caroline arrived the following day. She describes Maraghar as a place of Golgotha. It was a grey Spring morning and the sky was smudged by the smoke from the still smouldering homes. The survivors were in a state of shock. Elderly women reeled towards them, clutching battered photographs of relatives who had been killed. Blood was over the ground and on the walls. One man started to tell them he had seen 'children hacked to pieces like pigs'. Words failed him.

A woman whose two grandchildren had been seized as hostages fell at her feet and begged, 'Help us.' Caroline took her in her arms and explained that she, too, was a grandmother. 'I will remember you in my prayers,' she said. 'And carry your grief in my heart.'[1]

The survivors managed to tell them that Azeri troops had rounded up the villagers and sawn off their heads. It was almost too much to take in. Caroline surveyed the devastation and the villagers who were struggling to describe the indescribable. She took a deep breath and reluctantly asked the Armenians if they could see the bodies.

There was a moment's terrible hesitation. This woman was asking them to desecrate the sacrament of burial. Gently, but firmly, Caroline explained that evidence was necessary, because the world would not believe them otherwise. The remaining villagers withdrew into an intense, at times fraught, discussion about exhuming their dead.

Eventually, agreement was reached, and with a mixture of anguish and determination, they went through the process of digging up the freshly turned ground. While the spades continued to strike the grey soil, Caroline's eyes were drawn to a grizzled old man with a flat cap sitting silently beneath a tree. In his hand was a human ear. It was all that remained of his neighbour. It had been severed by the Azeris.

One by one the simple wooden coffins were opened. The old man with the flat cap stood by the graveside wringing his hands, his face a rictus of grief. Inside, just as the villagers had said, were charred and decapitated corpses, looking like oxen at a barbecue. The heads had been buried separately. Photographs were taken and evidence gathered. 'The whole place was just a scene of hell.'

Caroline had had enough. She noticed a semi-circular saw lying in a ditch. 'I should have photographed it; I should have brought it back, but it made me feel so sick I couldn't even touch it.' She rebukes herself for her weakness. Having insisted that others should exhume the victims, she had balked at handling the instrument of their deaths, 'I should have done; I should have done… because I would have had the evidence.' Her lips purse at the recollection. Her voice falls a semi-tone, a trace of cold anger behind it. Anger at what has happened, and anger with herself, for allowing squeamishness to inhibit the rigorous gathering of evidence of atrocity.

Moving on to the nearby town of Mardakert, in a region where 50 out of 56 villages were depopulated, they visited the hospital and met the senior nurse, a middle-aged woman, whose face was ravaged by grief. The previous day she had been made to watch as her own son's head was sawn off in front of her. Fourteen members of her extended family had been killed in the raid. All Caroline could do was hold her in her arms as she wept convulsively.

After her sobs had subsided, Caroline suggested gently that it might be a comfort for her to tell her story, to get the message of the suffering of the Karabakh people out to the wider world. She composed herself, steadied her voice and said, 'Thank you. I would like to give a message. As a nurse in this hospital I have seen how the medicines you've brought have saved many lives and relieved much suffering. Therefore, I just want to say thank you to all those people who have not forgotten us in our dark and difficult days.'

A message of thanks was not what Caroline had been expecting from a woman whose son had been decapitated the day before. 'That to me is one of the quintessential examples of the dignity of the people of Karabakh; that refusal to give in to hatred and bitterness.'

'Caroline's greatest contribution to suffering people,' says CSI's UK Chairman, Mervyn Thomas, 'has been physically showing solidarity with them and saying, "Look, I'm not just going to stand in Parliament and say we love you. I'm going to come out and see you and then I'm coming back to give you what you need."'

But by now, Caroline's combination of energy, drive and effective campaigning was also making a substantial impact on CSI. 'She put us on the map,' says Mervyn. 'We became more effective in our work as people took us more seriously.'

NOTES
1. David Moller, 'A Baroness Goes Into Battle', *Reader's Digest*, October 1992.

SEVEN

Calculated Risk

Few would trade their armchairs for a seat in a helicopter overflying hostile Azeri forces. When the shooting started, Armenia had seven such helicopters. Now they were down to three. As they passed over the military blockade, they saw the wreckage of one below. Caroline's first experience of being shot at was when a bullet ricocheted off her helicopter window. She was looking out of it at the time, and had it not been for the glass, the shot would have caught her right between the eyes. 'She gave no reaction,' says John Eibner, who was with her at the time. 'She is a woman of prayer and we just get on with the job.' The job in question was delivering medicine. Besides, the single round was spent by the time it hit the glass. But it was different at Shosh, where the rounds were artillery shells that were well within range, and aimed at her vehicle.

The village of Shosh could almost have been transposed from the English Lake District, before the Grads came pounding down that morning. Caroline went to gather evidence that civilians were being targeted and to give some encouragement to the people. Sun and snow were in the sky together. The mountain roads were awash with slush. An ancient green van, with a red cross roundel painted on its side, was trying to carry out the wounded, but was stuck in the sticky brown mud, its wheels spinning uselessly. Caroline and the others tried to shift it by wedging branches under the tyres, but only succeeded in splattering themselves with the sticky earth. A camera crew was present to record the undignified scene. The Karabakhtsis began fussing over Caroline's soiled clothing, but kissing the mud on her scarf, she said, characteristically, 'Don't worry; it's the soil of Karabakh and I love it.' The papal gesture was celebrated on Karabakh television. Cynical souls might accuse her of media manipulation, but if she is guilty of anything, it is sentimentality.

When they reached the outskirts of the village, pigs and sheep were lying shredded in the fields, dead and dying. Some villagers were sheltering under a stone bridge. Several others were rummaging through the timbers and stones to see if there was anything they could salvage. Their homes had

154

been reduced to matchwood, rubble and concrete dust. In the misty sunshine, the village had the look of a ships' graveyard. A woman of 105 had met her end when the Grads began falling at seven that morning. They couldn't bury her in the churchyard because it was too exposed. The funeral took place in her garden, her night-dress and a blue striped sheet her shroud, with the mourners taking care to stand well apart so as not to tempt Azeri artillery.

Caroline and the others walked back single file and well spread out towards the olive drab Warsaw Pact jeep that was waiting on the outskirts of the village. As they passed a farm building, they heard the sound of distressed cattle and paused to open the doors, not knowing whether the farmer was still alive to take care of his animals. The party of seven, including Zori Balayan and a brace of journalists, crammed into the vehicle, which picked its way along the mountain road.

The pounding of artillery started up again. It took a moment or two to realize they were the target. Shells were falling all around. The mountain road was a slash of ice and snow. The Armenian driver put his foot down, skidding and slewing frantically. The shells kept coming, and the gunner was getting their range. One exploded close enough to lift the back of the vehicle clear off the ground. Caroline was sitting on the left – the gun side. 'Just can't think why I volunteered to be on this side going back,' she quipped.

Temporary relief came when the jeep passed behind a shoulder of the mountain. But the driver knew the gunner would have his sights trained on the point where the vehicle would emerge back into view. Braving the ice, he stepped up the pace. They remained a target for the next two kilometres, when the jeep finally made its escape round a promontory. Caroline asked the driver what would have happened if they had taken a direct hit. He replied, 'A truck was hit here last week which was carrying 12 men. Only one of them was identifiable.' A lorry loaded with CSI aid was also blown up to the north of Karabakh, killing the driver. On Caroline's next trip to the region she awarded her jeep driver the Sakharov medal and asked him whether he was still ferrying supplies around Karabakh. He replied, 'No way.'

'We take calculated risks,' explains John Eibner, speaking slowly and carefully, with a New York State accent. 'We believe our work is in the will of God and we try as best we can to remain in communion with him when we undertake these dangerous missions. But both Caroline and I understand that if one is to show true solidarity with those who are suffering and experiencing martyrdom one has to be prepared to take casualties. This is something one senses has been lost in Western Christianity. Caroline doesn't seek martyrdom – nothing can be further from her mind. But she is intelligent and knows she cannot be immune from suffering, and on the front line she knows she is taking risks and is prepared for that.'

'You've got to die of something,' shrugs Caroline. 'It may be better to die doing something worthwhile than live to a ripe old age in a more cocooned kind of existence.'

That's the kind of answer Caroline's younger son, Jonathan, is used to hearing. 'It's very difficult to argue with her. She's not the sort to sit behind a desk. She has to go out there and try to be a voice for the voiceless, and that means identifying with them, not only in their cause, but potentially with the consequences of it.

'So many people go for the soft option, but at the end of the day that is numbing. If you don't ever put your head above the parapet, you never get to see what's on the other side. My biggest worry is that she will just burn herself out. Everyone has limits. Even Baroness Cox.'

Caroline would have drawn the line at going into war zones while her children were young, and admires the courage of CSI colleagues, like John Eibner, with small children, who still go on these trips. 'What would pull my heartstrings more than anything,' she says, 'would be to lose contact with the family. Robin, my eldest son, once said, "Your grandchildren want you to see them grow up. And *I* want to see them grow up."'

'We've got past the stage of being worried about her,' smiles Robin, a doctor in the Royal Navy. 'We know her work is dangerous, but nothing in the world will stop her doing it. We share her Christian faith, feel what she does is of the utmost importance and are fully behind her. We're very proud of her.'

But even Robin, whose naval career has taken him to hot-spots in Bosnia and the Gulf, admits to being nervous about Caroline's other aerial route to beat the blockade.

Air-bridge

With Karabakh cut off within Azerbaijan, the only way in was by air. The Armenians supplemented their dwindling helicopter fleet by taking standard, civilian passenger planes and training them to jump through hoops. Every surplus seat was ripped out of the twin-engined Yak 40s, and anyone going along for the ride would have to take their place amid the strapped-down fuel drums, medicine and food supplies. They would have to hang on tight.

To avoid the Azeri heat-seeking and radar-tracking missiles the pilots had to pretend they were flying MiGs. After take-off the planes would soar to way above their operational ceiling. The real hazard came during the descent over the mountains. To cheat the missiles the pilot would corkscrew down against the light, hoping the heat-seeking missiles would go for the sun and not for the plane. 'This manoeuvre is not included in the primer of civil aviation,' one flight engineer told *The Daily Telegraph*. Caroline did the trip many times. Fortunately, she has a cast-iron stomach. 'It was a very scenic way of arriving,' she grins. 'I would say my prayers and admire the skill of the pilot.'

As they reached the airstrip in Khojaly, the fliers would come in fast and steep and throw the plane down with a screech of tyres. The tactic wasn't always successful. In March, the plane following hers out of Stepanakert was raked by Azeri machine-gun fire. On another occasion, a plane flying back with a full load of 40 war-wounded took a direct hit. The pilot managed to keep it in the air long enough to crash-land over the border in Armenia at the airstrip in Sissian. Somehow they managed to evacuate all the casualties before the aircraft exploded. Astonishingly, there were no fatalities. Thereafter, blockade-running was carried out by ground-hugging helicopter. It became the standard way in for Caroline and her cargoes of medicine. She enjoyed the flights and, once again, found herself caught up in the emotional ambivalence of revelling in a journey undertaken against a backdrop of tragedy. Now, whenever she goes to Yerevan, she lays a wreath at a monument dedicated to the pilots who gave their lives to keep open that lifeline.

The air-bridge itself was not enough. Helicopters continued to be shot down. Karabakh is separated from Armenia proper by a tantalizing handful of miles. The usual way in was along the narrow, four-mile Lachin corridor. That had been captured and sealed off by the Azeris. To create a supply route by land it would have to be reopened. A *cordon sanitaire* would have to be created around the corridor to keep it free from artillery and missile bombardment.

In practice, it meant thrusting deep into Azeri territory, resulting in an exodus of Azeri civilians and giving rise to counter-claims of deportation and atrocity. Armenia was roundly condemned for the action by the international community. It was stoutly defended by Caroline Cox. 'If there hadn't been a blockade, which itself was a gross violation of human rights, there would be no need to open the corridor. If the international community was silent about the blockade, they had no right to condemn the corridor.'

The opening of the Lachin corridor for humanitarian and military supplies brought the war home to Azerbaijan and created a land-bridge with Armenia for military support. Caroline and her relief aid could now come in by car, though it was little safer than going by air. In one convoy ahead of her a vehicle took a direct hit from a Grad and all four occupants were killed.

The battle for Shushi

Another key target was the town of Shushi, a mountainous stronghold overlooking Stepanakert. Shusha, as it was called by the Azeris, had been occupied by Muslims since 1750, when Turkic forces were invited in to settle a little local difficulty. Today, it made an ideal Azeri base from which to send Grad missiles raining down upon the capital. The troops had pulled down the cross from the top of the church with a tractor and had only halted their attempt to demolish the building when they realized it would make an admirable storehouse. Knowing the Armenians would draw the line at attacking a church, it became the perfect choice for an ammunition dump for Grads. The missiles were stored inside, in a mountain of wooden lockers. Outside, a bunker was built using gravestones ripped up from the cemetery.

The bombardment of Stepanakert was supervised by an Azeri Lieutenant Colonel of the 366th Motorized Infantry Regiment. Three of his soldiers were killed and eleven injured in February 1992, when Karabakh forces turned a captured Grad against them. Shortly afterwards the Commonwealth of Independent States decided to call it a day and pull out of the conflict. Not all the troops decided to return home. The Lieutenant Colonel and some of his men stayed to fight Grad with Grad in Shushi. Others from the same unit defected and joined the Karabakhtsis, to take up arms against their former comrades.[1]

In May 1992, Armenia and Azerbaijan put their signatures to a peace agreement in Teheran. The following day, the Azeri offensive began. All attempts by the Conference on Security and Co-operation in Europe to mediate the conflict failed. Armenia's plea to the UN to send in peacekeepers fell on deaf ears. *The New York Times* warned: 'Without political intervention, the deadly little war will degenerate to the levels of Bosnia.' For the civilians of Stepanakert it was already at that stage, as the Grads kept hurtling down from Shushi. It became imperative to stop the missiles. And there was another compelling reason for taking Shushi – the town straddled the main road connecting Nagorno Karabakh to Armenia. Its fall would enable food and arms to go through unchecked. It could also turn the tide of the war.[2]

The battle for Shushi was a strategist's nightmare, for two reasons. The assault on the fortress town would put at risk a significant portion of the Karabakhtsis' already depleted forces. And as an historic centre of Armenian culture, Shushi had to remain as undamaged by further conflict as possible.

To try to persuade the Azeris they were being attacked by a far greater force Karabakhtsi troops were instructed to drive their few vehicles round and round, revving their engines and making as much noise and clamour as they could muster. A corridor was left open for Azeri soldiers and remaining civilians to escape and they fled *en masse*, resulting in fewer casualties on both sides than had been expected. The official figure for Armenian losses was 32 dead and 36 wounded. The fall of Shushi was a military triumph. The empty Grad storage boxes were seized upon by returning civilians and used for firewood and containers from which to sell produce. From Caroline's perspective, the whole conflict had acquired a Biblical dimension. It was like Gideon driving out the Midianites: 'The odds were impossible.' The whole of Karabakh had a remaining population of some 140,000, including women and children, against more than 7 million Azeris, assisted by battle-hardened mercenaries.

But the odds soon began to tell.

Counterattack

The following month an election in Azerbaijan swept to power the extremist Azerbaijani Popular Front, on a mandate to settle the Karabakh problem. A renewed military offensive was launched, with the advice and assistance of 40 senior Turkish army officers who had taken early 'retirement'. According to Karabakh, Turkish participation in the conflict ran deeper. Turkey was sustaining a crippling blockade of Armenia, and it was claimed that captured weapons bore Turkish insignia. Some 40 plane loads of Turkish weapons per day were said to be bound for Baku; the bodies of six soldiers had been identified as Turks, and a tank had been knocked out bearing the Turkish 'Grey Wolves' insignia. *Bozkurt*, the Grey Wolf, was venerated by the pre-Islamic Turks as the mother of their race. It was to become a symbol of pan-Turkism.

NATO mortar rounds bearing Turkish markings were handed to a visiting American Congressman from Virginia. Republican Frank Wolf, a lean George Bush look-alike in a blue polo shirt, cream slacks and sneakers, was led around tables creaking beneath the weight of weapons allegedly captured on the battlefield. They included a US-made military radio. Wolf called for pressure to be brought to bear on Turkey. That call was repeated in the House of Lords during debates initiated by Caroline. The British government reply was that there was no evidence of Turkish arms supplies to Azerbaijan, and Turkey had undertaken to respect an embargo of arms to the region.[3]

Frank Wolf was also worried about the growing Russian influence and intended to press President Clinton to send US diplomatic aid to end the conflict. Between 1992 and 1996, the USA gave half a billion dollars in aid to Armenia, more US aid per capita than was given to any nation except Israel. Yet Congressman Wolf was the first senior US politician to visit Karabakh. His motivation was essentially religious. 'I am a committed Christian,' he explained. 'My purpose is to bring about reconciliation. Christ said, "When I was hungry you fed me" and these people are certainly hungry. He said we should visit people in prison, and these people are basically in prison. Ecclesiastes talks about the oppressed having no-one to speak out for them, so my Christian faith drives me to get involved.'

Frank Wolf and Caroline Cox were kindred spirits. He described her as 'a passionate and articulate spokesperson for those caught in the hell-holes of political and military struggle – the voice of those who are not being heard'. And like Caroline, he denied being blind to the suffering of the Azeris. As he was quick to point out, he had campaigned to lift the arms embargo against the Muslims in Bosnia, and had sheltered with them against the Serb artillery in the basements of Mostar.

But if religious conviction had driven Frank Wolf to seek reconciliation in Karabakh, it was also motivating others to become involved in the conflict, with less benign intentions. Azerbaijan had recruited up to 3,000 mercenaries, including *mujahedin* veterans of the Afghan conflict, seeking fresh opportunities to drive back the infidel. And if the prospect of a *jihad* was insufficiently galvanic, then there was also the promise of wads of dollars – enough to have the hired guns queuing up outside the Iranian consulate in Pakistan. Saudi Arabian funds were said to be behind the recruitment drive.[4] Whatever the truth of either claim, the prospect of the conflict acquiring the panoply of a crusade was not far from the surface. The religious dimension was understandably played down within Karabakh. 'It is not a religious war,' said Bishop Martirosian. 'But there is a danger with the Azeris using *mujahedin* that they may internationalize the conflict and make it a religious war.'[5] As if to allay any fears, an Armenian team of restorers was dispatched into Shushi to make good the war damage suffered by the mosque.

But whatever the motivation of the Azeri forces and their allies, their renewed offensive began to take its toll. Armenian villages from the northern Mardakert and Shaumyan districts were the first to fall, under combined attack from aerial bombardment, missile and tank. Those who could, fled. Those who survived but could not, remained to face the troops. One young Armenian mother described the scene to Christian Solidarity International:

> They attacked the village and started cutting the villagers to pieces. I myself heard the screams of a man who was having his head cut off by a saw. Then we took our children and ran away. The next day we returned to the village. People were cut into pieces, their eyes were gouged out, their ears were cut off. We then saw the [body of the] man whom I had previously seen being decapitated. The saw was lying next to him and all the blood had flowed out of the body. Another man – our uncle – was tied to the back of a tank and was dragged 500 metres. After that we fled to Shaumyan. Ten days later, the Azeri-Turks did the same things. After that I took the children and fled. We walked for 40 miles. We arrived thirsty and hungry and with our clothes in tatters. We couldn't take anything with us. I've seen these atrocities with my own eyes.[6]

Forty per cent of Karabakh was overrun and Azeri troops were within ten miles of Stepanakert.

Longer range missiles were being used that were beyond the reach of Karabakh's defence forces. The civilian casualty rate soared. The enclave was rapidly becoming depopulated. Almost all the Azeri-Turk civilians had left or been driven from their homes. Now, many able-bodied Karabakhtsis were making the hazardous journey to a safe haven in Armenia.

In August 1992, the Azeris pressed aircraft into the conflict. SU25s started dropping 500 kilogram bombs on Stepanakert and the surrounding villages. An unexploded bomb that just missed a village bore the message, scrawled in red: 'Supper for the Armenians'. Each was the equivalent of five or more Grad missiles. In Stepanakert, the women listened for the bombs to fall, then waited. As soon as there was silence they knew they had up to 20 minutes to hang their washing, run their errands and return to their basements. It was as long as it took for a plane to reload. 'What is scary is the noise,' said an aid worker. 'The planes fly out of reach of anti-aircraft missiles and then suddenly swoop down to 100 metres above the houses. The most difficult thing is the constant alarms – five or six per day. It goes straight to your stomach.'[7]

By October, their payload had changed to cluster bombs, which are banned for use against civilians under international convention. Also banned was the use of flechettes, dart-like bullets with fins designed to maximize damage to human tissue. Surgeons were soon struggling to remove them from soldiers coming in from the battlefield. But the cluster bombs were far less discriminating. The attractive-looking silver balls, primed to explode on movement, drew children like magnets.

Twelve-year-old Pailak Haratunian was playing in the woods with his friends when he picked up one of the silver balls and decided to carry it home. He fell. The explosion tore out one eye, damaged another, injured his leg and chest, and perforated his colon. Maria Bedelian was also 12. She found a ball in her garden in a village near Stepanakert. As she was taking it to show her mother, she tripped. Seven people were wounded in the explosion. Maria's left leg was splintered like a twig and she suffered multiple injuries. The surgeons didn't know where to start. A doctor in Stepanakert said, 'This is not the front line. This is children.'

Caroline visited them in hospital and grimly gathered her evidence. She was determined to bring pressure to bear on the British government to condemn the atrocity.

'Ashamed to be British'

Armed with her photos, she arranged a meeting at the Foreign Office with a senior politician. She pointed out that Azerbaijan was a signatory to the major conventions on human rights and a member of the Conference on Security and Co-operation in Europe (CSCE). 'Therefore, would the British government prevail upon Azerbaijan to stop dropping cluster bombs on children, which is a gross violation of human rights?'

She is reluctant to name the senior politician, who coolly replied, 'No country has an interest in other countries, only *interests*. And we have oil interests in Azerbaijan.' She pressed the argument, but to no avail. What hope was there for Karabakh? she wondered. The odds were impossible, and if that was to be the attitude of the major players in the game of international politics, then it was another nail in the Karabakhtsis coffin. They couldn't fight the Azeris *and* the Turks *and* face the total hostility of the international community – because of oil interests. It was British policy following the First World War all over again.

She went back home and wept. And with that behind her, she steeled herself for a fight. She wrote to BP, demanding guarantees that oil profits would not be ploughed into weapons; that a share of the profits would be distributed among the victims of war, both Armenian and Azeri, and for BP to exert its influence to prevent Azerbaijan from imposing a military solution. BP declined. But as for Foreign Office policy, there was no way *that* was going to remain behind closed doors.

She rose to her feet in the House of Lords and quoted the minister. Before all the assembled peers, she announced, 'For the first time in my life, I was ashamed to be British.' There was an uncomfortable silence. She continued, 'I can understand strategic interests. I can understand commercial interests, but I didn't think it was the long-term interest of any country to let those obliterate concern for human rights. Moreover, I didn't think the majority of British people would actually want oil at the price of cluster bombs on children.'

Her anger is fuelled by seeing people *in extremis*, and feeling no relief or remedy for their anguish. When anger strikes, it goes deep down and becomes internalized. Instead of erupting, 'I become ice cold,' she says, 'and the adrenalin goes up, ready for a fight.' When she swears at all, which is seldom, it is usually in jest. When the anger is building, the words stop. 'I get very calculating, very careful... and vicious, too.'

The cynicism and amorality of the political arena drove her beyond anger to the point of despair. Internationally, the insistence of the CSCE on the inviolability of borders at the expense of human rights, drove her to distraction. But her attempts to cut through the political ice did not pass unnoticed.

In an address to the Anglo-Armenian Association, Chairman Odette Bazil thanked Caroline for putting Nagorno Karabakh on the map. She had 'urged influential people to take notice of the tiny "oblast" that Mr Douglas Hogg, then Minister of [the] Foreign and Commonwealth Office in charge of the Eastern European Desk, compared to a football stadium with its 130,000 people.'[8]

NOTES

1. *The Daily Telegraph*, 19 March 1992.
2. Jonathan Steele and Jonathan Rugman, 'Azeris Lose Control of Last Stronghold', *The Guardian*, 11 May 1992.
3. Baroness Trumpington, in reply to an unstarred question in the House of Lords put by Baroness Cox on 15 December 1992: *Hansard*, column 546.
4. Alleged by State Defence Minister, Vazguen Sarkissian and Zori Balayan in interviews with the author, September 1994.
5. CSI Karabakh Visit Report, 18–25 February 1994. The point was underscored by the World Council of Churches, which observed, 'This is not a religious war, but it does have religious dimensions, and if the conflict is not resolved soon, religious could be misused and play a decisive negative role': cited by the Lord Bishop of Guildford in debate in the House of Lords, 15 December 1992.

6. C. Cox and J. Eibner, *Ethnic Cleansing in Progress – War in Nagorno Karabakh*, Institute for Religious Minorities in the Islamic World, 1993, p. 54.
7. From interview notes by British journalist Hazel Southam.
8. Address to the Royal Academy, 17 July 1996.

EIGHT

White-out

CSI decided to show solidarity with the Armenian Christians by spending Christmas with them. According to the Armenian calendar, Christmas falls in January, the time of epiphany in England. Caroline flew to Yerevan on 5 January – Christmas Eve. The weather had closed in and the clouds were too thick for the helicopter. It meant travelling overland. Zori Balayan managed to commandeer an old red coach to take them in. The seats were hard and wedged so closely together that the passengers were unable to cross their legs.

As they headed up into the mountains, the snowfall became a blizzard, and by 7,000 feet, the blizzard became a white-out. The coach ran into a solid wall of snow. The mountain road was completely blocked. They settled down for a night of minus 23 degrees centigrade with a chill factor of the same again. The wind found every crack in the ill-fitting metalwork of the ancient coach, driving in small flurries of snow that clung to the seats, the floor and the passengers, and refused to melt. Diesel was at a premium, but the driver had no option but to keep the engine running to fight the cold.

No-one on board was equipped for the blizzard. There were curious glances when Zori Balayan huddled his overcoat around him and stepped outside. Before long he was back, and he was not alone. With him was another traveller, whose car had slewed to a halt at the same enormous snowdrift. Balayan ushered the grateful refugee on board then turned back into the blizzard, much to the concern of staff-nurse Cox, who was aware his blood temperature would plummet.

He went out again and again, rounding up his flock, bringing families onto the bus, relief written across their faces. One couple stepped in from the howling wind, cradling a child bound round and round in rugs, coats, and anything they could find. No sooner were they on board than they scrabbled through the coverings to find out if their baby was still breathing. It was.

They settled down for a long, bleak night. Caroline's thoughts strayed to the first Christmas Eve, when there was another family in the cold with nowhere to go. At least today they were able to offer some shelter. 'It was a blessed place to be.' At midnight they sang 'Alleluia' and shared whatever food they had.

When the wind dropped on Christmas morning, they were able to go out and survey the scene. The cars were completely covered in snow. Some of the passengers would certainly have frozen to death. By midday their diesel was coming to an end, when they saw three snowploughs from Goris struggling up the mountain. It took three hours to clear the road, and a further eight to make it to Stepanakert.

A year later, Caroline received a letter from the Karabakh authorities, saying there were children who would not have been alive to see another Christmas had it not been for their bus on that mountain pass that Christmas Eve.

What Caroline did not know was that the man who was to become CSI's national director was stuck in the same snowdrift. In fact, it was because he was stuck there that he became national director. Stuart Windsor had been making a film for Elam Ministries, an arm of the Iranian Christian Fellowship in London, which was delivering food and relief aid to Karabakh.

Their vehicles had been in convoy, with Stuart in the leading truck. Before long they realized they were the only truck. All the others had fallen behind and out of sight. The reason was obvious – another puncture. Stuart, a genial bear of a man, and Sam his sound engineer, decided to get out of their truck and send it back to help the others. Minutes turned into hours and they found themselves waiting by the roadside all night in conditions of minus 20 degrees. They were rescued by a police car the following morning which brought news that their truck had plunged down a ravine. Despite head and chest injuries, the two Armenian drivers had managed to climb the 120 foot ravine and get to a village hospital. Stuart and Sam eventually found them by following the trail of blood.

The remains of the convoy pressed on into Karabakh to deliver their aid. There was a near riot when they began to give out the food. The head of the civil defence tried to calm the hungry crowds. When that failed, he fired his gun in the air. 'Remember your dignity,' he commanded. 'You are Armenians.'

Stuart was returning from Karabakh in a Lada Niva jeep when they hit the mountain, and the blizzard hit them. Within 15 minutes they were unable to move. It was 8 p.m. on the Armenian Christmas Eve. When daylight returned, he realized they were not alone. There were other cars and a bus stuck in the same snowdrift, just a hundred metres away. Stuart braved the cold to shoot pictures of the scene. The tip of one ear caught frostbite and turned black. It was 2 p.m. on Christmas Day before they were rescued.

Stuart's pictures were shown on Sky TV. While they were being edited, Sky heard that Lady Cox had just come back from Karabakh and wanted to use footage of his trip with an interview of her. They had no idea she had been on the bus. As she was being interviewed, she recognized the pictures of the bus and asked in astonishment who had filmed it. Stuart was in the next room. Her first words to him were, 'Where have you been all my life?'

They agreed to go back to Karabakh together, when Caroline confided that CSI was in a crisis because their director, Tom Green, had been forced to resign due to ill health. 'Something quickened in me,' said Stuart. 'I felt, "That's my job."' Stuart, a curious combination of ex-RAF, ex-British Intelligence and Assemblies of God pastor, became CSI's national director in May 1993.

Foreboding

Caroline and the others arrived back in Stepanakert, the day after being rescued from the mountain, to see a coffin being carried through the streets surrounded by wailing relatives. In Karabakh, funerals are accompanied by public mourning. One cries out and others join in at the end of each phrase. In between there is gentle keening; the men and the women divesting themselves of grief in separate groups. The body was that of the 17-year-old son of a local doctor. The doctor had heard the fighting and had gone out with the local rescue service. The first body he had come across was that of his son.

Shortly afterwards, at 11 a.m., the ground was shaken by a massive explosion. Zori Balayan turned to Caroline and remarked, dead-pan, 'I think that's a Christmas present from the Azeris to you.' It was one of the new long-range missiles, nine metres in length, set to explode over Stepanakert and to rain down shrapnel upon the civilians. The huge tailpiece, containing the motor, fell harmlessly onto wasteland, and on this occasion no-one was hurt.

Some 50 casualties a day were coming in from the front line and Stepanakert was subsiding into rubble. It felt like the beginning of the end. The 13th-century stone monastery at Gandsasar, a monument to the enduring faith of the people of Karabakh, had become a symbolic target. Azeri air strikes had already hit the outbuildings, just 12 yards from the church. Bishop Martirosian described the attempt to destroy the monastery as 'an attack on our soul'. It seemed a matter of time before Gandsasar and the rest of Karabakh would go under.

Caroline joined a group making their agonized petitions at the monastery. All were well aware of the fate of civilians in other areas taken by the Azeris. In the stark, austere simplicity of that holy place she felt devastated by grief. As she left, the words came to her as a kind of rebuke. They were not what she might have expected. They spoke to her heart, 'What are you so worried about? Don't you think I can look after my own people?' The words were to her a reminder that God's will can and will be done. They brought comfort.

'Many is the time I've come back from Karabakh full of foreboding,' she recalls. 'I've been torn apart by grief. When the elderly women see you their faces light up with a radiant joy and they come and embrace you. Within about 20 seconds they have just broken down and are weeping in your arms, and as you hold them, they are as frail and as thin as a baby bird. All the pent-up grief just comes out and all you can say as you weep with them is, "I'll take your grief in my heart." And I do, and it hurts.'

What hurts most of all, she says, is the sense of impotence – that there is nothing one can give, nothing one can do, except just be there. 'Then I think of Mary, the mother of Christ, and at the end of Christ's life, all she could do was stand at the foot of the cross and be there with him, doing nothing, maybe feeling like I feel, utterly impotent in the face of the suffering, and yet being there in love. And maybe part of the Christian love which we are called to give is being willing to attend whatever Calvaries God may call us to attend. We do so in the sure knowledge that only through Calvary did Easter Day eventually come, but at the time, they didn't know Easter was coming. Sometimes in those situations I find it's much easier to believe in the reality of Good Friday than in the reality of Easter Sunday.'

Despite her many visits, Caroline has yet to reach the point where human suffering fails to move her. Often she returns feeling low or depressed, and apprehensive about what she will find next time. 'And then I think, "Don't be so self-indulgent." The Karabakhtsis interlace their suffering with humour. It's shot through with a radiance of faith, tremendous resilience, conviction and commitment – and no self-pity.'

Uneven contest

In an effort to boost morale, Stepanakert was being rebuilt even as it was being destroyed. It was an uneven contest. Cultural symbols took on the potency of icons. Resources had been marshalled to rebuild the Music

Academy, complete with a set of air-raid trenches in the main street opposite. One of the few undamaged buildings was the theatre. The upstairs had been converted into a church, since new church buildings had been forbidden under Soviet rule. Caroline attended a baptism. Afterwards, she asked one of the mothers if she had been baptized. She replied, 'No, I haven't,' then added, hastily, 'It's not that I don't want to be baptized, but when I grew up, I lived in a village under Communism and the Azeris. We didn't have a church, a priest or a Bible. Now I am here, I have a Bible, a priest and a church, and I really want to savour my baptism. I really want to enjoy it, so I'm not rushing it.'

It spoke volumes to Caroline, who was used to baptisms being treated as social occasions. Here, access to religion had been denied, but faith was treasured and sustained. It confirmed her impression of the deep spirituality of the people of Karabakh. They could teach Western Christians a thing or two, she thought.

Downstairs in the main theatre was an exhibition of art – the first since the beginning of the war. Among the woodcarvings and pictures was a painting by a farmer, which is now on display in Caroline's family home in Dorset. The oil painting, crudely framed in white-painted wood, is about 18 inches by 12. It depicts five objects: a chair, a night-dress, a book, a lighted candle and a Kalashnikov assault rifle. The farmer explained that the night-dress represented new life; the book, education; and the lighted candle, a living faith. He went on, 'For the protection of new life, we must always have education. We must always have a living faith. For the moment, we need the Kalashnikov. We pray for the day we no longer need the Kalashnikov.'

During protracted lulls in the bombardment, plays were still being staged in the theatre. Caroline was invited to a home-grown comedy. The cast explained at the beginning that they had wanted to put on a Shakespeare, but as most of the men were at the front they had decided to settle for satire. There is something about humour under intense adversity. Once the laughter begins, the worse things get, the funnier things become. The cast threw themselves into the performance with a vigour. Although the Armenian was lost on Caroline she laughed so much she almost fell off her chair. A potent pressure valve was being released.

Another potent release for the average Armenian is alcohol. No matter how scarce the food became in Karabakh, there always seemed to be abundant reserves of alcohol to raise the spirits and suppress the appetite. Wine grapes are, after all, Armenia's most important crop. Meals are punctuated by endless wordy toasts, usually washed down with excellent Gandsasar cognac. (The five star is the one to get. Don't be put off by the wonky label and the penny-halfpenny bottletop. It is silken fire. And don't be tempted by any lower-grade alternative. It would strip the skin off your tonsils.)

'A crown of thorns'

Armenian toasts are often a blend of high humour, heady sentiment and mutual appreciation. But today, despite the cognac, the mood was one of sober recollection. While they were awaiting the flight back from Yerevan to Moscow, the CSI team were taken to an Armenian home near the airport for lunch. Their host, a wiry farmer from Getashen, took them back to the days of Operation Ring, when the deportations began. Getashen, in Azerbaijan proper, was one of the first Armenian villages to be ethnically cleansed. Tanks and armoured personnel carriers of the Soviet Fourth Army closed in on all sides. Helicopters beat down on them from above. Soviet troops moved in, on the pretext of a passport control exercise. Next came the feared Azeri OMON. The farmer knew what was coming and, being a man of the mountains, knew how to use the hills to slip through the tightening cordon. He evaded the net, and managed to join up with the Karabakh forces.

It was May and the trees were in blossom. Desolated by the destruction to his community, he turned to them for consolation. The most exquisite of them all was the apricot tree. He sought out its beauty for comfort. But as he drew closer, he saw, amid the heavy blossoms, hanging from a branch, the body of a five-year-old Armenian girl. She had been cut in two. He wept. Then he vowed revenge.

Later, when his section of the Karabakh army captured Azeri villages, he couldn't bring himself to harm a child. He wept again, because he had broken his vow.

With Caroline was a Christian journalist, Michael Apichella. He stood up, took off his baseball cap and said, 'Thank you, sir. For the first time in my life I understand what it means when it says in the Bible, "'Vengeance is mine', saith the Lord." Thank you for the dignity you have shown.' To which the farmer from the hillside above Getashen replied, 'Dignity is a crown of thorns.'

NINE

Murray

It is the desire to respond to this dignity and lack of self-pity under duress that drives Caroline to continue her hazardous work on behalf of the Armenians and others. It is more than a desire. It is a need. She is a tireless campaigner, rising early, turning around armfuls of mail, constantly on the phone, whether at the office or in her car, driving frantically, working late, working continually. She has two London flats, back to back in a block in Kingsbury. One is her office, which she shares with her colleague, John Marks; the other is her *pied-à-terre*. The walls, shelves, even the floors, are covered with gifts and momentos of her travels. A Solidarity cross, given to Polish prisoners in jail sits on one shelf beside a matchwood model of an Armenian Orthodox church. Close by is the symbol of Karabakh, the grandfather and grandmother of the nation in traditional head-dress. There are certificates, pictures, and countless albums of photographs. Spread across the floor is a carpet from Karabakh, with the names Murray and Caroline woven into the design. Her life is interwoven with the people of Karabakh.

Again she returns to the theme of their suffering and her Christian responsibility, which she expresses in almost biblical terms:

Having been able to be with these people in their hour of need and witness their dignity, their courage, their graciousness, cheerfulness and lack of hate is an inspiration. Part of the debt I can pay back to them is to convey their message to the world that the world needs to hear. They show the triumph of the human spirit. That triumph is good news. It has come out of a terrible situation, from evil that has been inflicted upon them. But if people can redeem that evil in that way, that is good news. That's an inspiration. And that's the message I feel is a privilege, a responsibility and a burden to share.

Relief organizations like Tear Fund routinely offer counselling for workers in the field to offload some of the shock and trauma arising from what they have seen. It is regarded as an essential safety valve. In the field, the situations are too intense, too immediate to permit the luxury of reflection. The impact on relief workers and on Caroline alike is afterwards, when they return to the relative security, luxury and ordinariness of everyday life in Britain's relatively free and affluent society. Those are the moments when Caroline holds on to the ultimate issues of her faith.

On only a few occasions, when the weight of what she has seen has hung especially heavily, has she sought out someone to share with. But there are times when nobody can begin to touch what she feels, when visions of pain fill her eyes and even God seems remote. One such occasion was when she met a woman whose mother's head had been sawn off and her body tossed beneath a tank. It is beyond comprehension and beyond an answer. At times like those, she will go outside into the countryside to pray and release the tears. Those times eventually pass. 'God alone is the source of redemption,' she says, 'the grace which redeems that situation.'

Normally, she keeps her concerns to herself when she returns home, to spare her family. 'There's no point in spreading the gloom and the doom.' But coming back from Karabakh in the late Spring of 1994, when the war was at its height, she was filled with a sense of foreboding. She was out walking with her husband, Murray, in the hills around Stourhead, Dorset, but her heart was still in the Caucasus. She found herself hanging back, the tears welling up. 'I couldn't continue, visualizing what would happen to people I knew and loved.'

Her psychiatrist husband, respecting her need for privacy, gave her space, and then offered a single sentence, a paraphrase of Heidegger. The words gave her comfort. 'Only where there is great danger can there flourish that which saves.'

It spoke to her profoundly. 'In a way, that which saves can only come into full manifestation in the extremities of human experience. Recognizing that helped reconcile me to what I had seen: in terms of what people were going through, in terms of the triumph of the human spirit. Ultimately, that is what redemption is all about. It didn't negate the suffering, but it helped put that suffering in a wider context of redemption and hope. It didn't trivialize it, but it did remind one of the grace and the power of God which is mighty to save. If there is that which is mighty to save, there has to be that which is mightily in need of saving. There was hope even in the greatest suffering.'

Murray and Caroline complemented one another perfectly, believed Pippa, their daughter, now a nurse in Canada. He in the world of the theatre, a psychiatrist working with the Royal Shakespeare Company, concerned with the motives and emotions underlying dramatic events. She wrapped up in the politics and practices of a world where events were all too often stranger and uglier than fiction. 'Together,' Pippa believed, 'they could perhaps see the bigger picture, by recognizing what went on behind the scenes.'

Murray's love of language was infectious. He would often help her with her speeches, suggesting a good quotation to support a point or to complement what she was writing.

'He was a very creative person,' says Caroline, 'with an extraordinary sense of humour and an amazing way with words. Shakespeare was his treasure house. He was brilliant at mimicking dialects and people and had a phenomenal memory – much better than mine. He could sit at the piano and play anything from ear.'

'They sparked one another off,' added John Marks. 'It was a real battle of wits that went on between them most of the time – very lively. They were great talkers.'

Like Caroline, Murray's work took him away from home a good deal. But if anything, their relationship was enriched by it. 'Our last 14 years were among the happiest of our lives,' says Caroline. 'We always went walking on a Saturday when we had time to go to Dorset and went to dinner in the evening at a local restaurant. And we always said that people looking at us must have thought we were having an affair, because most couples who've been married for a long time don't talk an enormous amount at dinner. But we always had so much to talk about, piles of things to bring and share.

'We were both able to develop our own enthusiasms and commitments in ways that were not inhibited by worrying about the other person being at home on their own. We were blessed with years in which we were able to enjoy the freedom to do those things that we felt most passionately about. We used to write each other notes, saying "Roll on, weekend".'

'Caroline lived for her weekends in Dorset with Murray,' said Jana Pearson, her secretary. 'They were few and far between. They went through their diaries, putting in their weekends through the year. They were almost sacrosanct. They were always writing to each other, saying, "Looking forward to our walks in Wyke."'

Murray Newell Cox died unexpectedly on 28 June 1997, whilst undergoing heart surgery. He was 65. *The Times* observed:

The sudden death of Murray Cox has deprived forensic psychotherapy of a rare and creative talent who combined generosity of spirit with precise attentiveness and imaginative flair... Cox possessed a formidably retentive memory for creative quotation, which he used extensively in his work as a therapist... [He] refused to join 'the grey army of agnostic psychotherapists', and saw his work as in many respects a 'priestlike task'. He was concerned to enable each individual, with his or her unique story, to relate to the 'larger story' of which they were a part. The spiritual and theological were always important to him. A distinctive figure, with large sideburns, crumpled cotton suits, piercing eyes and an enigmatic smile, he was a natural enthusiast, possessed of the verve and excitement of new discoveries, encouraging others with sensitivity and warmth – and with, above all, a sense of fun... [He] commanded universal respect.[1]

Test of faith

In the 1960s Caroline became a third-order Franciscan, a commitment for those who wish to follow the basic principles of the Franciscan way of life while retaining their secular employment and family ties. She was drawn to the discipline by her appreciation of St Francis and fond memories of a trip to Assisi as a girl guide. She found the blend of good humour and spirituality attractive. When she heard about the third order she was keen to become involved. Her Franciscan spiritual director plays a part in helping her to ground and discharge her experiences. Central to that process is the need to find meaning in the suffering around her. Although there have been moments of depression, she says she has never lost hope. 'I have feared the worst in some situations. And in fearing the worst, I shrink from even acknowledging the possibility, say, that Karabakh could be overrun, or that people I know will be killed and massacred. I pray so much for Karabakh. A whole generation is dying.

'In political terms, I sometimes couldn't see any room for hope, in terms of a solution which could bring an end to this suffering. And then I have to hang on to other beliefs and hopes. I'm sure Marxists would say this was an opiate, but in the final analysis, we believe in a God who is able to do exceedingly abundantly above all that we ask or think. And he is a God who has worked through history, often in ways which seemed impossible at the time. That is my ultimate hope and anchor.'

There were moments in Karabakh when her faith was running thin. One was during the Azeri counter-attack, when 40 per cent of Karabakh was overrun. Another was during aerial bombardment and ground attacks, when casualties were coming in from the front line. The onslaught was at its height a month after the signing of a peace agreement in Moscow. 'These were times when Karabakh could not survive. It was a miracle, and I pray for the continuation of that miracle.'

'She was really shocked and worried,' adds Stuart Windsor. 'She had sleepless nights. She shared with me all the time, wondering what we could do, calling us to pray.'

Caroline continues, 'I have been with people whom I knew would probably be dead by the time I got back. Just the weight of their grief, the extent of their loss, was almost more than I could come to terms with.'

When Grads were hammering into Stepanakert, a woman came into the hospital whose two children had been ripped to shreds in front of her eyes. Her husband was in intensive care, fighting for his life. The woman had been thrown aside in the blast and had escaped physical injury. But she wished she was dead. 'What can you say to someone like that? How can you respond to something like that? Whatever the bigger panoramas, whatever the words of comfort might be – that God is looking after his people – here were people in conditions of extreme human suffering who had suffered physical torture.'

Confrontation with scenes like this, where suffering appears random and perfidious, where individual pain is too deep to reach and the problem too vast to begin to alleviate, let alone cure, are the moments when compassion fatigue could begin to set in. Caroline's response is to offer what she can – a smile, a touch, a tear, a moment of comfort. It is not the answer. But it is part of the answer.

She hesitates when asked if her faith has ever been shaken. At times, she admits, God's words of comfort seem to run pretty thin. It is moments like those when Calvary seems more real, more imminent, than the resurrection. 'I have wondered, I suppose like everyone does, "Why? Why does all this have to be part of the order of things?" I have wrestled with that. I have sometimes found it much harder to relate to God. God can seem very distant in some of those situations.'

Crying into a void

When she is in the midst of the problem, facing the suffering head on, the presence of God seems implicit: somewhere within and beneath the activity, if not overt and active. But in the questioning that comes afterwards, the comfort of his presence and the reassurance of her faith can elude her. 'Sometimes, it is almost like crying into a void.' It is a condition she finds herself in and out of much of the time. The suffering she has witnessed drives her on, but never leaves her. Faith, when the feeling has departed, becomes a choice, rather than an experience, which she says can seem like little more than an absence of flat panic. Comfort, such as it is, is expressed in inner calm and the finding of resources to cope.

She reads the Bible when she can and uses study notes. She pursues her faith with the same determination that she pursues physical fitness. She will pray before switching on the radio or opening her substantial mailbag. Prayer will be resumed in the car. On visits overseas she will take herself off for walks to meditate. Her Christian discipline is High Anglican, with more than a hint of Orthodox acquired from her attachment to Armenia, although she prefers to call herself Anglican Unorthodox. 'Anglo-Catholic with a good sermon, is my ideal. There is the liturgy, which I love, and good ministry of the word.' She will recite hymns and prayers as invocations of courage and strength. The words are her statements of intent; the setting of her will:

Dark and cheerless is the morn
Unaccompanied by Thee.
Joyless is the day's return
Till thy mercy's beams I see,
Till they inward light impart,
Glad mine eyes and warm my heart.
Visit, then, this soul of mine,
Pierce the gloom of sin and grief,
Fill me radiancy divine,
Scatter all my unbelief.
More and more thyself display,
Shining till the perfect day.

'Often that prayer has to be said with a certain amount of desperate conviction, because that gloom is very much a part of life.' She confesses she could find it possible to be depressed.

Yet Caroline is not a gloomy person. She is outwardly cheery, energetic and sunny. 'She laughs a lot,' wrote journalist Vanya Kewley, 'able to see the positive side of even the most disastrous situation. She is infuriatingly cheerful, even at six in the morning, as I discovered when we shared a room in Karabakh.'[2] The gloom is not hers, but she has chosen to carry the burden of it and run with it.

She works through her position on most things very clearly. She needs to know why and how and precisely what she believes. 'Faith and reason have to be interlinked,' she says. 'If you couldn't feel a coherence in the faith or the theology, it would shatter. I have to seek for and find a validity in what

I believe and how what I believe can address what I have witnessed, in order to continue to believe in it. I think if I felt any real major disjunctions, then the whole thing might fall apart. It's precarious to that extent... or authenticated to that extent.'

She has thought through her views on pacifism, and rejected the position. 'I have seen with my own eyes what has happened to people who have been overrun by an aggressor. They have an unenviable choice. Either they fight back, or they allow their women and children to be subjected to atrocities. And if you stand by and allow the vulnerable members of your community to be maltreated, tortured or killed, then, at one level that is almost to condone it.'

In theological terms, she is a just warrior, believing, and needing to believe, in the rightness of a cause before reluctantly taking up arms, and then as a last resort. 'I believe these people are fighting a just war against impossible odds for the right for their families to survive; the right to live in their own land, to preserve their religion, their culture, their tradition – things that are most precious to the human spirit. So I have to say, I am not a pacifist. You can't stand by. You have to see the evil, then speak out and try to address the injustice which lies behind the war.'

No half-measures

Her need for clear conviction unmuddied by shades of doubt could explain why her advocacy can sometimes appear so vehement and one-sided. 'She takes a line and she goes for it,' says friend and colleague, Christopher Besse of MERLIN (Medical Emergency Relief International), who has travelled with her to Karabakh. 'That's her great strength. She won't waver. She cuts off a lot of the stuff that would potentially take her off-track. But sometimes when she gets other reports she won't hear them. And that's what people find so frustrating.

'When you get close to the bone on certain issues you get this mighty door that slams down and she says what you are saying is a different issue altogether. That could be some sort of protective mechanism that has developed over the years. There's a very strong negation of things that are perhaps uncomfortable and she doesn't want to see. I find that quite frightening. I see it playing squash with her. She'll stand by something resolutely: the ball is either definitely in or definitely out. There's no halfway house. She's not a person who will dither or accept a grey area, and that's a feature of her life and what gives her clarity of commitment. She turns an issue into emotive language.'

There can be no doubting Caroline's personal and emotional commitment to Karabakh. She has placed her faith in the Karabakhtsis, and that faith will not be shaken. Her empathy is evident for a people fighting for their land and culture against a conscript army greater in number, but weaker in morale. Unlike the Azeris, the people of Karabakh had nowhere to run to escape the fighting. 'We all knew we could not go anywhere,' said the Minister of Education, Nellie Voskanian. 'I don't know if it was a miracle, or strength of spirit, or what. But we fought and persisted.'

Surrounded by the enemy, the women had little option but to remain in Karabakh. Nellie Voskanian believes that had a decisive effect on the morale of the fighting men: 'The men on the front lines realized the enemy could not come forward because the women and children were not far behind. So they fought extra hard.'[3]

That analysis was supported by Prime Minister, Leonard Petrossian, who told Caroline, 'The key to the military success of the people, despite the odds against them, lies in the fact that they are fighting for their families, their children, their land – for everything they believe in. The enemy does not have the same commitment and therefore has already lost psychologically.'[4]

The spirit of Karabakh was summed up by their spiritual leader, Bishop Martirosian, 'The people of Karabakh did not begin this war,' he said. 'We do not want to kill anyone. But we have been forced to defend our families and our own lives. The Azeris have repeatedly broken cease-fires and renewed the fighting, forcing us to kill. But we do not pray only for ourselves. We pray for the Azeris too, and we ask you to do the same.'[5]

NOTES
1. Dr Murray Cox, *The Times*, 26 July 1997.
2. 'Into Karabakh with Baroness Cox', *The Independent*.
3. Salpi Haroutinian Ghazarian, 'Entrusted with the education of the children', *Armenian International Magazine*, November–December 1994.
4. 'Humanitarian Aid Mission to Armenia and Nagorno Karabakh', CSI Report, 28 July – 3 August 1995.
5. CSI Report, 18–25 February 1994.

TEN

Turning the Tide of War

In February 1993, Karabakh forces captured the Omar mountain pass, a falcon-swept summit of rock and ice, 3,261 metres high where the air is as crisp as the snow and the altitude tugs at your breath. Up to 8,000 men died in the fighting: as many as had perished in the preceding year. French journalist, Myriam Guame described the scene:

> Eighteen-year-old boys, cut off from the rest of the world, froze to death at minus 40 degrees. Others suffered frostbite and had to have their feet amputated. The mountains look out over sheer emptiness. Fog one minute, sun the next. Endless whiteness – opaque, glittering, like fire in your eyes. An explosion. A shell comes whooshing in, leaving the snow filthy with grime and soot. The soldiers don't pause. Scarves pulled tight over their forehead... their faces taut, they keep climbing.[1]

The following month, Caroline and Stuart Windsor went to the front line at Martuni with a BBC producer in tow who had been harping on about getting pictures of the fighting and was getting under their skin. They were received by the commander, Monty Melkonian, an Armenian American who had given up his law practice in California to do battle for Karabakh. Monty, who borrowed his nickname from General Montgomery, was commanding the Karabakh Defence Forces for the Martuni region. Stuart called him to one side and said, 'Look, I've got a TV man here who wants some action.' Monty drew them together and explained the situation. 'We've got two observation posts,' he said. 'One is 19 kilometres to the north, the other is 19 kilometres to the south. We can't go to them both. One is simple and doesn't come under fire. At the other, there's a very sharp Azeri mortar gunner, who's pretty accurate. If you want action, we can go to that observation post in my car. We will be fired upon and we may be hit.' He turned to Caroline, 'It's up to you.'

She said, 'I'm game', and asked Stuart. 'What about you?'

'I want to do it,' said Stuart, but his sound engineer demurred. Then she turned to the BBC producer whose moment had finally come and asked, 'Do you want to do it?'

'No,' came the reply.

Shortly afterwards Monty Melkonian was killed.

Not all their experiences with film-makers were quite so tense. When things had quietened down, an American crew was making a film about Karabakh and wanted to liven things up. The director, a Catholic, asked Stuart and Caroline to pray. After he had finished Stuart looked up and saw a man and a donkey walking down the street. Zori Balayan grabbed the donkey, called for Caroline, swept her off her feet and put her on it, and the astonished crew filmed her riding into the village, quipping, 'This is where I become a fool for the Lord's sake.'

Keeping a sense of humour

Caroline is appreciated at CSI almost as much for her sense of humour as her campaigning skills. Stuart, Caroline and Mervyn Thomas, their Chairman, have built up the kind of rapport and camaraderie which enables close-knit teams to survive under pressure. A sense of humour keeps them sane.

It was a Saturday afternoon in Glasgow, between trips to Karabakh. Caroline was in Scotland with Mervyn and Stuart for their annual conference. That evening she would be flying out to Stepanakert again. 'We went shopping in Marks & Spencer,' says Mervyn, 'and she was in her typical Karabakh gear of jeans. Stuart is very proud of Caroline and the fact she's a Baroness. He turned to a lady in the shopping queue and said, "This is Baroness Cox, a Deputy Speaker of the House of Lords", at which the lady turned round and said, "Och, Aye; and I'm the Queen of England!" Poor Stuart was devastated.' The egalitarian aristocrat dismisses it all with a grin, 'I don't want to be the Queen Bee, the Baroness, overshadowing my colleagues.'

On the plane coming back from the conference Stuart and Mervyn were given seats next to a po-faced academic from Warwick University. Caroline was sat directly behind them and spent the entire trip prodding them in the back to make them jump. 'Will you please behave! You're like a little schoolgirl,' retorted Stuart. All the academic was aware of was that the passenger beside her, a slight middle-aged man with glasses, kept leaping out of his seat. 'Excuse my friend,' said Stuart, leaning across Mervyn. 'He's not with me.' But the academic's face had turned to thunder. Apparently unaware that the motive power for Mervyn's uncontrollable spasms was

Caroline, she rounded on the CSI Chairman at the end of the flight and announced, 'You're the most obnoxious man I've ever met!' At which Caroline looked at Mervyn and had to agree, 'Well, he is!'

'She's terrific fun to be with,' says Mervyn. 'She used to write letters to me – "Dear Doubting Thomas" – because of something I didn't have faith about once. When she phones up, she's always laughing and joking.'

That humour isn't always well-placed. What tickles Caroline the most is her sense of the absurd. And what set her shoulders shaking during Holy Communion one Sunday at her local parish church was a decision to conduct the solemn and sacred ceremony of foot-washing.

The first 12 members of the congregation were to have their feet cleansed, as Christ cleansed the feet of his 12 disciples. 'Which is fine,' says Caroline, 'except Maundy Thursday tends not to come at the hottest part of the year, so there were people with tights on. And I was one of those who volunteered to spend the rest of the service with soaking wet feet squelching around in shoes.'

There were smiles all round, but Caroline could contain that. The last straw came when the Vicar decided to experiment with a departure from the norm for Holy Communion. Instead of using wafers, he opted for real bread; in this case, an entire sliced white Wonderloaf. The first few slices were cut into squares, and a period of silence followed. 'When I looked up to see what was happening, there was the Vicar with the bread that had been consecrated, having to eat the whole lot. Two thirds of the loaf was still there and he was eating away, chewing, chewing.'

Caroline bit her lip and decided to say some more prayers. Two minutes later she looked up and the Vicar was still chewing, so in his desperation, he decided to draft in a server. 'It's very hard to swallow Wonderloaf dry,' says Caroline. 'Soon all the servers were standing around, chewing, chewing, chewing.'

Caroline and her family were neatly arranged in the very front pew. She choked. The children joined in the laughter. Murray was fighting to keep a straight face. Soon, the entire pew was shaking. 'I was desperate,' says Caroline. 'I daren't look. I thought, "Control yourself, say some more prayers." So I did. Next time I looked up, I saw not only the vicar, and the servers, but the whole choir chewing. I nearly left the church.'

Shifting sympathies

In Karabakh, the military stalemate was broken as Karabakhtsi troops moved west and south to bridge the gap between their enclave and Armenia proper, taking territory to the east between Karabakh and Iran. The aim was to secure a buffer zone which would deny ground to Azeri missiles and artillery. And civilians. It was a point in the war where the Armenians were deemed to have become the aggressors.

In October 1993, 60,000 Azeri civilians were herded across the Araks River into Iran. Refugees said they were shelled as they waited to cross. Many more drowned. According to reports, villages were looted, then burned to the ground. The head of the UN mission in Azerbaijan visited the front line. He told *The Guardian*, 'The Azeri side of the border was in flames. We could see entire villages burning about 500 yards from the barbed wire.'[2]

The plight of the refugees was highlighted by the Rapporteur for the Council of Europe, David Atkinson MP, who was at the time the UK President of Christian Solidarity International and Caroline Cox's predecessor.[3] Caroline was later to describe those reports of Armenian brutality as exaggerated.

No fewer than four UN Security Council resolutions called on the Armenians to halt the offensive and withdraw from Azeri territory. All were ignored.[4] Karabakh troops, aided by volunteers, and allegedly regular forces from Armenia,[5] fanned out to occupy a swathe of Azerbaijan almost to the frontiers of Turkey and Iran. Both countries nervously sent troops to reinforce their borders.

In the USA, fears were rekindled that Turkey, a NATO partner and ally, and Iran, an old adversary, could be sucked into the conflict, with all its attendant implications. Moves by the Council of Europe to draw up a peace plan were receiving tough Turkish opposition. The plan was proposed by David Atkinson, who reported, 'The Turkish delegation have attempted to thwart the initiative at every turn.'

In Yerevan, Armenia's hirsute State Minister for Defence, Vazguen Sarkissian was waxing apocalyptic, 'See how many countries are now involved,' he proclaimed to assembled journalists. 'Georgia may become involved because of communications. Russia has interests in this territory and may also be involved, and you may face a new world war.' Evidence was growing that Armenia was already an active participant in the conflict, despite all protestations to the contrary. Human Rights Watch / Helsinki sent a fact-finding group to the war zone. They found volunteers from Armenia side by side with regular soldiers from the Armenian national army.'[6]

An Azeri offensive in January threw thousands of young, badly trained conscripts at the Armenian guns, with predictable results. In a counter-attack, Karabakh troops moved out of the mountains and onto the plain stretching towards Baku, displacing, according to reports, upwards of half a million people. It brought the Armenians within 20 miles of the main railway line connecting west Azerbaijan with the east.[7] World sympathy was shifting decisively towards the Azeris. A US state department official told *Newsweek*, 'We see the systematic destruction of every town and village in their way. It's vandalism.'[8] Conspiracy theories in the press had switched from babble about pan-Turkism to fears of a drive to recreate greater Armenia.

Turmoil in Baku

If the Azeri war effort was faltering, it was because Baku had other worries. In Spring 1993, a military commander came under suspicion of planning a coup. President Abulfez Elchibey stripped the officer of his rank for disobeying orders, but Colonel Suret Guseinov would not go meekly. In June, the Colonel's men repelled an attack by government forces and captured the city of Gyandzha. That done, Guseinov promptly ordered his troops to march on Baku. A desperate President Elchibey called on a former Communist Party Chairman to come to the capital and help him negotiate. Seeking the assistance of ex-KGB head Major General Geidar Aliyev proved to be a fatal mistake.

Aliyev had been booted out of the Politburo in 1987 for opposing Gorbachev's reforms. He was not content with obscurity. He persuaded the Baku parliament to make him its Chairman, forcing the hapless Elchibey to flee. Acting head of state Aliyev promptly named Guseinov as his prime minister, and gave him control of the military and national security.[9]

With Azeri troops deserting the front line, Colonel Guseinov made an appeal on state television, 'Sons of Azerbaijan, I regret that some of the Azeri army soldiers are frightened by the Armenian forces and are leaving the battlefield. Those who show weaknesses against the enemy have no right to call themselves Azerbaijanis.'[10] Acting President Aliyev called on all Azeris living in Russia, the Ukraine and Belarus to come to the aid of their homeland. Russian military advisers were flown in to train Azeri officers, while the former hub of the Soviet Union continued to supply weapons to both sides. But it was too late for Azerbaijan.

By April, almost all of Karabakh was in Armenian hands and was holding. Karabakhtsi forces had fanned out to occupy Kelbajar, consolidating control of territory bordering Karabakh and Armenia, to further claims of Armenian ruthlessness. In a reply to observations from CSI, Foreign Minister Douglas Hogg wrote:

The principal escape route for Azeri civilians was through freezing mountains. Hundreds of civilians reportedly died from exposure before reaching safety, and many more arrived with severe frostbite or hypodermic [sic]. I do not dispute that Azeri treatment of Armenian civilians has been as bad, but we must be wary of portraying the NK Armenians as the victims in this conflict. Other reports we have seen, including those from Amnesty and NGOs and UN agencies active in the region also point to intense suffering on both sides.[11]

In June and July, the Karabakhtsis went on to take Agdam and the following month made inroads into Azerbaijan to the south, all in open defiance of the UN Security Council. In November, with its war aims secure, Karabakh offered to pull back from the ground it had occupied in return for independence from Azerbaijan. That independence was not forthcoming.[12]

Karabakh held its ground, and on 12 May 1994, Russia and the Organization for Security and Co-operation in Europe (OSCE, formerly the CSCE) mediated a cease-fire. It did not mean an end to hostilities. Clashes continued almost weekly, with the worst occurring in March and September 1995 on the border between Armenia and Azerbaijan. Even when the fighting stopped, casualties continued to come in at the rate of two a day from the combined efforts of snipers and the half million landmines scattered by retreating Azeris across Nagorno Karabakh. The mines, costing less than a pound apiece, were described by a former British soldier sent to survey the scene as 'permanent ethnic cleansing', a legacy that would last up to three generations.

Karabakh now occupied some 20 per cent of Azerbaijan, a sizeable chunk that was greater than their original territory.[13] All attempts to mediate a lasting settlement ground to a halt. Karabakh continued to call for self-determination. The refusal from Azerbaijan was equally adamant. The Speaker of the Azerbaijan Parliament, Rsaul Guliyev, warned on television that 'if the aggressor does not wish to liberate our lands by peaceful means, we have no other choice but to search for other ways to free the territories he has captured'.[14]

The war cost upwards of 25,000 lives, injured 50,000, displaced more than 1.5 million on both sides, and devastated industry.[15] Armenians began to settle in the occupied territories and prevented the 780,000 displaced Azeris from returning home.[16] According to the US State Department, ethnic Azeris were 'effectively banned from all aspects of civil, political and economic life'.[17] Azerbaijan showed itself reluctant to settle its own displaced for fear of compromising its claim to Armenian-held territories. Many Azeris continued to live in poverty in temporary camps, without adequate food, shelter or medicine. The world's relief effort was sometimes laughably inept: it included Danish pork for the Muslim Azeris, rotten apples from Italy, and malodorous Swiss cheese that was too strong for even the hungry.[18] The mass of displaced Azeris has been described as a ticking time bomb, and more than 60 per cent of the population remain below the poverty line.[19]

NOTES

1. 'Taking the mountains', *Armenian International Magazine*, November–December 1994.
2. 1 November 1993.
3. 'The Humanitarian Situation of the Refugees and Displaced Persons in Armenia and Azerbaijan', Council of Europe Report, 14 February 1995.
4. Resolution 884 (12 November 1993) confirmed Resolutions 822, 853 and 874 (1993). It condemned violations of the cease-fire and the occupation of Zangelan district and the city of Goradiz; called on Armenia to press the Karabakhtsis to comply; and demanded a cease-fire and unilateral withdrawal from occupying forces in Azerbaijan.
5. Alexis Rowell, *The Guardian*, 11 April 1993: 'Many of the soldiers I met on a trip to Karabakh last month were from the Armenian national army.' Also Felix Corley, *The Wall Street Journal*, Europe, 2 March 1994.
6. Human Rights Watch recorded, 'These units often occupy quiet sections of the front or guard communications lines and supply dumps, freeing up more experienced troops for offensive operations: 'Armenian military involvement in Nagorno Karabakh', 19 November 1994; also *The Washington Post*, April 1994
7. Hugh Pope, 'Azeris Square up to a Loser's Peace', *The Independent*.
8. 29 November 1993.
9. *Book of the Year*, 1994; *Encyclopaedia Britannica*.
10. *The Guardian*, 5 July 1993.
11. In reply to a letter to Robert Dunn, MP, citing observations from CSI's Chairman, Mervyn Thomas, 28 July 1993.
12. *Book of the Year*, 1994.
13. US State Department figure, in agreement with the Azeri estimate of one-fifth of Azerbaijan, an area of some 3,200 square miles, four times the size of Karabakh. In an interview with the author in September 1994, Robert Kotcharian, then Chairman of Karabakh defence forces, claimed the figure was nearer 10 per cent. He also asserted that Azerbaijan continued to occupy up to 17 per cent of Karabakh. In March 1997, President Aliyev of Azerbaijan told reporters the additional area occupied by Karabakh forces represented one-tenth of Azerbaijan. The wide discrepancy between these figures may depend on whether Karabakh itself is viewed as a part of Azerbaijan, or whether parts of Azerbaijan are viewed as belonging to Karabakh.
14. *Interfax*, 31 July 1995.
15. According to Reuters, 35,000 died. An estimated 70 per cent of the GDP of both countries had been spent on arms. Seventy per cent of Armenia's industry had been forced to shut down. What remained was operating at between 10 and 20 per cent capacity. Over a seven-month period to June 1994 the currency collapsed and prices rose twenty-threefold. One million Armenians were homeless and the suicide rate was rising. In Azerbaijan, up to 15 per cent of the population was displaced and industrial output was down to 65 per cent. Nearly every public building was turned into shelters for refugees and the displaced: 'The Humanitarian Situation of the Refugees', pp. 2, 7, 9, 11, 13; also *Hansard*, 15 December 1992.
16. US Department of State, March 1996.
17. US Department of State, March 1996.
18. 'The Humanitarian Situation of the Refugees', p. 16.
19. World Bank figure: cited in *The Nagorno Karabakh Time Bomb*, S. MacFarlane and Larry Minear, Brown University, Thomas J. Watson Institute, 2 July 1996.

ELEVEN

The Price of Oil

The fate of Azerbaijan could change decisively, as that nation seeks to exploit its oil resources in the Caspian Sea. The claims made for the Caspian are that it promises to yield as much oil as Kuwait and twice that of the North Sea. Within a matter of years, the Caspian could become the world's second largest source of oil and gas after the Middle East.[1]

Oil riches of that magnitude could change everything. Some say oil was the primary reason for the Karabakh conflict, and the reason that conflict will continue. Whoever controls Azerbaijan controls its reservoirs of black gold. Russia, Turkey and Iran want their share. Azerbaijan's corrupt and feuding politicians, with their private armies, are squabbling to secure their piece of the pie. And overarching all are the multi-national oil companies, who will do whatever is necessary to secure their multi-billion dollar investments. On 20 September 1994, a $7.5 billion deal was signed with BP and others to exploit the oil and gas fields. An $8 billion deal with the USA followed in 1997.

The name Azerbaijan has been linked with oil for more than a century. By 1900, more than half the world's oil came from the capital, Baku. It was from there that the world's first oil tankers plied their cargo of light crude to the Black Sea via the Volga river. It was to overcome the problem of the Volga freezing for three months each year that the world's first oil pipeline was constructed – from wood.

Pipelines mean power, influence and lucrative transit fees – more than £320 million a year at peak flow.[2] If you don't possess the oil, the next best thing is to possess the pipeline.

The route for Azeri oil favoured by the West is via Turkey and on to the Mediterranean, while Russia's preference is for a pipeline to the Black Sea, via Chechnya, leaving Russia in control and Turkey on the sidelines.[3]

Hedging their bets, the oil companies proposed multiple pipelines. And, when President Aliyev of Azerbaijan said the Turkish route should be the main route, Russia took one look at the emerging bloc and its own fading influence and threatened a new offensive by Armenian forces if Azerbaijan failed to meet Moscow's demands.[4] The threat is implausible, but what it revealed was Moscow's preparedness to pitch one side against the other in pursuit of Russian self-interest, and its self-perception as grand master in the chess-game of the Caucasus.

The West was not to be left out of the equation. Well aware that oil from the Caspian could reduce US dependence on the Persian Gulf – providing the pipeline did not run through Iran – President Clinton embarked on a whirlwind courtship with President Aliyev, who called for stronger economic and political ties with the USA, and the lifting of economic sanctions against Azerbaijan.[5] It left Russia fulminating in the background and Human Rights Watch accusing the USA of glossing over Azerbaijan's dismal human rights record in favour of its own economic interests.[6]

Suddenly, Western nations were queuing to bring stability to the region.[7] Some fear the price could be the final solution to the Karabakh problem, a Karabakh without Armenian Karabakhtsis.

It was oil that drew Britain to Azerbaijan after the First World War, and it was oil that lured Britain once again in the 1990s. Karabakh was the price paid to appease the Azeris the first time round, and Karabakh could be the price tag once again. *The Times* observed: 'The oil revenue will significantly alter the balance of power in the republic's favour as it struggles to retake Nagorno Karabakh.'[8]

In the House of Lords, Lord Avebury[9] condemned the rush for oil in no uncertain terms: 'British support of the Azeri government... will encourage it to continue mass murdering Armenians, knowing it is immune from criticism because we want Azeri business. True British interests are never served by turning a blind eye to oppression and cruelty.'[10]

'Sometimes politicians put aside truth to pursue material gain and commercial interest,' lamented the head of the Armenian Apostolic Church, in his wood-panelled palace in Yerevan. His Holiness Vasgen I, Catholicos of All Armenians, explained to Caroline: 'The history of our nation has shown that in the past, countries such as the USA, Britain and France forgot the Armenian tragedy of the genocide.[11] Some people in the West believe the political solution is to leave Karabakh as part of Azerbaijan. That cannot be right.'[12]

Talks to resolve the conflict broke down once again in November 1996, with Azerbaijan insisting that Karabakh should remain under Baku, albeit with a high degree of autonomy. The rebuttal from Karabakh was swift: 'Our people have paid too high a price for that,' came the message from their Parliament. 'We will never agree to become a chip in a big oil game.'[13]

It may already be too late.

Shadow of the Bear

Some observers say Russia is so determined to take a share in the oil riches that it instigated the coups in Azerbaijan in 1993 and 1994 as a means to that end. They say Russia has a second objective: to maintain influence in the region by pursuing a policy of destabilization.[14] Russia is accused of igniting the Karabakh conflict to bring to heel its breakaway republics and get its hands on Azeri oil – oil which Russia regards as its own.[15] Conspiracy theorists also point to Chechnya, and say the motive behind Russia's hapless incursion there was to try to seize control of its pipeline.[16]

Helsinki Monitor goes further. It claims Russia's intention is to maintain a constant state of warfare throughout the Caucasus.[17] That view is shared on the ground. Armenian medical worker Movses Poghossian accuses the KGB of instigating the massacres that sparked off the conflict. 'Armenia and Azerbaijan are fighting nations,' he says, 'and we have been set against one another.' He pauses, shaking his head. 'Russian politics is still the same.'

The same is heard from Azeri lips. Teacher Ali Sariev was captured and taken hostage by Armenian forces while out driving his car: 'Our nation did not come to war. It came from outside. The Soviet system is broken. It is maybe the KGB who started the war.'[18] Caught up in the throes and confusion of *fin de siècle* foreign policy, driven by fear and greed, it is little wonder that both Azerbaijan and Armenia are making overtures to NATO.

Yet among Armenians, fear of Russia is more than outweighed by a terror of Turkish involvement. Proposals for Turkish peacekeeping troops have been dismissed as a Trojan horse by Armenian and Karabakhtsi alike. 'Pan-Turkism is a terrible thing,' says Zori Balayan. 'It is a bomb which will blow, even if it takes centuries.'

Hawks in the Kremlin share his fear. Not only of Turkey, but of a shadowy Muslim 'menace' that could topple regions like dominoes until it reaches the heart of the Volga. It has suited them to play on that fear, and use it as justification for Russian involvement in the Caucasus.

To acquire greater leverage over the region, Russia took over the co-chair of the OSCE peace negotiations with the USA and France. The OSCE called for Karabakh to remain within Azerbaijan and hand back the occupied territories. Anything else would have been a clear and unwelcome signal to every other unruly enclave in the former Soviet Union. There were few surprises when Karabakh refused.

The Commander of Karabakh's Army, Samvel Babayan, summed up the prospects starkly: 'We are certain that there will be a final stage to the war.'[19] Fears continue to be expressed that Turkey, Russia and Iran could be drawn into the conflict, especially with the riches of the Caspian Sea coming on tap. If Karabakh looked set to be overrun, Armenia warns it would add its forces to the cauldron.[20]

By all accounts, both sides are building up for a battle with a new dimension. According to Karabakh intelligence, Azerbaijan has been using its oil revenue to stockpile missiles to extend the arena of war.[21] Azerbaijan in turn has accused Armenia of acquiring missiles capable of launching a nuclear strike (if Armenia had the warheads) and to have received Russian training in how to use them. Perhaps more significantly, Karabakh has let it be known that it now possesses missiles capable of penetrating deep into Azerbaijan. Their prime targets, if provoked, would be Baku and the oil fields of the Caspian Sea. It is an effective deterrent, designed to galvanize every vested interest in the world – including the oil companies – to push for a peaceful settlement of the Karabakh question.

'The Azeris' only solution to the problem is a Karabakh without Armenians,' Prime Minister Petrossian of Karabakh told Caroline. 'We are worlds away from that now. For us to return to [Azerbaijan] would be similar to the international community requiring the Commonwealth of Independent States to return to Soviet rule under the former Soviet Union.'[22]

Caroline echoes his words. 'The Armenians who live [in Karabakh] can never again accept Azeri sovereignty,' she observed in a report for CSI. '[It] would be tantamount to consigning them to another genocide or mass enforced deportations. The consistent pattern of events in recent history endorses this conclusion.'[23]

Yet by late 1997, the President of Armenia, Levon Ter-Petrossian, was driven to concede that the prospect of Karabakhtsi independence or unification with Armenia was 'unrealistic'.[24] His statement precipitated an explosion of anger that was to lead to his downfall. In February, hard-line nationalists led by Prime Minister Robert Kocharian – a Karabakhtsi – forced Ter-Petrossian to resign. Kocharian was later elected President, with the backing of the army, and pledged self-determination for Karabakh.

Azerbaijan, meanwhile, had its own election, which was roundly condemned for 'fraud and bias' by international monitors. Geidar Aliyev was duly returned to power. Among his election pledges was the resolution of the Karabakh conflict. 'I don't want any more bloodshed,' he told reporters. 'We will use peaceful means to solve it.' Yet he gave no indication as to how he would square that with an earlier election broadcast, in which he vowed never to give up Azeri territory.

Meanwhile Russia continued to strengthen its hand in the Caucasus, supplying Armenia with MiG 29 fighters and anti-aircraft missiles and expanding its military base there – amid Azeri protests that Russia was undermining regional security. Other circumstances also conspired against Azerbaijan. At the close of 1998, OSCE negotiators proposed turning Karabakh into a common state, similar to a confederation, giving the enclave equal rights with Azerbaijan. It was rejected by the Azeris.

Then doubts began to be raised about the extent of Azeri oil. Foreign companies had invested $40 billion in the Caspian, but on Christmas day, a US-led consortium pulled out after announcing disappointing drilling results. It came amid persistent rumours that the oil wealth of the Caspian could have been overstated.

'Can I forget?'

In the interregnum, while the fate of Karabakh is decided, the church is trying to rebuild the soul of the nation. Armenian bishops from the diaspora took advantage of the cease-fire to pay pilgrimage to the ancient monastery at Gandsasar. Caroline joined them, wearing an immaculate dark pink dress which had miraculously survived the trip in her rucksack. It was curious to see black-clad bishops and an English peer of the realm emerging from a camouflaged military helicopter sprouting a machine-gun from its nose. The late summer sun was cool on the mountain. It was cooler still inside the monastery. Four young girls sang a haunting liturgy of such potency that it filled the air and reverberated around the ancient walls. 'I cannot see any people in the world who have suffered as much for Christianity as the Armenian people,' said one bishop, the Primate of Switzerland. 'But let us follow the path of our Lord Jesus Christ and let us live together with our neighbours. Let us forgive our enemies.'

Someone interjected: 'It is hard to forgive when one's enemy is still intent on murder.'

The Bishop nodded, and replied in a quiet voice, 'Without forgiving, life will be very difficult for us. We have to try to find a way to live in peace with our neighbours.'

He paused. 'We cannot forget. That is the problem.'

'If there is one thing that keeps me, it is my belief in God,' said Galia Saoukhanin, who was driven from the village of Nakhichevanik by Azeri Grads and tanks. 'But can I forget the scene, when I saw the children without arms, without legs? That's not something I can ever forget.'

Movses Poghossian will also remember. The bearded rescue worker, whose job it was to scour the battlefield to see who might be saved, will not forget the crosses carved in Armenian flesh; the mutilated victims of the souvenir hunters who collect trinkets of human tissue; his friend who was captured and scalped; his colleagues who were killed. As Movses knows, it will not be possible to heal the wounds of his people lightly. Yet with a quiet spirit and infinite sadness he has made the hard choice. Movses has chosen to work out his forgiveness. 'Each time you start to find who began this, you cannot come to peace. You must forget it. We must come together and stop the war. We must live together and we must give our love to one another.'

'Go back to your history,' intoned the acting head of the Armenian Apostolic Church. 'Go back to your faith,' said Archbishop Torkom Manoogian. 'Our faith has not betrayed us. And only remaining faithful to the spirit of our people – Christian spirit – only then can we survive.'

NOTES

1. Olivier Roy, 'Crude manoeuvres', *Index Online*, no. 497.
2. Hugh Pope, 'Oil deal brings little respite from Azeri devils', *The Independent*.
3. Professor Stephen Blank, 'Helsinki Monitor, Russia, the OSCE, and Security in the Caucasus (1)', Strategic Studies Institute, US Army War College, PA, 1995.
4. Attributed to Vladimir Kazimirov, by the Turan news agency; cited in Hasan Guliev, 'Oil in troubled waters', War Report, April 1997.
5. 'Azeri, US leaders highlight commercial ties', Reuters, 1 August 1997.
6. 'Mixed year for Central Asia human rights', BBC News, 24 December 1997.
7. The players in the British-led Azerbaijan International Operating Company (AIOC) are BP, Statoil (Norway), UNOCAL, Pennzoil, Exxon (all of the US), Lukoil (Russia), Turkish Petroleum, Itochu (Japan), Ramco (UK) and Delta Nimir (Saudi Arabia).
8. Robert Seely, 'Oil can finance a Baku victory', 30 June 1992.
9. Chairman of the Parliamentary Human Rights Group.
10. Letter to *The Times*, 7 October 1992, co-signed by Caroline Cox and David Atkinson MP.
11. Turkey has been accused of waging a propaganda offensive to deny the existence of the genocide. Ankara has been funding seats in US universities on Ottoman studies, under conditions that would force scholars to overlook the genocide, and Turkey's US ambassador has been accused of sending letters to Jewish organizations claiming the Armenian holocaust was a hoax. Before embarking on his final solution against the Jews, Hitler is said to have asked: 'Who now remembers the Armenians?': Robert Fisk, 'Turkish money fails to blot out the stain of genocide', *The Independent*.
12. Letter to *The Washington Post*, 3 March 1997. The British position was explained in the House of Lords by government spokesperson, Baroness Trumpington: 'We have no vested interest in this dispute. All we want is to see it resolved peacefully, in a way which does justice to the legitimate hopes of all concerned. The conflict in Nagorno Karabakh is only one of many other real and potential disputes across the former Soviet Union...

'When the Soviet empire broke apart, we and all our Western partners agreed that the very abruptness of events ruled out any attempt to redraw boundaries and do justice to all the rival clans. The same considerations apply across the former Soviet Union as in Africa. There all the states have accepted, for better or worse, the fact of colonial borders. To do otherwise would open a Pandora's box of rival tribal claims with potentially terrible consequences.

'That is why the international community recognized as independent states only the former Soviet Republics. Hence under international law, the disputed area of Nagorno Karabakh is now part of Azerbaijan. No country, not even Armenia itself, recognizes it as an independent state.

'International principles do not rule out changes to the status of areas such as Nagorno Karabakh. But any changes must be made peacefully, with the agreement of all concerned. Azerbaijan will not cede independence to Nagorno Karabakh. So a realistic solution must start from the fact of Azerbaijani sovereignty. But the Armenian community there cannot be expected to accept this unless they know that their rights will be respected and their voices heard.

'This points to some form of autonomy, self-government, devolution of powers – call it what you will

– for Nagorno Karabakh. This basis for a solution – some sort of autonomy, under Azerbaijani sovereignty – is accepted by nearly the whole international community': in answer to an unstarred question in the House of Lords by Baroness Cox, *Hansard*, column 544, 15 December 1995.

But speaking in the House of Lords two years later, the Earl of Shannon insisted Karabakh had acted correctly under the former Soviet Constitution in holding a referendum on the right for self-determination, which resulted in a vote for independence. He added: 'Although Whitehall sanctimoniously wrings its hands and bleats about the sanctity of the later Helsinki Agreement to preserve the status quo, in fact, the legal status quo at the time was an independent Nagorno Karabakh': unstarred question on Nagorno Karabakh and Azerbaijan, 1 July 1997.

13. 13 December 1996.

14. 'In the early 1990s Moscow had actively encouraged conflicts in the Caucasus while presenting itself as an honest broker between the combatants. It openly supported the Ossetian, Abkhazian and Adjarian minorities in their rebellions against Georgia and provided military aid to Nagorno Karabakh. Russian mercenaries also fought alongside the Azeris. Despite its transparent involvement, Russia still shared the presidency of the Minsk group, charged with resolving the conflict': Olivier Roy, 'Crude manoeuvres', *Index Online*, no. 497.

15. Agence France Presse, 4 October 1994.

16. Elaine Holoboff, 'Internal threats to Russian security', Paper presented to the Conference on Russian Defence and Security Policy, London, May 1985.

17. Professor Stephen Blank, 'Helsinki Monitor, Russia, the OSCE, and security in the Caucasus (1)', Strategic Studies Institute, US Army War College, PA, 1995.

18. From interviews by journalist Hazel Southam, September 1994.

19. Radio Free Europe, 27 August 1996.

20. CSI report, October 1995, and in interview with journalist Hazel Southam.

21. CSI Report, 1–8 February 1996.

22. CSI Karabakh visit report, 7–12 October 1995.

23. CSI Armenia / Karabakh report, 27 May – 3 June 1997.

24. As stated by President Ter-Petrossian on 26 September 1997, according to 'Karabakh: are things moving?', BBC News, 25 October 1997.

TWELVE

A Land of Legend

Karabakh is a land of legend, where myths are woven about heroes ancient and modern. One such is Armen Melkoumian, Commander of the Matchkalashen Regiment. As the story is told, from the age of 19, Armen served in the Soviet army as a driver-mechanic, learning skills as essential to his future survival as fresh air. When conflict came, he was studying to be a teacher in Stepanakert. Laying aside his vocation, he took up arms as a volunteer and conquered the terror of death defending Pertatzor.

From the moment of his victory, until the moment of his death, Armen never retreated. In the summer of 1991, he took upon his tender shoulders the defence of the villages of the Amaras valley. That December he liberated Divanalar. Other villages followed – many of them. Armen, that humble, ordinary, level-headed, strong-willed young man, tempered by the fire of war, soon matured and mastered many kinds of firearm, and thus became a commander of conscience about whom was composed the legend: 'Whilst at Matchkalashen there is Armen, I will have no fear.'

On the battlefield of Tavalou Ghouty, he disabled 14 enemy tanks, fighting full of faith and victory, breaking all boundaries of the possible. He set his will like iron to capture the Ghadgar heights, from where ten villages in the valley had come under bombardment. On 8 October 1992, with triumph within his grasp, an enemy firebomb exploded beneath his feet. The bright spirit of Armen now hovers over Ghadgar heights, now renamed Armenasar, the Hills of Armen. His bright spirit also hovers over Matchkalashen, renamed Armenashen by its people. Armen sacrificed his life and became immortal. He repelled the enemy from the Amaras valley, gateway to Stepanakert. Now every small child sings songs and recites poetry about Armen.[1]

The 'Baronoohi' has also become something of a legend. Baroness Cox, as she is known elsewhere, is said to have escaped death some 22 times. When she asks how they arrive at that figure, her question is returned with an enigmatic smile. Armenians have been killed and injured nearby and several have died outside buildings that she was in at the time, but Caroline herself has remained unscathed.

Roads and buildings bear her name. She is recognized, stopped in the street and thanked. Awards have been heaped upon her, but like the best of celebrities, she receives her accolades with humility, batting back the praise towards those behind the scenes who have made everything possible.

Journalist Vanya Kewley described what happened as one of Caroline's aid convoys arrived in Stepanakert. It was typical:

> When the aid trucks arrived, the crowds that had been standing in the square in quiet groups, like moles not used to the light, became euphoric. The cry went up: 'The Cox has landed! The Cox has arrived!' Everyone wanted to see her, to shake her hand, to thank her. Wherever we went old ladies, children, soldiers, gnarled old men, everyone wanted to touch her. She was mobbed and always, out of nowhere, springs of wild lilac and voluptuous pink roses were pushed into her hands.[2]

In Yerevan, during an impromptu sight-seeing trip around the sprawling market, when the murmur went round that the Cox was among them, stall holders descended upon her and plied her with wares. She was surrounded by smiling faces, by Armenians bearing gifts, some standing by deferentially, others excitedly pumping her hand. A trickle became a flood of embroidery, paintings and nick-nacks, all received with a ready smile, an appreciative nod and a smattering of Armenian.

'All I remember hearing as I walked past', said CSI's national director Stuart Windsor, 'was, "Coxy, Coxy". As soon as they found out it was Caroline they went to their stall to find a present, or pulled her over and said, choose what you like. It was totally embarrassing, because we could not carry it all.'

Embarrassment of riches

Journalists and human rights workers accompanying the Baronoohi were co-opted to act as porters to haul back her *embarras* of riches to the hotel. The treasure trove filled a table and spilled on to the floor; 'Beautiful hand-made earrings and paintings: things that were precious, with a personal value, too,' said Caroline, surveying her homage with a hint of a frown. 'It means they've lost the money they would have got from selling them. That makes me worried that I have diminished their already meagre income. I don't cope with that easily.'

It was more than could sensibly be brought home by plane. Caroline chose a modest selection of items to display in her home and various offices, and shared out the rest among the party. As if to underscore the display of affection, Armenian radio made a special announcement: the birth of the Baronoohi's sixth grandchild.

There is no doubt from observing her that all the fuss really is an embarrassment, but one that is never allowed to show. The constant attention is to be received graciously, in the spirit in which it is given, with a smile of gratitude and a deferential tilt of the head, any reticence in the eyes hidden behind that heavy fringe of hair.

When people with nothing give everything, refusal is out of the question. Caroline met an old man in the village of Buzluk which had been overrun by the Azeris. His son had been killed in the fighting, and, as was the custom, he was buried in his best suit of clothes. While the Azeris were in the village, they saw the freshly dug grave, and exhumed the body to steal his clothes and extract his gold teeth. The old man invited the delegation to his home, which had been ransacked. All that remained to tide him through the winter was a pile of walnuts and apples. He was most insistent they should take his apples.[3]

'They want to give,' says Caroline. 'It comes with their heart, and I'm profoundly grateful and touched by that. Those of us who work with people in extreme conditions of deprivation have come to understand that it's a part of their self-esteem that they can actually give; that they are not just receiving.'

Having a psychiatrist husband helped with the human insights. The giving, which is both sacrificial and unnecessary, is an expression of normality. People respond as they would under normal conditions, sharing their food as one would offer a cup of coffee to a friend who had come to call. 'So I think it's important to respond with genuine gratitude and not let the embarrassment and awareness of the fact that it may be a sacrifice show.'

Caroline's affection for the Armenian people is returned in kind. In a speech at the Royal Academy, the British-based Anglo-Armenian Association thanked Caroline for lobbying 'fiercely and with great courage for [Karabakh's] welfare and its people's rights, to give hope when all hope was lost, to the desperate, the destitute, the displaced, the homeless and the orphans...' adding: 'She is truly loved and respected.'[4]

The Armenians love her because she has put her life on the line to champion their cause. They also warm to her sheer accessibility. Even when she is exhausted, she will smile, talk and offer a word of encouragement; she will maintain that personal touch with unfailing, genuine, humility. She appears never to fall for the temptation of seeking, using, or revelling in the attention. She cringes beneath her fringe when asked to comment on the adulation she receives in Karabakh, but her fame goes before her.

Absurd as it may sound, the Armenians seem to regard Caroline Cox as their very own Evita. At a Christian Solidarity conference two Armenian women were seriously discussing how to have her canonized, and Armenians in Jerusalem have asked to bury her bones in the holy city. The head of the Armenian church said her help to his people was 'beyond price'.[5] In Gandsasar a peasant woman hugged her and exclaimed: 'She is our own. She is our guardian angel. We love her and pray for her.' Another Karabakhtsi asked: 'Why do you do this work? You have no Armenian blood, so it is not your duty. This is magic for us that you are looking after us and sharing our dangers and our pain.' The Armenian Parliament has risen to its feet in ovation and the Prime Minister of Karabakh says he looks forward to the day 'when there will be children, streets and schools named after Caroline Cox'. To English sensibilities it seems ridiculous, and all the fuss makes the very English Caroline Cox intensely embarrassed.

'She is treated like a star, like a celebrity, like royalty,' says Stuart Windsor. 'She doesn't like it. I think she has difficulty handling it. It's against her natural instincts.' In Britain, all the adulation heaped upon Caroline (however modestly deflected), often turns to scepticism and suspicion. There is nothing the British hate more than to see a politician lionized. To make matters worse, to Caroline, the Armenians are the victims, and her credo is to stand on the side of the victim. That makes her an advocate. And to the media, any advocate is automatically a peddler of propaganda.

Hear no evil

When Caroline returned to London after witnessing the aftermath of the massacre at Maraghar, where villagers' heads had been sawn off, she took the story to the British press. Her reception was frosty. The previous month, there had been substantial coverage of an alleged massacre carried out by Armenians at Khojaly, ten miles from Stepanakert, which had been used as a base to fire Grads into the capital.

Armenian and Azeri versions of what took place differ widely. According to Armenian sources, every attempt to negotiate a safe passage for the town's 6,000 civilians was ignored. Warnings were given over the radio and a corridor was left for their retreat. But as they pulled out, Azeri troops mingled with the fleeing civilians and fought their rearguard action. Inevitably, and regrettably, civilians were caught in the crossfire. The figure for the dead was put by Helsinki Watch at 181.

But according to the Azeris, more than a thousand civilians were slaughtered after Armenian troops deliberately funnelled them into a killing zone. Many women and children were among the dead and there were reports of deliberate mutilations, including scalpings. International press reports gave credence to the view that a substantial massacre had taken place.

Wanton carnage, or disorderly retreat with civilians caught in the crossfire? Propaganda is a hall of distorting mirrors. Whatever the truth, the alleged atrocity was later used to justify repeated acts of retaliation.

The ripples spread all the way to Moscow and Baku. Thousands of Azeris marched on their Parliament to demand the resignation of President Mutalibov, who was later to describe the alleged massacre as a propaganda coup engineered by his opponents to bring about his downfall.[6] Some press reports claimed the assault against Khojaly had been a joint venture between the Armenians and Russian members of the 366th Motorized Infantry Brigade.[7]

Caroline had read the reports of the Khojaly massacre and believed the coverage was distorted by Baku to discredit the Armenians. She offered the story of the Maraghar atrocity to the papers in the interests of balance. The Daily Telegraph promised exclusive coverage, providing she kept it away from the other newspapers. Days went by and the exclusive never appeared. She grew angry. And each time she thought of the people of Maraghar, wringing their hands as they exhumed the mutilated and charred bodies of their relatives to provide the evidence for her report, it made her angrier still.

She phoned the foreign desk to ask about the hold-up, and was brusquely told they were not going to run the story. Talk of an exclusive had been a 'misunderstanding'.

Caroline's bile rose. 'Not so long ago, you and all the other papers had this massive coverage of a so-called massacre of the Azeris, and now we have real evidence of a genuine massacre of Armenians by the Azeris, you're not covering it. Whatever happened to balance and fair coverage?'

Back came the reply: 'I'm not interested in trading massacre for massacre.' The phone went dead. Her reaction was one of rage and frustration at what she considered to be a betrayal. The story had gone cold and there was no show of interest elsewhere.

There has been contention with the media since. There is often a reluctance to report her findings, for several reasons. It is notoriously difficult to get foreign news on the agenda, unless national interests are affected or the entire media circus is already on site for a large-scale shooting match. As there are usually several of these going on in the world at any time, minor conflicts, or logistically less accessible ones, tend to get relegated. There are only so many column inches for so many wars; so resources – and awareness – tend to be concentrated on the major players. Karabakh was eclipsed by Bosnia.

Caroline may also be a victim of her own ubiquity. Her endless visits to Karabakh and elsewhere result in Cox fatigue. There is a reluctance to run yet another Battling Baroness story. As one BBC World Service producer put it: 'She was on a couple of weeks ago; we can't have her on this week as well. Would it be possible to leave her out of the story?' She also credits the idea that the media has an anti-establishment bias and therefore objects to her because she is both a Baroness and a Tory.

But another thing that troubles some producers in the media is the question of balance. In some quarters, there is more than a suspicion of bias. The media can be reluctant to run with her evidence without confirmation or independent expert opinion from such as the United Nations. As so few independent observers are on the scene to offer the sacrament of confirmation, her evidence can often go unreported.

It is not only the media that Caroline finds reluctant to listen to her message. One demoralizing moment came during the National Prayer Breakfast, an annual event at the Queen Elizabeth Hall in London. Politicians of faith, irrespective of party, mingle with invited guests who have made some recognizable Christian contribution to society. Caroline was playing host at one table and invited her guests to introduce themselves. When the onus returned to her, she gave a brief account of the work of Christian Solidarity. Moments beforehand, the couple opposite had been expounding on the good works they did in their church. But as Caroline sketched out the sufferings of the Armenians of Karabakh, they visibly glazed over. One muttered, 'Oh, that's controversial' and switched off.

Caroline flashes her eyes in exasperation. 'If Christians won't engage in prayer and concern for the persecuted, especially when it is Christians who are being persecuted, where are they going to go for help and support?' She can hit the same problem when it comes to fund-raising. Donors are prone to back off at the first hint of controversy, especially the larger, more respectable trusts. She finds the reluctance to face up to suffering immensely depressing. When she is called on to speak, she will sometimes challenge Christian believers as to when they last prayed for the suffering church.

'The first priority of the persecuted church is prayer, yet half our intercessions are filled with the secular agenda: what we saw on television and in the newspapers that morning. We ought to weave in a commitment to continuing prayer for the persecuted church. Is that too much to give?' She recognizes full well that for individuals to be provoked to prayer about the events that concern her, those events must first find a place in the newspapers and on TV.

But despite some foot-dragging at home, the foreign media in particular are drawn to the swashbuckling nature of her activities and regularly send crews and journalists to accompany her. Some express suspicions that the trips are propaganda exercises. They are invited to bring their suspicions and find out for themselves.

NOTES

1. Adapted from the story of Armen by his cousin Arrmick Melkoumian.
2. Vanya Kewley, 'Into Karabakh with Baroness Cox'.
3. C. Cox and J. Eibner, *Ethnic Cleansing in Progress – War in Nagorno Karabakh*, Institute for Religious Minorities in the Islamic World, 1993, p. 62.
4. Chairman's address, 17 July 1996.
5. *Readers Digest*, October 1992.
6. COVCAS Bulletin, 9 April 1992, p. 4.
7. *The Independent*, 3 May 1992.

THIRTEEN

The Case against Caroline

Few of us, it seems, are prepared to face the possibility that war brings out the worst in people, whichever side they are on, regardless of the balance of injustice. Could the same be said of Caroline?

Questions are frequently raised about her objectivity, because of her close association with those she regards as the primary victims in the conflict. The case for the prosecution would point to her undeniable attachment to the beleaguered believers of Karabakh, a Christian oasis in the midst of a seemingly hostile Islamic desert. One British relief manager expressed it succinctly: 'Caroline Cox – Armenians Good; Azeris Bad.'

On the steamy afternoon of 3 September 1994, Caroline was called upon to address a passing out parade of graduates of the Military Training Academy in Karabakh. Row upon row of downy faced probationary lieutenants stood to attention in the simmering heat, clutching their weighty Kalashnikovs, smelling faintly of horses. Some shifted and squinted uncomfortably, clenching and unclenching their toes to keep the blood pumping, but to their credit, no-one passed out. The boy soldiers – officially aged 16 and up, but some looking little more than 14 – passed the test.

Their uniforms were Warsaw Pact camouflage, their footwear a tell-tale selection of hand-me-down boots and trainers. A former British soldier, working as a consultant for CSI, summed them up as: 'Rag, tag and bobtail', though as the parade continued he grew more complimentary about their professionalism.

The graduates stood straight-backed for more than an hour, their eyes screwed up against the sun, while uniformed officers observed from the sidelines; among them a number of senior Russians. It then fell to the Bishop, the senior ranks, and finally Caroline, to address them. It was Caroline's 21st mission to Karabakh. Her speech was a morale-boosting message of commendation for the soldiers' courage and their faith. Even after a cease-fire, it was a curious step for a human rights activist to take.

'When I first went to that area I went with complete impartiality, based on ignorance,' she replies. 'If I had any residual prejudice at all, it was probably anti-Armenian. I remember hazily reports of terrorist activity carried out by the Armenians in the past. I went as part of a genuinely independent international investigation. We bent over backwards to hear the Azeri point of view. In so far as I am now an unashamed advocate it's because the evidence which I have identified leads me to believe the Armenians of Karabakh have been the primary victims in a war not of their own choosing, against impossible odds and gratuitous brutality. The balance of oppression is against the Armenians.'

Her supporting evidence was given to an Armenian audience in 1994, and has been articulated many times since. It is as follows:

It was Azerbaijan, in conjunction with the Soviet Fourth Army, which carried out brutal deportations of thousands of Armenians from their villages in the spring and summer of 1991. It was Azerbaijan which imposed blockades on Armenia and Karabakh, causing immense suffering and economic damage. It was Azerbaijan which first used weapons of indiscriminate destruction against civilians, with Grad multiple-missile rocket launchers against towns and villages. Only Azerbaijan has used aerial bombardment of civilians, including the use of cluster bombs. Only Azerbaijan has used ground-to-air missiles against civilians.

It is Azerbaijan which has consistently tried to impose a military solution. The people of Karabakh never wanted a war – who would, with 150,000 against 7 million? The Azeris' combination of blockades and military offensives was intended to achieve a policy of ethnic cleansing of Armenians in Karabakh. As former President Elchibey of Azerbaijan said: 'If there is a single Armenian living in Nagorno Karabakh in October, the people of Azerbaijan can take me and hang me in the central square of Baku.' It is hard to find a more unequivocal statement of ethnic cleansing.[1]

A question of bias

Caroline will not concede that anger arising from the atrocities she has seen could tempt her into a loss of objectivity, because, paradoxically, to fall into that trap would damage her cause: 'If you can be demonstrated to have become partial, and they can prove that you have distorted the truth, then you lose credibility and therefore effectiveness for the cause for which you are speaking. So I always try to maintain the fundamental principles of objectivity, because I care about the cause.' And as an impassioned advocate, Caroline believes it is all the more beholden on her to get her facts right.

Not everyone is convinced she succeeds. Christopher Besse of MERLIN meets a good deal of scepticism towards his trustee, Baroness Cox. 'She's slightly on the edge sometimes,' he contends. 'The circus can arrive and sometimes information is gathered in a rather amateurish way. People are saying she comes back with all these one-sided reports which don't actually represent what is happening on the ground.'

Caroline takes issue with her friend. 'Often we are the only people in an area. At least we're out there gathering first-hand material which nobody else is getting. It won't be the whole picture, because we are speaking to the people in the no-go areas. Others will speak for the regimes who encourage the press and media in. So, yes, it is inevitably partial; inevitably collated at speed, because we are in high security areas and have to be in and out quickly. But we do try our very best to cross-check our information. And we are very careful to be clear about our sources, so they can be taken for what they are.'

And what that information should be taken for is propaganda, according to Moscow journalist Anatol Lieven: 'For Lady Cox in her work to concentrate purely on the sufferings of the Armenians, without even mentioning those of the other side, is not "Christian solidarity",' he maintains, 'it is simply nationalistic propaganda of the crudest kind. If I had been accredited to the First Crusade, I should certainly have listened carefully to what Baroness Cox's public relations' wagon had to say – but I should also have tried to see things from the Saracen point of view.'[2]

The accusation of bias is refuted by John Marks, who accompanied the British peer on her first precarious trip into Armenia and Azerbaijan. 'Some people say she doesn't take the opposition case on board, that she takes a partisan view,' he says. 'Well, she may have the odd blind spot – we all have – but we wanted so badly to get both sides of the story that we walked across the border into Azerbaijan with that white flag, on that crazy expedition.'

In her own defence, Caroline argues that she helped provide aid to the Azeris via MERLIN, of which she is a trustee; CSI co-operated with the Sakharov Foundation to provide relief for Azeri-Turk refugees, and she has visited prisoners of war on both sides of the conflict. Lord Pearson of Rannoch also points out that it was Baroness Cox who persuaded him to raise £150,000 on behalf of Azeri refugees, who 'would not have been helped without her intervention'.

'The criticism that we are pro-Christian,' says Caroline, 'to the extent of being opposed to those of other faiths is manifestly disproved by the facts. We work with those of other faiths, including Muslims and Buddhists. That is part of our credo and our action.'

When evidence came to light of the maltreatment of a captured Azeri officer whose injuries were being neglected, it was Caroline's complaint that prompted surgery to be carried out. She also investigated the deaths of three Azeri POWs in Yerevan and went on to confront Armenian officials. For the practice of hostage-taking, Caroline has criticized the Armenians and Azeris alike.[3]

'I have nothing but sympathy for the Azeris,' she says, 'but I am profoundly critical of the Azeri government which keeps trying to impose a military solution on a political problem.'

Some might accuse Caroline of passing judgment on the Azeris without an adequate knowledge of their country or their predicament. She has visited once, and has been invited back several times by President Aliyev to Baku. Her response has been to say yes, on two conditions: the lifting of the blockade, and the lifting of the price on her head. She has been told, and believes, that a reward has been offered for her death. 'She is public enemy number one in Azerbaijan,' says John Eibner.

'I think if people could get hold of her and kill her, they would like to,' adds Stuart Windsor.

Azeri criticism of Caroline's repeated visits to Karabakh has been unequivocal: 'You are a member of the House of Lords, you are in Azerbaijani territory without official permission and infringe Azerbaijani laws. The drugs and medicines you bring end up in the hands of people who are killing Azeris. If you want to help, distance yourself from the conflict.'

Inevitably, because the Armenians have her ear, Azeri atrocities will be uppermost in Caroline's mind. But she does not dispute that Armenians are also perpetrators of war crimes: 'It is not all right and all wrong,' she maintains. 'I'm not blind to the complexity of the situation or to the fact that in war both sides will commit atrocities, and that clearly will include the Armenians of Karabakh.'

'I don't think she does turn a blind eye,' adds Lord Pearson. 'Once people have been killed on each side the dog of war can bite indiscriminately. You get excesses – of course you do – that's just human nature. She doesn't condone atrocities. But she is always batting for the underdog, and when you do that you tend to be less severe on David than on Goliath.'

Both sides now

Much has been said about atrocities committed by Azerbaijan, but Armenia's human rights record is also far from exemplary. One medical relief worker, based in Stepanakert, witnessed horrors carried out by both parties to the conflict. 'We see people who have limbs amputated as a means of mutilation,' he said. 'The Armenians are guilty of this as well. They seem to appreciate cutting off the external part of the ear. They always say the other side is guilty. I have seen this on both sides.'

Both sides have been charged with the summary execution of would-be prisoners of war,[4] and in 1994, Armenia was accused of killing eight POWs then attempting a cover-up by saying they were shot trying to escape. UNHCR said the incident corroborated allegations of inhuman treatment of Azeri POWs and civilians.[5] Pictures by Armenian photographer Rouben Mangasarian rammed home the point. They showed Azeri prisoners hog-tied with their hands bound behind them to their feet. One was surrounded by hostile Armenians. In his mouth was wedged the kind of water bottle normally given to a gerbil. Another image was of an Azeri prisoner who had gone insane, clutching the rude wooden bars of his cell, his head held back, bellowing with every ounce of his frustration and rage.[6]

In defence of her impartiality, Caroline argues that she has criticized, and will continue to criticize, Christian nations when they violate human rights. But have those criticisms been directed at Armenia?

As the war with Azerbaijan ground to a halt, Armenia's political problems were just beginning. On 5 July 1995, the country elected its first post-Soviet National Assembly. The elections, which confirmed the mandate for President Levon Ter-Petrossian were characterized by independent observers from the OSCE as 'free, but not fair'. They were preceded, according to the UNHCR, by political assassinations, arbitrary arrests, torture and the onset of police-state tactics.[7] Demonstrators were beaten and journalists were harassed, intimidated and detained, along with candidates standing for the opposition. The conduct of the elections elicited a strong letter of protest to the President of Armenia from Caroline, urging the immediate restoration of fundamental human rights, justice and the rule of law. Her rebuke resulted in strained relations between herself and the President.

Religious freedoms have also been violated. Denominations are required to register and proselytizing is against the law. Violence has been committed against non-Orthodox believers, including Pentecostals, charismatics and Evangelical Baptists.

Caroline complained to the government and church authorities about the imprisoning of evangelicals. 'She was very strong over that issue,' says Stuart Windsor. 'I was amazed. She said: "If you continue to do this, then we won't be able to advocate on your behalf. We come from a democracy and believe in freedom of religion. I take the point you've got problems with pacifists who are causing havoc in your defence forces. I understand you are coming out of a period where Communists have been running your country and you are still finding your feet. But you cannot imprison people just because they are not of your persuasion." She made her point.'

But the most damning condemnation of Karabakh and Armenia has come from the USA's largest human rights organization, Human Rights Watch / Helsinki: 'Karabakh Armenian forces – often with the direct military support of the Republic of Armenia – were responsible for the majority of the violations of the laws of war in Nagorno Karabakh in 1993 and 1994 [carrying out] hostage taking and holding, violent, forced displacement of civilians, mistreatment and likely execution of prisoners, indiscriminate fire, and looting and burning of civilian homes.'[8]

That tit-for-tat brutality had taken place was acknowledged – and condemned – by Bishop Parkev Martirosian: 'From time to time it is happening here,' he confirmed, 'and by our people. But the Armenian is a Christian. He cannot do anything to soldiers, to prisoners. We do not allow them to do that.'

Yet happen it has. And through it all, Caroline has remained a fierce and unrelenting advocate of Armenian Karabakh. Her views run counter to Human Rights Watch because she believes that on balance, the scale of abuses is heavily tipped against Karabakh. Zori Balayan rallies, as ever, to the defence of his homeland: 'When Karabakh began to defend itself the West began to call us the aggressor. Now, if I can close your mouth and not allow you to breathe, perhaps you will hit me in the eye and hurt me, and you will be called the aggressor. It is natural to survive and defend ourselves. People will never leave their land. They would rather die there.'[9]

'Whoever has not visited Karabakh should not feel qualified to pass judgment on the issue,' cautioned the acting head of the Armenian Apostolic Church, Torkom Manoogian. 'He will base his judgment on hearsay and prejudice. Anyone who wishes to be just and fair must visit the mountains and see what civilization has developed, and see why Armenians cannot betray our history, our culture, our faith and our land, and why we have the right to live there. Fair judgment can only be passed by those with enough interest in knowing the truth to go there. I am grateful for the action that Baroness Cox has taken.'

A matter of motivation

It falls to Caroline's colleagues to play the apologist and provide further insight about their friend, the outspoken advocate of Karabakh. First Roger

Scruton: 'I wouldn't say she was blinkered. She is someone who sees the world as it is, largely, and has a quick capacity to see common concerns and act on them. She's been an admirable model of somebody who has stood up for truth and righteousness in a wicked world, and as a result has been very much scorned and attacked by just the sort of people who stand to lose from that policy.'

Behind some of those attempts to discredit her, believes Lord Pearson, lies a pecuniary motive: 'Don't forget she is up against vested interests. She is up against the whole oil industry. She is up against the greedy West which wants to be nice to Azerbaijan because it wants the oil.'

According to Roger Scruton, Caroline's strengths lie in two directions. Firstly, she is motivated by deeply-felt moral conviction. Secondly, she has the energy and the courage to carry those convictions through.

'Her weakness,' he adds, 'is perhaps being too taken up by her own causes and not sufficiently aware of the huge complexities that surround certain issues. She takes up causes in a very feminine way, and some people find that deeply objectionable, because always there is another side which one is going to have to overlook if one is going to have a cause.'

The Independent developed its own variation on that theme: 'Her opponents say her approach is founded on an emotional response to her own experiences.'[10]

But what finally prompts her to put those feelings into action, believes Roger Scruton, is religious conviction: 'She has a religiously inspired moral vision. Conflicts tend to become conflicts between good and evil but when anyone gets involved with a particular people in their national struggle, one has to remember that the people they are pitted against also have their national struggles. A nation is never wholly good.'

'She does need that tincture of the religious,' agrees personal friend, Christopher Besse of MERLIN. 'She is very spiritual in her approach and Christianity has to be involved. That's the sort of thing I get professionally uncomfortable about. That said, Karabakh would not be here today, I think, unless she had fought their corner and had been an advocate for them. They were politically naïve and unable to represent themselves at a high level.'

Several peers rallied to Caroline's defence during a debate on Armenia in the House of Lords, among them Lord Pearson: 'I am afraid there are a few people... who feel that my noble friend has mounted a crusade to help the Armenians of Nagorno Karabakh; that somehow she is not entirely balanced in her support for them. The Azeris and their friends go further, of course, and accuse [her] of pro-Christian bias. We must not fall foul of this obvious propaganda... I believe that it is true to say that without the huge personal effort made by my noble friend, first Chairman Lukyanov and then his Azerbaijani friends might have succeeded in burying their genocide of the Armenians of Karabakh from international view.'[11]

The gratitude in Armenia and Karabakh is tangible. At an award ceremony in 1994, Professor Hratch Zadoyan declared: 'I am confident that in decades and centuries hence [Baroness Cox] will be remembered [as] the Spirit of Armenia.'

Similar sentiments have been echoed elsewhere. Commending Caroline for her courage, veteran human rights campaigner, Elena Bonner Sakharov said: 'It is not from the words of press reports that she knows the misfortunes and suffering of the peaceful inhabitants of this region: women, children and old people. She has seen their suffering with her own eyes, spent nights with them in air-raid shelters and cellars and out in the villages in homes which might have been destroyed at any moment by a bomb or an artillery shell. She has shared their bread, when they had any, and wept for their dead sons and husbands. I do not know anybody in the West who is so deeply acquainted with everything that is happening in this region.'[12]

NOTES

1. From speech given 6 February 1994 to Armenian Children's Milk Fund.

2. Letter to *The Tablet*, 31 July 1993.

3. The practice of hostage-taking was documented by Amnesty International, August 1993 and 1995, and acknowledged by UNHCR in August 1995. Caroline argues that many Armenian hostages have been subjected to maltreatment and torture. She cites 38-year-old Eleanor Grigorian, who had been imprisoned in Baku. She was raped by an entire platoon of 30 and, with her four-year-old son, was kept without food or water for days. She was unable to lie down because of the wounds on her back. Another was 70-year-old Arevad Bogozian who was taken hostage during the 1992 Azeri offensive. On the first day, soldiers pulled out her fingernails on one hand. Then they raped her and sold her as a slave.

4. Acknowledged by UNHCR and US Department of State, 1995.

5. 'Background Paper on Refugees and Asylum Seekers from Armenia', August 1995.

6. In April 1997, three years after the cease-fire, Armenia was still handing over prisoners of war on the Red Cross list: Agence France Presse, 5 April 1997.

7. 'Background Paper on Refugees and Asylum Seekers from Armenia', August 1995; also Amnesty International, October 1996.

8. 'Ethnic Armenian Forces Major violator of Laws of War in Nagorno Karabakh for 1993 and 1994', 13 February 1995.

9. From an interview with Hazel Southam.

10. Celia Weston, 'The baroness of opting out', 8 September 1988.

11. Three other peers spoke out on Caroline's behalf on 15 December 1992, during the unstarred question on Armenia and Nagorno Karabakh. Lord Avebury observed: 'One admires her immense courage in placing herself in the front line of this desperate conflict when her anxiety is solely for the alleviation of the sufferings of the victims, whether they be Armenians or Azeris.'

The Lord Bishop of Guildford: '[Lady Cox has] vision, courage and determination... I am sure that there are many, not only in this House, who would like to place on record how much we profoundly

respect and admire the courage which she has shown in her daring visits to that troubled country...
I am deeply indebted to the noble Baroness, Lady Cox, for her persistent and courageous work.'

The Earl of Shannon: 'She has made many visits to the most dangerous areas of Karabakh, bringing humanitarian aid and has rightly earned the undying gratitude of all the people of Armenia and respect of us all.'

12. C. Cox and J. Eibner, *Ethnic Cleansing in Progress – War in Nagorno Karabakh*, Institute for Religious Minorities in the Islamic World, 1993, Preface.

FOURTEEN

Legacy of War

Caroline's visits to Karabakh continued even when the fighting stopped in 1994. Despite the cease-fire, one lasting legacy of war continued to claim victims: landmines. Ironically, most of the victims were mine clearers from the Karabakh army, who found the meticulous mine disposal methods taught by the British-based Halo Trust too tedious for their liking. A CSI report described the Armenians as still in 'battle mood' and impatient.

At least 450 people lost limbs as the result of the war. Amputees had to make the long and dangerous journey to Yerevan to be fitted with prostheses, and child victims whose limbs were still growing would have to make the trip several times. The authorities asked Caroline to become involved in post-war reconstruction of the most fundamental kind. CSI was invited to set up a clinic to provide artificial limbs.

By a stroke of providence Gunnar Wiebalck, from CSI Switzerland, managed to unearth a complete orthopaedic workshop in a container, which had been stranded in a field surrounded by cows. The workshop had been sent from Germany in response to the earthquake of 1988, and had sat there ever since, untouched. Strings were pulled and it was diverted to Karabakh.

Using their ingenuity, the Karabakhtsis set about incorporating the container as the centrepiece of an orthopaedic clinic. From the outside it looked much like an ordinary Stepanakert house. Inside, rooms and facilities were constructed around the container. Its designer was Howannes Tschugurian, a German-trained prosthesis specialist from Yerevan.

The clinic was opened in October 1995 by Bishop Parkev Martirosian. His message was that faith without works was dead, and love could only be expressed in action. By decree of Parliament, the centre was named after Caroline Cox. In further recognition of her work, she was awarded the We and Our Mountains medal by the Deputy Prime Minister, Lavrenty Gabrielian.

One of the first patients to be admitted to the centre was 68-year-old grandmother Chorasam Lalian. A Grad rocket hit her house in 1992 bringing the roof down on her leg. It had to be amputated almost immediately. After a three-year wait, she was finally mobile again. Until then, she had been totally dependent on her family for every necessity. Chorasam's middle son had been killed in the war. Now, with her husband, she was able to look after his widow and four children.

Howannes Tschugurian set about training local Karabakhtsis to make artificial limbs and appliances. Some were amputees themselves. As one explained, 'You have given us new life and we can give new life to others.'

When a senior consultant surgeon from the UK came to visit, he was challenged to watch a patient with a recent high-leg amputation walking down the corridor and to identify the real from the artificial leg. The consultant could not tell the difference. Another patient was back driving a truck for the mine clearance organization the Halo Trust within three weeks of fitting his prosthesis. In the first three months, Tshugurian fitted 40 artificial limbs.

'Many of the people who lost limbs in Karabakh were suicidal,' says Stuart Windsor. 'The clinic has given them new hope for the future.' There were rising numbers of suicides right across the population, as despair and shock set in following the cease-fire.

CSI went on to actively campaign against the trade in landmines and opened a rehabilitation centre in Stepanakert, named after its founder, Pastor Hans Stückleburger. CSI requested the authorities to allow Azeri victims of the conflict to be treated at both centres.

From the ashes

Caroline paid a visit to the Pastor Hans clinic during the freezing February of 1996. Low cloud over the mountains of Southern Armenia put paid to her helicopter flight, so the journey from Yerevan became an 11-hour ordeal by unheated bus – hard going for a woman who feels the cold and is happier in the tropics than in a snowstorm.

The centre's first resident, Edik Abrahamian, had been captured by the Azeris in 1989. Although a civilian they beat him beyond recognition because he was an Armenian and cut off his right ear. He was rescued by Russians, but was wounded again in the attack on Maraghar and paralysed from the waist down. At the centre, he turned his hand to craftwork, skilfully transforming old tin cans, boots and shoes into jewellery and ornaments. Caroline saw it as a picture of what God could bring about from the devastation of war. In the words of Isaiah, it was 'beauty for ashes'.[1]

The Pastor Hans clinic nearly didn't happen. The materials had been ordered and the plane was ready to fly out with them, when their builder rang to say he had made a terrible mistake on the costings. They were short of £20,000. Stuart Windsor called Caroline, who said, 'Let's pray.' With some trepidation, they decided to go ahead with the flight. Later that day she received a call from CSI in Zurich. An Armenian supporter in South America had called as they were praying and said he had £20,000 for their next flight. 'That's happened twice between Caroline and me,' says Stuart. 'Our working relationship is based on praying down the telephone, making decisions and seeing miracles happen.'

'In CSI we have a saying,' adds Caroline. 'We don't believe in miracles – we rely on them.'

During the visit, Caroline met seven men and a boy who had been blinded during the conflict. The child lost his sight after discovering one of the Azeri silver ball cluster bombs. His father had been killed in the fighting. Caroline asked them whether they had any requests to make. One man spoke for them all: a dignified figure with grey hair, Slavic features and the darkened spectacles of the blind. 'Just because we are disabled does not mean we are entitled to ask for help,' he replied. 'What is important is not material assistance, but your moral and spiritual support and the knowledge that we are not forgotten. What you have done is of priceless value.'

'But without practical aid as well from CSI,' says Zori Balayan, 'it would have been very difficult to survive.' Balayan has been responsible for many of Caroline's visits to Karabakh. Their negotiations over agenda are sights to behold. There is Balayan, the Soviet action man, in his open-necked shirt in his office barking down the phone, surrounded by more phones. Behind him are flags and other artefacts of nationalism, while his ubiquitous Artsakh enamel pin glints in his lapel. On the move, he is all scowl and bluster, requisitioning vehicles, procuring from nowhere impossibly scarce foul-smelling petrol, driving the timetable, tugging at Caroline, running late as usual, urging 'Sister, you come!' in a manner that contrives to be both patronizing and deferential, but always with an edge of humour. She, the diplomat, calling him 'Brother', remonstrating in unconfident snatches of pigeon Russian, hauling back the raging bull with a smile and swinging him around to her agenda. The styles are poles apart, the mutual respect explicit, a glint of amusement in both their eyes, the frisson between them almost tangible. 'I love Lady Cox,' says Balayan, simply. 'My love for her is very great. Cox is my sister.'

By 1999, the orthopaedic clinic had fitted more than 400 prostheses and Christian Solidarity had provided a new wing. The clinic and rehabilitation centre were not the only evidence of reconstruction in Karabakh. The bombed-out hospital where operations had been carried out without anaesthetic in wreaths of wood smoke was being rebuilt. Two banks were functioning in the capital and the first overpriced goods were appearing in the shops: tasteless cakes and ersatz versions of Pepsi-cola; sausage rolls without the sausage. In streets stripped clean of men, every stranger was regarded as potential marriage material. It was even known for a polite 'Good morning' to be greeted by 'I love you'.

The village of Talysch, just two kilometres from the border, had been the first to be overrun by the Azeris. Its civilians were the first to flee from tanks and bombs, leaving their houses to be destroyed in the scorched earth policy that had left gaping stone shells beneath the skies of Karabakh. Now the village was slowly returning from the ashes.

The school building had been flattened by an incoming Azeri bomb. The 150 pupils owed their lives to their headmaster, Valeri Babayon, who heard talk of the imminent bombing raid on Azeri radio and managed to sound the warning. Stone by stone the classrooms were being rebuilt. The resurrected school was to be named after a pupil who died in the war. But since so many children had been killed it was considered more respectful to leave the school without a name. The rebuilding was going well, the headmaster explained to Caroline. His faith had helped him overcome the horrors of war and with God's help the children would receive the strength and knowledge to do the same.

Even the massacre village of Maraghar was undergoing a resurrection – in a new location. The original was still in Azeri hands. Caroline and others visited to inspect the progress. They were given a speech of welcome by a village woman who seemed so cheerful and composed that Caroline assumed she must have been absent at the slaughter. Afterwards, when they lingered to talk, Caroline asked 'in my crass Western way' if the woman had been away when the Azeri troops moved in. The woman's face fell and she replied: 'No, but I wasn't going to burden you with my problems.' Kicking herself for insensitivity, Caroline invited the woman to continue.

She explained: 'On that day I lost all four of my sons who were trying to defend the village, but they had nothing to defend it with. They managed to hold the Azeris off just long enough for some of us to escape. They all died that day, and my daughter-in-law also died, therefore I am looking after the grandchildren. We have nothing, we didn't only lose our families, we also lost all our cattle. Our children have forgotten the taste of milk.'

Caroline looked around at the pale and peaky grandchildren and decided more needed to be done for Maraghar. Christian Solidarity undertook to replace the village's dairy herd. They provided an assortment of cows who were named after project staff, including a bull called Stuart. Stuart expired in the course of his duty and was duly eaten after leaving a field full of pregnant cattle. 'He had given his all in the service of his country.'

When Caroline later returned to New Maraghar she was greeted by the same woman with the words: 'Every family now has a cow and all our children now know the taste of milk.'

It is for reasons such as these that Christian Solidarity is regarded with such affection in Armenia. A war widow from the Association of Women said: 'Our only source of hope and comfort came from those who supported us in our darkest hours, such as CSI.' Said another: 'CSI shows that the value of blood is greater than petroleum.'

And for many, Christian Solidarity is embodied by Caroline. Added a third war widow: 'You show your Christian witness by sharing our hardship and enduring our suffering with us... All the people of Karabakh from the new-born to those aged 90 know your name. You have given us the energy and the hope to endure.'

CSI UK's former President, David Atkinson MP, stepped down from the post in favour of Caroline. Describing her as 'a modern-day saint' he called her work on behalf of Christians around the world 'amazing and inspiring'.

'Her greatest contribution,' he continued, 'is to bring hope and encouragement to those who are suffering for being Christians. Her greatest strength is her courage, in taking those initiatives for which she is so clearly at risk, in order to fulfil those missions. I have seen for myself how she sustains the hopes and the strength of the Karabakhtsi people. That is why their Christian life will now, in my view, be protected – because of Caroline Cox – Lady Karabakh Cox, as they call her.'

NOTES
1. Isaiah 61:3.

Part Three

Burma

'The Myanmar government does not condone human rights abuses. It is totally against human rights abuses.'

Foreign Minister, U Ohn Gyaw[1]

'I have heard [government] claims that there are no human rights problems in Burma. Claims like this make me want to laugh and cry.'

Corinne Armour,
an Australian teacher working in the refugee camps[2]

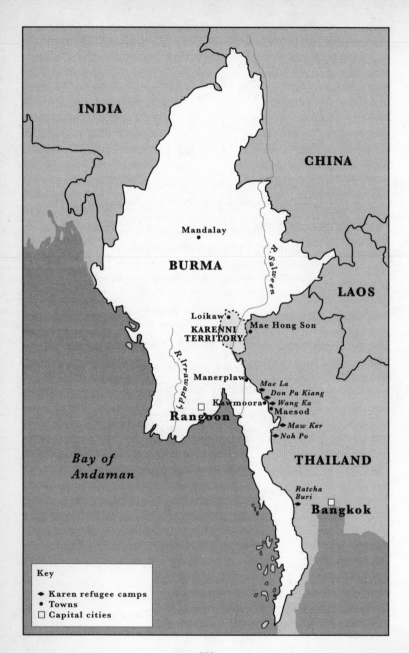

INDIA

CHINA

Mandalay

BURMA

R. Salween

LAOS

Loikaw
KARENNI
TERRITORY

Mae Hong Son

R. Irrawaddy

Manerplaw

Mae La
Don Pa Kiang

Kawmoora

Wang Ka
Maesod

Rangoon

Maw Ker

Noh Po

*Bay of
Andaman*

THAILAND

*Ratcha
Buri*

Bangkok

Key

◆ **Karen refugee camps**
• **Towns**
□ **Capital cities**

ONE

The Land of Light

The young Karenni woman was bathing in the river when a sudden noise or movement warned her to look up. Confronting her were the Tatmadaw, soldiers of the Burmese Army. She and the other refugees had fled from men like these across the border into Thailand. Now they had followed her there. There were four of them: men used to getting their own way. Today they gave her an ultimatum. It was as simple as it was stark. Submit to being raped by all four of them, or be executed. Faced with the choice of degradation or death, she accepted the former. Many others had had to settle for both.

Caroline rose early, sloughing off the nitrazepam pill she always took to help her sleep on foreign visits, and crammed on her trainers to take a run. Her standard way of dealing with jet-lag was to run or plunge straight into a game of squash. As squash courts were few and far between in northern Thailand, she set off at a brisk jog along the nearest grass track. Unusually, her heart was heavy that morning, and she decided to combine a physical work-out with spiritual exercise by praying as she ran.

It was November 1994. She had been invited to Burma by an English doctor working among the ethnic minorities, Dr Martin Panter. Myanmar, to give it its official name, is a land of mountains and rivers the size of Texas, adjoining Laos and Thailand, the other corners of the Golden Triangle, the opium belt of the world. It was the Land of the Golden Pagodas, one of the strongest enclaves of Theravada Buddhism in all of Asia. Caroline's mission was to gather facts about the Karen people who were being driven out of their land by Burmese troops, in a war that had been raging for decades and appeared to be drawing to a bitter conclusion. Caroline, Dr Panter and a team of British medics had spent the night in a mission station in the town of Chiang Mai in northern Thailand. From there it would be a voyage by longboat to the refugee camps in the borderlands, and then into Burma itself, the nation described by Amnesty International as a 'prison without walls'.

The weather at the tail end of the hot season was predictable: a cover of cloud which burns off by 10 a.m. to reveal brilliant sunshine and a vivid blue sky. On any other day, the beauty of the mountains and the vibrancy of the colours would have taken her breath away. But her thoughts went back a month to the Fifth CSI Annual Human Rights Conference in London. Dr Panter, a trim, precise figure in an elegant cream suit, spoke passionately and earnestly about the plight of the Karen and Karenni peoples of Burma.

'Terror regime'

The Karen were much in need of some Christian solidarity. Many had converted to Christianity in the early 1800s, fought with the British in the Second World War, and faced intense persecution from 1947, when the Burmese authorities set fire to 300 Karen Christians as they worshipped in a church in Tavoy State. Now this ethnic group, who made up less than 10 per cent of the population of Burma, were being driven from the country's coastal region.

Their land, in the eastern hills and delta was known as Kwathoolei; roughly translated as 'land of smiles', or 'land of light'. The Karen were among the earliest indigenous inhabitants of Burma, migrating from South Mongolia in 5BC,[3] hundreds of years before the Myen, who would go on to dominate the region. From generation to generation a legend was passed down that a white man would come from a faraway land and reveal to the Karen the truth about the gods through the golden book he would bring with him. Many visitors heard the legend and sought to exploit it for personal gain. But in the 18th century, the pioneer missionary Adoniram Judson reached the Upper Salween district of Kwathoolei and preached the Christian gospel. Satisfied their legend had been fulfilled, thousands of Karen embraced the Christian faith.[4]

'Successive authoritarian governments in Rangoon have harassed, brutalized, tortured and killed countless thousands of Karen villagers,' declared Dr Panter from the ornately carved pulpit at London's Westminster Chapel. 'They are liable to be murdered, raped, enslaved and pressed into forced labour.[5] Thousands of their young have been disabled. Hundreds of artificial limbs have been made. Dozens of young men have been blinded and lost one or both forearms as a result of anti-personnel landmines. It's a terror regime,' he told the assembled delegates at the human rights conference. 'Even if they flee to the refugee camps on the border, the conditions are severe and they may still be subject to attack.

After some 46 years of fighting, this peace-loving and gentle people are weary of war.'

With defeat looming, the Christian Karen leadership led their people in a day of prayer, fasting and repentance, seeking God for deliverance. But a glance at the military build-up against them suggested their prayers had come too late. Where the Karen had once fought for secession, today they would settle for autonomy, but even survival would take a miracle.

The grassy track soon led to a lake, which Caroline judged was just about the right size to run around. At the half-way point she came to a promontory, with a small, circular, brick-built shelter at its head which might have been used as a shrine or a temple. It was as good a place as any for meditation, and she needed it that morning. Caroline was having what she describes as one of her 'fits of faithless, fearful, dread'.

The crisis of confidence was sparked off by nagging doubts about whether what they were doing was sensible or right. CSI was a tiny organization with pathetically limited resources. She had heard so much about the suffering of the Karen. What did CSI have to offer them, apart from a little medicine and the promise of a little more to follow? Worse still, she wondered whether they would be raising their expectations falsely. Perhaps it was an act of cruelty to tantalize them by arriving, and then offer so little. It was a sticking plaster for an open wound: a form of mockery. The thoughts churned round in her mind, dragging at her steps as she ran, weighing her down.

There was a wooden bench beneath the shelter. She parked herself down and began to pray. She pondered about CSI's insignificant operational base and its meagre financial resources and prayed that God would nevertheless bless the mission and fulfil his will. Somehow. She flicked through the King James Bible she had brought with her, hoping to draw some inspiration or comfort. The pages flipped opened at 2 Kings 4. Her eyes ran down a passage she had never noticed before. It was the story of the prophet Elisha during the famine in Gilgal:

A man came from Baal Shalishah, bringing the man of God twenty loaves of barley bread baked from the first ripe corn, along with some ears of new corn. 'Give it to the people to eat,' Elisha said.

'How can I set this before a hundred men?' his servant asked. But Elisha answered, 'Give it to the people to eat. For this is what the Lord says: "They will eat and have some left over."'

Then he set it before them, and they ate and had some left over, according to the word of the Lord.

'I could relate so well to this poor guy and his crisis of confidence,' says Caroline. 'But he gave his 20 loaves and there was indeed enough, and some left over. If you were just prepared to go in faith with what you could and make that available, then maybe God could multiply that beyond anything you could imagine at the time.'

Her thoughts drifted to Nagorno Karabakh, where with CSI's encouragement, MERLIN (Medical Emergency Relief International) had set up an immunization scheme, and the Halo Trust had begun its programme of mine-clearance. What had started in a small way, hopelessly under-resourced, had multiplied. While it would never be possible for Caroline and CSI to solve all the problems they encountered, they could act as catalysts for change, and introduce others who could take the work forward. They could never be the complete answer – but they could be a part of it.

A phrase that Jonathan, her son, had used also stuck in her mind: 'God doesn't want our ability – he wants our availability.' It was like that with CSI. Little by way of resources, but a willingness to get involved. Maybe that was enough. She flipped her Bible shut and resumed her run around the lake with a lighter spirit.

A 'present' for the Chairman

They drove through northern Thailand to the river, to another of those strangely intense emotional juxtapositions. Exhilarating dramatic beauty all around – the high mountains, the startling colours as the sun chased away the mist, the vivid greens of the jungle, fast swirling waters and the graceful manoeuvring of the motorized longboats – all set against the tragedy that had befallen the Karen and others and which was unfolding daily.

That tragedy was in full evidence when they crossed the border and stepped onto Burmese soil. In a Burma the tourists would never visit, a war of ethnic cleansing was being ruthlessly waged. Minority groups were confined to the jungle, stateless, trapped, and subjected to a sustained military offensive. Those who were captured were forced to work without pay as porters for the troops or set to work building roads to boost tourism or railways to open up the country to foreign investment. Many were driven from their homes to make way for the projects. It was a reprise of the notorious Burma railway of the Second World War, which claimed the lives of thousands of allied prisoners of war, caught up in the Japanese advance through South East Asia. Asians had also been forced to toil on that railway then, and were being made to do so again. According to Human Rights

Watch some 2 million had been drafted into involuntary labour over a three-year period. The aim was to develop the infrastructure to bring in cash from abroad.[6]

It would begin with a summons to the head man of the village, demanding porters. 'If the letter comes with a bullet,' said one village chief, 'it indicates death if we don't comply. If it comes with charcoal, that's a warning the village will be burned; and if it comes with a chilli, it means we will be tortured.'[7]

The following summons was sent from the frontline 406 Light Infantry Battalion at Nat Gyi Zin Camp on 4 November 1994:

CALL FOR LABOUR TO THE HEAD OF THE VILLAGE

1) Regarding the above subject, we already called many times for the headman of XXXX village and 25 villagers for railway labour to come to Nat Gyi Zin Camp.

2) Therefore, as soon as you receive this letter, the headman and 25 people, along with rations and needed equipment [tools etc.], must come without fail.

3) Along with this letter, we are sending some presents for the chairman and secretary [of the village]. If you get these presents, come here. If you fail to come, we will give the next present to the headman of the village. Wait and see what kind of present.

[Sd.]
(for) Column Commander
Nat Gyi Zin Camp

The 'presents' enclosed with the order were two bullets. The document was used in evidence by an Australian government investigation into human rights abuses in Burma.[8]

The accounts of forced labour were supported by Amnesty International and the United Nations Special Rapporteur, Yozo Yokota, who observed, 'Persons taken for portering are reported to have been rounded up by the military in various places, such as schools, buses and market places. Large numbers... are reported to have died from ill-treatment, illness and malnutrition... Porters who attempt to escape are reportedly shot... elderly persons, women and children have been taken as army porters. These persons are often said to be used as human shields in military operations.'[9]

Unsurprisingly, the Rapporteur's successor was barred from entering the country. From reports obtained, Judge Rajsoomer Lallah described 'a culture of impunity' and called for a ban on forced labour and portering.[10]

It was a sharp contrast to the official picture presented by Myanmar, a signatory to the Forced Labour Convention of 1955. The Ambassador to the UN Commission on Human Rights claimed, 'It has always been a tradition in the Myanmar culture of donating labour in the building of monasteries, pagodas, roads and bridges. A belief persists that in doing so, it leads to mental and physical well-being... the authorities do all they can to provide for the basic needs of the voluntary labourers...'[11]

'If it were traditional and acceptable practice,' riposted the Australia-Burma Council, 'the people would not be fleeing it... Forced labour is slavery.'[12]

Manerplaw

Caroline spoke to the refugees. Witnesses told of people killed by stakes driven through their ears, of others who were burned alive. She was shown the photographs. But at the Karen administrative and military headquarters in Manerplaw it all seemed so unreal. The base resembled a well-kept English village, with a clearing in the jungle for a parade ground, sprouting a flag pole at its centre. Morning and evening, the red, white and blue colours, surmounted by the rising sun, would be raised and lowered with dignity and precision. The buildings, for the Ministry of Health and Defence, were spick and span and efficiently maintained.

They were greeted by General Hla Htoo, a veteran Karen freedom fighter in his 70s, who informed them with a wicked grin, 'Now you have really arrived in the jungle – the home of spiders, snakes and scorpions.' At which point, Caroline's Russian colleague, Nadia, turned a shade of green.

While Caroline and Nadia shared a mosquito net, a Russian Orthodox icon was placed on sentry duty outside. The icon had been brought along to extend divine protection against creepy-crawlies, and Nadia had considered it as essential as her first aid kit. But perhaps the icon was suffering from jet-lag, for within minutes Nadia's scream had summoned Dr Panter to the room. Straddling the top of the religious symbol with a glint of triumph in its many eyes was an enormous spider. Dr Panter dispatched it with the heel of his shoe, and, thus jolted into action, the icon performed tirelessly for the rest of the evening.

They had arrived at Manerplaw in November 1994. Within two months of their visit, the Karen base would be obliterated by a military offensive.

CSI's aims were as usual: to obtain firsthand evidence of violations of human rights; to assess the need for humanitarian aid; and to show solidarity with the suffering. With them were eye specialists from Britain to treat complaints and teach the Karen people how to carry out their own cataract operations.

It was Dr Panter's 17th visit to establish health care centres among them. The Karen, along with the Karenni, were among the last remaining minority groups in Myanmar to hold out against the military junta which seized power in 1988. Fourteen other groups had made their accommodation with the State Law and Order Restoration Council – SLORC. With the others subdued, the forces of the SLORC could be marshalled to bring them to heel. They were doing so with a brutality which brought universal condemnation.

Yet the eyes of the world were not on the jungles of Burma, but on a single house in Rangoon where the Nobel Peace Prize winner Daw Aung San Suu Kyi held court to the thousands of followers of the National League for Democracy who dared come to her gate to hear her speak.

This Oxford-educated woman was the daughter of Burma's nationalist hero, Aung San. He had fought with the Japanese in the Second World War in the hope that they would free them from their British oppressors. When the reality became apparent, he switched sides to fight alongside his former adversaries, who had subdued Burma during the 19th century. The twice victorious British gave Burma over to independence, and utter turmoil, in January 1948.

Years of turmoil

The nation's history dates back perhaps five millennia, to the first influx of migrants drawn along the Irrawaddy River from China and Tibet, the Mon. They were followed in the first century BC by the Tibeto-Burmese Pyu, who began to establish their city kingdoms in the north. In AD9, their capital fell to the kingdom of Nanchao, in southern China. The Myanmar people absorbed both the Pyu and the Mon, and subdued but never assimilated the Karen hill people. Dominion was exercised from their capital at Pagan, later to become the Buddhist 'city of a thousand temples'. Their reign was to end in 1287, with the Mongol invasion of Kublai Khan and the destruction of the dynasty by his grandson, Ye-Su Timur, who like Kublai Khan before him, exerted a rule of iron.

In his wake came anarchy. Some 300 years passed before this land of more than 100 languages could be reunited under the Toungoo dynasty, which was finally toppled by the Mon rebellion. Alaungpaya defeated the Mon and established Rangoon as his capital, but territorial ambitions brought Burma into conflict with a mightier empire. Incursions into colonial India drew Britain into the first of three successive wars which, from 1824, subdued Burma until it was recast as a province of India and a crown colony.[13] As the nation grew to become the world's largest exporter of rice, it began to disintegrate socially from within. Racial tensions were exacerbated by the British preference for Indians in the administration and Christian Karen in the army.

In the 1930s the nation was rocked by a peasant uprising followed by a student strike organized by Aung San. His Thakin movement cocked a snook at their British overlords, for whom the title Thakin, or Master, was normally reserved. In 1937, Britain agreed to the separation of Burma from India and partial self-government. But five years later, a wave of anti-British nationalism ushered in another empire: the Empire of the Rising Sun. The Burma Independence Army, founded by Aung San, fought alongside the invading Japanese to drive the British out of Burma.[14] But when Japan's promise of freedom turned to ashes, Aung San established the Anti-Fascist People's Freedom League (AFPFL) and resorted to helping the British regain control of his country. The Japanese were defeated at the nation's main artery, the Irrawaddy river.

That year, 1945, General Aung San sired a daughter, Aung San Suu Kyi. When she was two years old, her father was assassinated on the brink of achieving his dream of an independent Burma. With Aung San died another dream, that of a federal constitution offering equal status for ethnic minorities. After his death, the constitution, which provided for a Karen state, was amended. A unitary state was put in its place.

On 4 January 1948, at precisely 4.30 a.m., the moment regarded as most astrologically auspicious, full independence from Britain was granted. As the dominant Burmans sought to impose an artificial national unity on 135 disparate racial groups, the historic freedoms of ethnic minorities were ignored. The new socialist parliamentary democracy found itself embroiled in a civil war with the Karen National Liberation Army, the Karenni, the Mon and the Communists.

By 1958, the ruling AFPFL cracked under pressure, and gave way to an emergency caretaker government headed by General Ne Win, a contemporary of Aung San who, having once seized power, never truly relaxed his grip. Ne Win's Revolutionary Council swept aside the multi-party system and embarked on The Burmese Way to Socialism. For 12 years he ruled without a constitution before trading in his military uniform to become President of a one-party republic in 1974.

That year, in the former rice bowl of Asia, food riots broke out on the streets. Socialist isolationist policies, coupled with civil wars fought on multiple

Dr Murray Newell Cox, Caroline's husband. 'Together they could see the bigger picture.' ◄

Dima (centre), the child of the dream, once abandoned by a dustbin, now with his new family in Moscow. ▼

Blizzard bus. Christmas Eve shelter for Caroline in the mountains of Karabakh. ▲

Caroline with the man she calls the 'Lion of Karabakh', Zori Balayan. ➤

Caroline with the Bishops in the mountains of Karabakh. ▲

A converted water tank is home for refugees fleeing an Azeri pogrom. (Picture: Andrew Boyd) ◄

Celebration Armenian-style: the newly qualified soldiers of Karabakh. (Picture: Andrew Boyd) ▼

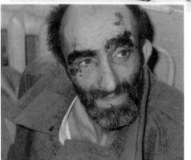

Maraghar, the place of Golgotha. A charred, decapitated body is exhumed as evidence of a massacre. ➤

A hostage maltreated by the Azeris, February 1991. ▲

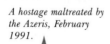

'Supper for the Armenians': the inscription on this unexploded bomb which just missed a village.

This Yak 40 laden with war wounded took a direct hit by a missile. Somehow, the pilot brought it down without fatalities. ▼

Two survivors amid the ruins of their home devastated by Grads. ▼

Child victim of a cluster-bomb attack on Karabakh. ▼

Producing artificial limbs for land-mine victims at the Caroline Cox orthopaedic centre in Karabakh.

Britain's former allies, the Karen, fighting for their homeland in Burma. ▲

Caroline with a Karenni long-necked girl, driven from her home in Burma. ▲

Unqualified Karen medics carry out an amputation in the Burmese jungle. Caroline was impressed by their professionalism. ▲

Victims of ethnic cleansing in Burma. Vastly outnumbered by the Burmese army, the Karen and Karenni are being forced out of their land.

◄

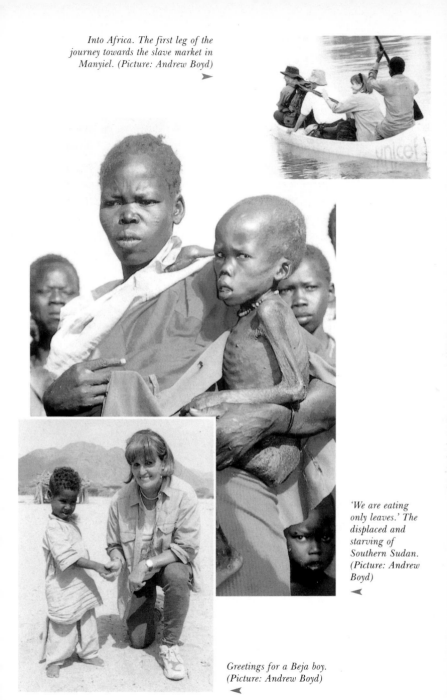

Into Africa. The first leg of the journey towards the slave market in Manyiel. (Picture: Andrew Boyd)

'We are eating only leaves.' The displaced and starving of Southern Sudan. (Picture: Andrew Boyd)

Greetings for a Beja boy. (Picture: Andrew Boyd)

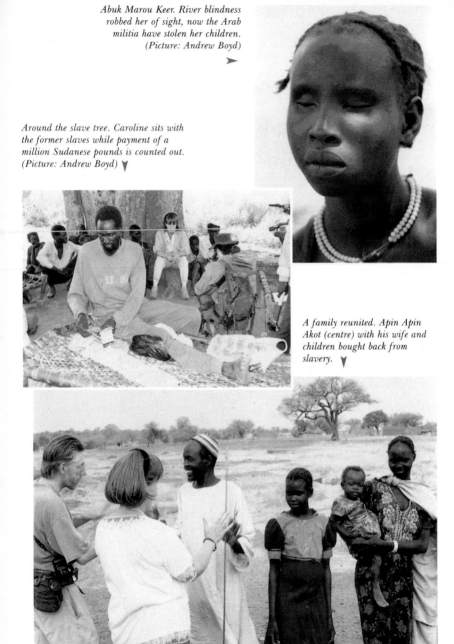

Abuk Marou Keer. River blindness robbed her of sight, now the Arab militia have stolen her children. (Picture: Andrew Boyd)

Around the slave tree. Caroline sits with the former slaves while payment of a million Sudanese pounds is counted out. (Picture: Andrew Boyd)

A family reunited. Apin Apin Akot (centre) with his wife and children bought back from slavery.

Gathering evidence. The author Andrew Boyd (centre) hears the story of a raid on Nyamlell, while Caroline makes notes. ▲

Landmine victim Matilda cradles Thomas (right), rescued from their burning home after an Antonov attack. ▲

Akuil Garang, still scarred from the attack on Nyamlell. Two of her children were burnt to death in their hut. Her third was taken into slavery. (Picture: Andrew Boyd) ➤

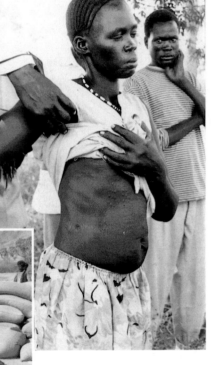

Caroline and John Eibner carry sacks of sorghum for the Beja on the Eritrean border. (Picture: Andrew Boyd) ◄

Southern Sudan – aftermath of a massacre: 'You could go for mile upon mile and see the corpses – civilians still wearing beads and bracelets, trying to flee from the raids.'

Shot in the face when he tried to stop the slave-raiders capturing a boy. ▼

Within walls pock-marked by shrapnel, worship continues in the church at Nyamlell. ◄

CSW's National Director, Stuart Windsor (right), presents a Bible to Santino Ring, a Sudanese catechist who has braved the slave raids to remain with his people.

 ◄

fronts, had driven the economy to its knees. A country rich in resources, including plentiful supplies of natural gas, was on the slide towards becoming one of the world's poorest nations. In 1975, non-Communist ethnic separatist groups united to form the National Democratic Front, with the aim of turning Burma into a federation. The army redoubled its efforts to prevent them.

In September 1987, students took to the streets of Rangoon. The following Spring, workers rioted. Students demonstrating on the White Bridge across Inya Lake were beaten to death by riot police. Forty-two were rounded up and locked in a waiting van and left to suffocate.[15] On 8 August, the army was turned loose and began shooting into the crowds gathered in Rangoon. In Mandalay, the armed forces were more restrained. Soldiers and Buddhist monks fought it out with slingshots. But elsewhere across Burma, between 3,000 and 10,000 unarmed demonstrators were gunned down.[16] An estimated 700,000 fled the country. Public protests and calls for democracy continued unabated. Multi-party elections were promised within three months. Instead, what the people got was a military coup.

General Saw Maung seized power on 18 September 1988, suspending the constitution, imposing martial law and transferring authority to a State Law and Order Restoration Council. Holding the reins was Ne Win.

It purported to be a new beginning. The country's name was changed to Myanmar and its capital became Yangôn; while the ruling BSPP became the National Unity Party. Steps were taken to liberalize the economy, even to stage democratic elections – of a sort. The leader of the opposing National League for Democracy, Daw Aung San Suu Kyi, daughter of the late Aung San, was placed under house arrest and barred from standing. Nevertheless, her party won a landslide victory at the elections in May 1990, claiming 82 per cent of the parliamentary seats.

Nothing changed. The military whose party gained just 10 per cent of the vote refused to recognize the election result and arrested many of the elected politicians. Thousands of pro-democracy activists were interrogated, tortured and imprisoned.[17] In 1991, Daw Aung San Suu Kyi, who had drawn her inspiration from the non-violent protests of Martin Luther King and Mahatma Ghandi, was awarded the Nobel Peace Prize. Meanwhile, a military crackdown was begun against the Christian Karen and the Muslim-led pro-independence movement. Within a year more than 100,000 Muslims were to flee the country.

In April 1992, Saw Maung was succeeded by General Than Shwe, a secondary-school educated postal clerk, who rose to the rank of Defence Minister. Behind the figurehead was the chief of military intelligence, Lt General Khin Nyunt, protégé of the ever-present Ne Win.[18]

To try to stifle opposition, a stranglehold was placed on the media. The press was censored; satellite dish ownership restricted; foreign language videos purged from rental stores, and anyone possessing an unauthorized computer capable of linking to the Internet faced a jail sentence of up to 15 years.[19]

NOTES

1. In a speech to the Thai National Defence College in 1994.

2. 'Human Rights and Progress Towards Democracy in Burma', The Parliament of the Commonwealth of Australia, Joint Standing Committee on Foreign Affairs, Defence and Trade, October 1995, p. 26.

3. Sources vary. Another claims they migrated to Burma in AD800.

4. Today, around half the 2.5 million or more Karen in the region are Christians: Dr Martin Panter, 'The Plight of the Karen People in Burma, CSI Magazine, February 1994.

5. The claim of forced labour is supported by other agencies, including the United Nations, Amnesty International, Christian Aid and Human Rights Watch / Asia: 'Burma: abuses linked to the fall of Manerplaw', March 1995, p. 2. The predicament of the Karen and Karenni was jointly highlighted by the UN Special Rapporteur on religious intolerance and UNESCO in discussions with the Myanmar Foreign Minister. He referred to 'reports of forced labour; and... military actions against certain ethnic groups, including the Karens and Karennis, resulting in further internal displacements and refugee outflows': Third Committee, 1a, 37th meeting (AM), 15 November 1996.

6. 'Worsening Human Rights Situation Requires Increased International Pressure', 26 July 1995. According to an Australian Parliament report there were two principal types of forced labour in Burma. Porters were conscripted under the Army Act, and should have been entitled to army pay, rations, medical assistance and compensation for injury. Corvee Labour was a traditional system of compulsory public labour contribution to infrastructure projects, said to be in use on a massive scale: 'Human Rights and Progress Towards Democracy in Burma', October 1995.

7. *Compass Direct*, 8 April 1997.

8. 'Human Rights and Progress Towards Democracy in Burma', p. 131.

9. 'Situation of Human Rights in Myanmar', United Nations, 28 October 1994. Mr Yokota's successor, Judge Rajsoomer Lallah was prohibited from entering the country despite repeated requests from the UN Secretary-General. Forced portering was also acknowledged by the US State Department, which said at the start of 1998 that it had remained a common practice, leading to maltreatment, illness and even death: 'Burma Country Report on Human Rights Practices for 1997', Introduction.

10. 'Country Report on Human Rights to Third Committee', 15 November 1996. The report was described by Myanmar as an 'unwarranted interference in our internal affairs', and was rejected.

11. Ambassador Maung Aye, letter dated 13 February 1995, exhibit no. 29.

12. Evidence given to UNCHR, 5 May 1995, cited in 'Human Rights and Progress Towards Democracy in Burma', p. 36. The International Confederation of Free Trade Unions concluded, 'The evidence is... overwhelming...; forced labour... is part and parcel of the Burmese population's everyday life': '1995 Report to the European Union', cited in 'Human Rights and Progress Towards Democracy in Burma', pp. 36, 37.

13. Burma became part of the British empire in 1886.

14. Burma became a Japanese protectorate in August 1943.

15. John Pilger, 'A Cry for Freedom', *New Internationalist*, no. 280.

16. More, according to Pilger, 'A Cry for Freedom'.

17. The International Committee of the Red Cross later withdrew from Burma because the government would not permit private access to prisoners.

18. *Encyclopaedia Britannica*; *The Hutchinson Encyclopaedia*; *Atlapedia Online*; *Compton's Encyclopedia*; *Funk and Wagnall's Encyclopedia*; 'The Last Two Million Years', Reader's Digest Publishers, 1974.

19. 'Human Rights and Progress Towards Democracy in Burma', p. 17; *Index on Censorship*, 11 October 1996. Two Burmese opposition Internet sites are: www.freeburma.org; and www.uvi.eunet.fr/asia/euro-burma.

TWO

Sleeping Dog Mountain

The proliferating refugee camps dotting the Thai-Burmese border were home to some 150,000 people who had been driven from their lands. A similar number had been displaced close to the border.[1] The camps consisted of rudimentary houses on stilts, with thatched roofs and thin woven walls through which the light came streaming. There was no shortage of camps to visit and no shortage of volunteers to tell their stories. Caroline sat and listened, clad in denims with her mandatory string of beads, pen in hand and interpreter by her side, and filled up the best part of a notebook. She heard further graphic accounts of people being abducted to be used as slave labour and even as human minesweepers. The United Nations had reported women and children being made to walk or ride in carts ahead of military columns.[2] Apart from proving effective at clearing mines, these human shields were intended to deter attacks by their own ethnic armies.

Seventeen-year-old Karenni, Go Lah, showed Dr Panter the bullet wound in his leg and explained how he had received it. 'I was a porter for SLORC with my elder brother,' he said. 'SLORC soldiers killed my brother, so I escaped from them. They followed and shot me.' He described how soldiers had taken him from his village of Pa Suang and forced him onto a truck in an army convoy. At each passing village they seized more porters, until there were some 600 in total, filling 60 trucks.

They were driven to a border town and confined to an old salt mill, where they were stripped of their money and possessions and denied any food. They took Go Lah's shoes, his torch, his matches – everything apart from his shorts. The next morning he was told he was wanted for 'service' in Karenni lands. He protested that he didn't want to fight his own people, so they beat him. Go Lah was made to carry 25 kilograms of salt and four landmines. He walked from five in the morning until six at night, with only a single break to eat a handful of rice. Their destination was the SLORC base, through the jungle and over the mountains.

'How did they make sure you wouldn't run away in the nights?' Dr Panter asked.

227

'We slept in a cage.'

'What was it made from?'

'It was made from bamboo. It was made by the porters.'

'How many people slept in the cage?'

'Sometimes there were 50 porters or more who slept in the cage.'

There were seven in Go Lah's group of porters. Six died, including his brother. Go Lah would have died too, after he was felled by a shot to the leg, but when nearby Karenni troops heard the firing, they came out of the bush and drove the Tatmadaw away.

Plague balloons

As well as guns and bullets, unconventional methods were also being employed to clear the jungles of the ethnic minorities. Strong circumstantial evidence began to emerge of the use of biological warfare.

Many of the Karen people had gone down with a form of cholera, which they believed was linked to the use of weather balloons and devices dropped into Karen territory. Instead of rising upwards into the stratosphere, where they would normally be used to track monsoons, the devices were dropped from low altitude and fell to earth. Soon afterwards, Karen people in the immediate vicinity developed virulent kinds of gastro-intestinal disease that they had never encountered before. The disease spread out in a pattern that could be traced along the watercourses from where the balloons had fallen.

Another effective way of spreading the sickness was on the hands of children. As Dr Panter put it, 'Children play with the balloons, the cholera gets on them, they spread it round the village, and a few days later the Burmese forces come in and most of the people are disabled or dead.'

Caroline was shown one of the devices which had been retrieved by the Karen. It was a polystyrene box, some 18 inches by 8, with a depth of three to four inches. Inside was a battery and an electric mechanism but the name of the maker and an identification strip had been ripped off. 'Interesting. One for the scientists back home.' She promptly persuaded Dr Panter to bring it back on the plane as hand luggage. 'We didn't exactly jeopardize everyone on board,' she insists. 'This was seven months after the event and the likelihood of any living pathogens being still capable of causing disease was zero.'

Dr Panter recalls: 'I was pleasantly surprised it wasn't detected by any of the electronic devices at Bangkok or Heathrow, but it was picked up straightaway on the X-ray into the House of Lords and I had some fairly quick explaining to do. When I said it was for Baroness Cox, the security officer gave a wink and signalled me through.'

Subsequent investigations by Dr Panter produced evidence of chemical warfare. Karen troops were displaying symptoms of blistered flesh indicative of chemicals like mustard gas. Forty-five-year-old Soe Aung was hiding from attack when his shelter was caught in a bomb blast. He recalled a pungent smell that was totally alien to him. Traces of some substance stuck to his skin, causing excruciating pain and inflicting third-degree burns. Victims of other attacks had been knocked unconscious and rendered weak and unsteady for days. The Karen claimed to have intercepted messages on Burmese military radio referring to chemical weapons, instructing their forces to burn all cases containing the chemicals, to leave no record of their use.[3] Burma was an original signatory to the Biological and Toxin Weapons Convention but had conspicuously failed to ratify the Convention.[4]

Under air attack and ground attack, thousands of Karen and Karenni had fled to refugee camps on the Thai-Burmese border. Conditions were spartan and the safety comparative. Even across the border, they were subject to raids and bombardment from SLORC troops and their allies, the Karen breakaway group the Democratic Kayin Buddhist Army (DKBA). The official view from Myanmar was that the camps were safe havens for the Karen military and their sympathizers and were used to launch attacks into Thailand.[5]

There was also the risk of forced repatriation by the Thai authorities, driving the refugees straight back into the arms of SLORC. CSI's aim was to reach people cut off from access to the major aid agencies and media attention – the forgotten peoples of forgotten lands. The Christian Karen and the Karenni – Christians, Buddhists and animists – fitted the bill. From CSI Australia came medical aid and equipment to make and grow food. Teachers were provided to show untrained non-medics how to carry out operations to save lives.

Caroline saw one such operation for herself. On the Sunday morning of their visit, in the middle of the jungle, a team of totally unqualified individuals carried out an amputation, complete with general anaesthetic, on a victim of a land-mine. Staff nurse Cox was impressed. 'It was superbly done.'

Their handiwork was a tribute to Dr Martin Panter, the driving force behind CSI's involvement and Caroline's visit to Burma. CSI first became aware of the predicament of the Karen in 1994. Stuart Windsor, their UK national director, had heard of a British doctor working among the Karen and wondered how on earth he could track him down. Scarcely knowing where to begin he prayed about it.

Some time later Stuart met a man in Bridgwater, Somerset, who had answered an advert in *The Daily Express* for a footman in the British Embassy in Moscow. The job gave Lenny access to the coats of almost every world leader. Into each he placed a Christian leaflet. He told Stuart of a friend who had been working with the underground church in Saudi Arabia and offered to put him in touch. Several weeks later they met, and to Stuart's amazement he turned out to know Dr Panter. Martin Panter had been consultant physician to King Fahd's brother, the Prince Sultan, before leaving to work in Australia. Stuart met him in the UK and told him about CSI. Dr Panter was fascinated and quickly recognized an opportunity to assist the work in Burma. A meeting was arranged with Caroline Cox at Heathrow airport, which led to her first visit to the Karen and the establishing of CSI down under.

Air attack

If there was a sense in which God was protecting and encouraging the work, it was never more apparent than on one of Dr Panter's earlier missions to Burma.

Dr Panter sat down for a meal with a member of Karen intelligence who told him the Burmese were planning a major offensive the following day. An air strike would be followed by an infantry attack. They had picked up signals on Burmese radio to suggest two battalions of soldiers were poised to move into the very area Dr Panter and his team were due to visit on the day they were due to arrive.

Dr Panter faced an agonizing decision. Not only was he responsible for his team, but also for his daughters, Rachel, aged 13 and Juliet, aged nine, and his three-year-old son, Nathaniel, who were with them. 'I knew from experience what the Burmese soldiers do,' he said. 'Not only do they rape and kill, but they torture. They use children to walk in front of the soldiers as human mine sweepers. So I knew what would happen if we were captured.'

Feeling utterly dependent on God, the team gathered to pray, and Martin felt drawn to Psalm 27. He looked it up:

When my enemies and my foes attack me, they will stumble and fall. Though an army besiege me, my heart will not fear; though war break out against me, even then will I be confident.

Encouraged, Dr Panter, his children and his team of eye specialists decided to go ahead with the visit. They set off into the potential war zone and were able to continue their work unhindered. The threatened attack did not take place, and the mission was declared a success.

It was only on his next visit to Burma that Dr Panter found out what had happened. The air strike had been scheduled to commence with the clearing of the morning mists, an event as dependable as the rising of the sun. But that day, something unprecedented took place. Instead of the mists being dispersed, huge cumulus clouds began to billow up from the river until they formed a deep and impenetrable bank. Somewhere, high above, SLORC fighter bombers could be heard, circling uselessly, searching for a break in the clouds. The freak weather conditions continued until the pilots' fuel ran so low they were forced to ditch their bombs and go back to base. 'Almost all of them fell on their own troops,' said Dr Panter, 'apart from one which killed two Karen chickens.' The planes returned to Rangoon and the soldiers withdrew.

Sniper alley

Dr Panter, Caroline and their team had made the border crossing along the Moei and Salween rivers. It was the same route taken by the longboats which had carried Caroline up to the front line. The fiercely contested Sleeping Dog Mountain was occupied by SLORC troops. The Karen were offering resistance on the opposing peak, a tree-covered slope which gave way to jagged outcrops at its tip. The climb began in the lush green valley beside the river and then up through dense vegetation. Higher up, the red soil turned into shale and rock and densely packed trees that conspired to block their way.

The long, steep haul up the mountain was hot and unbearably humid. The news cameraman was struggling with his video equipment, and even Caroline, decked out in her usual jeans, T-shirt and trainers, was finding the going arduous. Half way up, she remembers thinking: 'Caroline Cox, you're a grandmother with six grandchildren. It's time you grew up and stopped doing these crazy trips!'

Perhaps it was the message of the fridge magnet back at her home in London that spurred her on: 'Once you're over the hill, you pick up speed.' But there was still some way to the top of this particular mountain.

No-man's land was a narrow ridge dividing the opposing troops on one peak with their enemies on the other. The only way to the Karen soldiers was to walk along the crest of the ridge, in full view of any Burmese snipers who happened to be positioned some 300 metres away in the forest. Dr Panter spelt out the danger to Caroline. 'But with her usual manner, she refused to be dissuaded and simply said, "They are expecting to see us." Off she marched at a quick rate with us bringing up the rear in some trepidation.'

When they got to the top and met the soldiers they realized it was worth it.

These were the first outsiders to visit them at their mountainous outpost, and the Karen troops were amazed to see them. The features of these small, wiry men wreathed in smiles at the sight of this English baroness and others who had puffed and panted their way up the mountain. 'We thought we had been forgotten,' said one, 'that nobody knew about our battle.'

The soldiers wore the makeshift uniforms of a rebel army and were low on ammunition, food and all essential supplies. Trenches and dug-outs ran across their position to offer some shelter against attack from the air and from the attentions of the infantry nearby. Caroline was shown the places where it was unwise to walk. Conversation was punctuated by intermittent ground fire and it was necessary to keep down below the ridge.

'It meant a lot to them to know they weren't forgotten,' says Caroline, 'that people cared enough to come and visit them.' When they left to pick their way back down the mountain, the soldiers said their visit had given them the strength to carry on.

The going was getting easier towards the valley when Caroline heard what sounded like a bell ringing through the jungle. Incongruous as it seemed, she wondered if there could be a Christian community nearby. The group followed the sound. Sure enough, a wooden church emerged from the trees in front of them, complete with pews and worshipping children. She recalls their round faces and the trusting, open smiles of their greetings, but behind the shining sloe eyes were the unmistakable signs of suffering. Caroline caught sight of the bell and did a double-take. It had been fashioned from the sawn-off top of a Burmese bomb. 'Instead of swords into ploughshares,' she says, 'it was bombs into bells.'

SLORC offensive

In 1995, the SLORC renewed their offensive against the Karen and negotiated a cease-fire with the Karenni. It was cast aside within a matter of months when troops thrust deep into Karenni-held areas of Kaya state. To remove the insurgents, the SLORC employed the tactic of cutting them off from civilian support – by removing the civilians.[6] In a single month, they forcibly relocated 96 Karenni villages with a population of 30,000. Forced relocation to camps within Burma away from the battle-zones, where civilians would be starved of food and denied medical aid, was to become a growing feature of the conflict. Thousands more remained trapped behind SLORC lines. Many thousands more spilled over the border into Thailand. The renewed offensive was denounced as 'ethnic cleansing and genocide' by CSI.[7]

Even the Thai refugee camps were far from safe. Leaflets scattered by the breakaway Democratic Kayin Buddhist Army (Kayin was Burmese for Karen) warned civilians to return to Burma or be killed. They were not empty threats. Many lost their lives in the cross-border raids of the 'yellow men', so called because of the distinctive yellow scarves tied round their heads or thighs. According to Amnesty, dozens of refugees were killed and abducted in an attempt to force them to return to areas under DKBA control.[8] Reports from inside Myanmar suggested the DKBA had been given an ultimatum by SLORC: burn down the refugee camps, or face extinction.[9] They set about the task with rocket-propelled grenades and M79 grenade launchers. Dr Panter described 'a rapidly developing state of anarchy along the border and a widespread spirit of fear within the camps'.

The DKBA had split from the Karen National Union in December 1994 amid growing resentment from the Buddhists towards their ageing Christian leaders. Two thirds of the troops on the front line were Buddhist, yet two thirds of the leadership was Christian. There had been murmurings of the misappropriation of funds. Troops were kept on the front line for up to three months on sparse rations of rice, chilli and occasionally *ngapi* – fish paste. Sweets, chocolates and cigarettes, sent by donors from abroad were ending up with the officers in Manerplaw.[10] It didn't help. The potential for division was fuelled by an inflammatory anti-Christian propaganda campaign conducted by SLORC, which attempted to link itself with Buddhism to gain popular legitimacy.

Buddhist missionaries had started arriving at the crop of new monasteries and pagodas which were springing up at strategic vantage points. On 1 December 1994, at a monastery at the junction overlooking the rivers Moei and Salween, Buddhist abbot U Thu Zana engaged in the un-monk-like activity of blocking the river, halting all traffic and firing on boats that refused to stop. He was accompanied by a sergeant major and 29 others. A team of 16 Karen negotiators tried in vain to restore the peace. Seven were taken hostage.

On 28 December, the breakaway group announced themselves as the DKBA. They accused the Karen National Union (KNU) of the systematic oppression of Buddhists and, for good measure, arrested and tortured five Christian Karen soldiers. The men were given the choice – convert to

Buddhism or die. They were executed soon after. On 3 January 1995, the KNU declared war on its rebellious faction. Shots were exchanged around the monastery and soon after 11 a.m. the building caught fire. Before long the ground was shaken as an ammunition dump in the basement blew up in a series of large explosions, scattering the monastery to the four winds. On the same day, with all the appearance of a co-ordinated action, SLORC troops based ten kilometres away at Sleeping Dog Mountain began to advance behind an artillery barrage.

False propaganda – spread by SLORC – that the Karen National Union had executed a Buddhist brigadier and nine Buddhist monk,s swelled the number of DKBA recruits. Now more than 400 strong,[11] they retreated some seven kilometres to a village under SLORC occupation. Meanwhile, SLORC troops managed to break through Karen lines and reach the Moei River. By 20 January combined SLORC and DKBA forces had crossed the Salween and taken up position on White Mountain overlooking Manerplaw, where they were able to shell the Karen headquarters with rockets and heavy artillery.

On 26 January, the Karen leadership gave the order to burn their buildings and retreat. SLORC advanced with the DKBA troops ahead of them, calling out the names of their former friends and colleagues. KNU soldiers, not wanting to shoot their brothers, largely held their fire.[12] So fell Manerplaw, at 6 a.m. on 27 January 1995, and after it base after base as the DKBA turncoats showed the SLORC troops exactly where to go.

Manerplaw had been a haven for pro-democracy activists and several rebel ethnic groups. Its fall, and the subsequent rout, led to the loss of most of the remaining Karen territory and what Dr Panter described as 'an apparent collapse in the spirit of the Karen people'. Their army of 15,000 was whittled down to one third, following widespread resignations by disillusioned soldiers. SLORC, now in the ascendant, rejected calls for a nationwide cease-fire monitored and supervised by the UN.

Just a few kilometres down river, Pwa Ba Lu was like a ghost town. The hospital was deserted and an intravenous drip lay on the floor, where it had been hastily detached from a patient. The Karen Health Secretary, Dr Poo Thow Daw, took it philosophically. This man of faith believed that, in a measure, the Karen had brought defeat upon themselves. 'We need prayer,' he said, a sparkle still in his eyes. 'Some of our leaders look to themselves and care more for themselves than they do for their people. Please pray that they will repent and be prepared to work together in true love and humility, and maybe God will restore us.

'Pray also for reconciliation between Buddhists and Christians,' he added.

'There is hostility because of what has happened and only humility and love will help to restore these broken relationships.'

With the loss of their headquarters, the Karen military switched their strategy to guerrilla tactics while 12,000 new refugees swelled the camps on the Thai border. At Wang Ka Camp, tucked just inside Thailand, two kilometres from the remaining Karen foothold of Kawmoora, Dr Panter lay on his bed mat beneath a mosquito net listening to the thunder of exploding shells which lit up the night sky. For three days, some 40,000 SLORC shells had rained down on the thousand Karen troops holed up underground in a single square kilometre of swampy flatland within a C-shaped loop in the Moei River. Their retort shook and rattled the fragile bamboo dwellings of the refugees and plumes of smoke filled the air where stray shells had ignited the dry grassland. Over and between the bursts of thunder could be heard the voices of children crying in the arms of their fearful parents.

The camp commander, Major Mary On, was a tiny, irrepressible 61-year-old with the energy and vitality of an athlete and what one correspondent described as the disconcerting habit of bursting into song. A year ago, this pipe-smoking ex-footballer had entertained Archbishop Desmond Tutu and other Nobel Peace Laureates in her bamboo home.

Before dawn the previous day she had sprinted across the killing ground at Kawmoora under machine-gun fire to show solidarity with the soldiers. She told Dr Panter they had no antibiotics and not even an aspirin between them. They had rice, but to cook it would involve coming above ground and presenting a target for the artillery. So they went hungry. Tied around the thighs of the front-line troops opposing them were the unmistakable yellow scarves of the DKBA. Dr Panter borrowed a car and drove to Maesod to buy dried food rations and paracetamol tablets, as well as cotton wool and spirits to treat simple wounds. Major Mary thanked him profusely and said they would be taken to the troops at Kawmoora under cover of darkness. Her porters would go willingly, unlike the 2,000 Karen women rounded up the previous week by the SLORC to carry ammunition and be used for the amusement of the soldiers at night. Meanwhile the shells continued to rain down.

The commanding officer on the receiving end of the assault was Colonel Taou Lo, another devout Christian. Written on the walls of every bunker in Kawmoora were verses from the Psalms. Each morning and evening the Colonel would encourage his men by reading to them from the Bible. When he could, he would call up grieving relatives on his two-way radio to pray for them and comfort them.[13] Kawmoora was overrun in March 1995, some two months after the fall of Manerplaw.

Arms and oil

Some of the weaponry used against Colonel Taou Lo that night would have been Chinese. China had supplied some $2.5 billion worth of arms to Burma, including fighter planes and heavy tanks in direct contravention of a UN resolution.[14] At an international level, CSI had called for UN action to stop the arms trade. Lord Avebury had called for EU leverage to be brought to bear against China and was pressing for a boycott of all companies doing business with the dictatorship.[15]

While international pressure was growing for economic sanctions against the SLORC regime, Britain had been busily funding a London trade conference on Burma and co-sponsoring a business delegation to Yangôn. Britain's Premier Oil had sunk $30 million in Myanmar and since 1988, 65 per cent of all foreign investment in the country had been provided by the oil companies.[16] Other large businesses were being encouraged by the Department of Trade to follow suit. The British Foreign Minister pronounced himself 'heartened' by the progress made by the SLORC, and told the Commons that increased commercial contacts would expose the regime to 'democratic principles'.[17] Meanwhile Myanmar's democracy leader, Daw Aung San Suu Kyi, was calling for a boycott of Burma by foreign investors and tourists, arguing that the influx of foreign exchange would simply swell the coffers of the SLORC. The very day of her appeal for sanctions, a British official from the Department of Trade and Industry flew to Yangôn to evaluate the commercial prospects for further trading with the SLORC.[18]

Not for the first time, Caroline condemned her own party in the House of Lords. 'It appears incongruous and unprincipled,' she said, 'to be actively promoting trade with a brutal regime, when other countries are trying to put pressure on that regime to desist from its gross violations of human rights.'[19]

Caroline had her allies in the House, judiciously lobbied and briefed beforehand. Labour peers Baroness Blackstone and Lord Rea both called for sanctions. Internationally, Denmark had suggested an export ban and the USA was deliberating action. But the ASEAN states, those closest to Myanmar, were too afraid of surrendering territory to the growing influence of China to follow suit.

Britain had suspended non-humanitarian aid in 1988, imposed an arms embargo in 1991 and severed remaining defence links in 1992, encouraging other like-minded countries to do the same. Its policy, along with that of Europe, was one of 'critical dialogue', rather than isolationism. The government was opposed to a trade embargo, arguing that trade could provide leverage over the SLORC.[20]

The Minister of State Baroness Chalker told Caroline she shared her concern but found no evidence of international support. However, she added, the British government had no intention of supporting further trade missions.[21]

It wasn't much, but it was at least a movement in the right direction. 'Totalitarian and brutal regimes don't like international criticism,' says Caroline, 'so at least a refusal to condone what is happening was something.' It was also an encouragement to the Karen and Karenni.

In a way, it was Caroline Cox, not Martin Panter, who was responsible for CSI's involvement with the Karenni. Their democratically elected President, Catholic and former policeman Plyar Reh, told Dr Panter that he had first stumbled across CSI while reading a Cox speech in *Hansard* on human rights in Burma.[22]

Caroline gave the President more to read about in December. 'What is [Her Majesty's Government's] response to the continuing violations of human rights by the State Law and Order Restoration Council regime in Burma?' she demanded.

'Deeply concerned... condemning violations... we shall continue to put pressure' was the gist of Lord Chesham's reply.

Caroline followed through with her supplementary question: 'What about the suffering of the Karen and Karenni, including "slave labour, torture and massacres"? What is the government doing to raise these matters?'

Back came the reply that over the past four years the government had provided almost £160,000 per annum in humanitarian aid for the Burmese refugees. It was derisory.

Under parliamentary rules, Caroline had no other option but to sit tight and hope others would pick up the issue and run with it. Before her allies could respond, Lord Marsh rose to his feet and drew comfort from some 'small evidence of improvement in the receptiveness of SLORC'. But Baroness Park wasn't having it, 'We have had enough of quiet diplomacy.' Lord Avebury, a long-time champion of human rights went further, calling for a government health warning for all prospective tourists to Myanmar. Lord Chesham demurred, 'My Lords, we have no present plans to discourage tourism to Burma.'[23]

Even now, progress is slow, but the baroness is persistent. 'Caroline will fight her corner,' says Christian Solidarity's UK Chairman, Mervyn Thomas. 'She'll battle away and take every opportunity. She is gutsy and single-minded and will see a thing through right to the end.' For the Karen and Karenni, the end might not be long in coming.

NOTES

1. David Taw, Worldview International Foundation, addressing UN Commission on Human Rights, Geneva, 10 April 1997, UN Press Release HR/CN/798. CSI put the number of refugees at 90,000.

2. 'Situation of Human Rights in Myanmar', Interim Report, 28 October 1994. Confirmed by Freedom House, whose report for Burma, 1994–95 stated, 'In the border areas... soldiers rape women, force villagers to act as human mine-sweepers ahead of troops and compel civilians to act as porters, often until they die of exhaustion or hunger': 'Freedom in the World', 1994–95, p. 165. Freedom House rates countries according to their political freedoms. Burma rates 7 – the lowest rating possible.

3. CSI Report, 5–12 March 1995.

4. *Hansard*, 28 April 1995. In 1995, the Australian government urged the government of Burma to accede to the UN Chemical Weapons Convention, 'Human Rights and Progress Towards Democracy in Burma', The Parliament of the Commonwealth of Australia, Joint Standing Committee on Foreign Affairs, Defence and Trade, October 1995.

5. According to a statement by U Denzil Abel, the Myanmar representative at the UN Commission on Human Rights, Geneva, 10 April 1997.

6. 'Situation on Human Rights in Myanmar', Report of the UN Special Rapporteur, 8 October 1996.

7. CSI Report, 16 January 1996.

8. Amnesty International Country Report, 'Myanmar Kayin (Karen) State: The Killings Continue', April 1996.

9. Asian Tribal Ministries, 29 January 1997.

10. CSI Report, 6–10 February 1995, p. 2.

11. *Asiaweek* estimate. Dr Panter believes the number was up to 800.

12. CSI Report, 6–10 February 1995, pp. 3, 4.

13. CSI Report, 6–10 February 1995; also Dominic Faulder, 'In the Name of Money', *Asiaweek*, 9 May 1997.

14. Human Rights Watch / Asia, puts the figure at $1.4 billion. 'Burma: Entrenchment or Reform', 1995. The Australian government also put pressure on the regime to reduce its arms spending, reminding SLORC 'that the level of arms expenditure is a significant inhibition in the willingness of the international community to resume development assistance', 'Human Rights and Progress Towards Democracy in Burma', p. xxiii.

15. Unstarred question on human rights in Burma, House of Lords, 28 April 1995.

16. *Multinational Monitor*, Washington, 1992. By 1998, Australia, Britain, France, Indonesia, Israel, Japan, Malaysia, Thailand and the United States were clamouring to exploit oil and natural gas resources in twelve areas of the country.

17. John Pilger, 'A Cry for Freedom'.

18. John Pilger, 'The Burmese *Gulag*', *Covert Action Quarterly*, February 1996. Two years later Aung San Suu Kyi said 'Premier Oil is not only supporting the military government financially, it is giving it moral support and doing a great disservice in the name of democracy. Any company that is dealing with a repressive government contributes to repression in country': BBC, 30 March 1998.

19. Unstarred question on Myanmar (Burma) human rights, 28 April 1995.

20. Lord Inglewood, *Hansard*, 28 April 1995.

21. *Hansard*, 7 February 1996.

22. Draft report of CSI visit to the government and church leaders of the Karenni State, 16 January 1996.

23. *Hansard*, 2 December 1996.

THREE

Rearguard Action

Caroline returned to Myanmar on 7 December 1996, five days after addressing the Lords. With her were Dr Panter and a TV reporter. The situation had deteriorated considerably. Many soldiers had abandoned the fight, to cross the border and support their families in the refugee camps of Thailand. While Myanmar was busily promoting its Year of Tourism, a major SLORC offensive was building to drive out the remaining Karen and Karenni.

The Karenni, who made up a tiny minority of the population, had been fighting a rearguard action for their existence since Aung San clinched his treaty with Clement Atlee in 1947. The fact that the Karenni had been a sovereign state for more than a thousand years was somehow sidelined in the scramble to abandon empire. Yet in 1875, Sir Douglas Forsyth, on behalf of the British government had given sovereign rights to the Karenni to occupy their own lands in perpetuity. That treaty was honoured a decade later at the conclusion of the third Anglo-Burmese war.

It was an arrangement that was ignored by the Japanese during their occupation, and another oversight, this time by the Karenni, sealed their fate in 1947. Astonishingly, they remained absent from the concluding of the Panglong Agreement to unify Burma. They did so on the mistaken assumption that their British guarantee of independence excluded Karenni sovereign territory from the arrangement and rendered their attendance irrelevant. On 9 August 1948, the Burmese army marched into their capital, Loikaw, and has occupied sovereign Karenni territory ever since.[1] Britain's betrayal of Burma's ethnic minorities planted the seeds of the next 50 years of conflict.[2]

Almost half a century later, they were still fighting for their survival. Some 80,000 Karenni had already been displaced. Their army was down to 1,700 troops facing 30 battalions of SLORC soldiers in Karenni State.[3] Caroline met their Foreign Minister, Abel Tweed, in exile in Mae Hong Son. This quietly spoken, self-effacing man told her in perfect English that the process of ethnic cleansing was being carried out with systematic brutality and the displaced people were being rounded up and sent to death camps inside Burma. According to evidence given to the UN Commission on Human Rights, between half a million and a million refugees were trapped in the camps.[4] Those who fled to the jungle were dying from disease and starvation. If they were found, they would be killed on sight. Amnesty International described it as a de facto shoot to kill policy.[5] All aid organizations had been barred.

The process, Mr Tweed explained, would begin when the head man of a village received notice that everyone must evacuate within four days. They were to leave behind all their possessions and go to a relocation camp. SLORC troops would move in and attack the village, kill any remaining civilians, and then loot and burn the buildings to make sure no-one would want to return.

Caroline and Dr Panter set off to verify the minister's story. Their first port of call was Paduang village, in Thailand, to meet the 'giraffe neck' people who had been ousted from their homes. The necks of the women were adorned with brass coils, which pushed their collar bones downwards to give them the elongated appearance considered elegant within their culture. These were the long-necked people whose pictures were so prized by tourists responding to the SLORC's 'Visit Myanmar Year' campaign.

The SLORC was banking on a ten-fold increase in foreign visitors for its Year of Tourism. It was the very year which Amnesty International proclaimed 'the worst for human rights in Myanmar since 1990'.[6] But the SLORC were steadily driving away their tourist attractions. The Karenni had been forced to abandon their villages because extortionate taxes had made it impossible to survive. Deprived of their livelihood, at Paduang they were now dependent on income from sightseers who knew nothing of their plight and expected them to pose for snaps. Some Karenni women, it was later revealed, had been abducted by a Thai businessman and held in their refugee camp in a state of slavery, to create a human zoo for Western tourists.[7]

More than 3,500 lived in the refugee camp. Many were recent arrivals. They had been pushed out of Burma as a result of an accommodation between SLORC and the opium warlord Khun Sa, described bluntly by the US State Department as a narco-terrorist. In return for laying down his arms (and some say half a billion US dollars), Khun Sa had negotiated a commitment from the authorities to shield him from the US Drug Enforcement Agency. Confined to his house on Inya Lake, Yangôn, close to General Ne Win, he was allowed to continue to operate business interests based upon wealth accumulated through the heroin trade. And according to the USA, he continued to be involved in narcotics.[8] The accommodation was signed on 6 January 1996. Within a week SLORC troops had moved into the territory vacated by his forces and staged a series of attacks on the Karenni.

Shoot on sight

On 1 June SLORC issued evacuation orders to surrounding villages. Anyone not out by 7 June would be shot on sight. The villagers sent a delegation, pleading to be allowed to stay. It was the season for growing crops, the rain would make travel difficult, there was no school at the relocation camp, and besides, the very young and elderly would never manage to walk the distance. Their requests were met with a blunt refusal. The hasty evacuation got under way, abandoning those too old or too sick to travel. Among them was Paymo. SLORC troops burned her alive in her house in the village of Namay Doso. Everything was put to the torch, including rice-stores. Next, the soldiers slaughtered the livestock and gorged themselves on as much meat as they could eat, before leaving the carcasses to rot in the open. For the next few days, search and kill missions were carried out for the remaining civilians, before moving on to begin the process again at the next village.

Seven days later it was the turn of Buku. Everything was destroyed and the area was mined. When the villagers lit fires in the jungle for food or warmth, SLORC mortar gunners targeted the rising smoke with their 60 millimetre shells.

Saw Hey Noh was lucky. Three days later when troops marched into his village they spared him for use as slave labour. This middle-aged man with lines etched deeply around his eyes explained that he was made to carry loads for the army and to direct them to other Karenni locations. While he was working in the jungle, he saw soldiers murder six of his neighbours, stabbing them to death and throwing their bodies into the Salween River. He risked his life to escape to Thailand.

On 12 July, villagers from Puhokoo village heard the troops coming and fled into the jungle to avoid capture. To make sure the Karenni would never return, mines were laid in the houses: in the kitchens, the doorways and on the window ledges, as well as in the ground. Three villagers who went back to their homes were wounded and one was killed. The rest were too afraid to return and stayed in the jungle, where the troops came to hunt them down. The only alternative to death was Mochi relocation camp. Only it wasn't an alternative. There was little food and no medicine. Three children and a woman quickly died. Others wished they had stayed in the jungle. A number escaped and embarked on a three-week trek into Thailand, under constant threat of discovery by SLORC troops.

It was even worse in the relocation camps. At Pasaung 150 residents were sick. For three days they begged for medication. Eventually, the camp medic gave them injections. Within five days all who passed through his hands were dead.[9] A 30-year-old mother of six described conditions in the notorious Shadow Camp. If anyone asked to be fed they were beaten.[10] Many were dying around her. Disease was rampant, including malaria and TB. Some feared the little food they received had been deliberately contaminated, along with the water supply. Many became seriously ill after eating or drinking. She decided to escape with her children and make the hazardous six-day journey to cross the border. There she remained, with the other Karenni who faced the constant threats of repatriation to the death camps and cross-border shelling by government troops.[11]

Dismayed, Caroline and Dr Panter visited the Karenni President, Plyar Reh, and his Prime Minister, General Aung Than Lei. They were in exile in Camp 5, where the shelters were made of woven straw, patterned like parquet flooring. According to their estimate, there were some 10,000 Karenni in Thailand, up to eight times as many in the relocation camps in Burma, and possibly 50,000 hiding in the jungle or under severe restrictions in their own homes. Seven hundred had died in two SLORC camps in the past six months of disease and hunger.

Rather than be separated in different relocation camps one Christian family had preferred to flee into the jungle and take their chances. Bau La Gu was a 55-year-old widow. Her four children were aged between 10 and 22. They were caught, their hands tied behind their backs, and one by one they were thrown into the village paddy pounder, a foot operated machine to grind rice with a central wooden pestle weighing around 50 kilograms. Their 22-year-old sister looked on as her family was pulverized to death, then the traumatized girl managed to flee. Whether she gave the troops the slip or was allowed to escape *pour encourager les autres*, is not known.

'I have many things to say to you,' said the Karenni Prime Minister, 'but I am afraid you will not believe them, because these kinds of things could never happen in your country.' He spoke of children being hanged from branches and used as target practice, and of a ten-year-old boy and his eleven-year-old sister being tied up and thrown into a fire. All the Karenni wanted, he said, was to go back to their homes and earn their own living.[12]

Heed their cry

Tensions were being deliberately stirred up between Christians and Buddhists. Churches were being destroyed and crosses torn down. To acquire popular legitimacy, the SLORC were flying in the face of their public commitment to freedom of religion and proclaiming that the Karenni State should become Buddhist, the religion of only one in five. Most of the Karenni were Catholic or Baptist. Reports were also emerging of the Christian Naga peoples in the northwest being forced to convert to Buddhism and made to build Buddhist temples at gunpoint.[13]

For many, the war represented the ultimate trial of faith. Merdith Noo Noo, a 52-year-old widow, was a refugee at Nai Soi Camp 3. Her husband had been tortured and shot by SLORC troops, who burned her house to the ground. She was left with five children aged between five and twenty. Dr Panter asked her whether she was bitter about the killing of her husband. She hesitated briefly, then replied, 'Of course, I miss him, but I have to forgive, just as the Lord's Prayer says forgive us our sins as we forgive those who sin against us.'

'We need more help and prayer,' the Karenni President told Dr Panter. 'Ask the governments of England and Australia to help regain our independence. According to our history we are an independent free state, granted by international treaty and 1,000 years of tradition. We pray that God will show us the way to regain our independence and freedom.'[14]

Dr Panter recorded in his notes, 'This is a small Christian nation, suffering tremendous persecution. We fail in our Christian duty to be voice for the oppressed and the voiceless if we do not heed their cry.'

It was not only Christians who came into that category. The same treatment was being meted out to Muslims. Two Indian Muslims had been singled out by SLORC troops for their race and religion and had been forced to eat pork while soldiers joked about Allah in front of them. The Muslims of Arakan State had also faced persecution, and in the refugee camps, animists and Buddhists alike could be found in profusion.[15]

Child soldiers

With only a few days remaining of their fact-finding visit, Caroline and Dr Panter turned their attention again to the Karen. They visited the sprawling Behklow Camp, offering shelter for 25,000 refugees. CSI was supporting an orphanage for 21 children who had lost both parents, and a pastor and staff who were working with others traumatized in the war. It was another token gesture, but it was the only hope for those children in their care. There was a moment of relief and reflection, as the children sang in church a song they had composed themselves:

Thank you God, for brothers and sisters;
Thank you God, for people who care for us
like mothers and fathers.

Other children had found their own way of coming to terms with their trauma. They had taken up arms. Across the border, in Burma, Caroline found Pokalah, a small, black-haired 13-year-old boy with dark circles under his eyes, wearing oversized army fatigues. Pokalah, along with an estimated 2,000 others as young as 12, had signed up with the Karen army. He joined the troops in putting on a show for the TV cameraman; manoeuvring through the jungle behind a thicket of camouflage foliage wedged into the webbing that criss-crossed his army shirt. The Burmese are small anyway, but beside them Pokalah seemed tiny. And unlike the grown-up soldiers around him, his head was bare and unprotected. Hard to imagine much call for helmets his size. Later he sat in the green glow cast by the makeshift plastic roofing and explained: 'SLORC soldiers came to my village and tortured my parents and my family and burned down the village and rice stores. I could not take it any more, and decided to join the KNU soldiers.'

It was the same for 15-year-old Sayramon, who seemed, if anything, even smaller. Sayramon sported a purple baseball cap, with a military pack on his back over a voluminous army jacket rolled up at the cuffs. He had the almond-shaped eyes of the Karen and large red lips. 'I would like to be at school like other children,' he told Caroline, 'but because SLORC soldiers burned down my school the only choice I had was to join the army.' In his lap he cradled an American-made M16 assault rifle.

The boy soldiers were garrisoned in one of the last remaining Karen strongholds. They went out on a reconnaissance for the cameraman, a foray into the jungle to snipe at the SLORC officers who gave the orders to destroy their people. The adult soldiers were turned out in their smartest uniforms with puttees over their boots. Their faces were blacked up with stripes to conceal them in the tall grasses. Their mix of military hardware was culled from the arsenals of the US, SLORC, and who-knows-where, all using different and incompatible types of ammunition. Among their number were boys like Sayramon, and sad-eyed, thin-faced young women in full uniform.

The Karen village had the same air of making the best, come what may.

There was a school and hospital, as well as medical and teacher training colleges. Though how long they would last was anybody's guess. A fortnight earlier, at Kurtu, just two days' walk away, SLORC troops burned down the local church. And in the nearby village of Walea, forces aided by the Karen Buddhist breakaway group attacked and kidnapped six civilians. Reports were coming in of a large build-up of SLORC troops to the south. Karen intelligence put the figure at between 15 to 20,000.

SLORC demanded that the Karen lay down their arms and recognize SLORC as their legitimate government. 'We do not understand the word surrender,' the President of the Karen National Union, General Saw Bo Mya told Caroline. He was speaking at his mobile military headquarters, a cluster of temporary and, necessarily, disposable huts. 'We will always fight for the freedom of our people, otherwise we would just become their slaves.'

What the veteran soldier said next cut straight to the quick:

During the Second World War, like many Karen, I fought for the British against the Japanese. Many Karen soldiers were killed. The British did not give anything in return, but they gave the country to the Burmese who were fighting against them. We are very sad that what we did during the Second World War does not mean anything to the British. That's why we hope the British government reconsiders its position and thinks about the Karen who used to be their brothers in arms.

Mutiny in the ranks

The story of joint military operations between the Karen and the British is one of the stranger tales of the Second World War. It led to a rebellion by members of the British Special Operations Executive (SOE) that resulted in Briton fighting Briton in the jungles of Burma.

The story finally came to light when secret papers were released by the Public Records Office at Kew. It became the subject of a BBC television *Timewatch* documentary.

The SOE was established in 1940 to fight alongside resistance movements in occupied territories. British soldiers joined forces with the Karen to do battle with the Japanese and Aung San's Independence Army. They were known as Force 136 – and General Saw Bo Mya was among them. He and the Karen fought alongside the British on the clear understanding they would be given an independent state once the Japanese were defeated.

But in 1944, Aung San's Burma Independence Army switched sides.

They asked for – and were promised – an independent Burma which would include Kwathoolei, the land of the Karen.

At the end of the Second World War, Britain honoured its pledge to the Burma Independence Army and reneged on its promise to the Karen. A further military mission was despatched to Rangoon, this time to put down the rebellious Karen. Appalled by their country's shifting loyalties, former members of Force 136 ignored directives disbanding the Special Operations Executive and stayed on to fight with the Karen, only now their joint enemy was the British Army. Their leader was Lieutenant Colonel Cromarty Tulloch, a former commander of Force 136.

The Daily Mail reporter Alexander Campbell had also been a member of Force 136. Under the guise of foreign correspondent, he became their go-between. Campbell was supported by the *Mail*'s editor, Frank Owen, who had also fought in the Far East during the war. Owen apparently allowed the Karen to set up their London headquarters in the *Mail* building, and injudiciously raised the Karen flag, where it was spotted by the paper's proprietor, Lord Rothermere. Owen's demise from the *Mail* quickly followed.

An unrepentant Campbell explained his actions to the BBC, 'We were ordered to tell the Karen chiefs that if they would fight with us we would guarantee their independence. We just told them a bloody lie.'

Had Britain kept its word to the Karen they would probably not be fighting today. As it is, they have been fighting ever since.

'The Karen had just become an embarrassment,' said Dr Richard Aldrich, the academic who uncovered the wartime papers.[16]

Britain's wartime obligation to the Karen was a point that Caroline and others raised repeatedly in the House of Lords. 'I cannot agree that it would be anything but right for us to support the Karen who were our friends and comrades in a dangerous and difficult war,' urged Baroness Park of Monmouth.[17] The Earl of Cork and Orrery had actually fought with the Karen in the Burma Rifles and was wearing his medal – the Star of Burma. 'Their particular genius in wartime,' he said, in a debate initiated by Caroline, 'stemmed from the expertise that is natural to people who lived in the jungle. They were spies, information carriers and scouts. They were enormously brave and absolutely invaluable... General Wingate... himself said they were the finest body of soldiers he had led. That is a remarkable tribute from such a man... They are devoted to us. Can we not do something for them now?'[18]

But overriding any question of loyalty, it seemed, as ever, was the mighty petrodollar.

NOTES

1. CSI Report, 10–17 May 1997.
2. CSI Report, 16 January 1996; *Funk and Wagnall's Encyclopedia*, 1995.
3. The Karen National Union was little stronger. In 1994, it had an estimated 3,500 men at arms: 'Human Rights and Progress Towards Democracy in Burma', The Parliament of the Commonwealth of Australia, Joint Standing Committee on Foreign Affairs, Defence and Trade, October 1995, p. 44.
4. Evidence given by the National Coalition Government of the Union of Burma to the 51st Session of the UNCHR, Geneva, 20 February 1995, p. 8.
5. 'Myanmar Kayin (Karen) State: The Killings Continue', Amnesty International Country Report, April 1996.
6. *Asiaweek*, 16 June 1995 and 'Myanmar: 1996 Worst Year for Human Rights this Decade', Amnesty International, 12 February 1997.
7. Enver Solomon, '"Amazing Thailand" offers human zoo', BBC News, 16 January 1998.
8. 'International Narcotics Control Strategy Report: Burma', US State Department, February 1997, pp. 249–56.
9. CSI Report, 10–17 May 1997.
10. Supported by UN Special Rapporteur in 'Situation of Human Rights in Myanmar', 8 October 1996, para. 122.
11. The repatriation was opposed by the Worldview International Foundation, which called on the Thai authorities to move the refugee camps deeper into Thailand, at UN Commission on Human Rights in Geneva, 10 April 1997.
12. CSI Report, 10–17 May 1997.
13. 'Christians Forced to Convert to Buddhism in Myanmar', *Compass Direct*, 8 April 1997. Inflammatory leaflets denouncing Christian practices and beliefs were circulated around the Karen region: 'Human Rights and Progress Towards Democracy in Burma', p. 20.
14. CSI Report, 12–21 April 1996.
15. CSI Report, 10–17 May 1997; 'ASEAN Should Press for Human Rights Improvements', Human Rights Watch / Burma, 18 July 1996.
16. BBC *Timewatch*, 2 April 1997; 'Why Briton Fought Briton in Burma', *The Daily Telegraph*, 31 March 1997.
17. Burma: Human Rights, 2 December 1996.
18. Unstarred question on human rights in Burma, 28 April 1995. In February 1998, after a fact-finding visit to the Karen refugees, Lord Alton called for a war crimes tribunal to be set up to investigate atrocities committed by the Burmese junta. He added: 'The British government has repeatedly betrayed our former wartime allies, the Karen people. Now is the time to make amends. Britain should lead the way in securing tough world-wide economic sanctions. It is the international community's willingness to trade with Burma which strengthens the regime, enabling them to have money to buy weapons of destruction which they then use in their acts of genocide against the Karen people and ethnic minorities': 'Lord Alton interviews refugees on Thai-Burma border', Jubilee Campaign, 25 February 1998.

FOUR

Petrodollars

The French company Total and its US partner Unocal had signed a billion-dollar scheme for a pipeline to carry natural gas from an offshore field in the Andaman Sea to a new power station 270 kilometres inside Thailand. The deal, described by *Asiaweek* as the region's most controversial infrastructure project, represented a third of all foreign investment in the country. It would guarantee an annual income for the SLORC regime of between $200 and $400 million.[1] The pipeline was to run through Karen and Mon territory without consultation. It resulted in the forced relocation of up to 30,000 villagers, many of whom were made to burn their own homes and clear their own land.[2] Unocal claimed to have visited the area and found no evidence of abuses of human rights. The commander of the Karen National Union was calling for a complete pull-out by Total and Unocal from Burma. 'The pipelines they have built,' he said, 'are built with the forced labour of our people.'

The UN Special Rapporteur cited 'numerous reports from a wide variety of sources' that forced labour was being employed to build 'roads, railway bridges and gas pipelines'.[3] The National League for Democracy claimed extensive evidence of slave labour along the route of the pipeline. But according to the US oil company, Unocal, the claim was a 'fabrication'.

A lawsuit was brought against Unocal by Burmese politicians in exile, accusing the California-based company of complicity in human rights abuses. Unocal faced 19 charges including crimes against humanity, torture and wrongful death. The case would hinge on proof of 'vicarious liability' – guilt by association.[4] Unocal rebutted the charges as 'false, irresponsible and frivolous'. A political campaign was launched to force the company to pull out of the project.[5] If we did, came the reply, then companies across the Pacific rim would fight to take our place. To circumvent forthcoming US sanctions Unocal opened a 'twin corporate headquarters' in Malaysia.[6]

Meanwhile Unocal's French partner, Total, confirmed construction work on the pipeline would continue.[7] The Methodist Church in Britain and the USA promptly sold off its investments in Total[8] and human rights campaigner, Lord Avebury, called on the European Union to take legal action against the oil company.[9]

Burn the camps

Next to Myanmar, the country which stood to profit most from the pipeline was Thailand, for whom the gas was intended, and whose policies towards the refugees were being questioned. In 1993, the *Bangkok Nation* accused Thailand of burning down two refugee camps for reasons 'probably related to the gas pipeline'.[10] CSI's Dr Martin Panter believed the burning may have been encouraged or even orchestrated to compel Karen refugees to return to SLORC territory.

Thailand had made it clear that UNHCR and foreign agencies were not welcome in the camps. Now it was making the same message increasingly plain to the refugees themselves, though where else could they go? Most camps had fewer than ten Thai soldiers for security, who were allegedly under orders to evacuate if attacked. When requests for reinforcements were made, none were forthcoming. Nothing seemed to be done to stop the raids on the camps, which were located close enough to the border to offer an open invitation.

When the fire alarm sounded at Ta Per Po Camp at 1.30 one April morning in 1997, it was as though a signal had been given for the Thai militia to melt into the darkness. The guards departed promptly, to reappear only the following morning after a third of the shelters for the 2,275 refugees had been burned to the ground. According to witnesses, the Thai soldiers then proceeded to demolish any vacated buildings.[11]

Later, SLORC troops set fire to the Huay Kalok Camp, leaving its 5,000 inhabitants nowhere to live but among its ashes. To get to the camp, the SLORC troops had to pass through a Thai military checkpoint. It was mysteriously unmanned on the day of the attack, and manned again the day after.

'If anything,' Dr Panter recorded in his CSI report, 'it appears that the Thai army high command wanted the camps to burn. [The] local army commander... has often made it clear that he thinks all Karen refugees should be forcibly repatriated as soon as possible, and the burning of the camps seems to bring that day closer.'[12]

In 1995, the Australian government openly accused Thai officials of bringing pressure to bear on refugee groups in the vicinity of the pipeline.[13] Australian investigative journalist John Pilger went further, stating it was a requirement of the pipeline deal that the Thai military sent back refugees who crossed the border.[14] Many had already been forced to return to SLORC territory. After questions were raised at the UN, the Thai government reported it had taken steps to site refugee camps further away from the frontier to improve security.[15] Yet still the camps kept burning, as the economic links between Thailand and Burma grew ever closer.

In December 1997, Thailand expressed concern over rising unemployment and what it called 'economic migrants' flooding across its border. The two countries agreed to form a working party to deal with the problem of 'illegal Burmese labour and overflowing refugee camps'. The *Bangkok Post* reported: 'Thailand wants to send the refugees back to Burma.'[16]

Dr Panter set out to investigate claims that the Thai military had been shelling refugees and had executed several who refused to move on. His access to the camp in question was barred by Thai border guards. They even refused to allow him to give medical treatment to one of the wounded who had been shot in the stomach. The refugee subsequently died. The Thai Commander in Chief said later at a press conference: 'Thailand has a legitimate right to protect the country against intruders. In this case, we had the right to destroy them.'

When Dr Panter finally managed to get through to Karen refugees at another camp, he was presented with a painting by a nine-year-old boy which said it all. The child had drawn his village in Burma. It was burning, and his family was attempting to cross the river Moei into Thailand with all their belongings. 'As they cross,' said Dr Panter, 'Thai soldiers with fixed bayonets, point their weapons at them.'[17]

In Wang Ka Camp, Major Mary On was taking things philosophically. The numbers there had swollen to 9,000 refugees. It, too, had been almost destroyed by fire. 'The Lord has given us a bitter cup to drink,' said Mary, 'But we must drink it. We pray the Lord will have mercy on us and shorten our suffering.'

The Golden Triangle

Aside from fossil fuels, there was even bigger money to be made in Burma. In the Golden Triangle, which included Thailand and Laos, Myanmar was the most gilded corner – the world's number one supplier of heroin.[18] Its fields of opium poppies met 60 per cent of the global market and produced enough narcotics to satisfy the cravings of the USA many times over.[19] It had become the USA's primary supplier.

According to the Karen National Union, the peace talks had broken down because they refused to assist SLORC in the trade in heroin. They claimed other ethnic groups, which had made accommodations with the SLORC, had received concessions for trafficking opium to the military.[20] Former members of the Communist Party had set themselves up as warlords in the northern provinces then brokered deals with the SLORC to let them keep their arms and their areas of cultivation and control.

Distribution networks fed the drugs into China, Taiwan, Singapore, India, Bangladesh, Nepal, the USA, Europe and Australia. And along with the intravenous use of heroin came AIDS. Since the SLORC seized power, levels of drug addiction in neighbouring China had increased seven-fold, especially on the border, and most of China's AIDS cases were clustered next to Burma. Drug addiction in the Indian state of Manipur, adjoining Burma, had soared from 600 cases in 1988 to 40,000 leaving the province with the worst AIDS epidemic in the sub-continent.[21]

'The drugs trade corrupts every government and every region it touches,' said a report by the Australian Parliament.[22] According to the Pacific News Service, the deals with the drug barons had created a virtual partnership with the SLORC regime.[23]

At a local level, bribery ensured officials turned a blind eye to their activities. Witnesses said opium was warehoused at Burmese military bases and narcotics convoys were escorted by military vehicles to avoid inspection. Senior officers were amassing substantial personal fortunes. At a national level some believed SLORC was being bankrolled by the drugs warlords. An Australian government report noted the following:

> There is a curious discrepancy in Burma's national accounts. The IMF estimates of Burma's foreign exchange reserves for 1991 were $US310 million; however they showed no decline in 1992–93 despite a trade deficit of $US406 million and a current account deficit of $US112.7. Moreover, Burma has purchased arms to the value of $US1.2 billion in this period.[24]

The US State Department said a tidal wave of laundered drugs profits was flooding the Burmese economy: 'Drug traffickers and their families are among the leading backers of high-profile infrastructure projects in Burma.'[25] *The Thailand Times* claimed half the economy was driven by drugs money.[26] And a report by Southeast Asian Information Network said heroin refineries were located near military bases, and drugs dealers, traffickers and users acknowledged the involvement of the military in heroin distribution.

According to François Casanier, of the Paris-based Geopolitical Drugwatch, 'No drug operation in Burma can be run without the SLORC.' Casanier concluded that the Myanmar Oil and Gas Enterprise (MOGE) was 'the main channel for laundering the revenues of heroin produced under the control of the Burmese army'.[27]

It made things even steamier for the US oil company Unocal, whose major partner was MOGE. Robert Wages, the President of the Oil, Chemical and Atomic Workers International Union (OCAW), rounded on the company. If Unocal knew about MOGE's alleged involvement in the drugs trade, he argued, then the oil giant would have to bear a measure of responsibility for the rise in heroin use in the US.[28] Unocal described the charges as 'false and outrageous... An insult to think we'd involve ourselves in the drug trade.'[29]

'Climate of fear'

Caroline set about producing her report, as usual, in a marathon session on the final evening of her visit. Electricity had yet to reach this neck of the jungle so, instead of pounding away at her Apple laptop, she had to handwrite her missive by candlelight. The wooden houses were built on stilts to keep out the creatures of the jungle. A visit to the nearby privy showed why. It was swarming with rats; a tangle of white tails in the half-light.

Her report concluded: 'SLORC may soon succeed in their apparent intention to achieve the ethnic cleansing of the Karen and Karenni from their own lands... there is an urgent need to stem these developments before it is too late, and these peoples become entirely dispossessed.'[30]

She continued writing well into the night, while all around her slumped from sheer exhaustion. The infuriating thing was that everybody knew she would be the first to rise in the morning, as maddeningly bright and cheerful as ever.

Dr Panter later described her as a role model for his own work with the Karen. 'What impressed me,' he said, 'was the graciousness, kindness and respect she had for the simplest, the poorest and most wretched of the refugees. She spoke to them with love and compassion and always asked their permission before getting their story or taking their photographs. Her speeches in the House of Lords and robust defence of their rights has had a powerful effect on promoting spirit and hope among the Karen and Karenni, who have been greatly helped and supported by Caroline's unceasing efforts to be an advocate and a voice for them.'

Caroline's contribution was summed up by Philip Ambler of the British-based Karen Relief and Development Fund: 'She is a champion of many of the oppressed peoples in the world,' he wrote. 'It is through people like her that pressure is brought to bear upon our government to, in turn, put pressure on Burma.'

That was exactly what Caroline set out to do.

Her words echoed those of the new UN Special Rapporteur to Myanmar, Judge Rajsoomer Lallah, who had just submitted a report of his own. 'People live', he wrote, 'in a climate of fear.'[31]

It took Myanmar's Permanent Representative to the United Nations 19 days to respond to the charge. 'Since independence in 1948,' he said, 'Myanmar has never experienced such peace and stability in its modern history…'[32]

Crock of gold

Myanmar's Year of Tourism fell well short of being the crock of gold that SLORC intended but, according to Reuters, foreign investment in the country quadrupled within a year. More than a third of that was in petroleum and natural gas.[33] But the tide of international opinion was beginning to turn.

Moves to block trade with Burma gathered momentum. In a May 1997 statement condemning attacks against the Karen, President Clinton banned any further US investment in Burma. Some campaigners were disappointed the sanctions were not retroactive. It meant the controversial Unocal pipeline could still go ahead.

Other companies had begun to pull out in response to consumer protests. The Danish brewers Carlsberg had been the first to quit, abandoning plans for a £30m bottling plant. Now an organized consumer boycott in the US, led by Christians and students, prompted Pepsi, Mobil and Levi Strauss to follow suit, with Levi explaining it was impossible to do business in Burma without 'directly supporting the military government and its pervasive violation of human rights'.[34] Twenty-two states and cities went on to pass laws prohibiting companies that traded with Burma from tendering for contracts.

Then in November 1998, a state judge declared a ban by Massachusetts to be unconstitutional. That didn't stop Los Angeles imposing its own Burma trade ban almost immediately. A council spokesman declared the 'fruit of oppression is unfit for our consumption'. Los Angeles was the home of the oil company Unocal, which immediately declared the ban 'counterproductive and unconstitutional'.

Meanwhile, Caroline had raised the plight of the Karen with Britain's new Labour government, which had pledged to take an ethical stand on foreign policy, and urged them not to heed the 'many siren voices' representing business.[35] Labour took note of the Tory peer and cut off financial support for trade missions and promotions within Burma. In the Commons, Britain's new Foreign Secretary, Robin Cook, described the Burmese government as one of the few 'in the world whose members are prepared to profit out of the drugs trade, rather than seek to suppress [it]'.[36] Britain went on to play a leading role in persuading the European Union to tighten sanctions against Burma, earning British ministers a ban from visiting the country.

The UN Special Rapporteur again condemned Myanmar's record on human rights, backed up by Article XIX; the International Peace Bureau and the governments of Japan and Australia. Freedom House added Myanmar to its list of the world's most repressive regimes.[37]

Not before time, SLORC began to realize it had an image problem. In November 1998, at the suggestion of its Washington PR firm, the Orwellian-sounding State Law and Order Restoration Council was no more. It was dissolved in a government reshuffle to be replaced by the altogether chirpier-sounding State Peace and Development Council. But, as Lord Avebury observed: 'Unlike the rose, this regime has a nasty smell, whatever name it chooses to use.'[38]

The upheaval was ostensibly to iron out corruption, though observers pointed to a rift within the ruling party. Several senior figures were investigated for alleged involvement in the narcotics trade. The former minister of commerce threatened to retaliate by naming members of the regime with drugs connections. In the end, despite the makeover, the top leadership of the junta remained the same.[39]

Myanmar by now had been welcomed unanimously into ASEAN, the Association of South East Asian Nations. The USA opposed the move and Amnesty International called on ASEAN to halt human rights violations by Burma.[40]

It was against ASEAN protocol to criticize the internal affairs of member countries. But cracks began to appear in that united front after Aung San Suu Kyi was forcibly prevented from travelling outside Rangoon. Troops barred her way, leaving her to swelter in her vehicle for a week under the full glare of media attention. Thai and Filipino delegates to ASEAN were furious. Anger grew as the regime continued to arrest opposition members and force them to resign from the NLD. Suu Kyi began legal action against the government and the government in turn deliberated whether to arrest Suu Kyi for contacting illegal groups, including Karen guerrillas.

While the world was slowly waking up to what was happening to Burma's minorities, a fresh offensive had been launched by the Tatmadaw along the mountainous eastern frontier with Thailand. They attacked the Karen on up to six fronts, driving out their 4th and 6th Brigades, burning rice barns and displacing a further 20,000 civilians.[41]

'It would seem ironic', observed Dr Panter, 'that when any species of flora or fauna is threatened with extinction, governments around the world are quick to take action. Presently, we face the destruction of an entire nation.'[42]

KNU forces retained little of their own territory. At their peak, the Karen had boasted a fighting force of 20,000. But as the 50th anniversary of their struggle for freedom approached in 1999, just 400 fighters gathered in the jungle of eastern Burma to hear the presidential address of Saw Bo Mya. Together they vowed never to surrender the fight against the Myanmar military junta. They had formed an alliance with another beleaguered ethnic minority, the Shan. But they would have their work cut out. According to Thai military intelligence, Myanmar was building up for a major offensive – designed to drive every remaining resurgent from its borders.

As for the Karenni, Caroline warned the Lords: 'In Karenni state, troops have almost completely accomplished ethnic cleansing.' The British government declared itself 'appalled by the plight of Burma's ethnic minorities' and promised to use its EU presidency to bring further 'punitive measures against the regime'.

Caroline's verdict on new Labour's ethical foreign policy? 'I would like to see more of it in practice. The words are good, but I am not sure we have seen a fundamental sea change. Much of the attention has been focusing on Aung San Suu Kyi and the democratic opposition in Rangoon to the exclusion of the ethnic minorities. I would like to see more done for them.'

So Caroline took to the streets in demonstration with the Burma Action Group, author Salman Rushdie and playwright Harold Pinter. Together they presented a petition to 10 Downing Street, though Caroline's was the only voice at the demonstration to speak up for the ethnic minorities.

In April 1998, Caroline and Dr Martin Panter travelled again to Burma. They wrote: 'The plight of the Karenni is even worse. Twelve thousand are in border camps in Thailand. The remainder, some 200–250,000, are living in fear and danger in Karenni State.'

The relocation camps were still little more than places of lingering death.

The only choice facing the Karenni was how they would die. Anyone found escaping would be killed on the spot. Those who made it to Thailand were trapped in the border camps where death came by night in the raids of the DKBA.

They visited Wang Ka camp on the Thai border, where children played in the blackened embers of their home amid fragments of broken pottery, all that remained after the DKBA attack a fortnight earlier. At Mae La camp, a Muslim mullah reminded Christian Solidarity that his people also faced persecution. The policy of the junta, he said, was to divide one religious group against another.

Thirty-eight-year-old MaSu was nursing an injury from the shrapnel which had destroyed her fragile home. What she wanted above all else was to be allowed to leave the camp and go somewhere safer. But the Thai government had resisted all pleas to relocate the refugees further from the border. Caroline and Dr Panter asked MaSu about her attackers. She replied simply: 'I have no hate for them. I love them, because I am a Christian. The Bible tells us to love our enemies, so I love them and forgive the soldier who shot me.'[43]

NOTES

1. Dominic Faulder, 'In the name of money', *Asiaweek*, 9 May 1997; also *Covert Action Quarterly*, Fall 1996.
2. 'Human Rights and Progress Towards Democracy in Burma', The Parliament of the Commonwealth of Australia, Joint Standing Committee on Foreign Affairs, Defence and Trade, October 1995, p. 32; also International Labour Organization.
3. 'Situation on Human Rights in Myanmar', UN, 8 October 1996, para. 132.
4. Dominic Faulder, 'In the name of money'.
5. *Bangkok Post*, 4 April 1997.
6. *Asiaweek*, 9 May 1997.
7. *New Internationalist*.
8. A London spokesman for the Methodists explained, 'We are particularly concerned by allegations of the use of forced labour to clear the route of the gas pipeline', 'Methodists sell Total stake over Burma link', *The Daily Telegraph*, 2 June 1997.
9. During a debate on human rights in Burma initiated by Caroline Cox, 23 June 1997.
10. *New Internationalist*.
11. The burning took place on 24 April 1997, CSI Report, 10–17 May 1997.
12. Draft report of CSI visit to Thai-Burmese border, 12 November 1995.
13. 'Human Rights and Progress Towards Democracy in Burma', p. 86.
14. John Pilger, 'The Burmese Gulag', *Covert Action Quarterly*, Fall 1996. In 1997, there may have been a change of policy. Dr Panter reported that Burma would only accept ethnically Burman refugees back into the country – that represented just 1 per cent of the refugee population, CSI Report, 10–17 May 1997.
15. Statement in exercise of the right to reply by the delegation of Thailand to the 53rd Session.
16. 'New working group formed', 9 December 1997.
17. Report of visit to the Thai-Burmese Border, CSI Australia, 16–26 November 1997.
18. According to the US State Department, 90 per cent of the opium production of the Golden Triangle was sourced in Burma: Agence France Presse, 25 November 1996.
19. 'International Narcotics Control Strategy Report: Burma', US State Department, February 1997.
20. Alex Buchan, 'Myanmar's Karen Christians face slaughter for refusal to traffic drugs', *Compass*, 21 March 1997.

21. Dennis Bernstein and Leslie Kean, 'Hooked on heroin: the great SLORC Narco-Dictatorship and the world pays the price', *The Boston Globe*, 14 April 1997.

22. 'Human Rights and Progress Towards Democracy in Burma', pp. 45, 46.

23. Dennis Bernstein and Leslie Kean, 'Burma's dictatorship of drugs', Pacific News Service, 24 January 1997.

24. 'Human Rights and Progress Towards Democracy in Burma', p. 46.

25. Dennis Bernstein and Leslie Kean, 'Unocal Accused in Federal Court of Burma Narco-Traffic', *San Francisco Bay Guardian*, 23 April 1997.

26. 'Burma's military rulers live off opium', *The Thailand Times*, 2 May 1997.

27. Bernstein and Kean, 'Burma's dictatorship of drugs'.

28. 'Unocal's link to Burma drug laundering investigation call by Energy Workers' Union President', PR Newswire, 14 March 1997.

29. CSI Report, 10–17 May 1997.

30. CSI Report, 14 December 1996.

31. He observed, 'Violations of human rights remain extremely serious, including... torture... forced labour... and the imposition of oppressive measures directed, in particular, at ethnic and religious minority groups'. He related the account of a 20-year-old Karen from Bawgali village, who was made to join the infantry as a porter: 'Carrying dried rations and mortar shells, he allegedly had to go in front of the troops in order to detect possible mines. He reportedly stepped on a landmine and was seriously wounded, was left behind by the solders, and later died from his injuries': 'Situation of Human Rights in Myanmar'.

32. Letter dated 27 October 1996 from the Permanent Representative of Myanmar to the United Nations, addressed to the Secretary General.

33. Reuters, 4 April 1997.

34. Susan Peek, 'Oil companies' venture in Myanmar challenged by Methodists on both sides of Atlantic', United Methodist News Service, 29 May 1997.

35. *Hansard*, 15 May 1997, column 97f.

36. 'Burma: Human Rights', House of Lords, 23 June 1997; 'Malaysia hits back after Cook attack on Burma', *The Daily Telegraph*, 3 September 1997.

37. UN Commission on Human Rights, 9 and 10 April 1997, UN Press Releases HR/CN/796 and HR/CN/798, 10 and 14 April 1997.

38. Unstarred question on Burma and Sudan, 11 December 1997.

39. *Asiaweek*, 19 and 26 December 1997.

40. Reuters, 27 July 1997; *The Daily Telegraph*, 28 July 1997. ASEAN's own brief country profile of Myanmar, which omitted any reference to either the heroin trade or forced labour, concluded with the following: 'Religious intolerance or discrimination on grounds of religion is non-existence [sic] in the Union of Myanmar throughout its long history': 'An Overview of Union of Myanmar', www.asean.or.id/cv/cp-mya.htm

41. Agence France Presse, 4 April 1997; *The Observer*, 23 February 1997.

42. CSI Reports, 7–13 December 1996 and 10–17 May 1997.

43. Report of Christian Solidarity Australia and Christian Solidarity Worldwide mission to Karen and Karenni people, 31 March – 3 April 1998.

Part Four

Sudan

'There are two key elements to the story
of slavery in the 20th century. One is that it
exists at all. The other is what I call
the scandal of silence – the fact that people
don't want to even acknowledge
that it exists.'

Charles Jacobs, Research Director,
American Anti-Slavery Group[1]

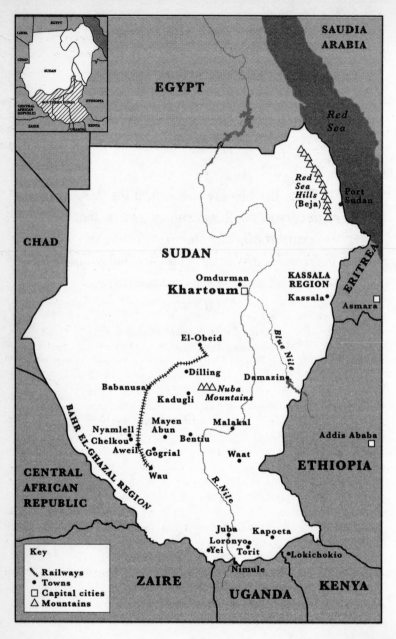

ONE

The Pounding of Hooves

25 March 1995, Nyamlell,
Aweil West County, Southern Sudan

Abuk Marou Keer has much to contend with this morning. As well as her own two children, her sister's pair are in the home, getting under her feet. Fortunately, her mother is with her to help keep order. Abuk is 25, a gentle-faced, attractive Dinka of the blackest hue, with twin rows of beads around her neck and her hair closely braided against her scalp. Later there will be sorghum to grind, but first she must deal with these children...

Outside, women balancing water pots on their heads walk with an indolent swing of the hips that could almost have come from the catwalk. An old man chides his unwilling donkey, and a youth clatters by on a bicycle, pursued by swirling red eddies of dust. A boy stokes a cooking fire, patting out a rhythm on skin-covered pots like bongos which pump air through pipes into the heart of the flames. A woman tosses bread like a pancake, on a large, flat circular dish. Others sit and weave straw.

Akuol Maroor is sweeping out the compound at German Agro-Action, the distribution centre for tools and farming implements. He is also 25. Watching him as he works is his one-year-old son, Athem. Agro-Action is one of the more substantial brick buildings in Nyamlell. More imposing still is the government residence, which overlooks a bend in the River Lol, a tributary of the White Nile. From its veranda, fishermen can be seen keeping a wary eye out for crocodiles as they wade across the blue-green horseshoe to throw out their nets. Others balance like acrobats in dug-out canoes, as they stand to fling their nets, while children plunge wicker pots into the shallows, hoping to trap a lazy fish.

The Roman Catholic Church is another of Nyamlell's fine buildings – or was. The thriving mission had been a prime target for the Arab militia since the 1960s. A decade ago, when the *murahaleen* occupied the town, they turned their mortar on the church and scored a direct hit. Now the corrugated iron roof is holed and shrapnel pock-marks the plaster walls. Still they gather to worship there, dressed in vibrant reds and greens, their hands lifted up, the rhythm clanged out on a makeshift metal bell.

Thanks to famine and war, Nyamlell is not what it used to be. It was once a thriving administrative centre – prosperous, by southern Sudanese standards; no roads, no electricity, no running water not withstanding. Nyamlell's principal asset was its sprawling population of some 100,000, drawn to the lush and fertile ground rimming the river. The River Lol fed the dusty red soil and the people with its fish. Homes for the tall, black Dinka were circular tukuls of sun-baked mud with conical thatched roofs, dotted around seemingly at random with no clear boundaries between them. Living, laughing, cooking and eating was a communal experience, under the trees. There was a market, a clinic and schools. A number of non-governmental organizations had bases in the town to ease the burden of famine, which had swept the region in 1988.

A quarter of a million died of hunger in the counties of Aweil East and West alone. Adding to their troubles was a civil war that had sputtered on since 1955 and had taken a turn for the worst. Nyamlell, blessed by its proximity to the river, was cursed by being too close to the military train. Twice a year, the train inched its way between El-Obeid and Wau along rickety tracks, accompanied by up to a thousand armed militia from the Arab Rizeigat and Misseriya tribes. The strategically important railway passed just 14 miles from Nyamlell, little more than an hour away on horseback. The train was painfully slow, giving the militia plenty of opportunity to flex its might against real or imagined opposition. It had undertaken to clear the area east and west of the railway line every year since 1992.[2] The danger for the local people – the Dinkas – was greatest during the dry season, when the ground was firmer for the horses.

For years there had been an accommodation between the Dinka, the largest black African group in Sudan, and the Arabs. Their Arab neighbours had been free to graze their cattle on Dinka savannah, and would bring their salt, sugar and brightly coloured clothing to trade at the open-air market. Arab and Dinka had generally lived in peace and mutual dependence; Muslim, Christian and animist side by side. But now the Arabs were being armed by the government and stirred up to wage holy war – *jihad* –against the infidel. They were not paid for so doing but, by way of inducement, whatever they could take they were permitted to keep. Ancient tribal rivalries were being rekindled, sanctioned by religious fervour and stoked by greed.

War is unpredictable, but life must go on. The grinding of the sorghum is like the rhythm of life: lift the pole and swing it down; lift and swing. Sometimes two work together, pounding sorghum in a single bucket. They keep rhythm like an engine: up goes one pole, down goes the other; up goes that pole, down goes the first. When there is not famine, there will be sorghum to grind; ground nuts to be harvested; goats and cattle to tend, and children, always children, to feed and to rear. Akuil Garang has her three to look after, while the four grown sons of 50-year-old Akuac Amet are looking after the cattle. Akuak's 14-year-old daughter Ajak, is occupied with duties of her own. The pounding of the sorghum sends its reassuring message through the ground.

But now there is another pounding: the pounding of hooves, the hooves of many horses. Now gunfire, and cries. Above the cries, urgent shouting in Arabic, getting closer. There is dust in the air. Frantically, Abuk's mother tries to hide their belongings, but the gesture is futile and before it is too late they all begin to run towards the river. But Abuk sprawls over a stool and falls. They are separated. Mother has the children, perhaps they will be safe. Abuk lies in the darkness that she has known for five years, since the river blindness stole her sight, and remains as still as can be, not daring to move, willing her children to escape, hoping that she will be overlooked. Then a fist closes around the rows of white beads around her neck, yanks them hard, and hauls her to her feet.

The gatekeeper at Agro-Action has been shot in the shoulder, but is running. Four women and a man in the compound are dead on the ground. Akuol Maroor has scooped up his son, Athem, and is running; running with the others towards the river, followed by the pounding of hooves.

A new sound fills the air, along with smoke and the smell of burning. Akuil's hut is on fire. She and two of her small children are trapped inside. What can she do? The militia are all around. She tries to run, but a knife flashes down, then a spear sends her reeling, then there is the noise of a gun.

Fifty-year-old Akuac Amet lost her husband in the great famine. Now the raiders are trying to take her 14-year-old daughter. She will not let them. The club swings up and down, up and down. Every possession in her tukul is seized, along with 14-year-old Ajak. With 281 others, Ajak is abducted and taken north – into slavery.

'God knows if we shall live'

Nyamlell was neither the first, nor the last township to be overwhelmed by the Arab militia. As well as the stirrings of a holy war, against the South, millions were being displaced and forcibly relocated to ramshackle camps. Reports were emerging that hunger was being used as an instrument of conversion, that food aid was being given on condition that recipients would turn to Islam.

In 1992, a radio message crackled out from Akobo on the Ethiopian border. The speaker described the slow deaths of southern Sudanese by starvation, as a result of a government ban on relief flights. 'God knows whether we shall live until next week,' said the voice. 'The situation is desperate. People are left to starve. Twenty-three starved yesterday... everybody is weak and waiting to die... We don't know if we will be on the radio next week. It depends on God's will... let the world know.'

The message was followed by an urgent appeal from the Catholic bishops in Lusaka. It was a warning of genocide, a plea to remember the forgotten churches of Sudan.

CSI was one of the first to respond to their request. Sudan was Caroline's old stomping ground. It was inevitable that she should accompany the CSI mission to that country. The rainy season was at its height when her Cessna tried to land at Akobo. The runway was more swamp than airfield. It was awash in mud. The pilot, looking dubious, tried a dry run that proved to be anything but. As the wheels touched down, mud splattered up and over the wings, and he swiftly pulled on the controls and took to the air again. The previous pilot who had tried to land at the same airstrip had crashed the plane. Reluctantly, he abandoned the landing and turned around, heading instead for Waat, where people were living in quagmires, dying of starvation and disease.

Landing at Waat was one thing. Taking off again was another. The runway was partially waterlogged, and not enough of the landing strip was clear to give the pilot a straight run. He would have to build up speed on a curve and then hit the throttles to lift the nose, before it could plough into the swamp that once passed for the runway. It would be touch and go. The pilot paced it out, marking his course with handkerchiefs and sheets of white paper. If the plane was not in the air by the time it reached the last post with a handkerchief tied around it, he would have to abort the take-off. All eyes were on that handkerchief, which fluttered beneath them as their wheels lifted off.

Conditions elsewhere were almost as desperate. At Aswa and Atepe refugee camps, north of Nimule near the Ugandan border, 42,000 people were living in the open or under plastic sheeting, with little by way of medicine. TB, dysentery and worm infestations were rampant. The weekly food ration was 2.7 kilograms of unground cereal per person. There were no implements to grind the cereal and no buckets to carry water. Getting fresh water meant a muddy trek of up to three kilometres to the river. Shortly before Caroline arrived, nine children and adults, desperate to slake their thirst, had been eaten by crocodiles.

Suddenly, the catalogue of misery was interrupted by the sound of singing. It seemed to be coming from three different directions. Huge processions were making their way from different parts of the camp. The three main Christian communities, Roman Catholic, Episcopalian and Presbyterian, had heard that CSI had arrived, and were gathering for worship. Many were dressed in rags, carrying thin African crosses made of reeds, and banners and flags saved from their churches, as government forces from the North overran their towns.

They gathered in a huge circle around the tiny CSI contingent, singing psalms and hymns and songs of praise. 'I saw more joy on the faces of the persecuted church living in rags in that quagmire than one sees on many a face in many an affluent Western church,' recalls Caroline.

During the service, their leaders made a plea for the needs of their people, in order of priority. First, they asked for prayer support, then for Bibles, and lastly for medicines and food. It was always the same with the persecuted church. Top of their list were always prayer and Bibles. Only after their spiritual requests had been made did they ask for items essential to physical survival.

At Aswa hospital exhausted staff were frantically trying to treat casualties from the war. The wounded were being operated on without anaesthetic or pain-killers. There was no running water and no electricity, so operations had to cease at sundown. The hospital had been built in 1982 and stripped to the bare walls four years later. Equipment and fittings were seized and taken North, leaving an empty shell to serve 700,000 people. Whatever medical supplies they had came from the Red Cross and UNICEF. In what passed for a maternity ward, pregnant women and babies were lying on the bare floor, unattended. Several babies were dying. Caroline asked permission to take pictures so she could show their plight to the world. Her translator was a man of few words. She took the shots, then wondered if the women had been asked, or if the translator had simply told her to go ahead.

The more she thought about it, the more the prospect of having taken their photographs without justification or explanation troubled her. The following morning, her mind was set at rest when the chief pharmacist relayed a message. 'The women are grateful for your visit,' he said. 'Although some of their babies died in the night, they are grateful someone cared enough to come and see them and take their photographs. They felt their babies had not died in vain.'

NOTES

1. Joseph R. Gregory, *First Things*, 1996.
2. 'Sudan – Progress or Public Relations?', Amnesty International Country Report, 29 May 1996; and highlighted again by Amnesty the following year.

TWO

The Collapse of Empire

In the dry season, when the flash floods are just a memory, Sudan looks very different from the air. From horizon to horizon, much of the South is a vast, flat plain, with the shadows of former rivers etched into the dusty soil. The terrain is harsh, open and empty, the domain of lions, leopards and gazelles.

The 'Land of the Blacks', as the Arabs call Sudan, is the largest nation in Africa – the size of Britain, France, Germany, Italy, Belgium, Holland, Spain and Sweden combined – with a population no larger than New York and Greater London.

That population of 30 million is scattered between 621 ethnic groups, speaking more than 200 languages split into scores of additional dialects.[1] Muslim Arabs dominate the northern two-thirds, while black African Christians and animists inhabit the South. Arabs form the largest ethnic group[2] and Muslims the largest religious group.[3] It is broadly between North and South, Arab and non-Arab, where the principal fault lines lie that divide this country. Sudan is a nation that has been at war with itself, for all bar 11 years, since gaining independence in 1956.

From as early as 7,000BC people lived along the Nile and its branches, which extend deep into the Sudan. Most of the population still does. Sudan's largest cities are located in the North where the White and the Blue Nile come together.

Sudan, with Ethiopia, is the biblical land of the Cushites, the twenty-fifth dynasty of Egypt, a civilization that reached its height many centuries before Christ and its nadir some 350 years after. The Arab influence can be traced back to 2,755BC, when Egyptian rule was extended to ancient Nubia, the area that is now northern Sudan. That rule was to endure until the Nubian revolt of 8BC. Coptic Christianity was introduced to the region from AD500. Its greatest challenge was soon to follow.

'Fight [those who disbelieve],' said the prophet Mohammed, 'until there be no more dissent in the land and religion is all for God.' It was a call to establish a spiritual and a political kingdom. Nine years after his death an Islamic army moved across the Gaza strip and into Egypt, the gateway to

Africa. What began in AD641 has continued into the present, with the Arabization of northern Africa, and the Islamization of some 250 million souls.

Coptic Christianity in Sudan was eclipsed by the black Muslim Funj in 1500. Within a century, the Funj capital, Sannar, was to flower into one of the principal cultural centres of Islam. Gradually, the kingdom became weakened by tribal infighting, and in 1822 the land fell once again to invaders from Egypt.

For the next 60 years, Egyptian Sudan, a province of the Ottoman empire, carved steadily deeper into the South, but failed to establish effective control. To feed the empire, the historic slave trade in non-Muslim blacks expanded and prospered, despite the best endeavours of the seconded British administrator, General Charles Gordon, who despaired of the task. Despite its legal abolition, the institution was so deeply rooted he was driven to observe, 'When you have got the ink that has soaked into the blotting paper out of it, then slavery will cease in these lands.'

It was prophesied that one would arise who would rid the world of evil. He would be called the *Mahdi*, he who is guided aright, the saviour and leader of the faithful, who would restore justice and conquer the world for Islam. In 1880,[4] Muhammad Ahmad proclaimed himself the Mahdi and declared holy war against Egypt. In 1883, his holy warriors – the *Ansar*, literally 'Supporters' of the prophet Mohammed[5] – annihilated the massed ranks of the Egyptian army. General Gordon was charged with the evacuation of Khartoum before the Mahdi's forces could surround the city. When his requests for military aid were rejected, he sought permission to forge an alliance with Zubayr Rahama Pasha, the military leader and slave trader he had once defeated. Once again, permission was denied. After a siege of ten months, Gordon was killed and Khartoum fell to the Mahdi on 26 January 1885 – two days before it could be relieved by an expeditionary force.

When the Mahdi died from typhus five months later, power passed to the Caliph. Abdallah at-Taaisha consolidated the Islamic state in the North and set himself to defeat the Nilotes (Nile people) of the South. But attempting simultaneously to conquer Egypt in 1889 proved an ambition too far. While the Caliph's forces were being overstretched on foreign soil, Sudan was collapsing from within. His reign was to be brief, but outlived by the potency of an ideal and a cause – that of an Islamic, Arabic Sudan.

Meanwhile, in London, eyebrows were being raised about the growing influence of the French in Southern Sudan. Both to dispense with the irritant of the Caliph and to head off any improper Gallic intentions, an

Anglo-Egyptian expeditionary force was despatched under the command of General Horatio Kitchener. Many of the men who fought in Kitchener's army were said to have been former slaves.

Success was assured at the battle of Omdurman, on 2 September 1898. The Caliph was defeated in the last great cavalry charge, in which the young Winston Churchill took part. The battle was recorded in the diary of Lt Robert Smyth, whose 21st Lancers bore the brunt of the fighting. He wrote: 'Horses lame and galloping aimlessly. Regular inferno. My left-hand man drops, his horse shot under him. Bullets whistling and splashing all around. Every side a compact mass of white-robed men, apparently countless, still firing and waving swords.'[6]

In reality it was neither Churchill nor the cavalry that conquered, but the new-fangled Maxim gun. Eleven thousand Mahdists were slaughtered by this mechanical marvel and 16,000 were injured.[7] Four months later, joint Anglo-Egyptian sovereignty was declared over Sudan, though the policies and most of the senior administrators to carry them out were British.

Divide and rule

In the years that followed, southerners were bombed into submission in the Nuba Mountains in a campaign of pacification, and railways and a modern civil service were constructed in the North.[8] The nation was divided between North and South and administered separately. 'The approved policy,' said Lord Killearn, the British High Commissioner in Cairo, 'is to act upon the fact that the peoples of the Southern Sudan are distinctively African and Negroid, and that our obvious duty to them is therefore to push ahead as fast as we can with their economic and educational development on African and Negroid lines, and not on Middle Eastern and Arabic lines, which are suitable for Northern Sudan. It is only by economic and educational development that these peoples can be equipped to stand up for themselves in the future, whether their future lot be eventually cast with the Northern Sudan or with East Africa.'[9] At that stage it could have gone either way.

But the future was not as distant as it seemed. In the very month those words were written, the Second World War came to an end, and all the globe's maps were in need of redrawing. Britain could see no long-term future for itself in Sudan and, heeding the growing clamour for independence, the policy switched to a fast-track move to coalesce North and South.

It was disastrous. In the words of one commentator, 'The first four decades of British rule were spent frustrating any links of culture and language that might have bound North and South together; and the last decade was spent trying to bind the whole country together.'[10]

The English-speaking South no more wished to be dominated by the Arab North in the latter half of the 20th century than they had in the 19th. Nevertheless, the timetable was set for a three-year transition to an independent, united Sudan. Tensions began to mount.

The first Sudanese parliamentary elections were held late in 1953 and at the Appointed Day – 9 January 1954 – a process of Sudanization began. Foreigners were removed from senior positions in the government and military. As far as the Southerners were concerned, Sudanization was a euphemism for Northernization. Southerners found themselves heavily under-represented, and not for the first time felt excluded from the corridors of power. On 19 August 1955, mutiny broke out among southern units of the army, and was put down by government forces. In an attempt to pacify the South, the Sudanese Parliament agreed the future of the country should be determined by referendum. On 12 November, Britain and Egypt withdrew their troops and Sudan was declared an independent state. Somewhere along the line, the referendum, which might have granted autonomy for the South, got bypassed. The stage was set for the civil war that still rages today – a stage set in the twilight years of British colonial administration.

Some in Britain described the collapse of empire as 'creative abdication'. Others, a hasty and ill-conceived cutting of losses, resulting in a scramble for power among the avaricious and those untrained in the art of government. 'Everywhere in Africa,' observed *Time* magazine, 'the European has waited too long before giving a share of responsibility to the black man.'[11]

Civil war

On 1 January 1956, the Republic of Sudan was established. Elections were held two years later and won by the *Ansar*-supported Umma (People's) party. The administration soon found itself paralysed by political jockeying and an enfeebled economy. Within nine months, the first elected government of an independent Sudan was overthrown by the commander of the armed forces. On 17 November 1958, Chief of Staff, Lt General Ibrahim Abboud suspended the constitution, declared martial law and himself Prime Minister. When it became clear that his promise to return the nation to civilian rule had evaporated under the Sudanese sun, dissatisfaction turned to unrest. In 1964, Abboud resigned and a wave of riots and strikes ushered in a new coalition government.

For the next three years, successive administrations failed to agree on a permanent constitution, to revive the economy, or to deal with growing ethnic unrest and factionalism. Simmering resentment in the South to domination by the more populous Arab North erupted into open revolt, which ignited into civil war.

In 1969, the crippled civilian government was ousted by a group of radical Army officers under Colonel Gaafar Mohamed el-Nimeiri, who abolished all political parties and declared a Socialist State. A briefly successful coup by the Communists was defeated after a few days in 1971. Nimeiri survived to become Sudan's first elected president the following year. To quell the unrest in the South, which had cost more than half a million lives, he granted a degree of autonomy to the region. The Addis Ababa accords drew a notional line across the country, and guaranteed the non-Muslim identity of the South.[12]

A decade of relative stability ensued, interrupted only in 1976 by a failed coup attempt by the *Ansar*, led by the great-grandson of the Mahdi, Sayyid Sadiq al-Mahdi, who had served as Prime Minister in 1966–67.

Then, in 1983, Nimeiri had what some saw as a lightning conversion to radical Islam.[13] An amnesty for political prisoners saw the release from Kober prison of Dr Hussan al-Turabi, the bespectacled British and French-trained lawyer and spiritual head of the National Islamic Front (NIF).

Despite a poor showing for radical Islam in the earlier elections, Nimeiri had recognized that the highly disciplined NIF was becoming a force to be reckoned with. Drawing its inspiration from militant Islam in the Middle East, the NIF sought to infiltrate the army, the civil service and the professions with a view to gaining control of the nation – with or without the ballot box. Nimeiri had tried to silence the NIF; now he was courting their support. Dr Turabi was appointed chief presidential foreign policy advisor, and other key positions were handed out to members of the Muslim Brotherhood.

With immediate effect, Nimeiri announced the incorporation into Sudanese law of the *Shari'a*, the strict Islamic penal code. The move drew protests from the Oxford-educated Sadiq al-Mahdi, who was promptly placed under house arrest. That same year, Nimeiri revoked the Addis Ababa accords of 1972, and carved up the South once again into three administrative regions, redrawing the map to incorporate newly discovered oil fields into the North. The backlash from the impoverished and largely non-Islamic South was inevitable. Mutineering troops under the command of Kerubino Kwanyin Bol attacked government forces on 16 May, followed by a second wave led by William Nyon Bany. The civil war was rekindled.

Nimeiri despatched an army Colonel to put down the revolt. He was unwise in his choice. The US-educated and Fort Benning-trained Colonel John Garang de Mabior joined the rebellion, along with his battalion, and took refuge in Ethiopia. That same year he took charge of the rebel forces, pronounced Kerubino his second in command and gave a senior post to William Nyon Bany. The embryonic Sudan People's Liberation Army (SPLA), with its political wing, the SPLM (Movement), became a focus for southern discontent and aspiration. Its natural constituency was a region almost the size of France, yet with a population less than that of Paris.[14]

On 6 April 1984, Nimeiri declared a state of emergency. Many constitutional rights were suspended, and 'decisive justice courts' were established in the North.[15] Crowds responded to media announcements of 'amputation day' to watch thieves lose their limbs in the courtyard of the notorious Kober Prison, and the public flogging of a Roman Catholic priest for the crime of being in possession of sacramental wine.[16] The state of emergency was suspended in September, but a new act was brought in to continue many of the practices of the emergency courts. Assurances were given, though not always believed, that the rights of non-Muslims would be respected.

The West watched with horror the events unfolding at speed. At a stroke, Sudan had apparently become a force for destabilization in Africa. The Iranian revolution was not yet a memory, and although Turabi publicly distanced himself from those events, proclaiming the revolution 'capable of destroying everything, including us', the defiant image of the Ayatollah was haunting the West.

Nimeiri abolished bank interest and replaced taxation with voluntary tithing and the economy went into freefall. Ironically, Western over-reaction may have helped usher in the fundamentalists. The USA suspended aid and the IMF demanded reform before further funds would be forthcoming. In response to international pressure, the Sudan government slashed its subsidies and the price of food and petrol soared. Suspecting the Muslim Brotherhood of planning a coup, Nimeiri purged his government and returned Turabi to jail.

As Nimeiri left for Washington to beg for the aid to be turned back on, his departure was greeted by riots on the streets of Khartoum and a general strike which shut the city. On his return in April 1985, with a pledge for $67 million, he was handed a communiqué from the Sudanese Army. It announced that he had been overthrown 'to save the country and its independence'. Among the flood of prisoners released from Kober was Dr Hussan al-Turabi.

The following April, in the first free elections for almost two decades, the transitional military council handed over power to a civilian government. Voting had been suspended in 37 southern constituencies due to the continuing unrest. When the northern votes were counted, Dr Turabi's NIF found itself beaten into third place with just under 17 per cent of the vote. Former Prime Minister Sadiq al-Mahdi, who was related to Turabi in marriage, was elected into office.

Al-Mahdi had inherited the leadership of the Umma party, and the party and its coalition government had inherited all the usual problems, alternately dissolving and reforming as the economy continued to sink into decline. In 1988 drought and famine claimed 300,000 lives. Faced with a raging civil war, soaring prices and mounting debt, the Mahdi's government teetered on the brink.

In a move towards reconciliation, the government had overturned the 1983 decree dividing the South into three regions. Now peace negotiations began in earnest with the SPLA. A plan was agreed with the Democratic Unionist Party (DUP) which would freeze Islamic laws, end the state of emergency and set in place a cease-fire. After some turbulence, the wheels were set in motion for a constitutional conference which would end six years of war.

But before the sun could rise on 30 June 1989, units of the Sudan army closed the airport, seized the presidential palace and army headquarters and set up road-blocks throughout Khartoum. Anyone turning for an explanation to Sudan's official Radio Omdurman would have discovered only ominous silence. More ominous yet was the martial music which began at 8 a.m., followed by the solemn announcement, 'The June revolution has come to restore to the Sudanese citizen his injured dignity and rebuild the Sudan of the future.'[17]

Under the command of then Colonel Omar Hassan Ahmed al-Bashir, leading politicians were arrested, the constitution suspended, political parties and trade unions dissolved and the independent press shut down. A state of emergency was declared and a 15-member National Salvation Revolutionary Command Council (RCC) was established.[18] Sadiq al-Mahdi, the Colonel explained, 'had wasted the country's time and squandered its energies with much talk and political vacillation'.

As for the cease-fire: the DUP/SPLA deal was repudiated, fresh negotiations came to nothing, fighting broke out again in October, and the war with the South resumed. The coup, declared the SPLA, was a negation of the peace process.[19] A failed attempt to overthrow the regime the following year resulted in the execution of 28 army officers.

Bashir may have brought the RCC to power, but the power behind the RCC was the NIF, even though technically banned.[20] The inspiration behind the NIF was the Muslim Brotherhood, a movement founded in Egypt in 1928, dedicated to the removal of Western influence and the establishment of a theocratic Islamic state.[21]

In his final days, Nimeiri had toned down the Islamic laws he had introduced. Now they were reinstated and extended by al-Bashir. The new Criminal Act of 1991 made provision for *hudud* punishments of amputation, stoning and the lash. Muslims who committed apostasy, by converting to another religion, could be punished by death.[22] Again, the southern states were exempted, but the Act made possible the eventual extension of the *Shari'a* to the South, should the state assemblies so decide. Two years later, all non-Muslim judges from the South were replaced by Muslims.[23]

The RCC launched a two-pronged initiative to Islamize the country.[24] Firstly, playing on a combination of tribal rivalry, greed and religious fervour, it handed out arms to Arab tribes in the southernmost parts of Northern Sudan and declared it was their duty to wage *jihad* against the infidel, the black African. By way of recompense, whatever they could take, they could keep. Secondly, the black Sudanese who had fled north to escape famine, two successive years of drought and the sword, would be herded into displaced camps or so-called 'peace camps', where they would be contained and indoctrinated in the ways of Islam.[25] As the US State Department observed: 'These practices all have a pronounced racial aspect.'[26]

In 1992 a peace initiative was launched in Abuja by the seven East-African nations which made up the Inter-Governmental Authority for Development (IGAD). It stalled after the leader of the NIF delegation, Dr Ghazi Salahudin announced, 'We came to fulfil a mission of Islamizing and Arabizing Africa, so the issue of self-determination is a non-starter.'[27]

'A nation is being destroyed'

It was against this backdrop that the Sudanese bishops had made their appeal for help, and had uttered their warnings of genocide, a warning echoed by African Rights,[28] and the former Secretary General of Médecins Sans Frontières, Alain Destexhe, who wrote: 'the deaths of tens of thousands of people in Sudan could well qualify as genocide. In the name of *jihad*, the whole population was either massacred or deported to the camps in the north of the country.'[29]

Caroline had seen firsthand the camps for the displaced, and having witnessed the misery of the people, she intended to make a second trip to Sudan, to confront the government in their capital at Khartoum. But first, she intended to bring the issue to the attention of the British government.

On 9 December 1992, she described vividly in the House of Lords all that she had seen, and made a plea for Britain to honour its historic obligations to the people of Sudan. 'The people feel forgotten and betrayed by the rest of the world,' she told the House. 'I hope that we in Britain will not fail them in their hour of need.'

Support on the floor was unanimous from across the parties. During an impassioned discussion, more came to light about Sudan. The House heard that Sudan had taken charge of 4,000 tonnes of Iranian arms and, according to *The Economist*, had sold £7 million worth of millet to Libya to pay for weapons. At the same time, it was calling on the European Community to provide 130,000 tonnes of grain to feed its western provinces. UN Personnel and NGOs had been barred from camps in the Kadugli area, where some 80 per cent of children were malnourished. In September, local workers employed by the European Community and the US Embassy were executed on suspicion of collusion with the SPLA. The US Senate had condemned Sudan for its 'gross violation of human rights'.

What should have been one of the richest countries in Africa, in terms of natural resources, was wracked by famine, upwards of $13 billion in debt, with a currency worth less than a tenth of its value before the coup. There was speculation about a possible Iranian-backed push to seize the abandoned Chevron oilfields in the South, which once promised enough petroleum to satisfy the needs of the entire nation. Oil reserves were estimated at some 2 trillion barrels. Exploration came to a halt in 1984 when SPLA rebels attacked a field crew, leaving Sudan dependent on imported petroleum for up to 80 per cent of its energy needs.[30] As one observer explained, 'Southerners feared that development of the Southern petroleum fields would primarily benefit the Arab North.'[31]

'A whole nation is being destroyed,' warned Baroness Park. 'We must speak out loudly and clearly... to tell the world what is happening.'

Lord Birkett took up the theme: 'No civilized country will countenance the suppression of all religions save one, all political opinions save one, and all racial types, save one. And yet the Sudanese government give every indication of doing exactly that... religious persecution is at the level of frenzy... atrocities are committed in the cause of *jihad*, the "holy war"... God save us from convictions which allow the ends to justify the means.'

The most outspoken of the bishops was Salisbury. He said the church had been under threat since the days of President Nimeiri, when churches in the

Nuba Mountains were burned down or bulldozed, and permission to build regularly refused. Now, increasing numbers of Christians were being murdered. In the education system, he said, young children were not admitted to primary schools unless they had first attended two years of instruction in the Islamic faith. At the other end of the scale, adherence to Islam had become a condition for admission to university.

'Let me say with all the force at my command,' he continued, 'that neither in the Sudan nor out of it do the churches see their plea for justice as an attack on Islam... What Sudanese Christians want is a constitution and system of justice which guarantees religious liberty for all – Muslim, Christian and indigenous African religion alike... for, make no mistake, it has been lost.'

Lord Avebury, always an ardent campaigner on human rights, reminded the House that Britain was historically responsible for the creation of modern Sudan. 'We joined the Arab, Muslim, North to the black, Christian, South. We delineated the boundaries of Sudan at the end of the 19th century and we handed [the country] over to the northern politicians who secured the acquiescence of the South by promising to consider federalism and independence. Of course they failed to deliver.'

Sudan, he said, had become a springboard for radical Islam to north and central Africa. 'It is impossible for us to convey in a few minutes the extent of the human rights violations in Sudan today, and the dangers posed by Khartoum's policies in the whole region. Not content with beggaring their own people, persecuting the intelligent, and driving hundreds of thousands of them into exile, they are trying to export intolerance and thuggery to Egypt, Algeria, Tunisia, Kenya, Uganda and Ethiopia,[32] and their acquisition of a sophisticated arsenal of weapons of mass destruction is a very serious threat to peace. We cannot afford to wait until the volcano erupts.'

Representatives of all major parties expressed appreciation to Caroline for bringing the plight of the Sudanese before the House. None put it more eloquently than Baroness Park of Monmouth: 'Without my noble friend, Lady Cox, her courage and persistence... in bringing what she has seen to the world's attention... we should apparently know virtually nothing about the forgotten war; the ethnic cleansing and the reported selling of some women and children into slavery; and the destruction of whole communities.'[33]

What nobody realized, least of all Caroline, was that her role as a witness to the forgotten war had only just begun. She called on the government to bring the warring parties together in a conference to try to achieve a peaceful resolution to the conflict. It was a challenge that the government refused to pick up. And presented with government inaction, Caroline and CSI resolved to do something about it.

NOTES

1. Africa News Service, 20 December 1998.
2. 40 per cent, according to Human Rights Watch / Africa.
3. 60 per cent, Human Rights Watch / Africa.
4. Some sources say 1881.
5. One of Sudan's main Islamic groupings.
6. John Vincent, 'Omdurman diary tells of the bloody cavalry charge to end them all', *The Times*, 26 March 1997.
7. *Compton's Encyclopedia*, 1995, and *The People's Chronology*, 1994.
8. 'Slavery in Sudan', Sudan Update and Anti-Slavery International, May 1997.
9. Khartoum Despatch to Ernest Bevin, 4 August 1945, cited by Sean Gabb, The Sudan Foundation, Politics File No. 2.
10. Politics File No. 2.
11. 7 March 1960.
12. 'Sudan's Crisis of Faith', MEC, 10 April 1993.
13. Robin White, *Sacred Rage*, Simon and Schuster, 1985, p. 201.
14. Dr Yasin Miheisi, *Independent Sudan Page*.
15. 'Sudan: State Department Notes', US Department of State, June 1995.
16. Robin White, *Sacred Rage*, p. 202.
17. 'An early morning coup', *Time*, 10 July 1989.
18. 'The tears of orphans: no future without human rights', Amnesty International, January 1995.
19. Policy Statement of the SPLM/SPLA on the Sudanese Peace Agreement signed in Khartoum on 21 April 1997.
20. 'It is an open secret that the government has been run from behind the scenes by this technically "banned" political party': Human Rights Watch / Africa, May 1996.
21. White, *Sacred Rage*, p. 178.
22. '1996 Human Rights Report: Sudan', US State Department. According to the same source, the penalties of amputation and stoning were informally suspended during 1995.
23. 'Sudan: State Department Notes'.
24. 'The NIF's stated aim is to create an Islamic state with only one language, Arabic, and one religion, Islam': Human Rights Watch / Africa, 'Behind the Red Line: Political Repression in Sudan', May 1996.
25. 'The Sudan', *Encyclopaedia Britannica*; *Funk and Wagnall's Encyclopedia*; *World Almanac*; *Webster's New Biographical Dictionary*; *Microsoft Encarta*.
26. '1997 Human Rights Report: Sudan', 6c.
27. Policy Statement of the SPLM/SPLA on the Sudanese Peace Agreement signed in Khartoum on 21 April 1997.
28. 'Sudanese troops are carrying out a genocide against the Nuba people', Associated Press, 5 August 1997.
29. *Rwanda and Genocide in the Twentieth Century*, New York University Press, 1995, p. 17.
30. *The World Book*, 1995. Other natural resources include chromium, gold, copper and uranium.
31. David W. Howes, Assistant Professor of Geography, Clarion University of Pennsylvania; *Compton's Encyclopedia*, 1995.
32. In August 1993, the USA denounced Sudan for being a safe haven for Islamic terrorists, claiming, 'Sudan has supported... insurrections and/or radicals in Algeria, Egypt, Eritrea, Ethiopia, Tunisia and Uganda.'
33. Unstarred Question on Sudan, 9 December 1992, *Hansard*, vol. 541, no. 73.

THREE

Cry of the Jihad

Caroline's debate in the Lords lasted 2 hours and 27 minutes. Watching the proceedings from the gallery with increasing discomfort, were the Ambassador and representatives of the Embassy of Sudan. 'If looks could kill I most certainly would not be alive now,' says Caroline.

After the debate, she was invited to the Sudanese Embassy to be informed of the many good and praiseworthy things that were being done in his country. In the interests of balance, she was pleased to accept. Eventually, she managed to interrupt what she describes as a monologue of self-congratulation to invite herself to Northern Sudan to witness the truth of what she was being told for herself.

The Ambassador courteously replied that a visit, of course, was possible, which was the cue for Caroline to jam a crowbar into the chink and lever for all she was worth. She demanded to be accompanied by John Eibner from CSI Zurich and a TV cameraman, and to be free to visit whomever they wished, wherever they wished, without any official presence, and with a cast-iron guarantee that there would be no reprisals whatsoever against whomever they did visit.

Reluctantly, the Ambassador agreed. While their breath was still hot in the air, she wrote to thank him and confirm she was very pleased to accept his kind invitation on the terms that she had set out and that he had agreed. Having acquiesced, Khartoum felt unable to back down.

Thus it was, that at 3.30 a.m., on 6 July 1993, Caroline and John Eibner found themselves in the capital of Sudan with Adam Kelliher, a cameraman from Frontline News. Their first day in Khartoum coincided with an indoor rally to mark the fourth anniversary of the coup which brought the military regime to power. On the balcony at the rear of the Hall of Friendship massed *mujahedin* (holy warriors) were bellowing Islamic chants. A bearded, white-robed imam, brandishing a great sword, led the assembled crowd in calling for holy war. All were urged to respond to the cry of the *jihad*, to close ranks and reduce their country's fragmentation.[1]

That spirit of *jihad* was on parade at the Hussein Ben Ali Popular Defence

Force training ground, where white-uniformed, Kalashnikov-carrying *mujahedin* marched up and down, chanting, 'There is only one God and Mohammed is his prophet', and 'We are soldiers of Allah.' Those who would give their lives in the Holy War would become *shu'hada* – martyrs – assured by the Koran of celebrating their deaths in Paradise.

'We noticed,' wrote Caroline in her report, 'that the virtually compulsory militia requires all its members – be they Muslim, Christians or animists – to sing Islamic chants. The pledge of the government to intensify its programme of Islamization is a cause of great concern to Sudan's non-Muslims.'[2]

A meeting was arranged with the leading figure of the NIF, Dr Hussan al-Turabi, who received them with courtesy in the wood-panelled reception room of his home. When they were settled on leather-clad sofas and had been offered tea and cool drinks, Dr Turabi, the Speaker of the Sudanese Parliament, began. A slight figure behind black-rimmed glasses and a close-cropped grizzled white beard, he spoke at length, using his hands for emphasis, and smiling reassuringly. But the meeting was less than convivial. 'He just opened his mouth and out flowed non-stop propaganda,' says Caroline.

Her blood rising, she cut across him and began to challenge his assertions. The more he persisted, the more she interrupted. Dr Turabi did not find the novelty amusing; the smile vanished and his face grew darker as the atmosphere between them became frostier by the moment.

'Unlike many Western politicians who go to meet these leaders, Caroline had done her homework,' says John Eibner. 'She was prepared and willing to challenge him on matters of fact. We made it clear we would not accept his lies or be part of his propaganda campaign.' John assumes Dr Turabi's strategy was to defuse Caroline's criticism by drawing her into a dialogue which she would be unwilling to jeopardize. 'It backfired miserably.'

When Dr Turabi remembered he was being filmed, he became angrier still, and terminated the interview forthwith. All courtesy dropped, they parted company without so much as shaking hands.

Into the 'peace camps'

Nevertheless, the rest of the visit went ahead as agreed, smoothly and well-ordered and without interference – until anyone tried to stray from the agenda. In Dilling, in the Nuba Mountains, security officers burst into a church while they were interviewing a clergyman. In a camp for the displaced near Omdurman, Caroline went off without prior agreement to talk to a Catholic nun who was based there. They had been together a matter of moments, when security guards pursued them in to her living quarters. In El-Obeid, it was the turn of the cameraman to break away from the main party. Adam Kelliher was talking to a priest in the cathedral when much the same thing happened. Security guards broke up the interview and began to rough up the cameraman. It hadn't taken much for the veneer to crack. 'Whenever we deviated in even the smallest way from the programme, we saw the other face of the fundamentalist regime,' says Caroline. 'We saw the kind of intimidation to which the local Sudanese are exposed.' One of their hosts troubled to explain the little difficulty, pointing out that it was against the national interests to say bad things about Sudan to Westerners.

One of their requests had been to visit areas of the Nuba Mountains, a range some 300 miles south of El-Obeid, rising 1,370 metres above the surrounding plains. The mountains were inhabited by people of the Nuba tribes, who were known for their prowess at wrestling. But their wrestling skills were of little use against government forces armed with modern weapons, who, according to reports, were systematically driving them from their land. Hill passes that had been used for centuries were cut off, watering points were captured and farmland was seized, as the people were driven higher and the troops moved to encircle the highlands. As Caroline flew into Kadugli, large white letters on the mountain, displayed for all to see, spelled out the ominous message, *Jihad Kadugli*. It stood like a flag of triumph over a town which had been captured by government forces.

Conditions in the camps nearby were depressing. The tumble-down, mud-walled houses were the same, but there was water, food and health care, though not always sufficient. An air of lethargy and demoralization hung over the place. The people explained they had been forced to go there after government troops had attacked their homes and villages, burned their houses and crops, destroyed their waterholes and left them with nothing. Short of death by thirst or starvation, their only option was the peace camps.

Foreign non-governmental organizations (NGOs) were denied access to the camps, and a propaganda campaign had been launched against them. The following message had been put out on Republic of Sudan Radio: '[The NGOs] are rooted in malice which knows no mercy. They are covetous of the material resources bestowed lawfully by God on the weak countries... The countries of arrogance continue to plant [them] as evil, parasitic plants which give succulent fruit on the outside, but poisonous colocyhth [bitter apple] on the inside... they did not take long to spread like cancer in the exhausted body of the nation.'[3]

With a bar on NGOs, Western relief aid could only be distributed by Islamic organizations, the sole agencies allowed to operate in the camps. 'Food is strength,' explained Robert Painter, a UN humanitarian co-ordinator. 'It provides people with the ability to continue... so I think the underlying rationale behind stopping the flights of these [relief] planes is to weaken the population.'[4]

In Khartoum the churches were permitted a small share in the distribution of aid, but in the peace camps in the Nuba Mountains rations would only be handed out to those prepared to go along with Islamization. To obtain food and medicine, many of the displaced said they had been driven to renounce their Christian names and adopt Islamic ones. 'It was the politics of hunger,' says Caroline.

The Dar Al-Salaam Camp near Khartoum was no less depressing. It housed those who had been forcibly relocated from the shanty towns of Omdurman and the outskirts of Khartoum. The Ministry of Housing had moved in and razed to the ground homes that, however poor, were at least within reach of the city and employment. The inhabitants were shifted against their will into the desert, where they found themselves marooned without transport.[5] There was no opportunity to grow their own crops or keep their own livestock. And for the southerners among them, conditions in the harsher northern desert were especially taxing.

Caroline's escort around the camp was the Minister for Planning for Khartoum State. Disturbed by the conditions and minimal facilities, Caroline wondered how long these people from the South would have to remain there. There was little comfort in the reply. The Minister said repatriation would not be encouraged. It was intended that these people should remain in the North, while northerners would go to live in the South, as part of the policy of integration. The displacement was to be permanent, a means of population control, akin to the policies of Stalin. 'They were in a state of despair,' says Caroline. 'They had been dislocated from their culture, isolated and deprived of all basic essentials. It was, in effect, a concentration camp.'[6]

The scale of the operation was staggering. Upwards of 2 million people had been displaced in so-called peace camps and hundreds of thousands had fled the country.[7] Some had gone to the camps to seek refuge from the war, others were forcibly relocated. Reports had filtered through of children being abducted from the camps and sent to PDF training centres from the ages of nine or ten. Muslim and non-Muslim alike would be indoctrinated in radical Koranic teaching and schooled in warfare by government forces to fight against the South.[8]

In a show of normality, a priest had been sent to accompany Caroline and John. Although most of the people in the camp were Christians, until that official visit, he had been consistently denied access to his own community. Other evidence soon came to light of hardship. Before their visit, John and Caroline had obtained a list of 150 prisoners of conscience from Amnesty International, which they presented to the Sudanese government. Many more cases were added to the list during their stay. They included the daughter of a Christian clergyman who had been arrested and sentenced to the lash for wearing African, rather than Islamic dress. Another was the Episcopalian bishop of Kadugli, Peter el-Birish, who received 90 lashes in public for alleged adultery. He denied the charge and claimed the court had prevented him from uttering a word in his own defence.

Splinter groups

But the government of the North did not exercise a monopoly over suffering. Severe infighting between rival factions of the SPLA was playing into the hands of the regime and driving people across the frontier into the peace camps. The SPLA had splintered and splintered again into a bewildering plethora of warring factions. Kerubino and others had gone their separate ways.[9]

There were differences about whether Sudan should be united, or split into North and South. Tribal divisions also came into play. Dr Riek Machar and another faction head were Nuer, while the Commander-in-Chief of the SPLA-Mainstream, Colonel John Garang, was Dinka. According to Human Rights Watch, the differences were manipulated by the government, which was financing the breakaway groups to serve as their proxies in attacking Garang.[10]

Their infighting added enormously to the burden of human suffering in the South, and factions of the divided SPLA found themselves condemned by the international community for carrying out atrocities of their own.[11] Caroline was aware of the fact. She had told the Lords, 'Although there are reports of some atrocities carried out by [Dr Garang's] forces, it is the belief of the people... that the SPLA is in general fighting a just war for the survival of the people of the South and for the protection of their basic human rights, including religious freedom, and that it has the general support of the population who now live in the South.'[12]

Once again, Caroline had made the controversial decision to stand on the side where the suffering was the greatest, even if it meant having to stand with men who were prepared to fight, and if necessary, kill, for their freedom..

During her visit to Sudan, Caroline had her first meeting with the opposition leader, Sadiq al-Mahdi, who had been placed under house arrest. Most of the opposition parties had come together under the umbrella of the National Democratic Alliance, and were operating underground and in exile. The NDA had accepted the principles of democracy, secular government and the right of self-determination. The contact with Sadiq al-Mahdi was to prove significant in the years to come.

More visits to Sudan followed over the next few months, all conducted without official permission, and all involving illegal entry to the country. Wherever possible, Caroline met leaders of the opposition groups, who, judging by the votes cast at the annulled election, represented some 90 per cent of the Sudanese people. In 1994, the year that a new government offensive sent 100,000 refugees fleeing to Uganda, she visited Dr John Garang. One of his principal sticking points with the North was the introduction of Islamic law. He dismissed Dr Turabi's insistence that the *Shari'a* would not be applied to the South:[13] 'It is impossible to exempt the South from the supreme laws of the land,' he explained to Caroline. 'The NIF will not accept a secular state; we will not accept an Islamic state.

Later, during that same visit, she met Garang's chief rival, Dr Riek Machar, the leader of the SPLA-United faction. Machar was prepared to negotiate with the regime and would settle for an independent South, but Garang believed the regime could not be trusted and was determined to remove it from power. 'My objective is a united, democratic Sudan which accommodates everybody,' Garang told the Egyptian magazine *Al Masowar*.[14] 'Separation is not one of our objectives.'

Nevertheless, Garang and Machar had much in common. Both were calling for a referendum over self-determination. Machar admitted to Caroline that more lives had been lost through inter-factional fighting than in battle with government forces. 'Reconciliation,' he said, 'can save the movement from collapse.' Church leaders across Southern Sudan were working to bring an end to inter-factional strife, and reconciliation was a task which Caroline and CSI resolved to support.

In the event, Machar's reconciliation was to be in a different direction, and the following month, February, he split again from the SPLA-United to form yet another faction, the mainly Nuer South Sudan Independence Movement (SSIM).[15]

NOTES

1. Human Rights Watch / Africa observed, 'The war against the South is characterized as a Holy War (*jihad*). At frequent government mass rallies the head of state and other government officials address the participants as Muslims and encourage them to continue with the Holy War against the South': 'Behind the Red Line: Political Repression in Sudan', May 1996.

2. Report of CSI Visit to Sudan, 6–13 July 1993.

3. Republic of Sudan Radio, Omdurman, 22 June 1993, reported in CSI Report, 6 July 1993.

4. Speaking on Channel 4 News, 13 July 1996.

5. Corroborated by Human Rights Watch / Africa, 'Behind the Red Line'.

6. MEC confirmed the description: '[They] have rightly been described as "concentration" camps. They are surrounded by desert and security forces guard the entrances, refusing access to anyone other than residents, relatives of residents and relief agencies': 'Sudan's Crisis of Faith', 10 April 1993.

7. Some put the figures far higher, at up to 5 million in peace camps and 2 million refugees.

8. US State Department, '1997 Human Rights Report: Sudan', 2c.

9. Kerubino's alliance with Garang had eventually erupted into armed conflict. Kerubino wanted a split between North and South, while Garang had resolved that Sudan should remain a unitary state.

The Nasir group had broken away in August 1991, following an attempted coup by SPLA regional commander Dr Riek Machar. A year and a month later, William Nyuon Bany formed a third rebel faction. A fourth was formed by Arok Thon Arok, who was expelled from SPLA high command after arranging a secret meeting with a government general on a trip to England. After escaping from an SPLA jail in Eastern Equatoria he went on to form the Bor Citizens Group.

All four factions had come together – briefly – to form the Unity group. They failed to live up to their name. The Nasir group split away and split again, into the optimistically-titled SPLA-United, led by Dr Lam Akol and the South Sudan Independence Movement (SSIM), under the leadership of Dr Riek Machar. One shard of the SSIM was to become the Equatoria Defence Force. There was a further defection from John Garang's SPLA-Mainstream in January 1997, with the formation of the Southern Sudan Independent group: Umma Party statement on the peace agreement signed in Khartoum on 21 April 1997; and Dr Yasin Miheisi, *Independent Sudan Page*.

10. 'Behind the Red Line'.

11. Human Rights Watch held the government responsible for atrocities committed by factions working with it: 'Behind the Red Line'. One violation committed by the government and Garang alike was the forced recruitment of underage soldiers. Amnesty observed, 'Armed opposition groups were responsible for serious human rights abuses, including holding prisoners of conscience, torture, abducting children... in August [1996] six Roman Catholic nuns and priests were detained for 11 days by an SPLA commander at Mapurdit after they opposed his efforts to conscript schoolchildren': Amnesty International 1997 Country Report: Sudan.

12. Unstarred question on Sudan, 9 December 1992, *Hansard*, vol. 541, no. 73.

13. A declaration that *Shari'a* would only apply to the North was made by Lt General al-Bashir in December 1992, but had not been constitutionally ratified, MEC, April 1993.

14. Reprinted in *Al Ahram Daily*, 25 January 1997.

15. Statement of the Umma Party on the Peace Agreement signed in Khartoum, 21 April 1997. Machar's SSIA was later superseded by the creation of the United Democratic Salvation Front, an alliance of several pro-government factions, including that of Kerubino.

FOUR

War in the Nuba Mountains

By June 1994, the situation was deteriorating rapidly. Severe fighting had led to the evacuation of 80,000 from the relief camps. Most NGOs had been forced to quit, and the food lifeline was severed. In Mayen Abun, Bahr el-Ghazal, people and cattle were starving. In the previous year, 90 per cent of their crops had been destroyed by drought. The rains had held off from July to April. Now even the seed had gone. Malnutrition was rife, along with malaria, TB, pneumonia and diarrhoea. Even leprosy was making a comeback; and it was only the beginning of the hungry season. There were four months to go before the harvest, and already most of the roots and grasses had been eaten.

If possible, things were even worse in the Nuba Mountains. There were some 3 million Nuba, from a variety of tribes; black Africans, most of whom spoke Arabic as their first language. Some 40 per cent were Muslim; up to 30 per cent were Christian and the rest were animist.[1] Yet Muslim, Christian and animist alike, were being systematically ousted from their homes by government forces. Around a quarter of a million were living in territory nominally under SPLA control and many more had been displaced.

The Nuba were no stranger to conflict with the northern Arabs. Their people had been driven from their ancestral homeland by centuries of Arab invasion. Gradually, they had been pushed back to the Nuba Mountains, an area of around 50,000 square miles that afforded some natural protection against their enemies, who today, came under the banner of the NIF.

The fact that a high proportion were Muslims did not deter the government from declaring a *jihad* against the people of the Nuba Mountains. Direct offensives began in the late 1980s, but inadequate numbers of troops floundered on the slopes and were picked off by those who knew the terrain. The tactic changed. The region was starved of aid and water supplies were cut off. Then the naked and malnourished were offered food, medicines and clothes as inducements to go to the 'peace camps' in the North. Once inside, anyone who tried to run away was shot.

'They were using hunger to force people to flee from their own land to seek survival,' says Caroline.

If inducement failed there was always coercion. By the end of 1990, some 35,000 soldiers, tribal militia and troops of the Popular Defence Forces had begun to move into the area. Settlements were systematically burned and their inhabitants deported to desert camps in Northern Kordofan, Khartoum and Port Sudan. Buffer zones were created, ostensibly to deprive the SPLA in the mountains of food and support. Educated Nuba who were captured were commonly tortured to extract confessions of SPLA involvement. There were repeated allegations of crucifixions.[2] Wells were poisoned to drive people from their homes, and mosques and churches alike were put to the torch.[3] Male captives were executed, while women and children were herded off to the camps. Children under the age of eight, it was claimed, were considered unproductive burdens and were killed.[4]

Hisim Khaleel had run from his village as the government troops moved in. His parents were too slow and both were murdered. The soldiers set fire to the houses and the Anglican church. They caught a Christian, Bolis Alhaj, and cut his throat. They did it clumsily and it took him three days to die. The only hiding place was the hills, but there was no food, and 124 died of starvation. The same thing happened at Kualib, but when the villagers split up to search the hills for water, monkeys came from the trees and took their infants. In January, troops shot at Anglican priest, Matta Noor, before dragging him to his house and setting it alight. 'They kill so many,' said Marcus Rahal Kuku, 'one can't begin to count them all.'[5]

Antagonism towards Christianity had come to a head with the imposition of *Shari'a* law, Caroline was told. An Episcopalian leader said that in 1986, Christians had been prohibited from preaching in the Nuba Mountains and the activities of catechists were curtailed. The government tried to close all the churches. Any priests or catechists who tried to resist were arrested. War soon followed. Churches, Bibles and hymnbooks were burned, pastors and catechists were killed. At that time, the troops left the mosques alone, attempting to drive a wedge between the Christian and Muslim communities. But the Muslims sided with the Christians, and since 1991 the troops had been burning mosques as well. Peoples of both faiths became subject to the *jihad*.[6]

'Many mosques have been burned down,' confirmed Sultan Hassein Karabus, Chief of the Koalib tribe. Christians who were captured, he said, were treated worse than Muslims and forced to convert to Islam. Those sent to the peace camps were made to pray to Allah five times a day. Women were divided among the soldiers and forced to have sexual relations. One woman who refused to commit adultery because she was a Christian was shot.

'Omar al-Bashir and the government are using religion as a political tool, for killing, raping and looting,' continued the Chief. 'Here in the Nuba Mountains we are a model where Christians, Muslims and [those who observe] traditional African religions live side by side. There are very good relations, to the extent of intermarriage. I ask Muslims abroad to understand that what we have in Sudan is a political conflict, not a religious conflict, and not to be blinded by al-Bashir.'

The SPLA commander, Yousif Kuwa, was both a black African and a Muslim, as were many of his fellow officers. 'I feel like a drowning man who is crying, "Help!",' he told Caroline, 'but no-one responds.' Commander Kuwa had been to Islamic school and spoke Arabic better than his mother tongue. Caroline asked him why he had joined the SPLA to fight the government of Sudan.

'I looked for recognition of the beauty of my Nuba land,' he explained, 'but I never found it in Arab poems. I looked for appreciation of the beauty of my people, and the only reference to beauty was to people with straight hair. I started to hate my own colour, my African self, my society. I started to feel this way in primary school, where the headmaster ignored and insulted us, saying, "Why should we teach Nuba people – they are only fit to become our servants." At secondary school, we were told that Arab women do not work; all the domestic work is done by Nuba boys.'

Commander Yousif had left his position and his people on the Nuba Mountains to appeal to the international community for aid. 'Since 1990, we have received no relief in our area – not even medicines. Even in terms of humanitarian aid, we are left to our doom. We feel we have been forgotten by the world.'

One relief operation which received a good deal of international publicity was the United Nations Operation Lifeline Sudan (OLS). It had afforded compelling TV pictures of aid packages tumbling out of the back of cargo planes. OLS was operating with the blessing and support of the Sudan government, an admirable humanitarian gesture – but it was only free to operate selectively. A senior OLS official, who preferred not to be named, told Caroline, 'The Nuba Mountains are not served at all by OLS. It is also prevented from meeting urgent needs in the South, where it does have a mandate.' He said UN food deliveries had been barred in areas where fighting had been taking place. Food barges to Juba, the largest town in the South, had been delayed while government weapons were given priority for river navigation.

The official described the psychological toll of the war on Sudan's children as the great hidden tragedy. Incontinence, nightmares, extreme introversion, and the cessation of menstruation in teenage girls were widespread. Only one child in five in Southern Sudan was receiving any education. War was producing a terrible legacy for the future.

'Exile is torture'

CSI was able to provide some aid, but it was also able to bring in a far more valuable commodity. Regularly attached to the CSI contingent was Bishop Macram Max Gassis of El-Obeid, a brown-skinned Roman Catholic of Arab extraction from the North, who had been exiled by the government. The only way back into his country was illegally, with Caroline. He went with her again and again. 'When I spoke out, I knew I would suffer,' he explained. 'I have not been whipped and lashed; I have not been tortured in a ghost house [interrogation centre]. But for me, exile is torture, because I want to be with my people.'

In the western Nuba Mountains, the bishop, resplendent in full ecclesiastical regalia, was dwarfed by a group of tall SPLA commanders in full combat gear. They were anxious about the suffering of their people and the suffering they, in turn, had inflicted. Bishop Gassis replied, 'Christ is calling us, the people of Sudan, to the privilege of sharing his suffering, to be with him on the cross, and to bring reconciliation and redemption through this suffering. We have not asked for this fighting,' he continued. 'It has been forced upon us. We can ask that the days of our suffering be shortened, but we cannot avoid the cross. God has helped us in our suffering. People from abroad are struck by our smiles and our serenity, even while we are suffering. I am not a gloomy bishop and you are not gloomy commanders!

'As for taking arms,' the bishop went on, 'If a man sees his child sold into slavery, his wife raped, his land taken, he is reduced to nullity. He has no option but to defend them. My vocation is to try to bring peace – but it must be peace with justice. It is no use talking about peace, or love, without justice. We must have justice.'

From witnessing the holocaust in the Nuba Mountains, Bishop Gassis went on to make an impassioned plea to the 50th Session of the UN Commission on Human Rights in Geneva. 'The population of an entire ethnic community has been caught in a web of the most inhuman measures perpetrated by the regime: killing, torture, rape... and denial of food... Children and women have been enslaved.' But the full force of his disapprobation was directed beyond Khartoum: 'The international community... has permitted the regime in Khartoum... to veto any provision of humanitarian relief for these unfortunate people... How can the international community fail to do anything to help?'[7]

The church in the Nuba Mountains had been cut off from the outside world for more than a decade, though their problems had begun in 1962 when the military regime of General Abboud had expelled all missionaries from the country. There were few clergy, yet the church had continued to thrive, kept alive by the catechists. They made up for their lack of education with zeal, braving snake-bite and malaria to travel round the country performing their Christian duties. 'These are the real heroes of the faith,' says John Eibner. 'They stayed with their people in the darkest days when many fled, and helped organize the church.'

The Nuba priests had nothing, so John and Caroline went back to give them Bibles and service books, even their wristwatches. In return, the hungry priests gave them a chicken, which Caroline entrusted back to them with a smile, promising to return to share a meal of eggs laid by their gift.

'You are the first Christians who have come to encourage us,' said the Rev. Barnaba, the Anglican Chairman of the Nuba New Sudan Council of Churches. 'We will never forget you.' He added, 'Please tell the Archbishop of Canterbury that Episcopalian pastors have nothing.' Once there were Sunday Schools and an Anglican primary school, but the teaching materials were exhausted along with resources for worship. He continued, 'We desperately need a bishop to come to tour, to witness, to minister to us and tell the world the suffering of the church in the Nuba Mountains.'[8]

In Pariang, in the Upper Nile, the catechist there had not seen a priest for a decade. John and Caroline were the first Christians from the outside world he had ever encountered. Yet his congregation was thriving and dynamic and well-versed in hymns and liturgy.

The story was the same at Mayen Abun, in Bahr el-Ghazal. Macram Gassis was the first bishop they had seen in ten years. He nearly didn't get there. They were late taking off because of a flooded airstrip, and the landing three hours later almost wrecked the plane. The sodden ground was so soft the aircraft sank into the mud. Amazingly, it was undamaged, but needed to be dug out.

The Bishop celebrated mass in the nearest thing they had to a cathedral: the shade of a great tamarind tree. In this church 'not made by human hands, but by nature and by God', children sang hymns and played drums, their faces radiant with pleasure. Caroline sat beneath the tree, refreshed by their singing.

Bishop Macram Gassis continued:

We must tell our brothers and sisters that the people here are still full of hope and that they still smile in spite of suffering and persecution. Those smiles put us to shame. Many of your people have been sold into slavery, but for me that is not to become a slave. The real slave is the person who does injustice to brothers and sisters, and who kills them. You, however, are children of God... no longer slaves but free: children of liberty, freedom and truth.

Many of the packed congregation were naked out of necessity, and visibly embarrassed. 'This is not real nakedness,' the Bishop explained. 'True nakedness is to be without love. Therefore to be clothed in love – this is Christianity. Wear the love of the Christian faith as a way of life and witness to it, even to those who do not believe in Christ.

'Do not think that we will leave you or forget you,' he continued. 'You will be remembered as people who are closest to God, because you are every day obeying Christ's command to take up his cross and to follow him.'

He concluded: 'I came, I saw, I heard, I touched – and I am enriched.'

All around, away from the embrace of the 'cathedral', people were dying of starvation. On the outskirts of the town Caroline came across two of hunger's victims. A man, aged 50, had walked for more than five days to find food, and had found none. The other was an 18-year-old girl who lay in the shade of a thorn tree, dying of starvation and TB. Her skin was stretched tight across her skull. She was beyond food and there was no medicine for her. She had only hours to live. Caroline did what she could. As John Eibner recalls, 'She was able to take time to say a quiet prayer with them, to hold their hands and touch their foreheads, to give them something for their discomfort. They were so weak they could not lift their limbs, but they responded with enormous smiles of appreciation.' The same thing happened with a woman caked in mud, unwashed for days, with all the symptoms of TB: 'Caroline can touch the untouchable.'

Akel Deng was naked to her waist apart from a locket. Her husband had died an hour earlier. She knelt in silence on reed matting, beside the dead body, her face a mask of grief and resignation, her hands lifted to God. For half an hour, Caroline knelt with her in her white sweatshirt, silk scarf and denim jeans, her arm around her, sharing her grief across the cultural divide, crying quietly, praying.

'My heart is breaking so much for the extent of the suffering and for the fact that so much of it is forgotten,' she said. 'The rest of the world doesn't know and doesn't care.'9

The body of Akel's husband was laid to rest in the red soil. Akel comforted one wailing child, while another hid behind a tree, unable to face what had happened to his father.

Father Benjamin Madol Akot, a Roman Catholic priest accompanying Bishop Macram, thanked Caroline for choosing to open her eyes to their need. 'We have felt deserted, even betrayed, by Christians in the West,' he added. 'We have suffered for 27 years, seeking help, but it doesn't materialize.'

Father Benjamin was ordained in 1981 and forced to flee his first parish, Rumbek, five years later, when it was overrun by government troops. After walking for three months, he found refuge in Ethiopia, where he ministered to the refugees. In 1992, he was expelled with all the other Sudanese after the fall of the Mengistu regime. So he walked to Kenya. He returned to Sudan in April 1994 to establish a mission in Thiet, Bahr el-Ghazal. Just six weeks later, it too, was overrun and set alight by government forces. Those too old or too sick to get away were put to death. The rest joined a tidal wave of some 300,000 fleeing the oncoming offensive.

After that, Father Benjamin was sent to Mayen Abun to re-establish the once thriving mission station that had been destroyed in the mid-1980s. In July 1995, he and the others were driven out again, by the renegade Dinka warlord, Kerubino. 'Because I was a Christian, living in a Christian area, I was shot by Arabs,' he told Caroline. 'We don't want to be ruled by Arabs. We would rather be ruled by the British, because they have a sense of humanity. But we feel the British have let us down.'

Although it was June, it was still cold at night. As Caroline settled into her sleeping bag, she was well aware of the many nearby who would be shivering with nothing to cover them. Her mind went back to the Mass beneath the tamarind tree and the contrast between the radiant faces of those praising God and the wilderness around them, with the ever-present threat of further attack.

Rumble of the Antonov

It was attack from the air which had proven the most effective instrument of displacement. Tens of thousands had been driven out by bombing and strafing from helicopter gunships. Further attacks had taken place at the end of the year, and the bombs were still falling during Caroline's visit in the first week of January. The air-raids extended well beyond the notional

North–South divide right to the foot of the country, where Caroline and John were to come under bombardment themselves. Their first attack was at Nimule, a once-flourishing town which had been reduced to bombed-out brickwork. Most of the relief agencies had pulled out, but Dan Eiffe of Norwegian People's Aid (NPA) refused to go: 'We won't leave,' he said, 'we can't leave the people. In South Africa, if one person died, everyone spoke out. Here, 25,000 people died in one massacre in Bor and the churches are silent. There is a vast population on the move – forced to move by continual attacks.' Their conversation subsides as a distant rumble snatches at their attention.

Shielding their eyes, they peer upwards into the brilliant blue of the sky. High, very high, the sunlight catches a sliver of silver. Making its approach is a Russian-built Antonov cargo plane. They suspend their interview and take cover in NPA's steel-reinforced air-raid shelter. They do so for good reason. The Antonov's cargo is bombs, which are rolled out of the back by hand onto the Southern Sudanese below. Four bombs fall around them that day, none of them nearby. It is not precision bombing, but the Antonov is used to great effect as a weapon of terror, to drive civilians from the area, by flying in on Sundays and targeting churches, or waiting till market day and dropping its payload on the shoppers. Flying out of range of the guns, it can make its attacks with impunity.[10]

Caroline and John's second taste of aerial bombardment came while the SPLA were laying siege to Kapoeta, in Eastern Equatoria. The town had fallen to government troops in May 1992. Most of Kapoeta's priests fled before the occupiers could move in. But the head catechist, Pio Lokuru Napomba, stayed behind to minister to the remaining Christian civilians and soldiers. The new Commissioner quickly began to implement his policies of Arabization and Islamization. He set up a Koranic school, and ordered Christian soldiers not to go to church. Any who disobeyed were arrested. After one was beaten to death, the others stopped going.

Pio Lokuru continued to minister to civilians, so the Commissioner ordered his arrest. He was taken to Kapoeta's 'ghost house' interrogation centre,[11] where a sack filled with red chilli pepper was placed over his head and tied tightly round his neck. It was a method of torture much in vogue across the country.[12] As the victim inhaled the chilli powder he would suffer agonizing convulsions. If the torture went on for long enough it would cause death by asphyxiation. Pio Lokuru did not die, but during the period of recovery after his release, his Christian duties were upheld by his son, Stephen, and his assistant catechist, Philip Lobalu.

Their arrest was ordered after children from the Koranic school attended church on the Feast of the Assumption, on 15 August 1993. They were accused of encouraging the Muslim children to go to a Christian church, and of sympathizing with the SPLA. They would be released, just as soon as they confessed their guilt. They refused. They were transferred to a prison in government-held Juba, the capital of the South. There, they too, were subjected to the red pepper torture. They were released without explanation one year and 13 days later. They managed to slip out of government territory as the SPLA lines began to tighten around Kapoeta.

The church building was a mile and a half from the town centre and close to the frontline. During the ensuing siege, its grounds were desecrated, fortified and mined by the defending forces. A government soldier was shot by the SPLA as he clambered up on the church roof to hack down the cross. On 10 November 1994, government troops were driven out of the church compound during a battle which claimed upwards of 35 lives. But the SPLA advance got little further. Ammunition was low and water had already run out. Plans to take Kapoeta suffered a setback when part of a government ammunition convoy broke through their siege lines and managed to get into the town. Under fierce renewed fire, the SPLA were forced to dig in and wait it out, as their supplies continued to dwindle.

The hum of the Antonov's engines interrupted Caroline's interview with the SPLA Commander, Thomas Cirillo, on the front line. They squatted in a foxhole, their heads just below the surface, while the sound of gunfire and artillery shells filled the air. Eight civilians died and three were wounded in that single raid. As the sound of the Antonov faded, they resumed their conversation.

Commander Cirillo was slight and wiry, with lively eyes and a youthful face with faint scars that betrayed a long and close acquaintance with war. The former altar boy, a practising Catholic, told them why they were fighting. Before every battle, before the bullets started to fly, the government troops always treated them to a barrage through their loudspeakers. The chant went up: 'We will force you to become Muslims, whether you want to or not.' Commander Cirillo told Caroline:

Our struggle is not against Islam or against Muslims, but against a fundamentalist regime that wants to destroy our African heritage and faith. It is discouraging to see the Islamic fundamentalist government in Khartoum receive moral and material support from other Islamic countries, while we receive no support from the Christian world. We see it every day – how they are helping their people. Even their personnel are coming and fighting us. But we will continue in our struggle for freedom, even if we are forsaken by Christendom. We will die for our faith and we will die as Christians. But please help my wounded – we have nothing.

Caroline asked to see the church, so they could witness the destruction and take photographs. The Commander explained that it had been mined by the enemy and was just a kilometre from their lines. It was risky, but if CSI insisted, he would call for an engineer to clear a path, so they could walk up to the church behind him, single file.

'It was then that I discovered her courage,' Cirillo said later. 'There was nothing that could give her that courage, that could push her to sacrifice her life in the mines, except her determination to see the people who are suffering. We are soldiers, ready to die for our land. But she was a foreigner, risking her life in that situation. The enemy was bombing, as usual. A shell could just come down and take them. But they followed me, and we went up to the church compound, walking in a line, and she took photos so she could show people across the world the persecution of our people. Two weeks later, I heard her talking on Voice of America about the situation, and I was very happy. She became the voice of the oppressed.'

CSI were the first outsiders to risk visiting Commander Cirillo's soldiers at the front-line. It meant a great deal to him. 'We were surprised to hear there was such a thing as Christian solidarity,' he said, 'because the only thing we knew was Muslim solidarity. And as Christians, we had been looking around, saying: 'Where are our brothers in Christ who will come to our help? Because unless someone really comes and shares our sufferings, they can never know.

'In southern Sudan we have a special honour and respect for Baroness Cox as someone who is sharing our sufferings and fighting in her own way to see that our people are really free and can keep their dignity as human beings. In our struggle and our history, we will not forget her.'

Marked by fire

Internationally, there was growing condemnation of Sudan's record on human rights. Eritrea and Uganda had severed diplomatic relations. There was concern in the West that Iran might be willing to exchange material and political support in return for a naval facility on the Red Sea at Port Sudan. Russia was seeking new allies in the Islamic world, having strained relations with its former Turkic republics. It had signed an agreement with Sudan to provide military hardware and train officers. A cease-fire negotiated by former US President Jimmy Carter had failed to halt the government of Sudan's military offensives in Eastern Equatoria and the Upper Nile. The cease-fire was supposed to facilitate a programme to combat river blindness and guinea worm.

Neither the relief programme nor the cease-fire reached the village of Loronyo in Eastern Equatoria. On 1 May 1995, it had a population of around 6,000. That day and the next, 48 bombs were dropped around the outskirts of the village. On 13 May, the Antonov scored a direct hit with a 600-pound bomb, killing five women, two men and three children. The bombing continued until the village became a ghost-town. The bombardment was combined with a ban on the delivery of humanitarian aid. The people were forced to survive by eating roots and leaves, or by deserting to government-held Torit, where it was claimed, help would be given to those who converted to Islam.

Two-year-old Thomas Obuka was a victim of the bombs which fell on Loronyo. On 19 May, he was alone in his mother's hut, when it was caught by flying debris. The burning shrapnel set the hut alight, and Thomas with it. By the time his mother managed to save him, Thomas had received severe burns to his arms, stomach and legs. When Caroline saw him, about a fortnight later, he was in constant pain. 'If he survives,' she said, 'he will be disfigured for life.' The government of Sudan would not allow the International Committee of the Red Cross to evacuate Thomas and the other wounded.

It was just the latest blow the war could administer to Thomas' mother, Matilda. Her face a study in grief, she told her story to Caroline as she tried to comfort her badly blistered son. It began in 1992. She was in Torit with her husband and two sons when it was occupied by government troops. 'I was separated from my husband and forced to live as the wife of an Arab soldier,' she explained. 'I was also forced by this soldier to become a Muslim and given the name Fatima. One of my sons, Okasah, was taken away from me by *Da'wa Al-Islamiyya* [an Islamic relief agency, authorized by the government of Sudan]. He was placed in a Koranic school and given the name Ahmed. One night, my real husband and I tried to escape from Torit. We ran through a minefield. My husband stepped on a mine and was blown up. I stepped on a mine, too. That is how I lost my leg. Since leaving Torit, I have never seen Okasah. He would be eight years old now, if he were still alive.' It was because she had lost a leg that it had taken her so long to rescue Thomas.

One of the soldiers who had fought against the South at Torit was Manut Agoth Ajak, himself a southerner. As a young boy, Manut had followed in his father's footsteps, making the trek from Bahr el-Ghazal in the South to El-Obeid in the North to try to establish himself as a trader. But first he had to complete his schooling.

A year after enrolling, soldiers came to the school and forced Manut and many of his classmates to go with them. Those who protested were beaten. Manut was just 15 when he was taken to army camp for training. Two years after having left his home in Southern Sudan, he and others were ordered to go deep into the South to engage in the battle for Torit. Those who refused were sent to prison. 'Our officers always put southerners in the front line,' he told Caroline and John. 'Many died around Torit. After about two years, those who remained were transferred back to El-Obeid… I have seen brand wounds on the necks of southerners who have been tortured by security officers. In the army, there is constant pressure on southern soldiers to become Muslims. Those who do, get special privileges. Those who do not usually have to perform the heaviest labour and are quickly and severely punished whenever they make even the smallest mistake.

'When we went on reconnaissance missions and came across Dinka women, the Arab soldiers would rape them. Some of my fellow southerners and I were very angry about this, and when we showed our anger, we were put in prison. On 15 January 1995, I saw an opportunity to escape. I attacked a guard, grabbed his gun and ran away.'[13]

Manut's assertion that branding was taking place was backed up by press reports and video evidence, but it was not just adult prisoners who were being marked like cattle. *The Washington Times* carried an interview with a ten-year-old girl who had been captured, taken into slavery, and branded with a red-hot iron by the wife of her master. 'After she marked me like an animal,' said the girl, 'I managed to cross the river to a hospital in Shendi.'[14]

Shendi had been infamous as a centre of slavery in the days of General Gordon. More than a century had passed. Could there still be slaves in Shendi?

NOTES

1. Some local community leaders say the majority are Christians: CSI Sudan Report, 31 May – 5 June 1995.
2. Crucifixion of the body usually takes place after death by hanging: Amnesty International 1997 Sudan Report; but CSI has been told of cases where individuals who had been crucified were still alive.
3. Human Rights Watch / Africa notes, 'Some Muslim sects critical of the government and the National Islamic Front have been harassed', 'Behind the Red Line: Political Repression in Sudan', 29 May 1996.
4. Claim by Nuba community leaders: CSI Sudan Report, 31 May – 5 June 1995.
5. CSI Sudan Report, 19–25 January 1995.
6. CSI Sudan Report, 14–20 August 1995.

7. Geneva, February 1994.
8. The Archbishop of Canterbury did visit, first in 1993 and again, to Khartoum, in October 1995.
9. From an interview with Sky News.
10. Eiffe came under bombardment again at Lubon, a camp for 45,000 displaced people six miles from the border at Uganda. A woman and her two children were killed; 12 others were wounded. 'We can see no reason for the government to bomb this camp,' Eiffe told Associated Press, 'it has no military significance': 'Sudanese air force bombs refugee camp killing six', 'CNNinteractive', 25 July 1997. On 23 May, a UNICEF-chartered relief aircraft, was bombed by a government Antonov as it stood on a government-approved landing strip at Aburoc, resulting in the temporary suspension of all UN and UN-related flights and a further loss of relief aid to the needy: CSI Report, 11–16 June 1997.
11. The existence of ghost houses was confirmed by various sources, including Human Rights Watch / Africa, in 'Behind the Red Line'.
12. The practice was confirmed by MEC, 'Sudan's Crisis of Faith', 10 April 1993.
13. CSI Sudan Report, 31 May – 5 June 1995.
14. Shyam Bhatia, 'Southern Sudan's kids vanish into slavery', 27 April 1995.

FIVE

Nyamlell

By now, Caroline thought she knew Sudan pretty well. But nothing could prepare her for what she found in Nyamlell. Nearby was an airstrip which the government had closed to aid. As usual, all entry was forbidden to NGOs. CSI ignored the injunction. No sooner had their Cessna Caravan touched down on the landing strip, whipping up clouds of dust, than people emerged from all directions to greet them, relief written large on their faces. 'Thank God you've come,' said Commissioner Aleu Akechak Jok, a clean-shaven, bespectacled man in Western clothes. 'We thought the world had completely forgotten us.'

Everything had changed on 25 March 1995, when the militia swept in. Encouraged and armed by the government of Khartoum, some 2,000 men descended on the village on horseback. They were Arabs from the Rizeigat and Misseriya tribes, along with soldiers and members of the Popular Defence Forces. They killed 82, mainly men, and wounded many more, leaving the old for dead. They put houses to the torch, seized livestock, stripped the village of every personal possession – even cooking pots – and rounded up the cattle. And herded behind the horses with the cattle went 282 women and children. The government's response was to close the airstrip to prevent outside aid from reaching the villagers, and outsiders' eyes from seeing what had happened.

Eight weeks had passed before Caroline arrived. In the blackened ruins of their tukuls, remaining townsfolk line up to bear witness. Others emerge from the bush, having walked for hours to describe similar attacks on their villages. 'We were armed with spears and they were armed with Kalashnikovs,' says Garang Amok Mou, who lost seven brothers – four killed and three captured. 'My brothers were killed because they were holding spears to try to rescue their family, and they were mown down by automatic rifles.'[1]

Blind Abuk Marou Keer wears a torn grey top over a pastel-coloured skirt. She tells how she was hauled to her feet and almost strangled by her beads. She was herded with the other captives, beaten, then forced to walk.

She stumbled blindly behind the horses, struggling to carry property looted by her captors. Their destination was an agricultural labour camp at Araith, 18 miles to the north. 'Four male captives were murdered by the Arabs,' she says, 'and many women raped.' She was among them. 'The soldiers said this was retaliation for the death of one of their leaders in the raid against Nyamlell.' She continues, referring to herself in the plural: 'It was early the following morning before we reached Araith. We were forced to grind grain from sunrise to sunset. All we had to eat was the left over waste from grinding. We were beaten, sometimes with whips, but they left our hands untied. We told our guards that we were going to stretch our legs. They probably thought we could not get away because of our blindness.'

Abuk's mother was also abandoned by the Arabs and managed to return, but her children were still in captivity. Little Deng Deng, and his older sister, Kadija Abuk, were captured by the militia, along with her sister's two children who had been in the tukul. Abuk's daughter had been her eyes, leading her to the river for water, and to the forest in search of coal. Now her mother must show her the way, walking ahead with a stick between them for Abuk Marou to cling to. Abuk misses her children desperately. 'I can't live without them,' she explains, in her soft, high voice. 'If I don't find them soon I will want to kill myself. Just die. If I live, I hope God will bring them back to me.'

Akuol Maroor explains what happened to him and his son, Athem, when the militia burst in to the compound at Agro-Action. Like Abuk Marou they had been forced to march, carrying goods looted from their village. People were beaten as they walked. Some were killed. Many women were raped. 'We were luckier than most,' said Akuol. 'When we reached our destination I was discovered by a relative who was working with the government of Sudan. He took us in and I performed domestic service for him. We were set free four days ago, when my family in Nyamlell arranged for two boxes of bullets to be given in exchange for us. Athem and I arrived back in Nyamlell two days ago.'

Fifty-year-old Akuac Amet tells Caroline how she was beaten unconscious with a club. When she came to, she could not move her legs. They were paralysed. Her four sons who had been tending cattle lay dead in the field. Her 14-year-old daughter, Ajak, had been abducted. 'The raiders left with all of my property,' she says. 'I am now completely destitute. The owner of this tukul is helping me to survive.'

That owner is Adut Wol Ngor, a slight, elderly woman with greying hair, who is somehow managing to care for 62 of the victims of the March raid. 'They beat Akuac so badly, it was impossible to know if she was alive or dead,' she says. 'I came and took care of this old lady and have looked after her. Her daughter can be returned, if the money can be found – but there is no-one to pay the money.'

When the raiders came, Adut gathered up as many children as she could find and ran with them to hide in the long grass. 'The enemy divided into two groups,' she recalls, 'some on horseback and some on foot. They found us and drove the older children away. Any who refused to go, they killed. Those who went were tied with a rope and pulled like cows behind horses. Some of them were as little as seven years old. We hope God will bring peace to us and bring back our children,' she adds. Her manner, like all who bear witness, is quiet and resigned but, like many others, she is afraid the militia will return. 'We are waiting for death under these trees.'

A reporter cuts in to ask how many militia carried out the attack. Adut shrugs, 'The dust was too much – and the one who wants to save his life does not stop to count all the horses.'

The raiders had stripped the clinic of all medicines and equipment. It had taken the Red Cross 21 days to come and evacuate the wounded. Five had died waiting. Yet, despite the uncertainty, about 1,000 people were making the long trek back to Nyamlell each month, preferring to die in their tukuls, rather than face the end in the North. They were heading into a crucible. The word among the community leaders was that Sudan was being funded by an Islamic league to open a route deep into Africa for their firebrand version of the faith. Their intention was to capture the continent for the fundamentalists. All that stood in their way was the Nuba Mountains and Southern Sudan.

On 25 March, Nyamlell's two Roman Catholic clergymen ran for their lives. They escaped, but never returned, leaving the task of leading the church to a handful of determined young catechists. One of them, Gino Aguer, is perched on a bench in the church, leaning forward to add emphasis to his words. It is almost dusk and the sound of crickets fills the air. Light is streaming in through the pock marks made by bullet holes and shrapnel across the corrugated roof. 'If the church does not remain with the people,' he says, 'all the children will eventually be assimilated into Islam. We older people can resist this, but the children can be manipulated by food and clothes.'

He is barely into his twenties, and as skinny as he is earnest. 'We are suffering from nakedness, disease and hunger,' he continues. 'It is the responsibility of the church to be here. Please tell the world that we are Christians and wish to remain so.'

CSI made its report, but the stories of Adut Wol and Abuk Marou and the injunction of the catechist appeared to be falling on deaf ears. While human rights organizations were beginning to speak out over Sudan, the media and world leaders were muted. Bishop Macram Gassis made an appeal to the international community, 'The silence of the leaders in Europe, USA and Canada, and their procrastination – tomorrow and tomorrow – is giving a helping hand to the government of Sudan to eliminate its people through genocide and ethnic cleansing. The indifference and silence of Christian leaders is condoning the inhuman acts being perpetrated by the regime, and their silence is killing our people.'

Caroline was determined that the Bishop's cry would not be ignored. CSI set out to place Sudan and its renascent slave trade firmly under the media spotlight. But before she could act, two events took place which propelled Sudan straight to centre stage. The first was an assassination attempt, the second a high-level visit to Khartoum.

Assassins strike

On 26 June, the armoured limousine of President Hosni Mubarak of Egypt was wending its way through Addis Ababa. The President had just left the airport and was bound for a meeting of the Organization of African Unity. Top of the agenda was political insecurity on the continent.

His motorcade slowed, and then stopped unexpectedly. Delaying them was a blue van, which appeared to be blocking the road. Suddenly, the President noticed a man lying flat on the ground. Then he heard the rattle of machine-guns. Mr Mubarak himself takes up the story:

> There were about five or six [gunmen]. Some of them were on the roof of one of the houses, the others were on the street. It was shocking. Then I realized there were bullets coming [towards] our car. It is an armoured car, so I was not afraid anything could come in. One bullet came at the glass, but with no effect at all. The driver was an Egyptian... and I told him to turn back to the airport.

The driver turned tail and pulled the President out of the cauldron. Mr Mubarak escaped to tell his story to waiting journalists. Meanwhile, his bodyguards engaged in a gun battle outside the Palestinian mission, riddling a grey Volvo with bullets and killing several assailants. President Mubarak promptly flew back to Cairo, where state television was transmitting songs of praise for his deliverance.

Journalists were later shown the would-be assassins' hide-out, a rented house near the scene of the attack. In it were assault rifles, rocket-propelled grenades, a suitcase bomb and Islamic literature.

President Mubarak came to power in 1981, after a successful assassination attempt against Anwar Sadat by Muslim extremists. Under Mr Sadat, Egypt had been the first Arab nation to forge peace with Israel – a policy sustained and nurtured by his Vice President and successor, Hosni Mubarak.

His re-election in 1993 was followed by an upsurge in violence by the Islamists, seeking to impose the kind of fundamentalist rule being exercised in Iran and Sudan. Mr Mubarak's response was to clamp down hard on the militants. Their reaction was to redouble their efforts to oust him.

There had been several plots against the Premier. Responsibility for this latest was claimed by the Egyptian terrorist organization, Gama'a al-Islamiya, which pledged to continue its holy war until Islamic law had been established in Egypt. Western sources believed Gama'a al-Islamiya was armed and supported by Sudan.[2]

Mr Mubarak and others named the terrorists' puppet master as none other than Dr Hussan al-Turabi of Sudan. The Ethiopian Foreign Minister, Seyoum Mesfin, claimed 'overwhelming evidence that Sudanese security officials were deeply involved',[3] and the Organization of African Unity added its voice to the accusation.

Egyptian and Sudanese border police clashed in the disputed territory of Halaib, and Dr al-Turabi made rumblings of war, before the tension subsided and the media focus moved on.[4]

Diet of violence

Sudan was dragged back into the news within a matter of months, when the Archbishop of Canterbury made his second trip to the country in two years. Previously, he had turned down an invitation by the government to come to Khartoum, opting instead to visit the rebel-held South. Then, as now, Dr Carey ignored the convention that visiting dignitaries should confine their remarks to benign generalizations.

At Khartoum's Green Square in October 1995, the archbishop addressed an audience of thousands. He apologized to Muslims for any persecution Christians had been responsible for in the past, which was 'directly contrary to the love which our Lord commands us to give to one another'.

He gave an assurance that he was not attacking Islam, but continued with a warning, 'The process of Islamicization imposed on a nation undermines fundamental freedoms.' It was a conscious echo of the words of Pope John Paul II, uttered during his own visit two years beforehand:

The immense suffering of millions of innocent victims impels me to voice my solidarity with the weak and defenceless, who cry out to God for help, for justice, for respect for their God-given dignity as human beings, for the basic human rights, for the freedom to believe and practise their faith without fear or discrimination.[5]

On the eve of that papal visit, the impoverished displaced of Khartoum were offered cows, goats and cash inducements not to go and listen to his address.[6] Now, like the Pope before him, Dr Carey called for greater dialogue and co-operation between Muslims and Christians.

Addressing them together as people of faith, the archbishop asked, 'When we attack one another, when we destroy our lives – physically, emotionally or spiritually – we are setting ourselves up in opposition to God. How can we, people of faith, do that?

'My Christian brothers and sisters who live in this great land of Sudan... are not treated as equals. They often feel persecuted by the laws of this land. The list of grievances which Christians feel is long and heavy. Religious tolerance, which should be at the heart of any civilized nation, is not being granted to them.' Then to the Christians in the audience, he added, 'I sometimes hear it said that you feel you are a forgotten people. You are not. The eyes of your brothers and sisters across the world are on you, and our hearts are with you in your suffering.'[7]

While the Islamists found Dr Carey uncomfortable, his welcome by the Christian community was jubilant. At Juba, vast crowds lined the streets from the airport to the Anglican Cathedral, where the archbishop held an outdoor service for a congregation of 50,000. In an address entitled 'The Crucified Church', he referred to 'terrible stories' of persecution in Sudan, including 'torture, rape, destruction of property, slavery and death'. He added, 'I challenge those who are responsible for such inhuman behaviour to stop.' Caroline was one of several people who had briefed the archbishop before his visit.

'In such a context,' he continued, 'I would not be surprised to hear stories of a dying church, of people losing heart and spirit. But quite the opposite. Christ crucified is risen and alive in Sudan, his message is spreading and his body is growing at a rate which is almost beyond belief. Amidst the pain which afflicts so many of the Sudanese people there is a courage and a fortitude which is truly Christlike.

'The constant diet of fear, suspicion and violence with which so many of you live is enough to break the strongest spirit. You have had to survive out in the bush, hunted and hated... To remain unbroken, you must, at least in part, hold fast to all the promises of God and the presence of the Lord in all you do.'

Then the archbishop went on to quote an unnamed Sudanese living in Britain: 'Sadness,' he said, 'is not the whole story. In times of trouble we discover that there is some spirit greater than ourselves which encourages us. We do not forget how to sing... We sing when we celebrate and sing when we mourn. Everywhere in South Sudan the people were suffering but they greeted us with singing... The tragedy will not be complete while the people sing.'[8]

Irresistible impulse

The unnamed Sudanese might equally have said, the tragedy will not be complete while there is still laughter. Caroline later opened a debate on the Sudan in the House of Lords, with the Archbishop of Canterbury as an ally. It was one of those singularly inopportune moments when her schoolgirl sense of humour, a lifeline in coping with stress, almost threatened to sink her.

Broadcasters understand the problem well – it is called *corpsing*. If the giggles are going to strike it will be during the reading of a news story of the utmost gravity. It is the same reflex that makes one laugh out loud when a person slips on a banana skin. The more out of place and outrageous it is to laugh at that moment, the more offensive, the more detrimental to one's career – the more there is at stake – the greater the impulse to give way to helpless, shoulder-shaking fits of mirth. Few things could be more incongruous or out of place than a fit of the giggles in the House of Lords during a debate about the calamity in the Sudan.

'I dreaded opening the debate,' says Caroline, 'because I knew I would have to refer to the archbishop as the Right Reverend Primate.

'There were all these people sitting in the gallery and, on this very serious and tragic subject, the absurd nature of that struck me.' Fortunately for herself, the Archbishop and Sudan, she succeeded in recovering her composure.

The Right Reverend Primate's visit to Sudan could not have been better timed. It attracted widespread international news coverage. It also gave Sudan's Ambassador in London the opportunity to defend his nation's openness to all who wrote in to protest about violations of human rights.[9] But three weeks later, another event took place which was to capture media attention across the world.

NOTES

1. A 1995 report by the Comboni Fathers, Catholic missionaries to the Sudan, concluded, 'Nothing has changed in the way of life of these Arab groups for the past hundred years. Their only progress has consisted in the provision of large amounts of modern weapons and up-to-date transportation. The time of long lines of enchained slaves marching north is over. Now truckloads of children are seen moving in the same traditional direction': cited by Joseph R. Gregory, *First Things*, 1996.

2. *The Daily Telegraph*, 15 August 1995.

3. *The Daily Telegraph*, 13 September 1995.

4. *The Daily Telegraph*, 4 July 1995.

5. His Holiness continued, 'Where there is discrimination against citizens on the basis of their religious convictions, a fundamental injustice is committed against man and God, and the road to peace is blocked', February 1993.

6. 'Sudan's Crisis of Faith', MEC, 10 April 1993.

7. Khartoum Address by the Archbishop of Canterbury, 7 October 1995, *Worldwide Faith News'* archives.

8. The Archbishop of Canterbury's Juba Cathedral Address, 8 October 1995, *Worldwide Faith News'* archives.

9. In correspondence from Fadl Abdulla Fadl, on behalf of the Ambassador, February 1997, the archbishop is listed among other prominent figures who 'were provided with opportunities to meet and visit any place they wanted to see (sic)'.

SIX

Redeeming the Slaves

Caroline and John Eibner flew out to Bahr el-Ghazal on 23 October 1995, with one aim in mind – to once and for all expose the slave trade in Sudan by whatever steps necessary. They took with them a reporter and photographer from the German news magazine, *Der Spiegel*, a freelance cameraman from Channel 4 News, and a freelance reporter for the BBC and *The Sunday Telegraph*.

Their mission was in two parts. The first was a visit to Nyamlell, to gather further evidence of abduction and slavery following the raid of 25 March. The second was a long and searing trek across the bush to a nearby market, where among the salt, sugar and other commodities, would be human beings.

It was touch and go whether it would be the Cessna or the sun that would go down first in Nyamlell. The prospect of landing in the dark at an uneven and unlit dirt airstrip concentrated the mind of Colin Nelson, the young Australian pilot. It had been a long day, which had begun at 4 a.m. with a call to evacuate UN officials under threat from a breakaway Dinka warlord. Kerubino Kwanyin Bol had aligned his militia with the government of Sudan. Using government-supplied weapons,[1] he was operating a kill, loot and destroy policy from the government garrison town of Gogrial, in Bahr el-Ghazal. Some 40 relief workers were at risk. The UN had called a Level 4 alert before sunrise, which meant instant evacuation.

The ebb and flow of war across the vast open plain made charting a flight path little more than an each way bet. Each night the UN called a security meeting to advise where the new fronts were moving so the civilian pilots could plot their course accordingly. Their information wasn't always accurate. Two air taxis had been shot at by forces on the ground.

The sun was already beneath the horizon when he throttled back the Cessna and the dust cleared at Nyamlell. First on the scene were skinny Dinka children, grinning and offering to carry bags. Next came the men, leaning on their long, thin thumbsticks. Caroline was greeted like a hero. She stepped out of the plane, beaming, her arms held wide, then clapping in delight at the sight of her long-lost friends. Her joy was their joy. The tents were thrown up quickly on rock-hard, rock-strewn ground by the light of torches.

The following morning word got out, and people appeared from the bush in all directions to relate their stories to Caroline and the reporters. Some limped in on sticks, still nursing wounds. However far they had come, however harsh their injuries, they stood or sat patiently, waiting to recount the events of the raid in quiet, even tones. There was never a hint of anger, nor a strident note in any voice.

Among them was Apin Apin Akot, a tall, skinny jet-black farmer with a goatee beard, dusty *djellaba*, and striped close-fitting cap, or *taqiyah*, in shades of brown and sand. In his hand was a Dinka stick, a long, thin switch for the cattle. There was something about his eyes – an earnest look of determination, blended with almost infinite sadness. Apin was from the nearby village of Sokabat, a two-hour walk from Nyamlell. The raiders had gone there, too.

'Hundreds of men on horseback charged on people and we ran away in panic,' he told Caroline and the assembled reporters. 'My wife was taken, and my children, too. I was powerless to do anything.' Apin managed to run to safety with their baby, but his wife and two daughters, Akec, aged nine, and Afaar, aged four, were taken as slaves.

Apin sold his cattle for roughly $900, then followed the raiding party north, determined to seek out the man who had abducted his family and buy back his wife and children. He searched for months, all the while working and saving. Eventually, he managed to pull together 150,000 Sudanese pounds, the equivalent of almost 40 cattle. Now he was ready to confront the slave owner.

He bribed an Arab informer to take him to the man who was keeping his family. The astonished slave owner took the money and sold back to Apin his wife and younger daughter. But he was reluctant to part with Akec. He had other plans for the Dinka girl. He intended her to be a concubine. If Apin wanted his daughter back, he would have to raise a further 50,000 Sudanese pounds. His funds exhausted, Apin Apin Akot was forced to leave the sobbing girl behind. Her parting words were, 'The worst thing for me would be to die. As long as I stay alive, I know you will come for me.'

His wife, Acai, almost as tall as her husband, with close-cropped hair and gentle eyes, took up the story, 'The Arabs came at dawn and captured us. On the way they did what they wanted with us.' Little Afaar had been unable to keep up with the others as they were herded towards the north. To force the four-year-old to go faster, her abductor tied her to his horse and dragged her behind. Her left leg was paralysed in the process, and today makes a strange looping motion as she walks, the foot sticking out at an awkward angle.

'We walked for two days,' continued Acai. 'We were taken to a camp where they built a fence around us and kept us there. We were beaten every day, any time they felt like it. Sometimes we had to work as domestic slaves or as water carriers. For food we were only given unground sorghum – no milk, no oil, nothing else. My husband was at considerable risk of being caught and tortured.'

'I was afraid they might kill me,' admitted Apin. 'So I gave my life to God as a sacrifice, to go and die. That is why God brought me back and saved my life.'

Sub-chief Noon Anguon Mauyual was another of those who walked in from the bush to testify. With the aid of a stick, he limped over to a small, backless woven seat which had been placed in the shade of a tree. He wore a pale, short-sleeved shirt and trousers rolled up at the cuffs; and a pair of leather sandals on his feet. His eyes were sunken and dark, ageing him beyond his 40 years. Caroline sat nearby on a log, in her white shirt, Alice band and jeans, taking notes, as Noon told his story with quiet resignation and unsettling dignity. 'When they attacked, they didn't differentiate between men, women and children, between soldiers and civilians. They shot me and left me for dead. My children escaped, but they took all my property, 30 cows and goods, and burned my home and crops. I am now lame, because of my wounds, and I cannot make a living. I have no cattle left.'

A reporter cut in with a question, 'How many bullets went into you?'

'One in my knee; one in my ankle; one in my finger.'

'What went through your mind when they shot you?'

'When I was conscious,' he said, 'I was thinking that God would bless my life and take me to heaven, because I was attacked in my house when I was innocent.'

The reporter paused, 'Christ asks Christians to forgive those who hurt them. Can you forgive those who hurt you?'

'Yes,' he replied, simply. 'I can forgive him. Because I will stand before God, who is the saviour of our lives, I can forgive.'

There were no further questions. Noon lifted himself to his feet with the aid of his stick, and quietly slipped back into the bush.

Watching nearby, on his own on the edge of things, was a barefoot young boy in a check shirt that he had outgrown, and a pair of tattered shorts. The reporter asked through an interpreter whether he would be willing to speak. He nodded, an awkward figure, clutching his hands respectfully in front of him, his eyes searching for a space, over there, where he would rather be.

Deng Deng Gong was 12 years old; too old to let slip the tears that pricked near the surface. His father had been the headmaster of Nyamlell. 'When the militia attacked I was with my mother and we were in front of my father. He said, "You run quickly." Those who ran quickly, got away. Those who were slower, didn't. My father stayed back to make sure no-one was left behind. When we ran ahead, he tried to follow us and then he died, along with my uncle.'

The reporter gazed at the ground, thinking of his own son, who was just a little younger, wondering how best to frame his next question. Eventually it came, 'How do you remember your father?'

Deng's eyes flicked down. 'When I think and remember my father, I do cry. Because I lose my very best father, and there is no way to get him back again.'

There is a point at which another's suffering sinks into the heart of the hearer with a thud. The reporter, who was also too old to let the tears show, retreated into professionalism, shook the boy's hand, briefly held his eye, and awkwardly moved on.

Fifty-year-old Akuac Amet was the woman who had been clubbed and paralysed in the raid. She had not been brought out to meet the group, so Caroline went to find her. When she arrived at her tukul, it was evident why. Under a mosquito net, lying on clean bedding, Akuac was oblivious to her visitors. Semi-naked, her bones stood out on her back like a relief map. Her organs were almost visible beneath skin which had acquired an unnatural translucence. Her breathing was as shallow as a bird's.

Seven months had passed since Akuil Garang had been attacked in her hut. She was recovering well from a spear wound, a knife wound and a bullet wound. She lifted her top, and across an abdomen dotted with tribal markings running from sternum to navel in rows of three, snaked an ugly zigzag scar. The flames that had consumed her tukul, also claimed the lives of two of her children. Her third, six-year-old Atong, was taken by the raiders and was still alive. She knew, because an Arab trader had sent word. 'He has said to prepare money and he will go and redeem the child,' she said. 'I will get money. I can pay this man and then Atong will come.'

'Have you got any money?' asked the journalist.

'I have nothing.'

'Then where will you get the money from?'

She paused, her eyes wells of sadness. 'I am looking for something to eat. The money is too much for me.'

The Dinka had made an arrangement with the local Arabs to get back their children. A deal was struck in 1990, under which the Rizeigat Arabs would bring back their enslaved children in exchange for cows, cash or Kalashnikovs. The middleman was a trader they called Ibrahim. He would send his scouts to find where the slaves were kept, who they were, and where they had come from. Message would be got back to the Dinka. When their families could raise the agreed fee they would commission the traders to steal or buy back their relatives to order.[2] 'I am a poor nomad and have only 100 head of cattle,' Ibrahim explained. 'I have not been adequately rewarded for my labour. But I will continue to do this work to help children as long as I live.'

While some may have found Ibrahim's 'altruism' suspect, he was proving a lifeline for families whose children had been stolen and sold. Between 1990 and 1995, he had brought back some 160. According to Ibrahim, the raids were organized by the government to serve its own political interests. The government-armed militia could keep whatever booty they took, including slaves. Most they sold off. Boy slaves were more expensive than girls. 'Before 1991,' continued Ibrahim, 'it was common to find slaves in the offices and homes of government officials in Southern Darfur and Kordofan. But the government in Khartoum has instructed the officials to keep them out of sight.'

It was a system that made slaves of everybody. The families who remained in Nyamlell had lost everything in the raid – their loved ones, their homes, their possessions, their cattle. Mere survival was almost more than they could hope for. On top of that, they were now having to scrape together a ransom to buy back their women and children.

Slave market

The following morning, as the golden light of dawn was breaking, Caroline, colleagues and assorted reporters set off for the market town where the slaves were sold. They were given an armed escort of SPLA soldiers, some uniformed, others in African or Western clothing. The two German reporters negotiated the use of the Commissioner's motorcycle. They spared their legs, but terrified themselves by running over a substantial snake in the bush. The only other vehicles were a brace of bicycles of ancient design, rust-free and gleaming, but with three pedals between them and only one set of brakes. Most chose to make the 14-mile journey on foot.

The trail was a well-trodden sandy thread running between clusters of tall scorched grass and stunted red thorn trees, like upside-down umbrellas, whose pale and unforgiving spikes clutched at anyone who strayed too close. A labouring journalist anxiously inquired of John, a lanky Dinka with perfect English and an easy, loping stride, how long the trek would take. 'For a Dinka,' he grinned, 'little time. For you? Three hours, maybe four. This is not the way we walk,' he nodded disparagingly at the Englishman's shuffling steps. '*This* is how we walk...', and with that he bobbed effortlessly into the distance, before rejoining the group, still grinning.

Government forces were 14 miles away. Kerubino's men were also known to be in the area. But the real enemy was the heat, which grew steadily more oppressive as the sun continued to climb. The evening before had been spent on the vital task of filtering water. The Dinkas strolled, hardly perspiring, their habitual spitting observed with envy by the dry-tongued, sweat-stained white contingent, who were fighting back the urge to swallow water continually.

After a time, even the wiry American John Eibner lapsed into silence, sipping liquid from his camelback pouch, his eyes shaded beneath a floppy white sunhat. Only Caroline seemed unfazed, keeping up a steady pace and a ready conversation, always asking, always inquiring, finding out about those around her, while every other Westerner in the party conserved saliva.

After three hours, Manyiel appeared out of nowhere. A cluster of tukuls, giving way to rows of market stalls, Arabs mingling with Dinka, selling their wares. Sewing machines chatter in the dappled light beneath woven awnings. Bicycles are repaired. The pace of transaction is lazy, constrained by the heat. So this is the slave market. Where are they? Low woven beds are pulled around in a circle beneath a large, spreading mango tree. Sudanese tea is served; hot and sweet in small glass cups. There are still no slaves; no women and children in manacles; only stultifying normality.

After drinking her tea, Caroline goes off beneath the shade of the market stalls to talk to turbaned Arab traders. Slavery is not their business. Their trade is clothing; far more mundane. The conversation is led by the journalist from *Der Spiegel*, whose elliptical, softly, softly interview technique eventually draws an acknowledgment that the slave trade does indeed go on.

For Jacob and his partner, Ali, Manyiel is a six-day journey from the North, avoiding those in government checkpoints who would take a dim view of their trade with the South and imprison them for it. 'The government arms the militias with AK47s,' says Jacob, sitting comfortably on his haunches, 'to fight the people in the South and act as escorts for the military trains. The militia raid villages to capture women and children and to loot whatever property they can get.' The militia had a term for it: *ghazwa* – slave raids.

'They are using their people to spread Islam by force,' Jacob adds. 'We, the ordinary Muslims, are not happy about that. They are using religion as a means of obtaining power. But Islam should not be enforced in that way.'

Attention is diverted when the Commissioner arrives, unruffled and incongruous in a blue Western shirt and neatly-pressed slacks, smarter than anyone. He is carrying a plastic bag printed with a calendar on the side. The bag is stuffed with brown Sudanese banknotes. It is placed on one of the woven beds beneath the mango tree where the Sudanese tea was drunk, and counted into rows of neat piles. A book is produced, of names – the names of the slaves that are to be redeemed today.

From nowhere, a small group has appeared, sitting quietly around the gnarled and mottled trunk of the tree. There are seven of them to begin with: boys, girls and a nursing mother in disarray with her naked baby. They sit in silence, conserving their energy in the heat, expressionless around the tree trunk. Caroline moves over to join them, smiling and greeting. These, it seems, are the slaves. There are no whips or wooden cages. Not even a slave trader, it seems. But then, who can say what a slave market should look like in 1995? Like sheep in a field with an open gate, the human livestock continue to huddle.

'1995' is the date printed on the blue plastic bag which contains the cash. The Dinka, John, is counting it out on the woven bed, his green tracksuit top embroidered with a single word picked out in multi-coloured threads: *Freedom*.

Then, unheralded, the trader appears. It is not Ibrahim, the man who controls the operation. Ibrahim, it seems, is camera-shy. He has sent one of his middle-men, a gaunt Arab with a white *taqiyah* and *djellaba*, who is blind in one milky-white eye. Names are ticked off on a list and money is counted out. The transaction is captured on tape for the BBC World Service:

'Commissioner, how much money is changing hands here?'

'One million Sudanese pounds.'

'And how many slaves are being bought for 1 million Sudanese pounds?'

'It's around 20... 22.'

'Caroline, can you describe what's taking place?'

'This is a sad situation here. These people could have been freed, but the local community does not have the resources to pay what the Arab owners demand. What we have done is give money to the local Sudanese authorities here in the South to use as they see fit. But in essence there is 1 million

Sudanese pounds, which is about $10,000, which will be buying the freedom of 22 people.'

'And this man here is the trader, is he? What will you be doing with the money?'

'I will work with it and eat from it. Eat and drink.'

It could be a scene from a previous century, but for the date on the bag; but for the almost too aptly embroidered sweatshirt, but for the videos, cassette recorders and cameras that click and whirr to record the scene, to take the story to the world.

Sleepwalking through a nightmare

The deal is over within minutes. The reporter and photographer from *Der Spiegel* have to be fetched back from the market before they miss the concluding handshake. Those who have been redeemed are strangely silent. They seem to be sleepwalking through a nightmare. Subsequent CSI visits were to be greeted with cheers of anticipation, followed by tearful, jubilant reunions. But today, Caroline and John are two white strangers, and nobody knows what their coming will bring.

Caroline sits beneath the tree and tries to chat with the boys who have yet to be reunited with their families. But they are schooled in the art of non-being, of sitting in silence, perfectly still, of avoiding engaging the eye or drawing attention to themselves in any way. To continue to be, they have learned how not to be. As well as an absence of animation – a studied passivity – their faces, their eyes, are devoid of hope.

Bol Kuol is an inscrutable 13-year-old, with a scar across his right cheek and eye. He squats at the foot of the tree, aped by his younger brother, Mohammed. Bol and his parents fled when raiders attacked their village. They hid in the bush until they thought it was safe to go back, but walked straight into another attack. His father was killed. The raiders snatched up Bol on horseback and made his pregnant mother follow on behind. They were taken to the North to live and work in a cattle camp, sleeping in the open or under plastic sheeting.

Mohammed was born in captivity and speaks only Arabic. The boys were given Arabic names and forced to adopt Islamic practices, though their mother 'acted stupid' and pretended she did not understand what was required of her. They were referred to as *Abid* – slave. If they refused to work, they would be beaten. They managed to escape and met some contacts of the trader Ibrahim. A price was set on each of their heads of five cows or one automatic rifle. So far, their relatives had only been able to find three cows. Bol and Mohammed will not be going back today. They will remain the property of the slave trader, until their price can be met in full. It must be this way for, without payment, the stream of returnees will run dry. Bol's face is devoid of expression and his eyes are completely unfathomable. He lives somewhere deep within himself, an exile in his own land.

In the shade of the tree, Aluat Majok sits in the dirt and struggles with her baby, who roots at her breast. Bikit is eight months old, conceived as a result of sexual relations forced upon her by her master. Aluat has dusty braided hair and wears a jarring combination of tattered floral prints. Her eyes convey suspicion, fear and deep resignation.

Gently, notebook in hand, Caroline asks for her story. Through an interpreter, Aluat obliges, 'When the Arab militia came on horseback, their first target was the cattle, but they also abducted many people, killing any who resisted and concentrating mainly on the women and children. My master took two boys as well as me. I tried to escape but was beaten.' That was in 1988. Aluat was 12. She grew up with her master, in the village of Abu Jabra, was given an Arab name, Fatima, and made to go to the mosque. She pounded dura, collected firewood and did the jobs that the master could not get his wife to do. Her only pay was barely enough food for survival. And when her master's wife went to the market, her master called her to his room. She could not refuse. Each time he called her, she could not refuse. 'He would say to me, "Come with me." I would say no, but he took me anyway.'

Twice she tried to escape, but was severely beaten. Eventually, she conceived. When her master's wife realized Aluat was pregnant she became angry and drove her out of the house. Away from her master's gaze, she was able to get word to the one who releases the slaves. It was arranged for her and her baby, Bikit Osman, to be sold back to her family for five cows. But now she has had sexual relations with her Arab master, no young Dinka would willingly marry her.[3]

The story was the same for Chok Dut. She too, was captured in 1988, and made to work without pay, tending goats and fetching water. While she was still a child, Chok Dut was sent to Islamic school. At first she refused to go, but was forced to relent. 'I would not be given any food or water,' she explained. When she understood they would let her die, she agreed to go to the school. Today, Chok Dut was waiting beneath the tree for her ransom to be paid by her relatives. 'If the money is paid,' she said, 'then I will be free to go home to my father.'

These are the tip of the iceberg. There are thousands of women and children in slavery in Sudan. Caroline and CSI could never free them all, and some fear their involvement at all could actually stimulate the trade they are so determined to stamp out.

Caroline throws the point back at the journalist who put it, 'But what would you do,' she insists, 'if *your* child had been taken into slavery? Would you let them stay in slavery, or would you pay the price to buy back their freedom?

'It's a strange symbiosis,' she tells another reporter. 'A tragic one. Macabre. Heartbreaking. Words cannot convey the distaste of being part of that transaction. But until the system of slavery itself is destroyed, it's the only way the Dinka parents here can ever see their children again.'[4]

'No other option'

Their mission accomplished, John and Caroline are back in Nairobi, awaiting the flight home. Away from the heat of the bush, in the air-conditioned cool of the hotel, John Eibner is agonizing over whether they have, indeed, done the right thing. He debates with Caroline about how to present the press release, whether to point up the buying of slaves, or to play safe and bury the story. How will the world receive what they have done?

He rehearses his justification: 'We've had parents of children who've been abducted come to us and beg for our assistance in the redemption of their children. These children are sent north to work as slaves, to perform sexual services for their masters. Some of them end up in Popular Defence Force Camps where they are brainwashed to become militant Muslims and are then sent to fight against their own people. These children have a horrible fate in the North. Their parents are desperate to get them back.'

'Yes, but a human rights organization resorting to buying slaves...'

'We have no other option. There is no other way to help these people. But what we are also doing is trying to abolish slavery in Sudan. As slavery is abolished in the Sudan, then the slave traders will not profit.'

CSI's actions, however controversial, are not without precedent. A century ago, American abolitionist newspapers did the same. True, buying back slaves may encourage the slave trade. But the dilemma is much the same as that confronting a relief agency in a war zone. If they patch up wounded combatants, what is to prevent those soldiers taking up weapons again and wounding and killing some more? Should medical aid be withheld from the injured for fear of perpetuating the conflict?

For Christian Solidarity International, there is a greater precedent yet for a redeemer able and willing to pay the price to rescue people from bondage. It is the price of forgiveness that Christ paid on the cross.

In the event, John Eibner needn't have worried. While *The Sunday Telegraph* blared: 'Slave trade nets profits from Christian cash', the general reaction from the media was sympathetic. The reality of slavery, exposed in the slave market of Sudan, was put before a global audience of millions via the BBC World Service, BBC Radio 4, BBC Radio 5 Live!, Channel 4 News, *The National Examiner*, *Der Spiegel*, *Insig* magazine and the Gemini News Agency. Along with it came the expected denial from the London Press Attaché of the government of Sudan. Such talk of slavery, he said, was false: 'An attempt to portray the government as barbaric and inhuman.'

'The Sudanese government flatly denies that slavery exists there,' observed *The Economist*. 'It is lying: the evidence from human rights organizations, exiles, traders and former slaves is overwhelming.'[5]

Journalists from across the world started queuing to join CSI on further missions to buy back the slaves of the Sudan. Nowhere in the world was the interest greater than in the nation that had fought a civil war partly to abolish slavery: the USA.

NOTES

1. According to Amnesty International Country Report, May 1996.
2. A trader, known as Nur, was blunter about the way the deal operated: 'I have a big network of agents in many towns and villages in Southern Darfur,' he told Caroline. The agents tell slave owners that they can get money for their slaves. If the slave owners are interested in a sale, an arrangement is made for a meeting in the bush. Usually, we are successful in striking a deal. Some slave owners try to make things difficult, but at the end of the day, money can make everything possible': CSI Report, 11–16 June 1997.
3. 'Slavery in Sudan', CSI evidence to the US Congress House Committee on International Relations, 13 March 1996.
4. 'Dateline: Sudan', NBC, London.
5. 'The flourishing business of slavery', 21 September 1996.

SEVEN

Slave Societies

If there is one thing the USA and the Sudan have in common, it is a history of slavery. In 1860, there were 3,953,760 slaves in the southern states of the USA, making up almost a third of the population. Their labour was crucial for the maintenance and survival of the English plantation colonies of the south. The southern states were, by definition, slave societies.

It was the unfortunate Slavs, a people captured and pressed into forced labour in Germany, who became a byword for man's inhumanity to man. A slave can be defined as a human being who is stripped of personal rights and freedoms, who is owned as property, and who becomes totally subject to the will of another. Slavery, then, is the most absolute and involuntary form of human servitude; the utter negation of human rights.[1]

Slavery has been a characteristic of ancient civilizations, from the Aztec to the Roman. Slavery was the inevitable fate of the prisoner of war and whole societies were built upon a plentiful supply of free human muscle-power. It was the slaves who built the aqueducts, the roads and the temples, who served as the oarsmen of the fleet, and who slaughtered one another in the Coliseum for the amusement of the crowds. There was a racist element to slavery, as it was usually foreigners who were forced into servitude. The ancient Sumerian symbol for slave suggested 'foreign'.

The coming of Christianity did nothing to abolish the practice. Slavery was considered a natural condition of man, and few voices were raised against it. The Christian crusaders enslaved Muslims and Muslim pirates enslaved Christians. To satisfy the Crusaders' newly acquired taste for sugar, slaves were brought in from Russia and Europe to work the plantations. Eventually these were replaced by black Africans, purchased from the Arabs of the North.

In Europe, slavery evolved into serfdom, but the practice continued to thrive in the Middle East. The Koran called for compassion in the treatment of slaves, and like the Bible, made provision for their release.[2]

The first Islamic society to be based on slavery was the Baghdad caliphate, spanning the seventh to the tenth centuries. Its forced labourers were purchased from Europe, Asia and Africa, including the Sudan.

The practice of enslaving Christian children, enforcing their conversion to Islam and pressing them into the Army has a precedent in the Ottoman empire. A tribute was exacted from Christian subjects. That tribute was paid in children. Presented with the need for more troops whose loyalty could be guaranteed, Sultan Murad I trained up these children of Christians to become his élite new recruits, or *Janissaries*. For 200 years until the 1500s they remained the crack troops of the Ottoman army until they, too, became a threat to the sultan's authority. Then they were disbanded, put down by force, and banished.[3]

By the 19th century increasing numbers of slaves were again required to bolster the ranks of the Ottoman army. To meet this growing market, and at the same time find the wherewithal to pay their heavy taxes, Arab Sudanese ventured south to round up slaves. As they were doing so, Mohammed Ali Pasha, the Ottoman viceroy of Egypt, set about the conquest of Sudan, founding Khartoum in 1823. By reputation, he ranked among the greatest slave owners in history. Slavery continued to thrive under the Ottoman empire until calls for its abolition were heeded in the mid-19th century.[4]

Slavery had long been the lot of Sub-Saharan Africans, who were being bought and sold by Muslim traders from around AD700.[5] Slavery was practised in what is now western Sudan from 1200, and with impunity in central Sudan in the 19th century.[6] But it was not solely the prerogative of northern Arabs. Black African tribes also conducted a lucrative trade in their captives. Between 1750 and 1900 up to two-thirds of western and central Sudan was in bondage. In Kenya and Zanzibar, that figure was even higher. Nine out of ten individuals were owned by another.

In Catholic Spain, it was Muslims who were pressed into forced labour after the land was recaptured from the Moors. Their efforts were supplemented by Africans imported by Henry the Navigator. From that small beginning, Portugal grew to become the principal western European slaving nation of the 15th century, trawling the west African coast for able-bodied men to work the land.

Every industry needs its middle men, to find the goods and take them to market. Arab traders obliged by rounding up blacks in central Africa, and herding them northwards, to Arabia, India and Iran. Black Africans did little better, seizing their fellow countrymen to store them in holding pens on the coast until the European slave ships of the 1500s could arrive. From there they were shipped to the New World, where the native Indians had been all but extinguished by European disease and forced labour in the mines and sugar plantations of the Spanish conquistadors. Those that made it alive, often fewer than half, were sold at auction. Seasoned slaves – those who survived the transition – were shipped on to North America, where the first blacks went ashore at Jamestown, Virginia, in 1619.

It took England more than a century to get in on the act, but the British made up for lost time. Britain, Holland and France had established colonies in the West Indies, and Bristol and Liverpool prospered under the growing trade in slaves. Under the Treaty of Utrecht of 1713, the British South Sea company defeated stiff competition to win the exclusive right to supply the Spanish colonies with their most important raw resource. When Spain tried to revoke the agreement in 1739, Britain went to war. Profits from slavery bolstered the British economy. Between 1680 and 1786, Britain is said to have shipped some 2 million slaves from Africa to the West Indies.

The dawning of conscience

But slowly, conscience was dawning. The abolition movement gathered momentum in England from the 1780s. Its leading light was William Wilberforce, whose conversion to evangelical Christianity in 1785 drove him to stamp out the slave trade. Wilberforce became the movement's chief spokesman in the House of Commons. His was neither the first nor the only Christian voice raised against slavery. Quakers on both sides of the Atlantic had long been calling for emancipation. However it was not England that became the first European country to abolish the slave trade, but Denmark in 1792. Under Wilberforce, Great Britain followed suit in 1807. Seven years later, at the Congress of Vienna, Britain ignited the conscience of the rest of Europe, and gradually, but inexorably, the slaves were set free. As the Latin American colonies seized their independence from Spain, slavery was immediately abolished. Wilberforce died just a month before the fruition of his labour: the abolition of slavery throughout the British empire in 1833.

That year also saw the establishment of the American Anti-Slavery Society, driven by a core of educated, middle-class Christians, under the banner of William Lloyd Garrison, founder of the *Liberator* newspaper. The stage had already been set for reform by Washington, Franklin and Jefferson, for whom slavery posed a challenge to the Declaration of Independence. 'I have heard their groans and sighs, and seen their tears,' grieved the black abolitionist Harriet Tubman, 'and I would give every drop of blood in my veins to free them.' An escapee herself, she led 300 slaves to freedom in Canada along the Underground Railroad.

Emancipation was resisted across the cotton, indigo and tobacco-growing south, where politics and society were dominated by slaveholding plantation owners, unwilling to relinquish their principal investment. It was widely held that if slavery were abolished, the economy would collapse. State laws prohibited the education and marriage of slaves and barred them from earning their freedom. Some defended slavery as representing the law of nature, where the strong dominate the weak. Others claimed the sanction of the Holy Scriptures.

In an effort to promote a slave uprising, John Brown raided the federal arsenal at Harpers Ferry in 1859. Civil war erupted two years later. Britain and France were restrained from intervening on behalf of the Confederacy by the strength of their own national anti-slavery sentiment. On 1 January 1863, Abraham Lincoln issued his Emancipation Proclamation, declaring all 'slaves within any State... shall be then, thenceforward, and forever, free'. It was a proclamation of liberty for more than 3 million American blacks.

By the conclusion of the war, the cost of union and emancipation amounted to some $4 billion in property, bonds and currency, and the loss of 620,000 lives. The 13th Amendment to the Constitution, which abolished slavery throughout the USA, was ratified in December 1865.[7]

In 400 years of the traffic in human flesh, some 15 million men, women and children were bought and sold, while millions more perished at sea.[8]

In 1951, a UN committee declared slavery to be in rapid decline throughout the world. In 1962, slavery was abolished in the Arabian Peninsula, and in 1980, it was – again – ruled illegal in Mauritania.

The abolition of slavery had been one of the stated aims of British intervention in Sudan at the end of the 19th-century. Sudan became a signatory of the 1948 Universal Declaration of Human Rights. Article 4 embodies the International Slavery Convention: 'No one shall be held in slavery or servitude; slavery and the slave trade shall be prohibited in all their forms.' But at the close of the 20th century, Christian Solidarity International and its UK President Baroness Cox, found slavery to be alive and thriving, once again, in the Sudan.[9]

The tradition of Wilberforce lives on in the USA, with the annual giving of the prestigious award which bears his name. The 1995 William Wilberforce Award was made to Baroness Caroline Cox, for her continuing efforts to expose the slave trade.

'As William Wilberforce was a voice for the voiceless and stood against his party and fellow parliamentarians in his campaign to end the slave trade in 18th-century England, so is Baroness Cox,' said Chuck Colson, at the award citation in Washington. 'With true Christian compassion, fused with fierce courage, Lady Cox continues to shun mere observation for front-line participation.'[10]

Political leverage

By now, the media was running with the story of the continuing slave trade, but Caroline and CSI were not prepared to stop at that. Their approach was typically two-track and controversial. Having achieved exposure, they were determined to apply substantial political leverage. Their first major initiative was to organize a meeting of the divided opposition factions in Bonn, in June 1994, at a conference entitled: 'Human Rights in Sudan, Past, Present and Future'.

The conference approved the statement of principles put forward by IGAD, the Inter-Governmental Authority on Development.[11] It was significant progress. It meant the opposition groups were agreed on the need for democracy, non-religious government and self-determination. With those key foundations in place, the ground was clear for a more structural alignment of the opposition. The Umma party and the SPLA were the first to stand together, before being joined by the DUP. This preceded a coming together of the full National Democratic Alliance at Asmara, in Eritrea. The Asmara declaration called for a four-year interim government, followed by a referendum to settle the question of self-determination.

In April 1994, further steps towards unity were taken with the signing of the Lafon Declaration, which committed Drs Garang and Machar to stop fighting one another and turn their attentions to their common enemy, the NIF. But by August, all that was in tatters. Garang's troops were accused of attacking Machar's, and Machar's powerbase was collapsing. There were defections to Garang followed by an attempted coup by Machar's own Chief of Staff, William Nyuon Bany, who joined the drift back to the SPLA.

On 29 November 1995, a month after returning from her mission to buy slaves, Caroline and CSI facilitated another conference, in the House of Lords. It drew together more than 30 leading members of the Sudanese opposition parties, with observers from Ethiopia, Egypt, Eritrea, Uganda, Norway and the UN. Riek Machar was present, but his former Chief of Staff, William Nyoun Bany, was not. Six weeks later he was killed at his hide-out in Gul during a 15-minute battle with Machar's forces.[12]

Another significant absentee was John Garang, who was leading the SPLA dry season offensive. 'Dr Garang's absence reminds us of the many still on the front line defending their people, their lands and their freedom,' said Caroline. 'The purpose of the conference,' she explained, was to help to establish 'agreement in agendas and democratic reforms [that] will hasten the day when you take your rightful places in your own country'.[13]

The stand taken by Caroline and CSI was as controversial as it was unequivocal. CSI's International President, Hans Stückleburger, made his justification of their position on the second day of the conference:

> From its inception, the NIF's self-perception has been that of an international revolutionary movement... Sudan has become an important nerve centre for an international terrorist network, the activities of which gravely endanger the peace and security of it and its neighbours...
>
> It is right under these circumstances that CSI... working for religious liberty... is also committed to facilitating meetings of the persecuted democratic opposition... which collectively represent over 90 per cent of the people of Sudan. We feel we have an obligation to help provide opportunities for the legitimate representatives of the people of Sudan, who cannot freely fulfil their public responsibilities in their own country, to come together to develop their programmes and strategies for restoring peace and democracy.[14]

The UN had no compunction about sitting alongside CSI and adding its voice to the condemnation of slavery, 'in the strongest terms possible'. The UN's representative was Alan Parra; a bearded man with round, tortoiseshell glasses. He added, 'The fact that the Sudan government know this is taking place and have not taken steps to address the problem and to intervene to stop the slave trade [means] one can hold them directly accountable under international law.'

The conference called on the UN Security Council to initiate an arms and oil embargo against Sudan.

Simultaneously, Caroline was pressing the case in the House of Lords. In view of 'widespread, systematic slavery in north-western Bahr el-Ghazal', she called for pressure to prevent further attacks against the Nuba Mountains and the South. That pressure, she said, should be backed by an arms and oil embargo.[15] She concluded, 'In the tragic calculus of man-made suffering, the tragedy of Sudan ranks among the greatest in the world today.'

Her opening shot drew volleys of support, as well as a fusillade of return fire. This time, Caroline didn't have the debate all her own way.

Gathering stormclouds

Lord Avebury, who had co-chaired the Sudan conference, was a staunch ally. He marshalled evidence to show Caroline was not isolated in her concern. The United Nations Special Rapporteur, Hungarian Gáspár Bíró, had reported an alarming increase in accounts of slavery and the abduction of women and children. Evidence was emerging of Sudanese attempts to destabilize the region. The US State Department had accused Khartoum of providing a safe haven for international terrorists, including Hizbollah and Hamas. According to the USA, they were being trained at a camp north-west of Khartoum. *The Guardian* had accused Sudan of assisting in Iranian arms shipments to terrorists in Algeria.[16] The Ethiopian Foreign Minister had claimed the assassination attempt against the Egyptian Premier was supported, assisted and facilitated by the Sudanese security services. It had diplomatic cover and the weapons used were directly traced to Sudan.[17] In the interests of balance, Lord Avebury also pointed out that the Sudanese Ambassador denied the allegations of supporting terrorism.

Baroness Park of Monmouth picked up the theme: 'What the government of Sudan are doing,' she said, 'is part of a widely recognized drive by militant Islamic fundamentalists, lavishly funded and armed by Iranian and Iraqi money, to create a new sphere of influence in East and South-East Africa and to destabilize.'

There was widespread disapproval in the House over terrorism and human rights abuses, but the waters had been muddied by talk of militant Islam. Apparent criticism of another religion smacked of un-British intolerance and provoked a liberal backlash. It was exemplified by the Earl of Sandwich, who, while acknowledging 'daily suffering, torture, slavery... and flouting of every kind of UN convention in Sudan', said there was one impression he wanted to help correct: 'namely, that Sudan is a country in which religious organizations are rampant and engaged in some kind of eternal crusade for souls'.

Viscount Waverley also rallied to Sudan's defence: 'Those who speak for the nation have set a moderate Islamic course,' he insisted. 'The Islamic faith... deserves to be regarded with sympathetic and respectful understanding.' And he went on to warn against assisting the rebels in their aim of self-determination for the South: 'For the Sudanese government, the degree of autonomy demanded would represent the break-up of the nation.'

Anxious to show impartiality, government and opposition ministers alike pointed to violations of human rights by both sides in the conflict.

Concluding for the government, Baroness Chalker said Britain took seriously claims that Sudan was supporting terrorism. She described its human rights record as 'atrocious', adding 'it is totally unacceptable in the 1990s that systematic slavery should still exist'.

Slowly, but surely, the once forgotten issue of slavery was being edged on to the public agenda, mainly thanks to Caroline. Her endeavours were praised by several speakers in the House, though none more eloquently than Lord Avebury: 'We are indebted to Lady Cox,' he said, 'for her intrepid missions to some of the most dangerous areas of the world, from which she brings back firsthand evidence... Her work in Sudan has already done much to focus public attention to the horrors of the conflict... and now, in addition, she has demonstrated that slavery is still alive and flourishing in Sudan.'[18]

Caroline was also congratulated by the Labour peer Lord Cocks of Hartcliffe, 'on her absolutely indefatigable efforts on behalf of the persecuted people in different parts of the world'.[19]

But outside of the House her controversial methods were not always so well received. 'She's not the most popular person in Sudan among the humanitarian aid people,' says Christopher Besse of MERLIN (Medical Emergency Relief International). 'She has her enemies, and some of them feel she is not well-enough informed. She recognizes a bit of the picture, but not all that's going on.

'As a personal friend, she is one of the most wonderful people I know. I would die for her. She is so committed and her heart is in the right place. It's her *modus operandi* that's a little bit questionable. Some people find her rather too one-sided.' Considering the backlash that was building, that was to prove to be quite an understatement.

NOTES

1. 'Slavery', *The Hutchinson Encyclopaedia*, 1995; 'Slavery', *Funk and Wagnall's Encyclopedia*, 1995; 'Slave', *Compton's Encyclopedia*, 1995.
2. 'Islam, Slavery in', *The Wordsworth Dictionary of Beliefs and Religions*, 1995, p. 248.
3. *The World Book*, 1995, and *Funk and Wagnall's Encyclopedia*, 1995.
4. By the Tanzimat enlightenment movement.
5. *Compton's Encyclopedia*, 1995.
6. By the Ouidah slave trading state.
7. 'The International Slave Trade', *Encyclopaedia Britannica*; also 'Abolitionists and Emancipation Proclamation', *Funk and Wagnall's Encyclopedia*, 1995.
8. 'Slavery', *The Hutchinson Encyclopaedia*, 1995.
9. Other organizations to expose slavery in Sudan include: the UN, the US State Department, Amnesty International, Human Rights Watch, Anti-Slavery International, Release International, the Comboni Fathers and the Coalition Against Slavery in Mauritania and Sudan, which maintained that in Mauritania, some 90,000 blacks remained the property of their Berber owners. As in the Sudan, slavery is illegal, but persists, because, in the words of an Africa Watch worker, 'No-one is interested in a French-speaking country of only 2 million and no oil': Charles Jacobs and Mohamed Athie, 'Bought and Sold', *New York Times*, 13 July 1994.
   World Vision observed, 'Over the past year, we have seen increasing reports of slavery and forced labour of women and children belonging to racial, ethnic and religious minorities': 'Sudan – Cry, the Divided Country', Policy Paper of World Vision, USA, 1996.

10. February 1985.

11. Under the auspices of IGAD, Eritrea, Ethiopia, Kenya and Uganda had pursued a peace initiative for Sudan.

12. According to the SSIM: Dr Yasin Miheisi, *Independent Sudan Page*.

13. Statement of welcome, 29 November 1995.

14. Speech given to the House of Lords, 30 November 1995.

15. Britain had been instrumental in the adoption of an EU arms embargo against Sudan in 1994, and abided by that, according to the Foreign Office, November 1996.

16. The claim was supported by Sudanese opposition leader, Fatimah Ahmad Ibrahim, who accused the NIF of providing men and money for Algeria's terrorists. In addition, Algerian border patrols had discovered weapon shipments aboard trucks allegedly shipped from Sudan.

17. According to US sources, the weapons used in the assassination attempt had been flown to Ethiopia on Sudan Airways and one of the assassins had escaped to Khartoum using the same airline, Harry Johnston and Ted Dagne, 'West should be tougher on Sudan's oppression in its Southern Region', 1997.

Western sources accused Sudan of supporting Gama'a al-Islamiya, the Egyptian terrorist organization which claimed responsibility for the assassination attempt against President Mubarak. The Abu Nidal group was also said to be sheltering in the country, and a former member of Hamas had acknowledged training there, *The Daily Telegraph*, 15 August 1995.

In 1993, five of the 15 suspects arrested in connection with the bombing of the World Trade Centre in February were Sudanese. Four of the ten who were convicted were believed to be Sudanese, and two Sudanese diplomats in New York were suspected of assisting the terrorists, Johnston and Dagne, 'West should be tougher'.

The following year, *The Sunday Telegraph* observed, 'Such is the importance of the training facilities provided by the Sudanese government, that there is hardly a terrorist group in the Middle East which is not linked to the authorities in Khartoum... Whitehall now accepts that Sudan is rapidly becoming the Middle East's main launch pad for terrorist acts': Con Coughlin, 'Sudan trains terrorism's new generation', 15 May 1994.

18. Unstarred question on Sudan, *Hansard*, vol. 567, no. 10, 30 November 1995.

19. *Hansard*, vol. 567, no. 10. It was also pointed out by the Lord Bishop of Exeter, that while Europe was operating an arms embargo, France was providing military training to the government of Sudan.

EIGHT

Backlash

Khartoum welcomed in the new year of 1996 with a mass rally to celebrate the fortieth anniversary of the independence of Sudan. The occasion was marked by President Bashir, who proclaimed that a 'spirit of *jihad*' had engulfed the entire nation.[1] CSI was about to find itself embroiled in an extraordinary battle for credibility.

In March and April, Caroline and John Eibner were called to give evidence to the UN Human Rights Commission[2] and the US Congress House Committee on International Relations. By now, they had been eight times to Sudan, and the government of Sudan was not well pleased. The Sudanese rebuttal set the tone for much that was to follow that year, as intellectual conflict raged to establish the existence of the unthinkable – modern-day slavery.

The Sudan delegation railed against Caroline, describing CSI as Christian fundamentalists, whose accusations were biased, unfounded, distorted and sickening. CSI and others were being used as covers for exiled politicians: political pawns, funded by governments pursuing an 'Anti-Islamic Agenda'. Sudan and others had 'become the subject of hatred... a target of abuse, vilification and conspiracies...' Rumours of slavery had been spread by CSI as part of a flagrantly partisan political campaign.[3]

It was neither the first, nor the last attempt by Sudan to deflect attention from its record on human rights by alleging an attack against Islam.

In the USA, John and Caroline met congressmen, think-tank scholars and human rights researchers. They encountered avid media interest, and again, the stirrings of organized opposition. They were confronted by placards waved by anti-CSI demonstrators gathered under the auspices of the Schiller Institute. The Institute was co-founded by the US conspiracy theorist *extraordinaire* and erstwhile presidential contender, Lyndon LaRouche, along with his wife, Helga Zepp-LaRouche.[4]

In a breathless counter-claim outside the US House of Representatives, the Schiller Institute accused CSI, in cahoots with the UN Special Rapporteur, of being engaged in 'witting fraud' against the Congress:

'[They] have fabricated testimony during several trips to Sudan… CSI… is, in reality, a vehicle of the intelligence services of Great Britain… Lady Cox is also a trained psychologist in psychological warfare… the Schiller Institute deplores the war-mongering actions of the CSI.'

LaRouche's touch-paper had been well and truly lit. In a radio broadcast he went ballistic. He accused Britain of being bent on destroying every nation state in Africa, in order to seize strategic minerals and petroleum, condemning the rest of the world to a state of:

terra incognita: uncontrolled areas, bandits, wild people, starvation, death en masse, so as to reduce the world into a New Dark Age nightmare, in which the thieves of London like a modern-day Venice gone mad, control the world, without nation states, controlling what it wishes through… feudal-like entities, managed and protected by mercenary bands, while the rest of the world is condemned to darkness.[5]

Opposition at home

LaRouche's claims against Caroline were to get wilder yet. Meanwhile, more articulate opposition was emerging in the UK, from the Sudan Foundation, an organization founded by British and Sudanese businessmen to promote commercial opportunities in Sudan. Its director, Sean Gabb, argued against an embargo in an open letter to the British Foreign Minister, Malcolm Rifkind. Abduction and forced labour were illegal in Sudan and allegations of slavery had been investigated by the government. Though Mr Gabb did concede: 'it is conceivable that chattel slavery continues to exist in some areas not fully controlled by the government'.[6]

'Pressure groups,' he continued, 'are notorious for exaggerating or even fabricating evidence to support their case… claims about inter-tribal abduction or chattel-slavery [should not] be allowed to be exploited by Christian fundamentalist propagandists and others with the intent of grotesquely distorting Sudan's international image.'

Calling for an end to sanctions, Mr Gabb said: 'Sudan is sitting on perhaps 1 per cent of the world's known oil reserves… it is the potential bread basket of the Middle East… It has immense opportunities for British businessmen.'[7] And, he might have added, for Hussan al-Turabi.

Faced with mounting international debt and inflation, the Sudanese government had promised to tap the nation's oil and mineral riches – much of which was in the South – to create a model economy. 'Oil will fly out of the Sudan tomorrow,' promised Dr Turabi. 'We were dependent yesterday;

tomorrow we will be independent.' His remarks were underscored in 1998, when Sudan signed a $600 million deal with foreign companies to build a 1,000 mile pipeline to carry oil to the Red Sea. Among those who signed up were companies from China, Argentina and Britain.[8] The oil was due to begin flowing in 1999. As Human Rights Watch / Africa observed: 'The... war in Southern Sudan is being fought over scarce resources – oil and water – for which the South is the principal source.[9]

Nothing mobilizes international will faster than a whiff of oil. And oil tomorrow is collateral today. The Malaysian state oil company Petronas was a member of the drilling consortium. According to reports, Malaysia had helped pay off some of the NIF's arrears to the International Monetary Fund, which at $1.7 billion were the highest in the world.[10] China was also involved in the oil exploration, and shells with Chinese markings had been used in combat against the South.[11]

The government of Sudan had allocated a crippling 80 per cent of its budget to defence and security, and the war was costing an estimated $1.5 million per day.[12] For Dr Turabi's NIF to get the benefit of southern oil, the SPLA would have to be held back, the fighting would have to end, and Sudan would have to remain a single nation; the South united with the North. Meanwhile, in the certain knowledge that oil revenue would be used to fund the war, the SPLA declared the oil fields a military target.

Propaganda?

The follow-up to the Sudan Foundation's letter to the Foreign Secretary was a broadside against Baroness Cox and CSI. It took the form of an open letter from David Hoile, an author on Africa. Mr Hoile was described by his publishers, the Sudan Foundation, as providing 'public affairs advice, from time to time, to the Sudanese embassy in London'. His letter was headlined: '*Baroness Cox Heavily Criticized for Propagandist and Unproven Claims*.' Copies were distributed widely to MPs and the media.

The gist was as follows: 'I have grave concerns,' wrote David Hoile, 'at the way you and Christian Solidarity International... have approached the issue of Sudan. Quite frankly, for all [your] sensationalist claims and allegations... the evidence... is simply not there.' There was no evidence of the slave trade, he argued, nor any alleged governmental involvement in such a thing. 'Reports on Sudan by Christian Solidarity International,' he claimed, 'have lacked any sense of balance and objectivity.'

But having dismissed the allegations of slavery as unsubstantiated, the author then attempted to have his argument both ways. If such a thing as slavery *did* exist, he surmised, then the blame would have to be placed at the door of no lesser figure than Sadiq al-Mahdi. The former Prime Minister, he alleged, had been the architect of the policy to create the Arab militia. His decision to arm the tribes had been made in response to a raid by the SPLA in the Nuba Mountains in 1985, which had killed and wounded more than 100 Arabs. The implication was clear: it meant the side for which Caroline had chosen to act as advocate was itself responsible for the revival of what she was describing as modern-day slavery in Sudan.[13]

And having slapped the blame for modern slavery on the previous democratic government, Mr Hoile went on to argue that the NIF regime had not only outlawed and condemned the practice, but had intervened legally to prevent it.[14]

If he was right, then Caroline and CSI were courting and condemning the wrong sides. Furthermore, what Caroline was labelling slavery was not slavery at all: 'What has been increasingly presented as slavery by anti-Sudanese and anti-Islamic propagandists can in no way be compared to slavery as we understand it,' asserted Mr Hoile.

His contention was that age-old tribal feuding and inevitable hostage-taking for ransom had been mistakenly reclassified as slavery. 'What Christian Solidarity International has presented as slavery is in fact the taking of captives during tribal raiding... followed in some cases by equally illegal forced domestic servitude... Quite frankly,' he continued, 'if this is the best evidence that can be gathered to support allegations of slavery or the condoning of slavery by the present government in Khartoum, then there is not much of a case to answer.'

Mr Hoile went on to attack CSI's policy of buying back those it insisted were slaves. 'While undoubtedly done for sincere reasons... CSI is then party to a process whereby it pays ransom to people who claim to have in turn kidnapped children from their original abductors, with no means of ascertaining whether this is indeed the case...

'CSI's involvement... while providing media sensationalism, does not in any way provide evidence of slavery... Additional attempts to project the present government of Sudan as either explicitly or implicitly supporting or condoning these practices is fundamentally dishonest.'

Elements of the argument seemed compelling – compelling enough for several BBC interviews to get bogged down on the question of whether the women and children of Nyamlell were actually slaves or hostages – not that the difference mattered much to those who were abducted and forced into servitude.

When is a slave not a slave?

The argument turned on several points. Firstly, when is a slave not a slave? According to the Supplementary Convention on the Abolition of Slavery:[15] 'Slavery is the status or condition of a person over whom any or all powers attaching to the right of ownership are exercised.' There may have been no *right* of ownership over the women and children abducted from Nyamlell and elsewhere, but brutal *powers* of ownership were certainly being exercised over them.

Some observers, to satisfy their own agendas, prefer to sanitize what is happening by calling it hostage-taking. But far from being put up for ransom, many of the abducted women and children were being kept and used as chattels and remained as such for years.[16] In the words of Sudanese lawyer, Asma Abdel-Halim: 'Should we call it slavery? Yes, because there is slavery in Sudan, by any definition... to call it anything else would lift the pressure on the government to co-operate in ending the practice.'[17]

A further criticism was that CSI's actions could have stimulated the market in slaves and encouraged the trade. If so, one would have expected the price of slaves to rise and the frequency of the raids to increase. But local agreements between Arab and Dinka had prevented that. The price had actually fallen from five head of cattle to three.[18] CSI experienced some fluctuations, but the trend was downwards. From a peak of $500 per head, the going rate for a human being dipped to just $100.[19] And the slave raids did not increase in frequency.

Next, there was the question of the arming of the militia. But if the militia were to blame for reviving slavery under Sadiq al-Mahdi, then who was to blame for the continuation of that slavery today? Mr Hoile may well have provided his own answer to that question: 'In November 1989, the new government passed the Popular Defence Forces Act which absorbed the militia into the Popular Defence Force.' The aim of the PDF Act, he wrote, was to instil 'professionalism and discipline into these militias,' and to bring them under government control.

The inference, therefore, was that since the coup the militia had been incorporated into the Popular Defence Forces and were operating under the control and with the authority of the government of Sudan.[20]

In 1995, Human Rights Watch, like CSI, interviewed children who had escaped from slavery, and their relatives who sought their freedom. And its report: 'Slaves, Street Children and Child Soldiers', accused Khartoum of turning 'a blind eye' to the illegal capture of southern and Nuba children and subjecting them to slavery.[21]

Mr Hoile's argument, that because the regime regarded slavery as illegal it could not be said to be condoning the practice, was suspect because the rule of law was simply not working. 'Things rarely get as far as the courts,' said Anti-Slavery International. 'When families of slaves do try to get their children back through the courts, prosecutors and others usually drag their heels and do nothing, or help the slave-holders.'[22]

A case in point was raised before the UN Commission on Human Rights by Bishop Macram Gassis. When eight-year-old Hanna Akwal was taken to El-Obeid for sale as a chattel slave, a relative saw her and reported it to the police. The owner declared in court that the PDF, who had kidnapped the girl, was part of the Islamic Dawa (call) and *Jihad*. The girl was considered booty of the holy war and therefore legally his property.[23]

Forced conscription

But Mr Hoile pursued one further allegation which was uncomfortable for Caroline and CSI. And that was the claimed involvement of John Garang's SPLA in the very practice that Caroline was determined to stamp out. According to the US State Department, Garang's SPLA had 'forcibly conscripted at least 10,000 male minors' into its ranks and had used southern men for forced labour and portering.[24] Human Rights Watch / Africa had referred to the 'warehousing of children for subsequent use in the war... resulting in the training and recruitment of thousands of underage soldiers who were thrust into battle'.[25]

Mr Hoile's argument was supported by a former SPLA member who told journalists that he used to train child soldiers in Ethiopia. Farouk Saleh Mohamed Abdellah claimed: 'We took them by force from their homes, from their parents and guardians. We confined them to one place. The children that we usually took were between the ages of 5 to 16 years.'[26] The issue was raised in parliament by Lord McNair, who demanded: 'Mr John Garang [should] account for those who are missing. I hope [Lady Cox]... will press him to do that and to deliver the surviving children from what is a form of slavery.'[27]

Further capital was made from the point by Sudan's delegate to the United Nations Commission on Human Rights, Fathi Khalil Mohamed. Insisting that CSI was politically motivated, he observed it had 'totally neglected to make any reference to the thousands of children... who had been abducted and subjected to forced labour and forced conscription by its SPLA allies.'[28]

But despite the range and variety of voices raised in accusation, Caroline remains sceptical of the allegations of forced conscription: 'I don't say that it doesn't happen,' she says, 'but I have been to Sudan many times and I have yet to see any evidence of it. If I saw it, I would oppose it.'[29]

There were further accusations to come of other human rights abuses by the SPLA. According to Human Rights Watch, the SPLA had launched an attack on Ganyiel in July 1995, resulting in the killing of 53 women and 127 children. The SPLA claimed the attack had been unauthorized and promised to investigate, but did not.[30] In the words of Amnesty International: 'Both government forces and the armed opposition have committed abuses with complete impunity.'[31]

Caroline, of course, had met the SPLA's Commander-in-Chief and was encouraging closer co-operation between Dr John Garang and other opposition leaders. Could Caroline's opponents have a point when they suggest she is ignoring the abuses of one side while condemning the other?

Her response is characteristically robust: 'Do we turn a blind eye? We never deny the fact that obviously in any war, human rights violations are committed by everybody. We also recognize the fact that the SPLA are not immune to human rights violations themselves. Yes, abuses happen, and we have taken issue with the SPLA and publicly criticized them. But nowhere does the SPLA carry out the *systematic* violations of human rights of the NIF regime under their policy of *jihad*. The SPLA and the NIF are a world apart.

'Secondly, when the SPLA does find that its own members have committed serious violations of human rights, as when a rogue commander behaved brutally with some Roman Catholic missionaries, the moment we heard about the incident we raised it immediately with John Garang. He immediately investigated, condemned what had happened, apologized for it, took disciplinary actions against those who had done it – they are now in prison – and those missionaries are now back and working in the area.[32]

'We do criticize where there is cause for concern, but yes, there is bound to be a one-sidedness in our advocacy, because we want to be a voice for those who don't have a voice, and the regime, with all its resources, has every opportunity to speak up for itself and state its case.

'Lastly, there is also a huge asymmetry in the way the parties respond to abuses that do occur. The SPLM/A showed a very real commitment to human rights by organizing a conference on civil authority and civil society. In that context, some commanders did admit that they had done wrong things, especially in the early stages of the war, but realized they were wrong, regretted them, and said they wouldn't happen again. It is quite an unusual guerrilla army that will do that.'

Cynics and opponents of the SPLA would read her words as an

expression of naiveté; others as a statement of faith. There was a partial endorsement for Caroline's view from African Rights, who said at the least the SPLA was trying to curtail abuses by its members, compared with a total lack of effort by the government of Sudan.[33]

Discrediting campaign

Nevertheless, writing for the Sudan Foundation, Mr Hoile pressed home his argument: 'Baroness Cox... your work on the issue of slavery and slavery-like practices within Sudan is somewhat undermined by your close association with... those men who are directly responsible for them... What is even more questionable is that you have actively argued their case within the US Congress and at Westminster.'

He concluded by urging Caroline to consider 'a more balanced and less partisan personal approach to the Sudanese civil war' and to 'bring pressure to bear on John Garang... to end the slavery-like practices to which he has been so closely associated'.[34]

In what was to all appearances an organized discrediting campaign, printed copies of the letter attacking Caroline and CSI were sent to 200 British MPs. Hundreds more were distributed to the media. A thousand more went to business and community leaders and academics. Perhaps tens of thousands were distributed via the Internet. Copies were posted on many different web sites. It was translated into Arabic, Urdu and Italian.

'The doubts cast on the value of the work being done by Baroness Cox and Christian Solidarity International are influencing the media treatment of that work,' wrote Sean Gabb of The Sudan Foundation.[35]

Caroline's reply is as brief as it is frosty. She believes many of the voices raised against her and CSI have a clear political motivation. 'This is an attempt to discredit us in order to deflect attention from the criticisms that we have made. Our allegations are rooted and grounded in hard evidence, independently corroborated by the media and human rights workers. This is an attempt to distract attention from those really carrying out violations of human rights.'

Across the floor in the House of Lords, Baroness Symonds, Labour's front-bench spokesman on foreign affairs rose to speak on Sudan:

> [Lady Cox's] accounts are more compelling because she is not giving us second-hand accounts. She is telling us dispassionately but very clearly what she has seen for herself. She has not only been where the Sudanese government has sent her. She has been where she felt she

ought to go in order to get a clear, first-hand account... we all respect her courage for doing so.[36]

But the final few words belong to Dr Sean Gabb of the Sudan Foundation, who has worked so hard to discredit Christian Solidarity. Describing himself as 'a leading member of the Libertarian Alliance' Dr Gabb 'edits its successful quarterly journal *Free Life*'. His signed Editorial, number 24, entitled 'Why defend nipple rings?' observed: 'We defend the rights of sado-masochists, of autoerotic asphyxiationists, of pornographers, of racists, of holocaust revisionists, of believers in strange religions, of militiamen, and of anyone else we think to be persecuted.'[37]

Defending the rights of all, it seems – including the militia – over and above the slaves of Sudan.

NOTES

1. Broadcast by Republic of Sudan Radio, 1 January 1996, 13.00 GMT.

2. They had also given evidence to the UN Human Rights Commission in Geneva the year before.

3. From statements by the Sudan delegations to the sessions of the UN Commission on Human Rights, 1995, and 10 April 1997.

4. The Schiller Institute 'aggressively campaign on behalf of the regime', according to former congressman and member of the Africa subcommittee, Harry Johnston and Congressional Research Service African specialist, Ted Dagne. 'The group sponsors "fact-finding" visits to Sudan to show how much "progress" the NIF has made', and has organized trips for several state legislators. Its campaign, they say, targets African-Americans: Harry Johnston and Ted Dagne, 'West should be tougher on Sudan's oppression in its Southern Region', 1997.

5. *EIR Talks*, interview with Lyndon LaRouche, 29 January 1997.

6. In defence of the *Shari'a*, wrote Mr Gabb, 'It must also be accepted that there is a solid majority in the United Kingdom for restoring the death penalty for murder, and there seems to be some approval for the idea of castrating rapists and mutilating thieves – especially housebreakers.'

As for terrorism, Sudan had consistently denounced the assassination attempt against the Egyptian premier, and claims that Sudan was training Hizbollah and Hamas terrorists had never been proven. The coup that brought the NIF to power had cut short an period of 'riotously corrupt semi-democracy' that none should mourn; the torture and ill-treatment of detainees in Sudan was illegal and the SPLA had kidnapped children and forced them to fight in the rebel army. The Sudan Foundation's commercial connections with Sudan were made clear in their publication, *A Response to Baroness Cox*, March 1998.

7. Anglo-Sudanese Relations: An Open Letter to Malcolm Rifkind, Secretary of State for Foreign Affairs, December 1996, by Sean Gabb, director, The Sudan Foundation.

8. Associated Press, 22 February 1998. The previous year, 1997, the Canadian Arakis Energy Corp. announced plans for a 1,540 kilometre export pipeline to Port Sudan with a capacity to shift a quarter of a million barrels of oil per day from an oil field in southern Central Sudan.

9. 'Abuses by All Parties in War in Southern Sudan', 7 July 1994.

10. *Africa Confidential*, 9 May 1997.

11. In January 1998 a British company was among those awarded a $1.2 billion oil contract in Sudan. The US-based Occidental had withdrawn from explorations amid reports that America was providing military training to the SPLA's ally, Uganda. Uganda itself had a vested interest in supporting the SPLA – it was driving back the NIF-sponsored guerrilla groups in Sudan that were trying to overturn the Museveni government.

12. According to the Inter Press Service, 25 October 1997 and the BBC, 29 October 1997.

13. His authority for the statement was Human Rights Watch / Africa: 'The practices described as slavery in Sudan have their current origin in the human rights abuses committed in the civil war by government troops and militia in the south and the Nuba Mountains. These abuses did not start with the current

government which took power in June 1989. They routinely were committed by Arab militias armed by local government and the Umma Party under the democratically-elected government (1986–89) of Prime Minister and Umma Party president Sadiq al-Mahdi': 'Children of Sudan: Slaves, Street Children and Child Soldiers', Human Rights Watch / Africa, Human Rights Watch Children's Rights Project, New York, 1995. The allegation is reinforced by Anti-Slavery International, which argues: 'Nimieri... used al-Mahdi to encourage the deployment of Meseriya militia forces – initially armed by the Umma – against Ngok Dinka villages... many were killed at random and others were seized as slaves.' The allegation that it armed the tribes is denied by the Umma party, which claims the weapons were given out instead by the transitional government after attacks on tribesmen by the Nuba and SPLA: 'Slavery in Sudan', May 1997, pp. 9, 11. Mr Hoile pressed home his point: 'That the Umma party and Sadiq al-Mahdi opened a Pandora's box of inter-tribal violence is clear... And it is out of this deliberate policy that the allegations of slavery started to emerge.' Hoile drew support for his argument from the journalist Julie Flint, writing in *The Guardian*, 24 April 1993, and an African Rights report, 'Facing Genocide, The Nuba of Sudan', London, 1995.

14. A fact disputed by Amnesty International, whose Country Report of May 1996 maintained: 'Amnesty International does not know of a single case where a kidnapper or person suspected of holding domestic slaves has been prosecuted.' Evidence of legal intervention is provided, however, by Human Rights Watch.

15. 1956, Article 7.

16. The principal trader himself, Ibrahim, had been most insistent that he was not colluding with the slave owners: 'The slaves that I bring are those I and my friends have abducted from their owners. I do not negotiate for the return of slaves.' That position, however, was always suspect, and a trader confirmed to CSI in 1997 that money was indeed changing hands in exchange for slaves. 'We have to raise money ourselves to buy the children from their owners of from the cattle camps,' he told Caroline Cox. 'We therefore need the money to purchase the children. We do this on a commercial basis': CSI Sudan Report, 11–18 March 1997.

17. 'Slavery in the Sudan', Sudan Update and Anti-Slavery International, May 1997, p. 23.

18. A reporter from NBC observed that CSI was paying $500 per slave to a trader whose normal rate was $300, and suggested CSI could be driving up the price of slaves: 'Dateline: Sudan', NBC, London.

19. Linda Slobodian, 'The Slave Trail', Part 5, *The Calgary Sun*, 1997.

20. Mr Hoile went on to cite two academics, MA Mohamed Salih and Sharif Harir who supported that position against his own argument. They wrote: 'There is no reason to suggest they [the militia] were all under the full control of the government, a fact which prompted the government to promulgate, in 1989, the Popular Defence Act.' The implication is that the militia which attacked Nyamlell in 1995 could no longer be regarded as lawless mavericks pursuing ancient tribal rivalries, but as agents of government.

A second Human Rights Watch report spelt out the situation: 'Slavery experienced a resurgence when the Baggara [Arabs] were armed with automatic weapons by the central government to attack their Dinka neighbours in the mid-1980s... Following a common but illegal counter-insurgency theory of draining the 'sea' of people so the 'fish' or rebels cannot swim, the tribal militias were given a free hand to raid the Dinka, killing those who resisted, looting cattle, and violently capturing women and children [as] war booty to be used as slaves in unpaid domestic labour.' It went on, 'This practice continues today': 'Behind the Red Line: Political Repression in Sudan', May 1996.

The significant difference today is that the practice continues under the auspices of the Popular Defence Act brought in after the coup to bring the militia under government control.

21. September 1995.

22. 'Slavery in Sudan', May 1997, p. 15. The US State Department Human Rights Report on Sudan, 1997, said: 'In some instances, local authorities did something to stop slavery; in other cases, the authorities did nothing to stop the practice.'

23. Evidence given to the 50th Session of the Commission on Human Rights, Geneva, 1994.

24. US State Department Country Reports on Human Rights Practices for 1991, p. 382. That figure was revised upwards in 1996 to 17,000 and the allegation of forced recruitment was repeated in the report of the following year. It was alleged the boys, aged between 12 and 15 were forcibly recruited in the late 1980s and trained in camps in Ethiopia. When needed, they were inducted into battalions known as the 'Red Army'. According to one commander, '[When] the Red Army fought [it] was always massacred... they were not good soldiers, because they were too young': 'Child Soldiers and Unaccompanied Boys in Southern Sudan', Human Rights Watch / Africa, November 1994.

New ground rules were signed in 1995 by John Garang and Riek Machar of the rival South Sudan Independence Movement / Army, agreeing to support the provisions of the international Convention on the Rights of the Child. Garang told CSI: 'Since our convention last year, we have been working to allow the establishment of civil society and improve respect for human rights in Southern Sudan. We are doing so in a very difficult war situation, so progress is slow. We are not angels, but we are moving in the right direction. Our record is there for all to see': CSI Sudan Report, 14–20 August 1995.

Yet in June 1996, Human Rights Watch / Africa reported that the SPLA had again recruited underage boys from UNHCR refugee camps, and had forcibly recruited others in Western Equatoria: 'Sudan: Military Recruitment of Sudanese Boys'.

In 1997, Anti-Slavery International observed, 'Both sides in the war... have conscripted young teenagers to fight': 'Slavery in Sudan', Peter Verney.

The government of Sudan was also accused of the forced conscription of underage boys in violation of its own laws by the US Department of State, '1996 Human Rights Report: Sudan', and Human Rights Watch / Africa, 'Children of Sudan: Slaves, Street Children and Child Soldiers', September 1995, which reported: 'Army officials... set up checkpoints throughout the Khartoum area, and rounded up children as young as 12... during the training period... they were subjected to forced conversion attempts... and trained... as holy warriors.'

25. 'Children of Sudan: Slaves, Street Children and Child Soldiers', Human Rights Watch / Africa, Human Rights Watch Children's Rights Project, New York, 1995, pp. 31, 75.

26. Inter Press Service, 18 December 1996.

27. Unstarred question, Burma and Sudan, 11 December 1997. The previous month Lord McNair had visited parts of north and south Kordofan and had concluded that allegations of slavery against the government of Sudan, made principally by CSI, were without foundation.

28. Speaking in Geneva on 10 April. He said adults were also being abducted: UN Press Release HR/CN/798, 14 April 1997.

29. She dismisses one persistent claim of the hijacking of children as 'a misrepresentation and fabrication. Many of those children left their homes because life was untenable. They went to Ethiopia, partly to survive, partly to get an education. When the Mengistu regime fell, the SPLM/A actually took them back through Sudan to a large refugee camp in Kenya where they were able to get an education in peace. If they wanted to keep them as boy soldiers, they would have kept them in Sudan. Now the SPLA are gradually sending them back into Sudan to reunite them with their communities.'

30. Human Rights Watch, May 1996. Both factions of the SPLA – pro- and anti-government – had been accused of atrocity. 'The two factions of the SPLA [pro- and anti-government] have engaged in indiscriminate attacks, destruction of property, looting, and long-term sieges that starve civilians': 'Civilian Devastation: Abuses by all Parties in the War in Southern Sudan', Human Rights Watch, June 1994 .

Later, a number of women soldiers who quit the SPLA claimed they had been ordered against their will to have sexual relations with other soldiers. One lieutenant said she had been tortured for refusing to sleep with her commander: 'Sudan human rights: Women ex-rebels speak of neglect and abuse', Inter Press Service, 3 April 1997.

SPLA and government forces had both been accused by Gáspár Bíró of taking no prisoners. But by 1996, that had changed. The US State Department said the SPLA was taking prisoners and permitting Red Cross visits, and had 'begun to observe some basic laws of war'. It added: 'The government still does not apply the laws of war to the southern insurgency and takes no prisoners': 1996 Human Rights Report, Sudan.

31. Country report, May 1996.

32. The Sudan Foundation later claimed that no report or hearing had taken place into the incident, citing Human Rights Watch World Report, 1998, and the Sudanese Catholic Information Office: *A Response to Baroness Cox of Christian Solidarity UK, Regarding Criticisms of Her Work in Sudan*, March 1998.

33. 'Facing Genocide: The Nuba of Sudan', 1996, cited by the International Women's Committee in Support of Nuba Women and Children, Africa Policy Information Centre, Washington, 26 October 1997.

34. Sudan, Propaganda and Distortion: Allegations of Slavery and Slavery-Related Practices. An Open Letter to Baroness Cox and Christian Solidarity International, David Hoile, The Sudan Foundation, 20 March 1997.

35. *An Exchange of Correspondence between the Sudan Foundation and Caroline, Baroness Cox, Regarding David Hoile's 'Open Letter to Baroness Cox'*, 25 April 1997. The claim that Mr Hoile was a part-time public affairs advisor to the Sudanese embassy was made in *A Response to Baroness Cox*, Sudan Foundation, March 1998.

36. Unstarred question on Burma and Sudan, 11 December 1997.

37. Dr Sean Gabb: Brief biographical overview, and *Free Life*, No. 24, December 1995. Http://freespace.virgin.net/old.whig

NINE

On Whose Orders?

Caroline was not the only high-profile individual speaking out about slavery to be taken to task by Dr Sean Gabb's Sudan Foundation. Another prime target was the UN Special Rapporteur of the Commission on Human Rights, Gáspár Bíró.

Mr Bíró's report to the UN General Assembly outlined the following abuses:

- Aerial bombardment of civilian targets by government forces.
- Food and relief used to force people to convert to Islam.
- The killing by soldiers in uniform of some displaced people in the South who refused to convert to Islam.
- Arbitrary rounding up of children to be sent to special camps; to be ideologically indoctrinated and forced to become Muslims.[1]

Mr Bíró acknowledged an 'alarming increase in the number of reports' from a wide variety of sources on cases of slavery. The Special Rapporteur backed CSI's finding that the militia which had raided Nyamlell had been travelling aboard the Wau to El-Obeid military train. According to his evidence, Nyamlell was not the only town to be hit. 'PDF troops left the train in Aweil and... took thousands of cattle and abducted some 500 women and 150 children between five and twelve years of age.' The captives were loaded on the train and taken to Babanusa.[2] Once there, 'children are taken by *Da'wa Al-Islamiyya*, an Islamic non-governmental organization active in the field of education, while the government claims that they are displaced children. Big boys are distributed as workers... they work in the fields or as servants.'

In some cases, UN relief trains were followed a few weeks later by military trains. People who went forward in the hope of receiving more food were abducted... 'easy victims for the captors'.

'Girls,' he continued, 'become concubines or wives, mainly of soldiers and PDF members in northern Sudan... Dinka boys as young as 11 or 12 years reportedly receive military training and are sent by the government of Sudan to fight the war in Southern Sudan.'

The Special Rapporteur cannot but conclude that the... traffic in and sale of children and women, slavery, servitude, forced labour and similar practices are taking place with the knowledge of the government of Sudan... The manifest passivity of the government of Sudan... after years of reporting... leads to the conclusion that abductions, slavery and institutions and practices similar to slavery are carried out by persons acting under the authority and with the tacit approval of the government of Sudan.[3]

Playing the player

The Sudanese government's response was both lengthy and vehement, and published in full by The Sudan Foundation 'in order to correct... a gross imbalance in the reporting of Sudanese affairs'.[4] It demonstrated once again the old adage, if you can't play the ball, play the player.

The government of Sudan played the player hard. Gáspár Bíró lacked 'experience and professionalism... credibility and reliability'. His report was 'mere collections of allegations and hearsay...' motivated by 'intolerable bias... purposely to discredit the government of Sudan'.

'It is not always easy to tell lies', the rebuttal continued, before making the straight-faced accusation that Mr Bíró had conspired with the Eritrean government to fabricate 'all kinds of allegations against the Sudan'. Mr Bíró, they continued, sympathized 'with the rebel factions, in particular the SPLA-Mainstream of John Garang', and had endeavoured to 'cover up crimes perpetrated by the SPLA'.

As to the allegations of abduction and slavery by members of the Popular Defence Forces, Sudan's reputation was spotless: 'in fact these forces are carrying on a noble mission of protecting the relief routes and fighting banditry and outlaws who regularly interfere with the relief operations. Those forces should have been commended... manifesting the bias and political motivation of the Special Rapporteur.'

Slavery had been shunned and prohibited for hundreds of years by Islam, the government went on. Similarly, killing those who refused to convert was 'against the fundamental principles enshrined in the Koran'. Therefore, because these practices were illegal and contrary to the faith, they could not be going on in Sudan.

The Sudanese government then deflected fire from its own appalling human rights record by accusing Gáspár Bíró of attacking Islam. According to Sudan, the Rapporteur had overstepped his mandate by calling for the abolition of the Shari'a laws. The principled response was therefore to ban him from the country and call for his sacking, and Sudan appealed to all of Islam to endorse its condemnation:

'The noble issue of human rights has been manipulated to wage war against Islam... What we are really confronted with [is] a flagrant attack on Islam which goes far beyond the Sudan... No Islamic nation on earth should tolerate such a measure, since it would prevent all Islamic countries, not only the Sudan, from applying Islamic laws.' As a result of his 'contemptuous and blasphemous statements... against Islam and its laws...' the government of Sudan, there and then declared Mr Gáspár Bíró an unacceptable person to visit the Sudan, and refused to have any further dealings with him.[5]

The discrediting exercise was extended to Amnesty International, which had also questioned the *Shari'a*, by calling for the 'the punishments of stoning to death, crucifixion, mutilation and flogging [to be] removed from the Penal Code 1991'.[6] Therefore, Amnesty International, and anyone else who dared to question such laws, had to be similarly 'politically motivated against Islam'.

The discrediting strategy was spelt out by Amnesty: 'The military government has sought to deflect human rights criticism by accusing its critics of being motivated by a desire to oppose or insult Islam. This message exploits the beliefs and values of the Muslim majority in Sudan, and Muslims in other countries as the government tries to deflect criticism and build public support.'

'A second dimension of the strategy,' observed a later report, 'is to portray criticism as the product of a Western conspiracy... Dr Hassan al-Turabi went as far as to claim that Amnesty International was in the pay "of the British intelligence service".'[7]

'[But] Amnesty International takes no position on the political goals or ideology of either the government or opposition... Its concerns arise when those in authority violate internationally recognized human rights standards.'

And Amnesty was utterly unrepentant in pointing out exactly where such violations were happening: 'Since 30 June 1989, virtually all sectors of Sudanese society in all parts of the country have experienced the persistent and gross violation of human rights... by a political and security establishment that behaves as if it is unaccountable.'

The same propaganda techniques continue to be employed against a similarly unrepentant CSI and Caroline Cox, believes John Eibner. According to sources inside Sudan the NIF has launched a media campaign against Caroline at home and abroad: 'Every other day there is some negative reference to Caroline in the Sudanese media as the mastermind of some international conspiracy plotting to undermine the NIF regime. If Western governments take a strong line, they attribute it to the wicked influence of Caroline Cox. We are told there is a price on her head by our Sudanese friends.'

'I fully expect to be assassinated,' Caroline told a Canadian journalist. 'But I'm not going to be silenced.'[8]

Through the fog

Once the fog of obfuscation has cleared, one key issue remains – *is slavery taking place today in Sudan?* On that point, Amnesty was emphatic: 'Women and children have been abducted and sold into domestic slavery by government-controlled militia...[9] PDF and *murahaleen* militia appear to regard women and children as legitimate spoils of war.'[10] And of the women and children of Nyamlell, Amnesty reported, 'Some are known to be in the homes of militia members in South Darfur, where they are being held as little more than domestic slaves.'[11]

As to the notion that the slave trading was merely an extension of traditional tribal hostilities, Amnesty would refute that:

There is nothing 'traditional' about militia members being armed by the Sudanese authorities... Nor is the trade in children 'traditional' – the seizing of children in raids was stamped out in the early 20th century by effective government intervention.[12] The Sudan government provides bases and weaponry to militias and co-operates in military operations with them. The continuing failure of the authorities to act to prevent human rights violations by forces over which it has control, or with which it is prepared to co-operate or to arm, leads to the inevitable conclusion that the authorities support the actions of the perpetrators.

The meaning is clear and unequivocal: slavery is going on, and with the knowledge and support of the government of the Sudan, in direct contravention of its own laws.

Two days after Amnesty published its report – which was dismissed by the NIF – *The Times*' leading columnist, Bernard Levin proclaimed Sudan, 'A slave state of our time':

Would you like a few dozen slaves for Christmas? Well, not Christmas exactly, because the people selling these goods are very down on

Christmas and even more so on Christ. Moreover, the Christians very frequently are the slaves, and when they are, they are very likely to be tortured or murdered, or usually both. I should add that... those taken for slavery are used not only for the normal work of slavery, but for sexual services. Yes, yes and yes again, I am talking about the horrors of Sudan, which may well at present hold the Blue Riband of savagery...

There are many who are working hard to bring them peace, one being Baroness Cox... she has, with a very powerful team, brought to the world's attention the fact that sooner or later – more likely sooner – Sudan will be nothing but a charnel-house, where madness reigns and does not even know that it is mad.[13]

Bernard Levin's broadside prompted a predictable backlash from Sudan, and its apologists, The Sudan Foundation, which accused the commentator of hyperbole, and of recycling Baroness Cox's used information. The unblinking response from the Sudan Embassy in London was as follows: 'At no time has my government encountered a single case of slavery in any part of the country, let alone the existence of 12,000 southern slaves in the North.'[14] What the author would have made of the SPLA's claim that the figure was nearer 40,000 was anybody's guess.

Those who took part in a letter-writing campaign orchestrated by CSI hit the same stone wall. On behalf of the Ambassador, Fadl Abdalla Fadl replied, 'The unfounded allegations regarding slavery in Sudan are most outrageous... [and] not supported by credible evidence.'[15] In a later missive, he added for good measure, 'Sudan has always been an oasis for religious coexistence and tolerance... if there is a source of threat to this situation, it would be attempts by Christian Solidarity International, who have a consistent track record of hostile activities to overthrow the government of the Sudan.'[16]

In the heat of debate it is easy to overlook a central allegation of Gáspár Bíró that would have created considerable consternation in Sudan – that not only was the PDF abducting civilians under government authority, but members of the PDF were taking slaves and concubines for their own use.

The Washington Times alleged another, if possible, yet more sinister use for the PDF slaves – as living blood banks for northern soldiers wounded in battle.[17]

Bombshell

By now, Sudan's record on human rights had been condemned by, among many others: the UN General Assembly, the UN Commission on Human

Rights, the African Commission for Human and People's Rights of the Organization of African Unity, Human Rights Watch / Africa, Amnesty International, the British Foreign Office, and the US State Department, which observed: 'Slavery persists... the number of cases... have increased alarmingly... Government security forces were responsible for forced labour, slavery and forced conscription of children.'[18]

But it wasn't just white Westerners who were throwing the accusations. The Arab Lawyers' Union described human rights in Sudan as going from bad to worse. The General Arab Women Federation said much the same.[19] And it would be hard for Sudan to dismiss The Arab Organization of Human Rights as anti-Islamic. Yet it said among the most 'dangerous and worrying' reports it had received all year was information that slavery was still practised in Sudan despite the government's insistence it had put an end to the banned trade.[20]

Within a week of the statement from the Arab Organization of Human Rights came a further bombshell that blew a hole right through Sudan's denials: official confirmation of the slave trade from government sources actually within Sudan.

Two prominent Southern politicians had investigated allegations of slavery and had come to one inescapable conclusion: 'That many children from northern Bahr el-Ghazal are taken as slaves by Arab tribes... who live in areas bordering on the South.'[21]

The report's authors were the Rev Ambrose Adi, deputy chair of the National Assembly's Human Rights and Public Duties Committee, and Santino Deng, the political adviser to the government of northern Bahr el-Ghazal. Deng, a former government minister, had cause to be certain about the slavery, whatever the official line might say. The children of his own relatives had been abducted and enslaved by Arab raiders. Adi went on to urge the United Nations to send a fact-finding mission and his own federal government to take measures to curb the slavery.

But the revelations didn't stop there. Deng and Adi's investigation also supported the claims of forced Islamization and went on to allege the complicity of other Arab nations. 'Some of our children are taken as slaves and sent to Koranic schools in Djibouti, Mauritania, Gabon and Cameroon, the Kingdom of Saudi Arabia and Libya,' Deng told the Inter Press Service. Their findings were verifying all that human rights campaigners had been saying, and making a mockery of all Sudan's denials.[22]

Other voices were also being raised in Sudan, acknowledging the slave trade. Two lecturers from Khartoum University set out to investigate a massacre of the Dinka in Ad-Da'ein in which more than 1,000 men, women and children had been slaughtered by armed Rizeigats. The first to die were churchgoers, who had gathered for evening prayers. Many were later burned alive. The lecturers uncovered evidence of slavery by the Rizeigat militia, and exposed the government's lack of intervention to stop it.[23]

And another Southern Sudanese investigator Lawrence Tung concluded: 'There are genuine slaves, slave raiders and slave traders in contemporary Sudan.'[24]

NOTES

1. Other allegations included torture in secret detention centres and arrest without charge of suspected political opponents.

The practice of forced conversion was also identified by the US State Department. Its 1996 'Human Rights Report: Sudan', 30 January 1997, stated, 'Popular Defence Force (PDF) trainees, including non-Muslims, are indoctrinated in the Islamic faith. In prisons, government-supported Islamic NGOs offer inducements to, and [put] pressure on, non-Muslim inmates to convert. Islamic NGOs in war zones are reliably reported to withhold food and other services from the needy unless they convert to Islam. Children, including non-Muslim children, in camps for vagrant minors are required to study the Koran. In rebel-controlled areas, Christians, Muslims and followers of traditional African beliefs, generally worship freely.'

The allegation of forced conversion is supported by Human Rights Watch / Africa. In 'Behind the Red Line: Political Repression in Sudan', May 1996, it claims, 'The most serious religious rights violations, however, occurred in conjunction with the government's efforts to proselytize in prisons, the armed forces, the civil service, the universities and other sectors of society. The PDF is the principal vehicle for carrying out this agenda. Participation in 45 days of its religious-military training programme, intended to create holy warriors to fight in a holy war in the South, is mandatory for civil servants, university students, and others. The mandatory training, infused as it is with Islamic religious fervour, creates an atmosphere of coercion on all participants to convert to Islam in violation of freedom of religion, or if they are already Muslim, to join in the government's particular interpretation of Islam.'

2. Boys released from slavery described being herded into a carriage like a cattle truck and given one cup of water each day. They were referred to as 'Abid' (slave) and 'Gengir' (non-person): CSI Sudan Report, 11–18 March 1997.

3. 'Interim Report on the Situation of Human Rights in the Sudan', prepared by Mr Gáspár Bíró, Special Rapporteur of the Commission on Human Rights, in accordance with Commission Resolution 1995/77 of 8 March 1995.

His words were echoed in the House of Lords, by the Earl of Sandwich: 'By using those who practise slavery as part of their military campaign, whether or not as a deliberate policy of condoning slavery, they are allowing this major abuse of human rights to persist, at least by default': Unstarred question, Burma and Sudan, 11 December 1997.

Anti-Slavery International (ASI) took a different view, pointing out that the militia were not instructed to take slaves, but 'to kill everything that moves'. 'If charged with engaging specifically in the slave trade,' ASI continued, '[the government] may escape blame. A rigorous inquiry would probably find that it is condoning enslavement, but would not be able to demonstrate a policy of slave trading... Yes, there is slavery in Sudan – and it is a crime': 'Slavery in Sudan', May 1997, pp. 14, 20, 23.

4. November 1996.

5. That ban was to remain in force until August 1996, when Sudan again allowed him to return to the country. Caroline Cox paid tribute to Gáspár Bíró's work, which she described as 'outstanding' in her preface to evidence to the 51st Session of the United Nations Commission on Human Rights in Geneva, March 1995.

6. 'The tears of orphans: no future without human rights', Amnesty International, January 1995.

7. Amnesty International Country Report, 'Sudan – Progress or Public Relations?', 29 May 1996. The third strategy, maintained Amnesty, was divide and rule, by co-operating with some human rights agencies and disenfranchising others. The fourth was misinformation.

8. Linda Slobodian, 'The Slave Trail,' The Calgary Sun, 1997.

9. 'The tears of orphans: no future without human rights', Amnesty International, January 1995.

10. Amnesty International Country Report, 1996.

11. Amnesty International Country Report, 1996. Amnesty reinforced the point in its country report the following year, 1997: 'Scores of children were abducted by paramilitary forces; the fate of hundreds of children abducted in previous years remains unknown', Amnesty International Country Report 1997: Sudan.

12. Amnesty reiterated the point in its report the following year, *Sudan: Progress or Public Relations?*, which observed, 'many kidnapped children appear to be held in domestic slavery'.

13. 31 May 1996. He added that, according to the civil authorities, some 12,000 children were enslaved and the numbers were growing.

14. *The Times*, 10 June 1996.

15. Correspondence, 30 September 1996.

16. Correspondence, 27 February 1997.

17. It gave its source as an eminent southern lawyer, who felt it safer not to be named: 'Southern Sudan's kids vanish into slavery', 27 April 1995.

18. US Department of State, Sudan Country Report on Human Rights Practices for 1997, 30 January 1998. The report of the previous year also acknowledged: 'The taking of slaves, particularly in war zones and the export to parts of central and northern Sudan continued... Representatives of Christian Solidarity International have also confirmed the practice of slavery by arranging the purchase of children... There continue to be credible but unconfirmed reports of the existence of special camps in the South in which people from the North or from abroad came to purchase women and children for work as domestic servants.' A 1996 report by Human Rights Watch also concluded: 'Slavery continues today as tribal militias capture women and children as war booty': 'Behind the Red Line', May 1996.

19. In evidence to the United Nations Commission on Human Rights, 9 April 1997. The Sudan representative went on to accuse the spokesman for the Arab Lawyers' Union as being a member of the Sudanese rebel movement: UN Press Release HR/CN/796, 10 April 1997.

20. 'Rights Violations Widespread in Arab Countries', Associated Press, 29 July 1997.

21. The Rev. Ambrose Adi, deputy chair of the National Assembly's Human Rights and Public Duties Committee and Santino Deng, political adviser to Northern Bahr el-Ghazal, Inter Press Service, 24 July 1997.

22. But there was a crumb of comfort yet for the NIF. According to Deng's co-investigator, Ambrose Adi, in recent years, some of the Dinka had also resorted to the slave trade. He alleged Dinka were capturing Arab girls and taking them to their areas. Some had been bought back by their parents. Others were sold as wives.

The fact of intermarriage was acknowledged by representatives of the Rizeigat and Misseriya tribes, but the allegation that marriage took place against the girls' wills was contested by the Dinka: Nhial Bol, 'Sudan human rights: children still being sold into slavery', Inter Press Service, Khartoum, 24 July 1997. 'I have seen no evidence of that,' adds Caroline, 'and would have thought it quite against Dinka culture.'

23. The incident took place in March 1987: 'Slavery in the Sudan', Sudan Update and Anti-Slavery International, May 1997, p. 12.

24. 'Slavery in the Sudan', Sudan Update and Anti-Slavery International, May 1997, p. 14.

TEN

An Ominous Turn

Events were taking an ominous turn. Egypt and the Organization of African Unity accused Sudan of staging the assassination attempt against the Egyptian premier. The UN Security Council called unanimously for Sudan to hand over the three assassination suspects sheltering in its borders and to cease all support for terrorist organizations.[1] As the year wore on, the UN ratcheted up the sanctions, and in December called on Sudan once again to abide by the Convention on the Abolition of Slavery 'and put an immediate end to these practices'.[2]

All was not well between Sudan and its neighbours. Sudan accused Uganda of supporting the SPLA and retaliated by arming the Ugandan opposition force, the Lord's Resistance Army, which had bases in Sudan.[3] Eritrea went several steps further. It handed over the Sudanese embassy in Asmara to the NDA, and offered to supply the NDA with arms. 'We do not intend to show any courtesy with regard to toppling the Sudanese regime,' said the Eritrean President, Issaias Afewerki, 'and we are not working secretly in this context.'[4] Sudanese guerrilla groups were permitted to establish bases along the Eritrean border. Sudan accused Ethiopia of attacking its border posts.

Within Sudan, security forces staged a crackdown against suspected leftists and liberals. Sadiq al-Mahdi was arrested for alleged subversion and held for three months in solitary confinement in Kober Prison. Prominent party figures and religious leaders were rounded up, army officers were purged and trade unionists and activists were arrested after handing in petitions calling for the government to step down.[5] Bread riots broke out, following changes in the price of flour, and bakeries closed in protest. Fighting erupted in Khartoum, Omdurman and Khartoum North. Demonstrators took to the streets, to be met with tear gas and live ammunition. Up to 11 were killed. Communists and Ethiopians were accused of stirring up the protests. Scores of refugees were arrested, along with suspected left-wing activists. The economy was in ruins and inflation was soaring. The civil war intensified.

In March 1996, presidential and national assembly elections were held, under government decree that all candidates should stand as independents. Political parties remained banned under the state of emergency,[6] effectively sidelining the opposition, which boycotted the elections. Sadiq al-Mahdi was arrested again, as were a number of members of his banned Umma party. The American Ambassador to Khartoum described the elections as a sham,[7] and the US State Department condemned them as structured in such a way as to ensure the NIF would retain control of the government.[8]

The following month the Sudanese government achieved a genuine political coup. On 26 April 1996, Riek Machar of the South Sudan Independence Movement (SSIM) abandoned any further attempt at reconciliation with John Garang and made his peace with the government. Both sides signed a political charter pledged to preserve the unity of the nation, while giving wider autonomy to the South. *Shari'a* law was asserted as the paramount source of legislation (permitting regional variations), and guarantees were given that 'no citizen shall be coerced to embrace any faith or religion'. The way was cleared for a merger between both forces into a single national army.[9]

In May, a conference of the SPLA's political wing endorsed a charter on human rights and pledged to build a strong civil society in Sudan. It was a sign that John Garang's SPLA was beginning to address criticism about its own abuses.[10]

The ban on Gáspár Bíró remained in force until August, when the UN Special Rapporteur made his fourth trip to the country. Shortly after his departure, rioting broke out again in the capital.[11] Mr Bíró reported that circumstances in Sudan had deteriorated for the fourth year running. He observed, 'The whole range of internationally recognized human rights was violated by agents of the government... The practice of slavery also continued.'[12]

Sudan discounted his sources as dubious, political and unsubstantiated.[13]

September saw an assassination attempt against the former Prime Minister, Sadiq al-Mahdi. By his account, a government security guard pointed a pistol at his head in a mosque in Omdurman. According to the Umma party, the gunman was disarmed before he could shoot. Twelve other agents were involved in the conspiracy, they claimed. The Sudanese government's version differed on the detail. An innocent civilian had been beaten up by al-Mahdi's supporters – for trying to tape the sermon.

At the same time, Iran was making overtures to Sudan to consolidate its existing ties. No fewer than 300 advisors accompanied the Iranian President on his two-day visit to Khartoum. Teheran Radio described Sudan as of strategic importance to Iran in its 'international struggle against the [USA] and its followers in the region'.[14] President Mubarak of Egypt had earlier accused the Iranian Revolutionary Guard of training extremists at 17 camps inside Sudan. The camps were disguised as farms and the terrorists posed as workers, while training under cover in explosives and firearms. Unsurprisingly, Iran again headed the list of countries designated by the USA as sponsors of terrorism. But up there with Iran was Sudan, which was deemed a 'refuge, nexus and training hub' for international terrorist organizations.[15]

Now the two were planning to work even more closely. President Rafsanjani's visit was followed up, according to *The Daily Telegraph*, by a $9 million programme to install Iranian intelligence units in key areas in Africa. The aim was to establish 'a network of terror cells throughout Africa which can be activated at any moment to launch terrorist attacks, particularly against Western targets'. At the same time, the intention was to 'persuade the Muslims of Africa to accept the fundamentalist principles of the Ayatollahs' Islamic revolution.'[16]

That policy of persuasion was at that moment being spelled out in the villages of the Nuba Mountains. Government troops bided their time, waiting for the crops to ripen. It had been a good year and the harvest was plentiful. Then they descended on the villages. Families scattered to the hills and returned to find their homes, their crops, everything, burned.[17] Caroline spoke to families whose villages had been utterly destroyed, down to the last cooking pot. She met a father, mother, grandfather and five children living in the rubble. They said, 'We know why the government is doing this. They are trying to force us off our land, to go to the peace camps, to turn us into Muslims. But we are Christians. We will never go.'

In November 1996, the British Foreign Office added its own condemnation of Sudan's 'appalling human rights record', including forced Islamization.[18] It continued, 'The British government condemns slavery in all its forms... The British Ambassador in Khartoum is urging the government of Sudan to take action to stop the practice.'

'We are coming to get you'

In the midst of all this, Caroline and John Eibner continued their illicit visits to Nyamlell, to buy slaves and to bring the media to record it. Their work was creating ripples in the USA. Louis Farrakhan, the bow-tied leader of the militant black Nation of Islam, had added his voice to the sceptics. 'Where's the proof?' he demanded of the National Press Club in Washington, in his staccato, emphatic, pulpit rhetoric. 'If slavery exists, why don't you go as a member of the press, and look inside Sudan? And if you find it, then you come back and tell people what you have found.'

There was a scramble to pick up the gauntlet. Gilbert Lewthwaite and Gregory Kane – one black, the other white – of *The Baltimore Sun* got there first.

But before they could go, there were two issues to settle. Did CSI's account of slavery check out? And could the buying of slaves ever be justified?

They spoke to Sister Lucy Paganoni, of the Comboni Missionary Sisters, who had spent years in the Sudan. 'The government sends the Baggara warriors from the tribes of the desert,' she told them. 'They attack villages, burning produce, killing people. They take away young men and women.'[19]

So could buying back those men and women be justified in the name of journalistic – and humanitarian – endeavour? William O. Lowrey, an expert on Sudan with the US Presbyterian Church, didn't think so. 'It passes money onto the merchant, which is a way of supporting the ongoing slave trade,' he said. 'Do we make deals with terrorists? Do we pay a ransom? Won't that just encourage hostage-taking? Buying back slaves – doesn't that encourage additional slave trading?'[20]

Kane and Lewthwaite consoled themselves with precedent. The same debate had been raging before the American Civil War. Pro-abolitionist newspapers had placed the issue in the public eye by buying slaves. Almost 150 years later, they were going to do the same.

Their first impression of Caroline was the warmth of her smile and her boundless energy. John Eibner, they said, was professorial and 'driven, like Cox, by enduring outrage over humanity'.

It was April, the traditional time for the slave raids. En route, in Nairobi, the SPLA sent a message telling them not to go to Nyamlell for security reasons. The military train was passing through, raids were taking place and it wasn't safe. Caroline and John ignored the warning. If, when they landed, the civilians on the ground asked them to leave, they would do so; otherwise they were going.

When their Cessna Caravan touched down at the airstrip, they were warmly welcomed, although a sense of anxiety was tangible. Soon after their arrival, news came through that raiders had attacked the nearby town of Chelkou. It was the home of Commissioner Aleu Akechak Jok, with whom they had worked to redeem the slaves. His house had been raided and his cattle and belongings stolen. They even took his bicycle. The PDF sent the following warning to the Commissioner at Nyamlell, couched in a curious blend of Islamic protocol and the language of the gangland movie:

In the name of God, the Merciful:

Dear Outlaws,
   Peace be with you. We ask you to be alert, for we are coming to you at Nyamlell. Our force is 1,800 soldiers strong. We ask you to prepare yourselves, for we are coming to get you at 3 a.m. – so be prepared. Be patient and courageous.
El Sabur Company.
El Tewakalna Company, Commander of the Forces,
Captain Younis
Tag-Eldin Babo

You idiots. If you want peace, you should surrender before July, at the latest.
Commander PDF Hebeid
Hassan el-Hamer, PSE Colonel in Kordofan State

Thank you.

Wounded were already coming in. Caroline and John despatched their plane to fly them to safety, leaving themselves stranded. Apprehensively, they tented down for the night in Nyamlell. Unsurprisingly, sleep eluded her, so Caroline chased down a sleeping pill with a swig of sherry. In the event, Nyamlell was spared because the militia attacked another village instead.

Fate of the women

For the first time, they had the opportunity to talk to a couple of PDF officers, one captured, the other a defector. Farjellah Wada Mathar was a herdsman from Darfur, with no formal education: 'cattle were my school'. He had been recruited in 1992 and tasked with building and organizing PDF forces in three areas. His men were supplied with guns and ammunition but paid no salary. 'Whatever was taken belonged to the PDF and was our income,' he explained. They burned houses and collected children, livestock and cattle. The children were pressed into slavery. 'If the President said it should not happen, then it would not happen,' he said. 'But while the President doesn't stop it, the people think it is allowed and is normal... no-one has forbidden it.'

The second officer had defected from Kadugli, where he said there was growing disaffection among his colleagues. He said captured women would be taken back to the barracks, where the most beautiful would be divided up amongst the senior officers. The less attractive were sent to peace camps, where they would be collected at night to perform sexual services for junior members of the PDF.

Some of those had now been freed, and Caroline, John, and the journalists from *The Baltimore Sun* walked again to Manyiel to buy back slaves. The slaver had brought 28. Caroline had the funds for only 15. The trader warned, 'If the community leaders do not come up with the fee, I will not be able to bring back more children. This work is dangerous for me.'

The slave owners, he explained, were Arab extremists, who had been integrated into the NIF. 'All the slave raids since 1985 have been organized by the government,' he continued. Many slaves could be found in areas around Meyram and Fashar.

Cash changed hands, and once again cameras clicked and whirred as the journalists documented the traffic in human beings. But as well as bringing reporters, CSI had brought much-needed medical aid. 'You have rescued our people with these medicines,' said the Commissioner.

Not every well-intentioned attempt at relief was greeted with such enthusiasm. For a brief period the NIF temporarily removed Nyamlell from its list of prohibited airstrips. Another NGO took advantage of the respite to fly in a Buffalo plane full of seven tonnes of sand and stones to build a sanitation project. But if Nyamlell had one thing in abundance, it was sand and stones. The materials were locked away in an empty building, taking up a valuable resource, and abandoned. On another occasion a relief flight had landed to be greeted by expectant villagers. The plane was empty. It had been sent there to take away a pick-up truck that had been donated earlier as aid.

While Caroline and the Commissioner were catching up on events another casualty was brought in from Chelkou on a makeshift stretcher. His lower jaw was shot away and he was in pain and shock. Caroline dressed his wound as best she could with gauze and wadding and gave him some analgesic. He was the village sub-chief, who had run into Chelkou at the sound of the raid. He intervened to try to stop the PDF from capturing a boy. The militiaman turned his gun on the sub-chief instead, and shot him in the neck. The bullet passed through his mouth and took off his lower jaw. A woman was also brought in with gunshot wounds. CSI commissioned a plane to come in and evacuate the casualties to Lokichokio, in Northern Kenya.

The village of Majok Kuom was one of many that had just been raided. Despite the risk, Caroline, John and the journalists decided to go there to gather evidence. They set off on antique bicycles until the tyres became so full of thorns they were forced to continue the journey on foot.

What confronted them on their arrival was a desolate scene of burned-out tukuls and charred rubble. Nothing was left intact. The crops were blackened and the livestock stolen. Twelve women and children had been captured. Three had escaped. One survivor, Tong Anei, had heard them shouting, 'Allah-u Akbar, Allah-u Akbar!' People were running everywhere, trying to get away, but he stayed to protect his wife and 15-year-old daughter. It was an unequal struggle. Eight militia surrounded his hut, beat him and abducted his wife and daughter before his eyes. He watched as the children were tied together and women, including his wife, were made to carry the looted sorghum and peanuts. When they were loaded up with every ounce they could carry, the militia burned what remained.

A small, frail woman, with thick matted hair, was standing in the charred remains of her home. The raiders had taken her daughters, aged 13 and 15. It was the second attack on her village within a year. This time, along with her children, the raiders grabbed her few remaining goats. Last time, they had overlooked some cattle. The villagers had used most of them to buy back their children. Now, the last of their cattle had been stolen, too. Amidst the rubble that had been her home, in a dress that was torn, the elderly woman observed simply, 'I shall die. I have nothing left. All we have to eat is leaves.' There was no hint of self-pity in her voice. She smiled and said to Caroline, 'Thank you for coming, thank you for caring.'

At another village, Caroline spoke to survivors. They included a young man who had been tending cattle. He was shot in the arm, his hands were tied together and he was dragged behind a horse until his arm was severed from his shoulder. Then they left him for dead. He was found by other villagers who had run from the raid.

Caroline talked to a young boy who had been captured and kept in a cattle compound with several hundred others. They were regularly beaten. If a master took a dislike to a child, he would pour boiling water in his ears. Eleven children had suffered in that way. Most had subsequently died. If any tried to escape, their masters would slash their Achilles tendons. It made them less useful as slaves, but they could still hobble after the herds, and a slave that could hobble was better than a slave that took flight.

Thirteen-year-old Lual Deng, from Nyamlell, still carried a legacy of the

March 1995 raid. He had been abducted and caught whilst trying to escape. To prevent any further recurrence, his captors had thrust a knife deep into his hips and left him lying on the ground. Despite his injuries, he managed to crawl away and drag himself home. His wounds were still visible.

Anger like ice

Caroline's reaction to all this atrocity is to become steely determined to stamp it out. As she describes such things, her jaw sets, her eyes gaze into the middle distance and her words become clipped and clinical. The horror of what she has seen turns to an icy, controlled anger, which is expressed in an utter resolution to act.

'The feelings are so deep and so complicated, it's hard to verbalize them,' she says. 'Immense, deep grief. If you talk to a mother whose children are currently slaves, what do you say? There aren't any words to describe it. Deep anger, that this is part of a systematic policy, being pursued and encouraged by a government that is sitting in Khartoum. It makes me feel intense anger and a passionate commitment to try to do something about it, to try to expose it, to try to get it stopped, to try to get anyone who is at the moment a slave, set free.'

But Caroline draws the line at hatred. 'One thing I most admire about the people we meet in these situations is that they are the ones who are suffering, yet they don't feel hatred. It would certainly not be right, as a Christian, to feel hatred. And if they who are suffering don't feel hatred, why should I?'

Journalists Kane and Lewthwaite purchased slaves of their own, who they handed back to their father, and returned with some excellent copy. Their coverage was tipped for a Pulitzer and was syndicated around the world. Armed with irrefutable evidence, they confronted Sudan's Ambassador to the USA, Mahdi Ibrahim Mohamed. He was unmoved.

'There are no slaves,' he explained. 'Slavery is not the practice of the government of Sudan.' What the reporters had witnessed were tribal disputes over grazing and water. The militia were there to protect the villages against rebel attack, he reasoned. They were not authorized to take slaves. If such a practice could be established, the government would 'take all measures' against it.

He said much the same when confronted by another set of reporters from NBC. Having watched a videotaped confession by a captured PDF militia leader, he cast doubt on the man's veracity and declared, with the flag of Sudan behind him, 'This is just outrageous. It cannot happen. The practice of taking people, enslaving them and, as you term it, chattel slavery: that is contrary to the policy of the government.'[21]

Perhaps he believed his own line. Perhaps he was unaware, even as he was offering his ritual denial, that two of his government's own politicians were investigating – and confirming – the slave trade.[22] But the only thing Kane and Lewthwaite could find themselves nodding to in agreement was his final statement: 'The practice of slavery is something that amounts to an abominable act to every single individual, every citizen, to every responsible person. It is also contrary to the spirit of the soul of every individual, to our religion, our traditions, to Muslims and to the enemy.'[23]

As for Louis Farrakhan, the leader of the Nation of Islam, who had throw down the challenge to prove the existence of slavery; his own newspaper, *The Final Call*, denounced *The Baltimore Sun*'s story as Zionist lies and propaganda. In all his travels to Sudan, he maintained, no-one had told him about slavery.

But Bona Malwal, a former Sudanese cabinet minister and editor of the London-based *Sudan Democratic Gazette*, begged to differ. In 1994 he had spent a week with Farrakhan in Nairobi. 'We talked about slavery,' he told *The Boston Globe*, 'It came up very often. He said he had been told about the slave camps.' A senior SPLA official said he, too, had informed Farrakhan about the slavery.

Boston Globe columnist, Jeff Jacoby, was forced to conclude, 'To speak out on behalf of Sudan's black slaves would be to forfeit the patronage of Khartoum's Arab dictators. That was a price Farrakhan wouldn't pay.'[24]

NOTES

1. Resolution 1044 (1996), adopted by the Security Council at its 3627th meeting, 31 January 1996. When Sudan failed to comply, it called on member states to restrict the number and travel rights of Sudanese diplomatic staff (Resolution 1054 (1996), adopted by the Security Council at its 3660th meeting, 26 April 1996). When that made no difference it called for a flight ban over members' airspace on planes operated by Sudan Airways (Resolution 1070 (1996), adopted by the Security Council at its 3690th meeting, 16 August 1996).
2. 82nd plenary meeting, sections two and three, 12 December 1996.
3. Amnesty International Press Release, 29 October 1996.
4. In an interview with *al-Hayat* newspaper, reported in *Sudan News and Views*, No. 17, January 1996.
5. 'Amnesty International Country Report 1997: Sudan'; UN 50th Session, agenda item 112c, 18–19; *Sudan News and Views*, No. 17, January 1996.
6. 'The regime of al-Bashir', BBC News, 29 October 1997.
7. *The Daily Telegraph*, 31 July 1995.
8. Human Rights Report, Sudan, 1996.
9. Political Charter of 26 April 1996, between the Sudanese government and the SPLA (United).
10. Building on that in June 1997, the New Sudan Council of Churches and the Sudan People's Liberation Movement (the political wing of the SPLA) formed a joint committee to establish guidelines for the future of Sudan. They included a commitment to develop peace initiatives and respect human rights, 'Church Forging New Relationships in the Sudan', *AfricaNews*, 30 June 1997.

11. 'Amnesty International Country Report 1997: Sudan'. When Mr Bíró returned the following year on a scheduled visit to Khartoum on 14 January, the authorities were in the middle of another round up of detainees. Because his safety 'could not be guaranteed', it was necessary for the Rapporteur to leave the following day. 'Amnesty International believes the government's action amounted to expelling the Special Rapporteur at a time when it was engaged in arresting political opponents': 'A New Clampdown on Political Opponents', Amnesty International, April 1997.

12. UN Press Release HR/CN/795. The Special Rapporteur also criticized investigations by Sudan into the issue of slavery for glossing over the data and shedding little light on the horror. Slavery and slavery-like practices in Sudan were condemned once again at the 53rd Session of the UN Commission on Human Rights on 18 April 1997, UN Press Release HR/CN/808.

13. Ahmed el-Mufti complained that he had taken more cognisance from the armed opposition which 'had raised the banner of human rights to camouflage their political and military objectives': UN Press Release, HR/CN/795, April 1997.

14. *The Guardian*, 11 September 1996. In 1994, *The Sunday Telegraph* reported that there were 3,000 Iranian revolutionary guards in Sudan, acting officially as military advisors, but thought to be training as terrorists. The Iranian navy was using Port Sudan for resupply, and special landing rights had been granted to the Iranian airforce': 'Sudan trains terrorism's new generation', 15 May 1994.

15. *The Washington Post*, 30 April 1997.

16. Con Coughlin, 'Ayatollahs find fertile soil for seeds of terror', 9 March 1997.

17. Scorched earth campaigns are acknowledged by Human Rights Watch / Africa: 'Behind the Red Line: Political Repression in Sudan', May 1996.

18. 'Sudan: The Civil War and Human Rights Abuses', Foreign and Commonwealth Office, November 1996.

19. Cited in Gilbert Lewthwaite and Gregory Kane, 'Witness to Slavery', *The Baltimore Sun*, 18 June 1996.

20. Cited in Gilbert Lewthwaite and Gregory Kane, 'Witness to Slavery', *The Baltimore Sun*, 16 June 1996.

21. 'Dateline: Sudan', NBC, London.

22. The Rev. Ambrose Adi, deputy chair of the National Assembly's Human Rights and Public Duties Committee and Santino Deng, political adviser to Northern Bahr el-Ghazal, were investigating slavery the same year, before concluding the following July that Arab tribesmen were abducting Dinka children. They called on the government to curb the slavery, Inter Press Service, 24 July 1997.

23. 'Witness to Slavery', *The Baltimore Sun*, 18 June 1996.

24. 'The Slave Traders and Farrakhan', 1 April 1997.

ELEVEN

Playing the Ansar Card

In June 1996, Caroline and John stepped even further into the political arena to try to bring an end to the slave trade. Under the auspices of CSI, they took the General Secretary of the exiled NDA illegally into Sudan.

Mubarak al-Fadil al-Mahdi was a former minister under Sadiq al-Mahdi. With him was Hammad Salih, the East Africa representative of the Umma party, and also the former government minister, Bona Malwal, editor of the *Sudan Democratic Gazette*. With them were press and TV reporters. Caroline's actions might have been controversial, but they would be carried out under the open scrutiny of the international media.

CSI was playing the Ansar card. The Ansar were the followers of the Mahdi who arose at his call in the 19th century and defeated the Egyptians in Sudan, along with General Gordon. Mubarak al-Mahdi was the grandson of the great Mahdi and cousin of Sadiq al-Mahdi. Among the Ansar were members of the nomadic Rizeigat and Misseriya tribes. Many had shown themselves reluctant to join the government's *jihad* against their black African neighbours.

Before the coup, both tribes had been represented by the Mahdi's Umma party, a major player in the National Democratic Alliance. In 1991, the Umma had signed a co-operation pact with the political wing of the SPLA, the Sudan People's Liberation Movement. A series of local trade agreements followed between Rizeigat and Misseriya leaders and their African counterparts on the frontier. Markets were established, like Manyiel, in SPLA territory, where the Arabs could go to sell much needed sugar and salt and other wares. The arrangement allowed the Arabs to graze their cattle on the lush vegetation around the River Lol during the dry season. It was also important to the Dinka, because it opened up a supply route to return their captured slaves. It was important, therefore, to the government to prevent it, so they countered by harassing and arresting known traders.[1]

If the Rizeigat and the Misseriya could be reunited behind the NDA and turned back to the Ansar cause, then the militia would be weakened and the will to continue the slave raids would be undermined.

The market at Warawah, in Aweil East County, had been razed during a government attack in November 1994. It had since been rebuilt and the trade between Arab and Dinka – Muslim, animist and Christian – was thriving. It was there CSI chose as the location for the main meeting.

The need for secrecy was crucial to the security of the operation. If advance notice were given, a crowd could be guaranteed, but so, too, could the unwelcome attentions of government forces. They were too close to the front line to risk broadcasting their intentions. Yet despite the total lack of prior warning, more than 600 Arabs and Dinkas responded to hasty word-of-mouth invitations. The reception for the exiled political leaders was euphoric, with outbreaks of cheering, backslapping and hugging. 'We were so excited, we nearly fainted,' said one Arab. 'Having the grandson of the Mahdi come here gives us great happiness,' said another.

'All democratic parties are united in opposition to the government of Sudan,' said Mubarak al-Mahdi, a blend of cultures in his *djellaba*, and white turban (*imamah*), with his walking-stick, gold-rimmed glasses, wristwatch and neatly-trimmed moustache. 'We all oppose the NIF regime because they have destroyed our nation; they have looted the country in their own interests. We must all unite to defeat the government of Sudan and bring an end to the NIF.'

Before him, rows of Arabs sit on the ground, listening attentively. Behind the sea of white skull-caps are the Dinka. Addressing the Arabs specifically, Mubarak al-Mahdi continues, 'The NIF has nothing to do with Islam; they are using religion for their political advantage and their own agenda… Allah will not tolerate wrong-doing; Islam does not allow [you] to attack innocent people. Spread the message… that you do not want this war; you do not support the NIF and you will not fight for them any more.

'The government has been using you Arabs here in this part of Sudan as slaves, reflecting their saying, "Use a slave to kill a slave"… I want to ask you all to refrain from any fighting between Arabs and Dinkas and to unite against the common enemy of the NIF… There will be no peace in Sudan if you do not live in peace with each other here in the borders.'

Dinka elder Bona Malwal had also been given a hero's reception. He had fled the country after the coup and was risking his life to return home. On the flight in with Caroline they had read together Bernard Levin's column in *The Times* condemning the slave trade. Along the route of the river they had seen rows of burning tukuls, their smoke billowing up into the evening sky. Now he was in a position to do something about it. The tall, middle-aged Dinka in his yellow straw hat was given a front seat in a camouflaged pick-up bristling with chanting SPLA soldiers. Later they danced for him, firing their assault rifles into the reddening sky.

He told the crowd that for the first time they had achieved political alliances, uniting all the opposition parties in the North, a unity symbolized by this historic visit. Then addressing the Arabs before him, he pleaded, 'Some of your people have taken our children as property... please tell your people to stop the practice of enslaving our people.' He also promised the Arabs that they would always be welcome to graze their cattle and to trade in Dinka territory.

Then it was the turn of Hammad Salih, a senior figure in the Umma party: 'Turabi and the NIF regime have been trying to confuse the Sudanese people,' he said, 'inciting them to fight each other, to eliminate opposition, so that they can run the country in their own way, to serve their own interests.

'Muslims have been attacking Dinkas, burning houses and killing people; this should not be our way... we must stop doing such things.'

Finally, the local representatives of the Rizeigat and Misseriya tribes stated their position. Their ancestors had long lived in peace with the Dinkas, even intermarrying among them. They were mutually dependent: the Arabs needing the grazing land, the Dinka their sorghum. There had been benefits in resisting the call to *jihad*. The NIF had incited the Arabs to violence, providing them with arms and horses. Where that had failed they had used intimidation and bribery. The local leaders called for the establishment of permanent Umma party headquarters in the region and pledged to help their northern brothers avoid conscription into the army.

CSI's strategy had worked. It had been their 13th visit to Sudan. How those words would translate into deeds, and the effect they would have on the slave trade remained to be seen.

Their effect on the NIF was profound, judging by a report which got back to Caroline.

Back in Cairo, Mubarak al-Mahdi was visited by his brother who had been to worship in a mosque on Friday night in Khartoum. The Imam stood up and raised his arms to lead the congregation in prayer. His first petition to the Almighty was for the destruction of Baroness Cox and Mubarak al-Mahdi. At which point his brother put down his arms and disassociated himself from the prayer.

Prayer aside, evidence was emerging of a more temporal weapon being employed against civilians hostile to the NIF – cluster bombs. At least six had been dropped on the village of Chukudum, scattering anti-personnel devices which could explode at any time. One fell near the primary school, where 475 children were attending classes. Another flung bomblets in front of the Roman Catholic church. A third bomb exploded 300 metres from a hospital run by Norwegian People's Aid. There was no time to evacuate patients who had just undergone operations. The use of cluster bombs was outlawed by the Geneva Convention. It was the 17th time Chukudum had been hit by air-raids since 1993.

CSI called for condemnation of the use of cluster bombs, and the focus of Caroline's attention turned to events in another area of Sudan: its north-eastern border.

The Beja

In Southern Sudan Christians and animists were the targets. In the Nuba Mountains, the *jihad* extended to Muslims who sided with Christians. But in the borderlands near Eritrea, it was Muslims specifically who were being reduced to starvation and driven out by the Islamist regime in Khartoum.

The Muslim Beja people of the Red Sea Hills may seem strange beneficiaries for Christian Solidarity, but the charity's mandate extends beyond Christian believers to all victims of repression, regardless of creed, colour or nationality. Their policy is never to proselytize. 'Our priority,' says Caroline, 'is to reach those people who cannot be reached by other aid organizations.' That certainly held true for the Beja.[2]

The Beja had fallen foul of their government for two compelling reasons. This non-Arab people possessed both fertile land in Eastern Sudan and a guerrilla force in Eritrea, operating under the banner of the outlawed Beja Congress.

Eritrea was happy to play host to Sudan's armed opposition for reasons explained to Caroline by the country's President, Issaias Afewerki, during an informal meeting at his residence. Sudan, he said, was attempting to destabilize his nation. 'It is Eritrea's duty to co-operate with the Sudanese opposition to get rid of the NIF regime,' he told her. 'It is in the interests of Eritrea and her neighbouring countries.' *The Economist* quoted the President as saying he would 'give weapons to anyone committed to overthrowing them.'[3] It had the effect of making Sudan all the more determined to overthrow him.

The Foreign Minister briefed CSI on the background in the capital, Asmara. After the coup in 1989 Eritrea had hoped the military-dominated government would shake off its dependence on the NIF. Gradually, they had become aware that they had witnessed an NIF coup with military window-dressing, that would never yield to a civilian government.

It also became clear that Sudan was bent on exporting militant Islam to its neighbouring countries. It had forged links with the Afghanistan *mujahedin*, had set up training camps and, since 1992, had been recruiting Eritrean refugees. Sudan, he claimed, had created and funded the Eritrean Islamic *Jihad* organization to establish a government in its own image in Eritrea. Money was being funnelled into businesses and fifth columnists were infiltrating mosques and the community. The same techniques were being used in Ethiopia, Egypt, Somalia, Tunisia and Algeria. Documents subsequently captured from government forces north of Kassala, detailed the NIF's involvement with Eritrean rebel groups.[4]

At a secret meeting in 1994, Eritrea informed President al-Bashir that it would not accept any interference and that he should desist from spreading his fundamentalist ideologies abroad. In reply, the Sudanese General inquired why Eritrea was opposed to Islamic activism and demanded to know what was wrong with converting people to another religion.

Realizing any meaningful dialogue would be hopeless, Eritrea began supporting the Sudanese opposition. One fruit of that was the Asmara agreement, which pulled together the NDA. 'The success of the opposition groups and the establishment of a stable, peaceful Sudan are a must for us,' the Foreign Minister explained, 'because unless we have peace in the region, we cannot develop. We cannot have a country next to us which is working to destabilize countries from Morocco to Burundi.'[5]

Starved out

Caroline went on to meet the SPLA leader, Dr John Garang, whose organization was now in alliance with the Beja. The Beja occupied a strategically important position around Port Sudan. If a stranglehold could be put on imported supplies coming through the port the NIF war effort would collapse.

In 1996, Caroline and John Eibner made a series of visits to the Beja people. As usual, it meant entering Sudan illegally. They found a people who were being gradually starved off their land. They were taxed exorbitantly on all they sold, then often forced to pay bribes to be allowed to keep the little that remained. Lack of food led to disease. Malnutrition and creeping illness put the people to flight. Government press-gangs were a further incentive to leave, as Beja young men were rounded up and forced to fight against the South. Many had made the crossing over the jagged mountains into Eritrea.

Of the 3 million Beja, representing some 6 per cent of the population of

Sudan, approximately 100,000 were displaced in the Gadaref area; 15,000 had sought refuge in Ethiopia and 10,000 had made the journey into Eritrea. A further 100,000 were thought to be on the verge of leaving.

Traditional Beja territory extended a quarter of a million square kilometres from the Egyptian border, along the Red Sea coast to Eritrea. Many Beja worked in Port Sudan, until creeping economic collapse cost them their livelihood. The middle classes were little better off. After the coup, professionals and community leaders found themselves dismissed from their posts, to be replaced by individuals loyal to the NIF.

Mussa Osheikh Tahir Onour, a 32-year-old land owner, was one of the many who abandoned Sudan for Eritrea. He was taking his sorghum to market when he was arrested by militia and his crops were confiscated. The soldiers said his sorghum belonged to the government. Mussa protested. It belonged to him, he said. Besides, what about his wife and the nine members of his extended family? The soldiers offered him 10,000 Sudanese pounds for his produce – a third of its market value. If he refused, they said, he would have to go to jail. He refused, and jail is where he ended up. After three days he was brought before a judge, who asked him whether he would prefer to take the money or stay in prison. Faced with the choice, he sold his sorghum. When he was released, he was forced to pay half his money in bribery to corrupt police officers and soldiers. He and many others left for Eritrea.

In July 1996, Caroline and John Eibner received a request from the Eritrean People's Front for Democracy and Justice. There was concern about impending famine in north-eastern Sudan, which could result in a flood of refugees into Eritrea, a nation which could barely feed itself. The situation was critical.

NOTES

1. CSI Sudan Report, 10–15 June 1996.
2. Though it did cause consternation among some members of the CSI board of a more evangelical persuasion. 'It's a question of balance really,' explained national director Stuart Windsor. 'If we find people, like the good Samaritan, we help them, but it doesn't deter us from our main business.'
3. 14 October 1994.
4. NDA forces captured Togan in April 1997, after encountering stiff resistance from NIF, PDF and Eritrean Islamic *Jihad* forces: *Africa Confidential*, 9 May 1997. According to US sources, Sudan was also assisting the Eritrean Liberation Front: Former congressman and member of the Africa subcommittee: Harry Johnston and Congressional Research Service African specialist, Ted Dagne, 'West should be tougher on Sudan's oppression in its Southern Region', 1997.
5. CSI Sudan Report, January 1996.

TWELVE

Speaking Islam by the Tank

At breakneck speed, Caroline and CSI put together a package of medical aid, found a journalist to accompany them and flew out to the Italianate capital of Eritrea, Asmara. Then followed a long drive by Landcruiser, down from the rugged highlands, along the highway until the highway petered out, then into the desert and towards the border. Their driver and escort was a wiry soldier, Malachi, whose loaded machine-gun jolted alarmingly around the footwell, while his back-to-back cassettes of East African pop music were curiously interspersed with the distant drums of Jim Reeves.

Night was spent at an army camp in a secret location. Security, they were told, was high. A huge satellite dish in a clearing hinted at secret surveillance; but seated in rows in military formation, the troops were tuned in to nothing more subversive than the Olympic Games on CNN. They considerately offered front row places to Caroline and her group and switched to the US News in English, which was incomprehensible to all save John Eibner. The rainy season had yet to begin and the air was cool and mercifully free of mosquitoes.

Caroline and her companions bivouacked the night in a clean, if basic, military bungalow. She settled them down with the ideal bedtime story, a tale told with relish and a hint of mischief about a man who had gone to the dentist because of a swelling in the jaw, which he took to be an abscess in a tooth. Curious thing was, his mouth had gone numb and it didn't hurt a bit. The dentist began his inspection, then paused, looking visibly shaken. The abscess turned out to be nothing of the sort. In the dark, moist recesses of the patient's cheek a camel spider had taken up residence. Having anaesthetised its host, it was slowly proceeding to digest the soft living tissue until, in the fullness of time, it would emerge once again into the daylight. The moral of the story, said Caroline, was: don't sleep with your mouth open. Every mouth was tightly shut that night, save for that of Caroline, of whom, it must be said, by way of revenge for that story – and for the record – snored.

Breakfast was a communal enamel bowl full of pasta – a legacy of the

Italian occupation of Eritrea – and sweet, fresh goat's meat. To soak up the juices were two kinds of dura bread. One was flat and grey like a crêpe, but sour and honeycombed with holes, the product of three days' fermentation. The other was soft and billowy like a tortilla, but with added sugar.

Breakfast over, the Toyota was back in the bush before 7 a.m., the morning light casting a red glow across the craggy highland backdrop. In late July, by 10.30 a.m. most Eritreans are back in their huts, sitting out the heat. The bleached landscape is made even harsher by the periodic rusting remains of tanks or trucks from Eritrea's 30-year war of independence. Outside the Landcruiser, the only evidence of other living creatures were the huge termite mounds, and even their inhabitants seemed to prefer the cool of the indoors. By 4.30 p.m., the warm, rich tones started to return, and the falling sun modelled the landscape, providing welcome relief and stimulating the cool breezes that accompanied the magenta sunset.

The sun was already down as Caroline reached her destination: a guerrilla camp in the Barka region. She peered around in the gloom for a flat spot to pitch her tent, relatively free of stones and shale, and found just such a place. The former girl guide set up her dome tent in a matter of minutes, and handed spare pegs over to others less well prepared. As the moon rose, the outlines of grass huts of different shapes and sizes became distinct. To the right there were camels behind the trees. Ahead was a mixture of civilians and guerrilla troops of the Beja Congress. Every tent erected, Caroline and her party went across to join them, stepping over a curious line of stones that seemed to pick out the perimeter of the cleared area. Only when the familiar, halting, repetitive chant began, did Caroline realize what she had done.

Many of the Beja strode over to the middle of the cleared area, and with their faces to the East, began their intonations. Caroline had pitched camp in the middle of their mosque. Thankfully, the diplomatic incident seemed to pass unnoticed.

The following day, food distribution to the local Beja people was to take place. Ninety tonnes of dura had been transported across the desert to the camp, to be picked up by Beja from Sudan and taken back over the mountains to their starving families. The grain started coming in by military trucks, in roughly sewn hessian sacks. Many of the bags were ruptured from the journey, and eddies of grain flew out to mingle with the sand as the trucks pulled up to unload their cargo.

Guarding the growing hill of grain are Beja Congress soldiers, dressed incongruously in green camouflage fatigues that pick them out against the desert. Some are boys: trainees, according to one grey-haired warrior, whose face is a medley of wounds and tribal scars. Seedi Mohammed Hadal explains that he is not an officer. There are no officers in his army, although some are leaders. He is among them. 'Before this government came all people in Sudan are one, believing they are Sudanese. The government is creating a great gap between them. They take products from the poor by force. I am a Muslim,' says Seedi, 'but I refuse their Islamic ways.'

'When the government say they represent Islam, they lie,' adds refugee Humush Koreb. 'Islam is from Allah and should lead to good works. But they speak Islam by the tank. Many are dying of disease,' he continues. 'We cannot buy medicines because the prices are so high and we have no money.'

Seedi Mohammed takes up the refrain, 'Here in the East,' he continues, 'all our people are hungry – approximately 3 million. If they find the chance, if they find the way, all of them will come to Eritrea.'

This is not what Eritrea would like to hear, and this is why Caroline and John have been invited to bring the impending famine to the world's attention.

Taken by force

The mountain of sacks which Seedi's men judiciously guard overlooks the rough-hewn peaks that separate the two countries. Soon the hungry will come, to claim their dura.

Seventeen hundred had already made the crossing into Eritrea. A further 3,000 were expected imminently. There were 25,000 more a little way inside the border, who could follow. Eritrea would be hard-pressed to feed them. Overseeing the relief operation is Tewelde Tesfay of the Eritrean Rehabilitation and Refugee Commission, who ticks off the names on his ledger. 'If all the people came from Eastern Sudan,' he confirms, 'it would be a disaster, like the 1984 famine in Ethiopia and Eritrea.'

Among the first across the border is an old man on a donkey, his grizzled face gaunt with hunger. He is followed by tribesmen with tessellated swords in bell-ended scabbards, decorated with strips of red, yellow and blue. But no-one carries a heavy sword across a mountain merely for the purposes of ornamentation. These are not Arabs, which is why Khartoum does not want them. Nor are they as black as the Dinka; they are from the same stock as the Eritreans; lean, fine-featured men, with neat moustaches and close-cropped beards. Some come on camels laden with plastic water containers. Others trudge in on foot.

Mustapha Issa Omer comes with the aid of a pair of crutches. 'All my people are starving,' he shrugs. 'There is nothing. If we go to the market it is very expensive and we cannot buy the food. There is nothing to buy and no-one to give anything.' Mustapha used to be a shepherd. That was before he took two bullets escaping a Sudanese army snatch squad, contracted gangrene, and lost his leg. Somehow he has picked his way over the mountain, and somehow he intends to take back a sack of dura.

Mustapha is 35, with tired doe eyes that dart this way and that. Last summer, while on his way to buy food and coffee, he was picked up by a PDF press-gang to fight the SPLA in the South. When he tried to explain he was shepherd, not a soldier; that he had elderly parents and a wife and two children to support, they threw him into a locked compound with their other new recruits.

At 2 a.m. he found a gap in the wire and tried to slip through. The soldiers saw him and shot him in the arm and leg. He managed to scramble under a thorn bush and remain hidden all the following day while the troops continued searching. That night he heard a passing camel driver talking to his animals and recognized the accent. He called out to him and the driver took him home.

But by then his leg was becoming infected and potentially gangrenous. His family were too afraid to take this 'deserter' to the hospital, so they called on the services of a quack doctor to remove his leg. 'The operation cost my brother five camels,' said Mustapha, clutching the stump.

Mustapha came to Eritrea two months ago, but his family were still in Sudan, hungrier than ever and totally dependent on a one-legged man to bring them their food.[1]

Several others had been victims of the press-gangs. Issa Mahmoud Ahmed was among them. He had been buying food for his family in Kassala, he tells Caroline. His mistake was to call in at a café for coffee. As he drank, the café was surrounded by regular soldiers of the Sudanese army. He and nine others were bundled into trucks and taken to the Army base in the city, where they were herded together with 20 more like them. They were informed they were being recruited into the PDF to fight in the South. Issa and another teenager managed to club together 4,000 Sudanese pounds and bribed a guard to look the other way while they went to the toilet. 'We ran and ran,' he said, 'while the guard just shot into the air.' Issa took refuge with his uncle who helped him escape to Eritrea. All the others were sent into battle in the South.

A delegation was sent to Khartoum to appeal for an end to the practice of forced conscription. They returned with a warning that if the Beja refused to join the PDF and the militias, no assistance would come to the area.

Omer Musa also hailed from near Kassala. He is in his late 40s, moustached, and a dusty green waistcoat hangs open over his loose white *djellaba*. Omer managed to escape when the government troops surrounded his village, and watched from a distance as the trap closed tight around his children. 'Three of my sons were taken by force,' he says, as Caroline and John scribble in their notebooks. 'They took all the men in the village and all the young boys to use in the war.'

Next, they came for his crops. 'They took all my produce, and all that of my friends and colleagues – all our dura – to buy weapons for the fight in the South.' He poses before the mountain of grain for the camera, holding his hand aloft and letting the dura run through his fingers.

Even being a teacher of the Koran was no protection, as Taha Ahmed Taha found out. His ability to organize famine relief in the mid-1980s secured his return as a Member of Parliament during Sudan's short-lived democracy. As an MP, he served his constituency by building a Community Centre, a Koranic School, a regular school, a clinic and a bakery and installing a generator for electricity. In short, he was a pillar of the community. But then the NIF seized power. 'One of the NIF leaders began to offer me money for the [community] centre,' he tells Caroline. 'I refused, and they arrested me, accused me of not being a real Muslim and of being unfit to manage the centre.' Taha Ahmed Taha ended up in jail.

'After seven days in prison, I feared for the well-being of my poor family and agreed to give up the centre. I was released from prison but was banned from fulfilling my duties as a teacher of the Koran. The government closed down the centre and it is now falling into disrepair.'

The scholar, with his sparse moustache and white *imamah* speaks quietly, but earnestly, raising his hands rather than his voice for emphasis. 'The NIF,' he insists, 'are afraid that if the Beja become educated and advanced they will start speaking out about their human rights and assert their rights as Beja.

'The *Sufis* and *Ulema* [Islamic jurists] are the true representatives of Islam. The leaders of the NIF are liars and do not have the interests of Islam or our people at heart. During the NIF rule, violations of the tenets of Islam have multiplied rapidly in Sudan.'

The NIF were unwise to make an enemy of Taha Ahmed Taha. Then head of the Beja Congress in exile in Eritrea, Taha was determined to see the regime ousted from power. And with Caroline's help he was to return to his people and urge them to resist the rule of Khartoum.

But first Caroline had to find a way of persuading her escort, who had been charged with her safe-keeping, to let her cross into Sudan. She had started making her case the day before in the Landcruiser. Malachi merely sucked his teeth and shook his head and made no promises.

Caroline raised the subject again. And again. She pushed the point well beyond the bounds of politeness, explaining her reason for going into Sudan from every conceivable angle, at exhaustive length, and then again for good measure. It was an eye-opening example of what her friends would call tenacity, and her foes, sheer bloody stubbornness. Poor Malachi sucked his teeth and shook his head and fixed his eyes on the road ahead, doing his level best to be non-committal, all the while his Kalashnikov rattling in the footwell, its spare magazines jammed into the pocket of the driver's door. Any hope that she might drop the subject was soon dispelled as he got to know her better. She bullied him ruthlessly, endlessly, persuasively, acutely, and with utter charm.

It is hard to know what would have been worse for Malachi: the prospect of letting his charge wander across the border or of facing yet more ear-bashing if he refused. He was damned if he did, and damned if he didn't. To Malachi's credit, he stuck to his ground.

But it would take more than that to deter Caroline. She was determined to go into Sudan to see this famine in the making with her own eyes. There could be any number of hungry Beja crossing the border to pick up provisions, but the only thing that would satisfy her desire for hard evidence was the sight of the starving on their own territory.

When her charm offensive and cajoling looked set for failure, Caroline did what she was best at. She applied leverage. She and John managed to contact the Beja commander, Basara, a bearded, thoughtful man who was in the habit of carrying his assault rifle across his back, his arms locked around the barrel and the butt.

He and his men had no compunction about going into Sudan. Their eventual aim was to go all the way to Khartoum. In the meantime, they were content to carry out guerrilla raids on roads and bridges. If Caroline wanted to cross the mountains he was game and his men would provide an armed escort. The only condition was that his scouts in Sudan must judge it safe to do so.

Caroline complied. Malachi capitulated.

Dinosaur of the desert

The journey across the mountain was a roller-coaster ride over rocks as sharp as dragon's teeth. The Russian-made military truck grunted and wheezed like a soon-to-be extinct dinosaur of the desert, its olive drab all too visible against the sand-blown boulders. The grinding and clashing of its gears could have been heard for miles as it inched its way up the mountain, flattening trees that stood in its path. It was a sitting target for a single soldier with a rocket-propelled grenade and an intimate knowledge of the twists and turns of the terrain. It was all too easy to see how the might of the mechanized Soviet army could be defeated by handfuls of *mujahedin* on their home ground in the mountain ranges of Afghanistan.

Hanging on for grim death in the back of the truck were Beja Congress guerrillas. Behind, in a Toyota Landcruiser, was the head of the Beja Congress, Taha Ahmed Taha. A light Toyota pick-up bounced and rattled up ahead, with a brace of Beja Congress guerrillas riding shotgun. Inside the bucking, swaying cab Caroline sat braced with her foot against the dashboard, humming with satisfaction. The windscreen was decorated with a halo of demurely dressed but amply-endowed Arab pin-ups. Beyond the glass, dust dervishes whirled and the horizon did a giddy dance. A camel, being led by a boy up the narrow track, came face to face with the green leviathan, and reared and bolted, its panniers and their contents flying, the hapless boy running and calling uselessly after it.

Eventually, the convoy cleared the mountain and came in sight of a Beja village, a mixture of mud huts and tents stretched like spinnakers along the windy ridge. Aside from a few Beja who came out to greet them it seemed strangely deserted. Caroline later found that the villagers, unsurprisingly, had mistaken the convoy for a Sudanese army snatch squad and had promptly fled. What happened in 1992, when the army had come and rounded up several hundred of their young men, was still etched in their memories. In case there were spies in the camp, it had been impossible to give the village advance warning of their visit. The Sudanese army would like nothing better than to get hold of a certain outspoken Baroness and the head of the Beja Congress.

The village elders were reassured, and gradually the people returned. That is, the men: the women were nowhere to be seen. Water was brought and a single Beja with a goat and a knife was trying to beckon the party towards him. But the leader of the Beja Congress guerrillas told Caroline she had just an hour to complete her business, and the man and his goat were left behind.

Famine never stalks alone. Its invariable companion, and often precursor, is disease. Along with tell-tale signs of malnutrition, such as rusty hair, had come TB, which was already widespread. 'If a man is not starving,' explained an elder, 'it means he is a spy of the Muslim Brothers.'

One man was suffering from terrible headaches and asked for medicine, but this was one occasion when CSI had nothing to bring. Caroline fished around in her handbag for something to give him. The best she could offer was paracetamol.

As the villagers gathered, old men were coughing and younger men looked gaunt and drawn. There were no distended bellies or sobbing, skeletal babies at this early stage of starvation, and the reporter realized with mixed feelings that the absence of conspicuous suffering meant the story would never make the networks. Half-blown horror could never compete with images of mass destruction available across the globe. A listless, hungry people, moving in slow motion to conserve energy would be unlikely to satisfy the networks' endless appetite for the violent and the visceral.

John Eibner had brought with him a satellite phone, which had survived the crossing, and which he now erected in the desert with the aid of a compass. MBC (Middle East Broadcasting Corporation) were able to conduct an interview with Taha Ahmed Taha from his own land.

Caroline asked to speak to the Beja women and was escorted to where they sat, huddled together beneath a woven grass shelter like rainbow-coloured sheep. Only her husband may look upon a Beja woman, so each was swathed from head to toe in a garment of red, blue or green, a vivid contrast to the drab desert colours worn by their menfolk. The women gathered in the shadows, and, according to custom, presented their backs to Caroline, this strange unveiled one, who addressed them from a distance. Only the little children returned the gaze of the watching reporter. A single Beja woman sat apart from the others, twice-veiled in the shadows, and acted as interpreter.

In this village of 500 families, she explained, some 300 people had already died from hunger and the disease that it brings. Despite the mountain breeze, which rasped across the TV reporter's microphone, the heat was hanging in the air.

Now Taha Ahmed Taha addresses the men. They gather round him in a broad arc within the circle of their huts and tents, the mountainous border a jagged backdrop. Taha has doffed his Western anorak, and stands before them in white, speaking fervently with his hands to the hushed and respectful gathering.

'There is no difference for someone to be a Christian or to be a Muslim,' he says. 'Both of them are divine morality. Instead of going to fight your brother in the South, it is better for you to come to the Beja Congress to fight against the government, because they are not Muslims.' His reception is as enthusiastic as it could be from a people who find it enervating merely to stand.

One elderly Beja grandfather has a word to say to this British baroness: 'Life was better for us under British rule,' he informs her, 'because the British met our needs. The British also used a policy of divide and rule. But since 1989, the government of Sudan has adopted another policy, ruling by the saying, "Make your dog hungry, so that it will follow you."'

Their evidence gathered and their work done, John and Caroline deliver their soundbites to the reporter. If TV will not take the story of the Beja, then maybe radio will, and if not radio, then the newspapers; if not in the UK, then overseas.[2]

'What we are seeing is a famine in the making, a crisis that's about to become a catastrophe,' warns Caroline, her eyes screwed up against the sun, sitting against a backdrop of Beja women who pretend not to look at the camera.

'The government of Sudan is making the famine,' asserts John Eibner, peering out from beneath his sun-hat. 'It is an extension of their *jihad* against their political enemies.'

It is time to leave. Caroline makes her farewells and opts to ride out the return journey standing in the back of the Soviet truck with the Beja Congress guerrillas. It means several hours of clinging to splintering woodwork, ducking and diving to avoid the thorn trees, as their vicious two-inch spikes scree and squeal along the sides, and riding the truck like a surfboard as it sways and plunges over the mountain. Quite a pastime for a 59-year-old grandmother of six. She disembarks in Eritrea, dusty and bloodstained from a close encounter with a thorn tree. She sucks her bleeding fingers, grinning.

NOTES
1. Andrew Boyd, 'Hunger and oppression force Bejas over the border', *The Guardian*, 3 September 1996.
2. In the event, Channel 4 News carried some of the footage to balance a propaganda set-piece by Sudan, otherwise TV reacted as expected, dismissing the pictures as undramatic. Reports were carried by BBC World Service radio, Radio 4, *The Guardian*, *The New African* and others.

THIRTEEN

Challenge at the Border

With the food distribution under way and the mountain of sacks reduced to a molehill, next stop is a refugee camp. During the journey, Caroline's mind is working, working. She discusses with John how to encourage other agencies to provide relief; relief that should ideally be distributed by Eritreans who understand the situation on the ground. There will be many meetings to arrange back in London and Zurich.[1]

The Landcruiser pulls into Gash Barka Camp. There are refugees a-plenty – some 10,000 in all. 'This is the hospital,' the administrator points out to Caroline. 'We still have over 63 inpatients, suffering from night and day blindness.'

'They'll need vitamin A or antibiotic cream,' says Caroline, scribbling it down, along with her list of other essentials for CSI's next visit, like syringes, to replace the handful here which are used over and over without proper sterilization.

In the camp are several Dinka boys who have escaped from slavery. One had been taken to Chad, where he said there were many other slaves from Sudan. Others said they had been taken to Libya,[2] Iraq, Iran and Saudi Arabia. The previous year *The Washington Times* reported that Shendi, the major slave-trading post in the days of General Gordon, was still functioning. It was being used as a staging point for Port Sudan, from where slaves were shipped out to the Persian Gulf, while those destined for Libya, Chad or Mauritania were sent west to Northern Darfur.[3]

Clement Deng, a Catholic catechist, tells Caroline that captured boys are being taken to an Islamic training camp near Khartoum, and later sold as slaves to rich Saudis, Libyans and Iranians. He helped one escape just before he was due to be sent abroad with his new master. Clement himself was later abducted by members of the PDF and taken to a ghost house for interrogation. He was tortured with electric rods for seven days before being dumped semi-conscious at a church centre.

Today, at the camp, there is no church building, just a tree with a cross crudely carved into the trunk. Beneath its branches, many gather to worship, dressed in their colourful Sunday finest, or what passes for best among refugees. Leading the singing is another catechist, Anglican Simon Mayuat Bol. He sits in a striped Western shirt and pale grey trousers, holding open the pages of a blue Holy Bible. The congregation of all ages sit facing him on logs arranged on the ground. They sing from their hearts and pray with their heads bowed.

The hymns could have come from the *Redemption Hymnal*; the tunes are vaguely Victorian, but the language is alien. Caroline nods and beams and hums along as best she can. Then Simon calls on her to address the people.

'Many people pray for you,' she says, 'that soon you will be able to go back to your land and live in peace and justice there. We believe in a God who can do these things. And we pray he will do them quickly.'

Afterwards, scores of people line up to give their testimonies to John and Caroline, while Simon tells the reporter how he, his wife and their ten children had been forced to move again and again in Sudan. It began when his home town, Atar, was put to the torch in 1992 during a government offensive. Things were safer in Malakal, but the only food aid was distributed by *Da'wa Al-Islamiyya*, and it was given on condition that all the recipients became Muslims. Simon would not renounce Christianity, so he and his family went without aid. The local church had no food or medicine, so many became dependent on the Islamic distribution agency and were pressed to renounce their faith. It was time for Simon to move on, again.

He took his family further north to Wad Medani. There was no work, so his wife set up a tea stall at the market. When the other stallholders found out she was a Christian, they confiscated her cups and hounded her out. His children were made to study Islam in school. Any who did not attend were given the lash. Permission was granted for Christian instruction once a week on a Thursday afternoon. But the *mujahedin* regarded it as their religious duty to disrupt the classes, and teachers were repeatedly detained and interrogated by security police. Simon headed south-east towards the Eritrean border and into exile.[4]

Close call

It is a gruelling two-day haul back to Asmara that has everybody clinging to the handles of the vehicle to avoid being thrown from their seats. The journey is conducted to the accompaniment of endless Eritrean pop music, a far cry from Caroline's beloved Elgar, with its lush evocative images of England's well-watered fields and villages. The only other vehicles on this wind-blown highway are ancient Bedford Bedouins, their paintwork sandblasted down to gleaming grey metal, their passengers spilling over onto their roofs. At a town just beyond the border, several battered trucks line up for repairs, while men scramble beneath with spanners, struggling to find a way to keep them going for another few decades.

Malachi pulls in for a well-earned drink and a siesta. The Cokes are years past their sell-by date with even less sparkle than an ageing Bedford Bedouin, but one gives way to another and then another.

Here in the shade, as the Cokes slip down, the Beja seem far behind. 'It seems so unreal,' says Caroline, 'so horrific, so outrageous, that it's hard to comprehend the reality, except when you are with the people, seeing those who are suffering from this policy.'

The fact that the suffering this time are Muslims is profoundly irrelevant. The reporter asks her whether she believes Muslims worship the same God as Christians. She replies that God's love knows no boundaries. Whether she is free to love as she does because her theology is liberal, or whether her theology is liberal because she loves as she does is indeterminable, and equally irrelevant.

The reporter's mind flips sideways, seeking refuge from the deep issues in trivia. Has she ever been on the BBC's *Desert Island Discs*? No, she laughs. The BBC is not interested in Conservative politicians. Her conviction of left-wing bias in the media is heartfelt.

Malachi, who would once have been branded a Communist guerrilla by the BBC and Conservatives alike, yawns and stretches and takes to a bed to recover from the journey. The English baroness takes the opportunity to stride off for a walk in the midday sun. She is drawn relentlessly back towards the Sudan and, despite Malachi's warnings not to stray too far down the road, she walks clear of the houses to get a better view of the mountains, beyond which lie the Beja.

She returns later and recounts, a little sheepishly, that she must have wandered too far because she was challenged by a Sudanese border guard who demanded to see her passport. She shrugged, smiled and murmured a few words in Arabic, before turning around and stepping back into Eritrea. Had the guard's superiors known the prize that had slipped through their grasp, that soldier's life would not have been worth living. Sudan's response to news of her visit, when the news finally reaches Khartoum, is to threaten to sue for contravening its passport and immigration laws.[5]

Malachi will be more than pleased when the Baroness is back in Asmara. For the second time in two days her life has been at risk. 'I'm not the only one,' she demurs. 'I have a far greater admiration for my colleague John Eibner who still has young children. My children are grown up.'

'She's willing to give her life,' says CSI Chairman Mervyn Thomas, back in the UK. 'There's absolutely no doubt about that. Nothing will stop her.'

The Sudanese government has underlined the risks she is taking. During her first visit to Khartoum she and John Eibner challenged a senior minister about the government's refusal to allow access to human rights organizations. It was met with blank indifference. To which Caroline retorted, 'Well, we will have to go if you won't allow access.'

'In which case,' replied the minister, 'we will have to shoot down your plane. We shoot down any plane which goes into areas which we do not authorize.'

John Eibner nods in recollection. The conversation is printed in his mind. 'She's regarded as an enemy of the NIF regime,' says the American. 'There are many people who would love to harm her and would do so willingly.'

'We're scared for her,' admits Mervyn Thomas, 'very much so. And she's scared, too. She'll call me from the car phone on the way to the airport and we pray over the telephone. She's constantly aware she may not come back. She prays the Lord will keep her safe, but always finishes with "Nevertheless, not my will, but yours be done."'

'It is imperative that we go,' maintains Caroline. 'The situation must be exposed. I would not be happy resigning myself to a comfortable life back in England when there is still something we can do to ease the suffering. We are privileged to be with people such as these. We always come back feeling we have received, even though we have gone there to give. It is not one way.'

As she pauses to reflect, drawing on a fizzy orange Fanta, the reporter's mind wanders back to the welcoming Beja with the goat, to be sacrificed in hospitality to well-fed strangers, when all around are hungry.

Caroline's own thoughts have returned to a Sudanese man she met dying of starvation on the path. 'I remember giving him a drink,' she said, 'purely to make him feel a little more comfortable. The gracious smile he gave me will be printed on my heart forever. That famous Sudanese smile. The next morning, he was dead. They maintain their dignity, their graciousness, their generosity. Like so many people in extreme circumstances, they have nothing, but they will give you everything. They don't complain, they don't beg. They maintain this staggeringly impressive faith. The joy on their faces when they worship in the wilderness, without clothes, without food, hungry and ill, yet full of radiance; they radiate more joy than you see on the faces of many Western Christians in many of their relatively well-off churches.'

It is a constant theme with Caroline, and a hint of disgust creeps into her voice at the contrast. This Conservative peer would make a marvellous socialist, but not one of the bleeding-heart variety. She will talk readily about the emotional toll exacted by hardship on others, but baulks when it comes to discussing her own feelings. When asked for her emotional response to the suffering, she side-steps the question by referring to CSI policy. Only when pressed repeatedly to talk from her heart rather than her head, will she reluctantly do so. Later, it releases a floodgate. For a while she remains on her own in the Landcruiser, she admits, to cry.

It will be another long day before the Toyota can make it back to Asmara. The night is spent at what passes for a hotel in a dusty Eritrean town. A jug is brought round for communal hand washing and, after a reviving plate of spaghetti bolognese and a mineral water, her mind resumes its racing. She assails John with ideas about which levers of power to pull, which organizations to tap, how best to make sure that aid is delivered to the Beja. Perhaps USAID would build roads, so a market place could be set up at the border, where the Beja could cross to bring goods to sell, in exchange for food. Taxes could be levied on the goods, some of which would be marked for the Beja, some for the Eritreans. So instead of receiving hand-outs, these people would receive food and aid in exchange for goods and services. And the roads would still be there to serve the people after the crisis had passed.

Nightfall curtails the conversation. Caroline, the eternal girl guide, protests that she would rather take her tent out into the bush, but settles for sleeping on the veranda under the stars head to toe with almost everyone else in the hotel. She is not an admirer of politicians who go on media junkets in foreign lands and step out of their expensive suites, to pose before huddles of starving refugees.

At first light she is sitting up on her bed, applying lipstick and eye-liner, ready for the road.

'Man-made famine'

Back in Asmara, at a faded hotel with tinkling bakelite telephones, whose uniformed staff wear ill-fitting hand-me-downs made shiny by years of pressing, a reporter has a meeting with Yemane Ghebreab, Head of Political Affairs of the People's Front for Democracy and Justice.

There is no love lost between the governments of Sudan and Eritrea. This man with his boyish face, wispy hair and tired eyes, stands on the balcony and accuses his neighbour of attempting to destabilize the region.

'The government of Sudan is wasting its resources in financing regional and international terrorism,' he accuses, to the hooting of ancient Italian taxicabs. 'It is waging war against its own people. It is a very rich country, it could feed the whole region, but its economy is in ruins. This is a man-made famine, and it could have been avoided.'[6]

His own country has little enough food for its own needs, and now it faces a flood of refugees. But there are two compelling reasons why Eritrea cannot turn its back on the Beja. Yemane Ghebreab explains: 'The borders between us were created in the colonial era, but we are one people. We are Beja. There are intermarriages between Sudanese Beja and Eritrean Beja.' And their protracted war for independence gave many Eritreans an intimate understanding of what their Sudanese brothers are going through. 'We have lived as refugees for 30 years in Sudan, and we know what refugee life is like.'

Evening comes, and Omer Nur el-Dayem, the General Secretary of the Umma party, takes the CSI entourage out for an expensive meal at a fashionable Asmara restaurant – all bare wood and zebra skins, back-to-native chic. It seems curious to be presented with more food than one can eat, having just returned from a famine zone. To cap it all, the topic of the conversation is starvation: 'When the regime came to power a sack of dura was between 45 and 60 Sudanese pounds,' says the politician, bald, plump, smiling. 'Today it is 45,000 Sudanese pounds – a thousand times more in a matter of seven years. Thousands are dying from malnutrition.' The reporter loses his appetite.

Back at the hotel, Omer Nur El-Dayem confides in the reporter, 'Baroness Cox really is exceptional. She is the outstanding woman of the twentieth century, a humanitarian with concern about the poor. In the Sudan she has done a lot to alleviate the misery of those who need help. We are proud of her and appreciate her.'

In the hotel room, it is the first time in days that Caroline and John have been properly clean, properly fed, properly able to sit down. But the mission isn't over until the report is finished. Caroline pounds at the keys of her Apple laptop until almost 5 a.m., while fatigue overtakes John and the reporter who appear to be moving in slow motion. Still, her fingers peck at the keys. There is a problem with the portable printer. Regardless of the time in the UK, she cajoles the hotel switchboard to untangle their jackplugs and put her through to her office companion in London, John Marks, to talk her through the computer's printing program.

'Any chance of a quick run-around when we get home?' she adds over the crackly international line. 'I've had enough of sitting on my bottom in a Landcruiser all week and could do with a game of squash.'

Caroline retires to her room, and the other John, John Eibner, gropes for the travel alarm and sets it for 8.30 a.m. No sooner has he slumped onto the pillow than its insistent bell jangles him awake. Moments later, there is a tap at the door. It is Caroline, fresh and ready to travel, bags packed and beaming, explaining that she plans to skip breakfast because there is still work to do.

The sleepwalking reporter mumbles something about her being indefatigable. 'If Caroline wasn't so charming,' words to that effect slur out, 'she would be terrifying.'

John, who always sounds like he has hayfever, is more than usually nasal this morning. 'She isn't always so nice,' he says, 'just like the rest of us. And then she *can* be terrifying.'

On the return plane at Addis Ababa, a complete stranger comes up to Caroline and hands her a letter. He explains that he has seen her on television. The letter, from a Muslim, reads, 'May God bless you for the efforts you exert and the risk you take for my people.'

More than a year later, Caroline was to revisit the Beja. Little had changed. She wrote: 'We heard eye-witness accounts of torture and saw the scars which testified to the truth of their ordeals. We found people dying from malnutrition and disease which could not be treated, as the NIF had taken all their supplies.'[7]

NOTES

1. In Switzerland, a UN spokesman confirmed, 'There is a serious food shortage in Eastern Sudan. We are talking about a famine where literally hundreds of thousands could possibly die.' Subsequent visits to the Beja showed the problem to be more one of malnutrition, and the illness that follows in its wake. By mid-1997, the expected mass-exodus of Beja into Eritrea had not taken place.

The plight of the Beja was also discussed by the UN Special Rapporteur on human rights in Sudan, Gáspár Bíró. In his 1995 report he writes that members of the Beja tribe, 'were being subjected to various abuses and violations of human rights ranging from arbitrary arrest of leaders and confiscation of property to the denial of the relief and health care services currently being enjoyed by all Sudanese citizens... the motivation for the discrimination against the Beja tribe is mainly political, since they are a part of the traditional constituency of the banned Democratic Unionist Party.'

2. Reports that slaves are sold on to Libya were considered 'credible' by the US embassy in Khartoum, 'The Flourishing Business of Slavery', *The Economist*, 21 September 1996.

3. Shyam Bahtia, 'Southern Sudan's kids vanish into slavery', 27 April 1995.

4. CSI Sudan Report, 24–31 March 1996.

5. Reported in *Sudan News and Views*, no. 27, June 1997. 'She uses human rights issues as a pretext to realize her political aims against the Sudanese government,' an official was quoted as saying.

6. Interview with the author.

7. CSI Press Release, 19 December 1997.

FOURTEEN

New Offensive

In the closing days of 1996 the combined forces of the Beja Congress and SPLA, under the banner of the NDA, began a new offensive. It was launched by an attack on a mechanized brigade close to the Eritrean border. What actually took place is submerged in the propaganda offensives of both sides. What is for certain is that a major onslaught to liberate Sudan had begun, and that an eastern front had opened up, bringing the war closer to the capital than ever before.

According to the Sudan government and the London-based Sudan Foundation, a US-sponsored invasion by 6,000 regular soldiers of the Ethiopian army had taken place, supported by armoured units and accompanied by John Garang's SPLA. At the same time rebels trained by Israel in Eritrea and commanded by Eritrean officers had crossed the border. Uganda was offering military support and the UK had given the invasion its benediction.

Ethiopia, Eritrea and Uganda denied any involvement, and President Yoweri Museveni of Uganda threw it back at Sudan, accusing the NIF of supporting rebels fighting the Ugandan government. He warned that both countries were on the brink of war.

According to *The Economist*, the USA was supplying 'defensive' weapons to Eritrea, Ethiopia and Uganda to help protect them from neighbouring Sudan. The Sudan Foundation claimed the USA was training troops and terrorists to be used against Sudan and was 'playing with fire'.[1]

In what *The Times* recorded was 'a mood bordering on panic', President al-Bashir called on his people to rise up in holy war against the aggressors. Khartoum University was closed to encourage students to swell the ranks of the army. 'A million martyrs for a new era,' was the rallying cry. But according to one report, when only 250 answered the call, the PDF resorted to rounding up youths on the streets, some as young as 15.[2]

Fierce fighting ensued in Bahr el-Ghazal with the breakaway Kerubino faction, which had sided with the government. More significantly, Kerubino, Riek Machar and other splinter groups confirmed their support for the regime by signing a treaty with Khartoum. The 21 April peace agreement offered a referendum for the South after a four-year interim period, giving the choice of unity or secession. It was confirmed that the *Shari'a* and traditional law would form the basis of all legislation.[3]

'This agreement is not a sell-out. We have not betrayed our people,' Machar told the Panafrican News Agency.[4] The treaty offered Machar the prospect he had hoped and fought for – an independent Southern Sudan under his presidency. A disgruntled Kerubino would have to make do with the post of deputy.

The SPLA-Mainstream dismissed the treaty as a 'desperate retreat to divide and rule' that should be 'rejected in its totality'.[5] Machar, it said, had signed a war agreement against the SPLA.

The Umma party went further, accusing the government of scheming to hand over the South to separatists, so it could transfer its forces North to 'defend the battered regime'. That would leave the factions to fight it out amongst themselves, transforming Southern Sudan into the next Zaire. 'The agreement is not a peace agreement,' warned the Umma party, 'but a plan to replace the holy war with a tribal war of mutual elimination... in the style of... the current pattern of Hutu and Tutsi tribal ethnic destruction.'[6] Both sets of rebels – those for and those against the regime – had aspirations that ran against the grain of history. Both had placed their faith in unnatural allies. Machar and Kerubino wanted independence for the South; a political settlement based upon a referendum, entirely dependent on the will and co-operation of their masters, the NIF. But to untether the South and let it go would run contrary to centuries of Arab and Islamic ambition. It would also mean forfeiting the oil riches that were ready for exploitation.

For his part, Garang would settle publicly for nothing less than the downfall of the regime and its vision of an imposed Islamic theocracy. In its place, he wanted a democratic, secular Sudan, united with the North in confederation. What the North wanted was a federal system with power remaining in the capital.

In 42 years of fighting, the military defeat of the North had never been possible. And, should the impossible be achieved, who could guarantee that this new and disparate alliance could hold? Or would the ancient tribal and religious fault lines tear it apart? After all, Sudan's last democratic government under Sadiq al-Mahdi had been at war with the SPLA under John Garang. And would al-Mahdi, who had previously committed to print his intention to Arabize and Islamize the South[7] be prepared to relinquish that hope?

Whatever the future might hold, it was plainly in the NIF's present interests to divide the opposition and to erode Garang's power base in the South. How to handle the payback to its allies was tomorrow's problem.

Khartoum's worst fear was that the rebels would overrun Damazin, and capture the hydro-electric dam controlling 80 per cent of the capital's water supply. According to observers, the NDA's strategy was more ambitious. Stage one was to capture Juba, the capital and final government bastion of the South. In the words of John Garang, 'Whoever controls Juba, controls South Sudan.' Stage two was to topple the government of Khartoum. The rebel strategy, observed *Africa Confidential*, was to 'follow military successes with civilian uprising'. From Cairo, the NDA called on the army to mutiny and the people of Sudan to rise up and overthrow the regime.

It's that woman again...

Sudan's troubles, it seems, were all Caroline's doing. That is, according to the fevered imagination of US radical, Lyndon LaRouche. Having accused CSI of being a vehicle of British intelligence, his claims were to get wider-eyed yet. During an interview on his satellite radio show, *Executive Intelligence Review Talks*, Mr LaRouche took it upon himself to expose Caroline as the mastermind behind the putative invasion of Sudan by Eritrea and Ethiopia: 'an invasion, by the way, which was organized by people such as Lady Baroness Caroline Cox, the Speaker of the British House of Lords'.

Mr LaRouche warmed further to his theme in print. Caroline, he wrote, was a 'British war-Lord...[8] the woman personally directing, and even openly funding the British Commonwealth's London-directed military invasion of Sudan'.[9]

A press release by his Schiller Institute accused her of being part of 'a London-directed, raw-materials-grabbing, colonial war in Sudan...'[10] However off-the-wall, conspiracy theories have a habit of taking root. The notion resurfaced at a US State Department briefing. Records reveal the spokesman, Nicholas Burns, being harassed by a persistent but unnamed reporter. The journalist accused Baroness Cox of being John Garang's master, of persuading Garang to pay Eritrea to support the rebels, and of being a 'main player' in Executive Outcomes, a company which hired out mercenary soldiers to the diamond merchants of Sierra Leone.[11]

It was but a reflection of the paranoia being expressed in Sudan. According to the official Sudanese news agency, SUNA, Attorney General Abdel Aziz Shido went even further, accusing Baroness Cox of being the mastermind behind *all* plots against his country...[12]

Caroline chuckles. 'It's *so* bizarre. I think they rather overestimate my capabilities. Apparently, I'm a specialist in psychological warfare, related to the Royal Family, *and* in MI6.'

So can we take that as a denial that she is linked with British intelligence? 'Absolutely! I wish it were true!'

Meanwhile, it seemed, Sudan was hatching a plot or two of its own against Eritrea. According to the Eritrean embassy, a plan to assassinate President Issaias Afewerki was blown apart by the Sudanese opposition alliance. On 14 November 1996, secret agent, Captain Nasr el Din Babiker Aba el Khayrat Bush, of the Sudan General Security Services, slipped across the border into Eritrea. He had until 30 April the following year to kill the President. Should he be captured, he was primed to give a confession absolving the NIF of any involvement in his mission.

The contingency plan was a spectacular failure. According to Eritrea, el Khayrat's confession ran deep, though the methods used to extract it were not open for discussion. As well as confessing the assassination plot, el Khayrat admitted Sudan was running terrorist training camps for the Eritrean Islamic *Jihad* organization, the Ugandan Lord's Resistance Army, Egyptian *Jihad* and the Chadian *Mujahedin*, who were attempting to overthrow their own country's President, Idriss Déby. Arms and money were being supplied by Iran, Iraq and other fundamentalist groups.

Training for the assassination attempt against President Afewerki had been provided by no lesser terrorist than Carlos (the Jackal) who had taken refuge in Khartoum in 1993, before being kidnapped by a French snatch-squad and removed to Paris to face trial. Sudan dismissed it all as a 'mere fabrication' to mask Eritrea's involvement in plots against Sudan.[13]

The alleged assassination plan was exposed on 20 April 1997, the day before splinter opposition groups in the South signed their peace pact with the NIF. United States reaction to the plot was decisive. The US was worried that the war could spread to Eritrea and Ethiopia, nations central to US strategy for the region. Policy swung away from 'constructive engagement' towards a tougher line which would isolate the regime and support the NDA opposition.[14]

'We are praying and running'

With the NDA uprising well underway, Caroline and John headed out to Sudan again, to Yabus, in Southern Blue Nile. In response to military gains by the SPLA the NIF had been conducting a scorched-earth policy against civilians. The PDF were joined by Riek Machar's South Sudan

Independence Army in a campaign to burn and bomb 50,000 people from their homes. 'We walked from one burned-out village to another, over terrain stretching for many miles,' says Caroline. 'We were told it was possible to walk for eight hours through such areas of complete devastation.' In many of the ruined tukuls the remains of Christian symbols were still visible.

Bara Deidi displayed the smouldering remnants of his tukul. 'You can see the place where the bomb fell from an Antonov,' the 40-year-old told Caroline. 'I was out gathering food. My wife took our eight children to safety. I came back to see what had happened and I was devastated.

'I saw 20 die in the bomb attacks,' he continued. 'After the bombing, the soldiers came. More than 100 tukuls were burned. Crops and stores of grain were burned, too. Now we are living under these trees, just eating grass, roots and fruits. The small children cannot digest this food and they get diarrhoea. The children cry as they are hungry. I give them water, but that is not enough. Two of my own children have died.'[15]

There were no humanitarian aid organizations working in the region, so medical supplies and food aid were non-existent.

In March Caroline and John were back again, to the Nuba Mountains and Nyamlell. Just as they were about to leave Kenya, they met a group of Christians from Release International, returning from supplying aid to the area. The news wasn't good. They had seen evidence of fresh, systematic destruction. The aid workers had themselves come under fire from low-flying helicopter gunships as they tried to distribute their LifePaks of hoes, jugs and mosquito nets.

Kevin Turner had to dive into rocks for shelter. Three Sudanese children were killed instantly and four others were injured by shrapnel. 'The children who were being attacked were crying out to the pastor,' he recalled. 'They asked him, "What have we done to these men that they are trying to kill us? Why do they hate us like this?"' The onslaught created a wave of 50,000 refugees in just three days.[16] According to community leaders, some half a million had run out of food and were on the brink of starvation.[17]

Caroline and John witnessed the devastation for themselves. Despite the destruction, singing and dancing crowds lined the airstrip to greet them. Christian Solidarity was a ray of hope when despair was all around. They were greeted by their old friend, Reverend Barnaba, who confirmed what they could see with their eyes: 'The NIF has escalated its policies of burning churches and church property,' he explained. One Pastor, Kamal Tutu, had been thrown on the glowing embers of his own church. His feet were severely injured and both hands were burned off up to the elbows. By 1994, more than 160 places of worship had been set alight in the Nuba Mountains. That number was continuing to grow. 'We thank God,' added the Rev. Barnaba, 'that we are not alone despite our suffering. God has sent us brothers and sisters.'

From her earliest involvement in human rights, and from her first days with CSI, there were two injunctions that Caroline believed were from God, and by which she had tried to live. In a truck in the middle of Poland, in the middle of the night, she had felt a call to share the darkness; and it was the aim and mission of Christian Solidarity to be a voice for the voiceless. The Rev. Barnaba encapsulated both in his words to her: 'The churches in the Nuba Mountains are carrying the cross of Christ. They want you, who have been sent by God, to be a voice for them – to try to bring some help in their dark days.'

Their dark days were far from over. In the coming months, government troops and their allies began what they called a liberation offensive, driving back the SPLA deeper into the mountains.[18] It prompted condemnation from Africa Rights, who reported: 'Sudanese forces have systematically burned dozens of villages, looted cattle, raped women, kidnapped thousands of civilians, and killed hundreds.'[19]

Yet despite or perhaps because of the persecution, the church in Sudan was growing. In the face of the threat from militant Islam, Catholic and Anglican congregations had been thrown together. There was a revival of interest in Christianity. According to one report, the number of Christians in the South had grown from 5 per cent in 1950 to 70 per cent in 1997.[20] 'The church grows despite many difficulties,' said Roman Catholic lay leader, Eliu Ullam. 'The church loses some people to Islam, because they are willing to accept money for their conversion.' The going rate was 10,000 Sudanese pounds – the price of a shirt. 'But many more are becoming Christians,' he added.

'We are praying and running,' said another. 'We have lost many, but Jesus Christ is our life and we live in him.'

'Always in crises people look for solutions,' explained Catholic catechist, William Aryoun. 'There had never been a church here before this war, but now people come to the church. And now that you have visited us,' he told Caroline, 'what we are doing and saying has become meaningful to the people. They now understand Christian solidarity.'

William Aryoun had studied at Nyamlell. For the first time in years the slave raids had abated. The clincher had been the visit by Mubarak al-Mahdi the previous year. Caroline and John had flown him in to appeal directly to the leaders of the Rizeigat and Misseriya tribes. He had implored them to withdraw their support for the government's *jihad* – and his message had hit home. Without support from their militia, the number of slave trains had declined and the attacks had diminished.

More tribesmen were now signing up to the peace agreements, allowing Arabs to graze their cattle on Dinka land and sell their wares in Dinka markets. It also furnished the Arabs with another ready market – for the trade in returned slaves. The government had retaliated, Caroline was told, by arming the Zagawa tribe to attack those Arabs who had opted for peace.

Hopes were high that it was the breakthrough they were looking for, and for a time it was. Peace lasted six months. Then the raids began again. The militia returned, attached, as ever, to the military train. They came once when the train was on its way to Wau, bristling with weapons and fresh supplies of ammunition, and again when the train was returning.[21] Village after village was burned and looted, until finally, the raiders were beaten back by the SPLA. It was the first time the militia had encountered stiff military resistance.

The NIF had been furious about the visits of Mubarak al-Mahdi and others. They were turning many Rizeigat against the government, explained Joseph Akok Akol, the Executive Director of Aweil West County. 'The NIF is also very angry about the international attention that is being given to slavery as a result of CSI's work in the area. We are convinced these raids are directed here with a view to stopping the [peace].'

His analysis was backed up by a slave trader helping the Dinka, whose task was getting tougher by the day. The NIF had begun patrolling the borders in Landcruisers, forcing the returning slaves heading south to travel at night, and the security police were clamping down on anyone suspected of being connected with the trade. To replenish their haemorrhaging support, the NIF was recruiting more militia. 'The Rizeigat believe the NIF wants to destroy peace between themselves and the Dinka,' said the trader. 'Many Rizeigat are opposed to the raids. The government tells them that the people in the South are pagans who want to take over the country. They say they must fight to protect Islam, and that they should circumcise the Southerners and make them Muslims.'[22]

Family reunions

The backlash was inevitable. But news of CSI's exploits in trying to stem the slave raids had reached far beyond the NIF. With the help of a Canadian organization called Crossroads, CSI was able to buy back a record 220 slaves, bringing the total redeemed to 300. It was good news for the people of Nyamlell.

To greet Caroline on her return visit was Apin Apin Akot, the farmer who had gone north to rescue his wife and two children after they had been kidnapped by the militia. He had been forced to leave behind his nine-year-old daughter, Akec, who had been chosen to become a concubine and was priced beyond his reach.

The last time they were there, Caroline and John had left Apin Akot enough money to buy his daughter back and, once again, he had risked his life to cross the front line and confront the slaver who had taken her.

'The owner told me it was wrong to come back and bother him,' said Apin, a slender, inoffensive figure in his sand-stained *djellaba* and brown striped *taqiyah*.

The slave owner had tried to dismiss him, saying, 'We refused to give you your daughter, and yet you still come back.'

But Apin had risked all for this moment, and was not about to walk away. He looked him in the eye and said, 'You took my daughter at gunpoint. If you had a spear like me, you wouldn't have succeeded in taking her. I love my daughter and you took her from me. You agreed to part with her for money.'

Whether the slave owner was unnerved by this feisty father's determination, or moved by an unfamiliar inkling of compassion is not known. Either way, he produced a copy of the Koran and made Apin Akot swear that he would never return. Apin gave him the money and received his daughter's freedom. Together they walked the seven miles back across the frontier.

His daughter Akec was with him now. 'Today I am so happy,' said Apin. 'I cannot forget the help you gave me.'

Akec, whose face and legs still bore the scars from her beatings, described what had happened the day the militia came. 'When I was captured, my hands were tied with strong rope,' she said. 'All the bad jobs were given to me – grinding dura in the house and carrying water from the well at night. If I was slow fetching the water, my master beat me with a big stick. All the family beat me. I was just given left-overs on the plates for food.'

She had been forced to pray like a Muslim and wear the head-dress of a Muslim woman. She was told by her owner that this was the year she would be married to his son.

When her father had come the first time, he had seemed like a vision. She could not believe her eyes. But when he had said good-bye and had left her behind, she had not been able to eat for days. Now, she said, she was very happy.

'You created me again,' beams Apin Akot, 'like God, giving me a new life.

When you gave me the money and I got my daughter back, I felt as if I had been born again.'

Akec's mother, Acai, chimes in, her gentle face wreathed in smiles, 'I will never forget the people who raised the money. At night I dream of you and the news that you were coming here. I will always dream of you.'

Blind Abuk Marou Keer had also been given money to buy back her two children. An Arab trader said he knew where they were. With the cash from CSI, her brother went north and found her boy. Her nine-year-old daughter, Kadija Abuk, was being kept as a slave in another village. On the day of the raid she had tried to run, but had been captured and put in a trailer with many other children. This year, she was due to have been circumcised, and after that would have been fit for use as a concubine. Circumcision was routine, for chattel girls as well as boys – without anaesthetic.

'Thank you for all the people who gave money for my children to come back to me' said Abuk Marou. 'Although famine and hunger may kill us, we would rather starve together than live apart. I am so happy, I could dance.'[23]

'The joy of reunited families,' wrote Caroline in her report, 'has to be witnessed to be fully appreciated.'[24]

Within weeks of Caroline's return to the UK from Sudan, the British people voted out the Conservative government and ushered in Labour by a landslide. Two weeks after the election, from unfamiliar opposition benches, Caroline was returning to her familiar theme. There was no time to waste. There was a new government to persuade, with a declared commitment to take an ethical stand on human rights. There were new ministers to educate and inform, lobby, harry and harangue. 'In the cruel calculus of man's inhumanity to man,' she began, surveying the red leather seats opposite, 'Sudan ranks as one of the greatest tragedies in the world today... We estimate that tens of thousands of African Sudanese are now enslaved...[25] Will the government do everything possible to put pressure on the Sudanese government to desist?'[26]

The greatest pressure on the Sudanese government was coming not from the international community but from the forces of the NDA. Garang's deputy, Commander Salva Kiir, outlined their strategy in the clearest possible terms: 'The war... will continue northwards until the government is removed.'[27] It was left to *The Economist* to wonder out loud whether the North/South alliance could survive victory,[28] and for the BBC to observe: 'The opposition... is so divided that some opposition leaders talk of a complete disintegration of Sudan – in the manner of Somalia.'[29]

Physical disintegration was almost complete. Many roads had become so choked with undergrowth and littered with landmines that they were almost impassable. UNICEF accused both sides of preventing humanitarian aid, and warned that a whole generation of children was at risk. Africa's longest war had sent malnutrition and child mortality rates soaring to among the highest in the world.[30] Famine had broken out once again in the South, forcing the displaced to live on a diet of leaves. As one Sudanese politician observed: 'The South is back almost to the Stone Age.'

World condemnation of the man-made horrors continued. The World Bank suspended its operations in Sudan, claiming corruption was preventing the money from reaching the ordinary people.[31] The USA imposed severe financial sanctions, which were denounced by an unrepentant President al-Bashir at a massed rally in Khartoum, who pledged: 'There will be more campaigns for *jihad* and more training of *mujahedin*.'[32] Meanwhile Sudanese church leaders were warned to sever relations with Christian organizations critical of Khartoum – especially the UK-based Christian Solidarity. They were told 'a 'bombshell' would explode in their midst, unless they refrained from spreading 'rumours' of slavery and the alleged persecution of Christians.'[33]

Those rumours will prove hard to quash. A report by Anti-Slavery International confirmed: 'Slavery exists in Sudan today.'[34]

The stench of death

In March 1997, Garang's forces captured Yei, near the Uganda / Zaire border, creating a vital supply route and opening a way to Juba, the capital of the South, a prime but elusive goal since the modern phase of the war began in 1983. The SPLA launched a six-front offensive and began to close in, before suffering reversals in the battle for the strategic town of Torit.

The Daily Telegraph described the capture of Yei as Garang's 'most significant victory... a turning point.'[35] It also brought home what a brutal, bloody business war is. Hundreds were killed along the main Yei road in what turned out to be a turkey-shoot. Caught in the ambush alongside government soldiers were civilians seeking shelter in the nearby garrison.

Sudanese journalist Andrew Allam was at the scene soon after: 'On Good Friday we saw the cost of liberation. The smell of bodies rotting filled the air. Maggots crawled and rats ran. Were these once human beings made in the image of God? Women had died, begging for mercy, goats at their side. It is said that, in war, everyone loses, because war brutalizes even the winners.'[36] Allam was so haunted by the smell and the sight of the carnage that the task of reviewing his video footage was beyond him. The stench hung in the air for three months until it was washed away by the rain.

Those who survived and were captured included boys aged 15 and younger, Southerners press-ganged by the government to go to war against their own people. As the fighting grew fiercer, so did the protests in Khartoum against forced conscription. But, if such a thing is possible, worse was to come.

Caroline returned to Sudan in May 1998, this time under the aegis of Christian Solidarity Worldwide. CSI-UK had split acrimoniously from the Zurich-based Christian Solidarity International. The reasons were largely ones of agenda and control. CSI (Zurich) had withdrawn support for Nagorno Karabakh while CSI-UK continued to be committed to the enclave and the work there. By agreement, Zurich also withdrew from the Russian child care project, leaving Caroline's British organization pulling in an increasingly divergent direction with a different set of priorities. There were other problems. CSI (Zurich) wanted access to CSI-UK's database of donors, then there was an angry falling out over the handling of a school project in Nepal, resulting in CSI-UK taking it over. It led to, in Caroline's words, 'deep divisions and disagreements... I am very sad about the bitterness that is there.' CSI-UK went its own way and became CSW. Other active branches in Germany and Australia also split away. CSW went on to set up its own branches in the USA and Hong Kong with its sights set further afield.

As far as Sudan was concerned it was mixed news. It spelt the end of the fruitful relationship between Caroline Cox and the quiet American, John Eibner, who remained in Zurich, furious about the division. The upside was that both CSI (Zurich) and the new CSW were as committed as ever to exposing the slave trade. Now there were two organizations working to drag the issue into the media spotlight.

When Caroline and CSW returned to Sudan in May, that spotlight was already on Sudan. Images of famine were being beamed around the world. The NIF was self-righteously opening up selected areas of the country to relief agencies. But where Caroline went was still an official no-go zone – for reasons that became all too apparent.

While the NIF regime was basking in accolades for its humanitarian gestures, at the same time it was carrying out massacres on an unprecedented scale. By going to the areas the world was not meant to see, we saw systematic carnage on a scale I had never before witnessed.

The stench of death was overwhelming. You could go for mile upon mile and see the corpses – civilians still wearing beads and bracelets, trying to flee from the raids, followed into the bush and slaughtered. Cattle that wouldn't go willingly with the raiders were killed so there would be no food for anyone who might survive. Crops and homes were put to the torch. Pilots told us they could fly 60 miles in every direction and see burning villages. Areas which before had been rich pasture with thousands of cattle were now completely desolate. Huge swathes of land were treated in this way, a population of about 2 million were affected, facing what was now a totally government-made famine in fertile lands. I think it no coincidence that this area is significant in the development of oil; it is an area of tremendous potential. The reason for genocide was to cleanse the Dinkas off that land. The last night I just sat under a tree and wept.'

One area believed to have been targeted by the raids was Nyamlell. Again.

Caroline was in a different part of Bahr el-Ghazal and unable to verify the fate of Nyamlell. But the civilians she met in Wuntok told a familiar story. They had been attacked on three sides by Arabs on horseback, sometimes two or three to a horse. As the people fled, the net closed around them and they were herded towards the waiting guns. Thousands of children were rounded up and abducted into slavery. But there was a crucial additional strand to their evidence. Many of their attackers had been in army uniforms, suggesting the direct involvement of government armed forces in both the genocide and the taking of slaves.

Those same troops had also attacked Mayen Abun. Caroline reached there just ten days after the soldiers had left, to hear of women and children tied up and slaughtered like goats and men thrown alive into a burning tukul. Catholic catechist Santino Ring showed Caroline the brick-built church which the raiders had been unable to burn. Instead, they had set fire to prayer books, slashed the drums used for worship and shot at the cross on the roof. He said: 'These people are suffering because they are Christian; if they were Muslim this destruction would not have happened. I am appealing to the churches to rescue us, the Christians of Mayen Abun.'

Grandfather Ajak Ring brought Caroline his four grandchildren. The raiders had killed his daughter and her husband, rounded up his 70 cattle and burned his home. All he had to feed the grandchildren were tamarind seeds. He echoed Santino Ring's sense of utter abandonment: 'Doesn't the church want us any longer?' Commander Salva Mathok made a direct appeal: 'We are angry. The international community came to help in

Somalia, Sierra Leone and Kuwait. Why can't we have safe havens for our people?'

Caroline took up the Commander's cry and her report called for air exclusion zones to protect the civilians of the South. She returned with video footage, pictures and witness accounts that attracted widespread media coverage. It was roundly denounced by the Sudan Foundation as 'shamefully bad journalism'. They poured cold water on Caroline's claims of collaboration between Sudan and Iraq and added: 'Baroness Cox is a supporter of the rebel movement.'[37]

In October, she flew out again with Stuart Windsor, to meet representatives of the Muslim community in territory liberated from the NIF. Christians, animists and Muslims were living peacefully together, as they had done in the days before the regime. Abdulla Ibramhim was the Muslim administrator of Yabus. Yet because he was also an African the NIF had barred him from higher education.

Terefi Babikir was another African – an Imam. 'The NIF regime was not pure Islam,' he said, 'it was highly politicized. The regime talked about a *jihad*, but their *jihad* was to take freedom away. I would be ready to fight against them, because as an Imam, I do not believe [we can] bring people to faith by force.'

He concluded: 'Thank you for coming and asking about our religion. You are the first people to do this, and I will always be grateful that you cared enough to come.'

Caroline and Stuart visited a church and a mosque and promised to send Bibles – and Korans – as quickly as possible.[38]

Chemical stockpile

At the close of 1998, events in the Gulf eclipsed those in Sudan. The US and Britain launched air-strikes designed to whittle down the military machine of Iraqi leader Saddam Hussein because of his refusal to allow the UN to inspect and destroy his stockpiles of chemical and biological weapons. Earlier, a US cruise missile had pounded the Al-Shifa factory in Khartoum which was allegedly making a key ingredient for the deadly VX nerve gas. Baghdad had stood up for Khartoum, promising to make resources available for Sudan to withstand American 'aggression'.

The first indication of what those resources might be had come earlier from Wau, the regional capital of Bahr el-Ghazal, which was still in government hands. According to *The Sunday Times* Wau was the secret location for the production of mustard gas to be used against the SPLA. The gas production plant was said to have been a joint venture between Sudan and Saddam. Khartoum had given its blessing to the Iraqi invasion of Kuwait, which triggered the Gulf War. When Baghdad was defeated, the Iraqi dictator negotiated a deal to move some of his Scud missiles and chemical weapons production to Sudan to escape the UN embargo. Sudan had used the mustard gas against the SPLA on at least two occasions, rolling canisters off the back of cargo planes onto rebel positions below. They missed their targets.[39]

During Caroline's visit to Sudan in October she had heard more about chemical weapons. Admittedly the source was an SPLA commander, who might cynically have been seizing the chance for a propaganda coup. But what if he were telling the truth? Commander Malik was the Governor of the Southern Blue Nile. He said a chemical shell had been used against the SPLA in Ulu; government gas masks had been discovered in Rumbek, and in Kelei, a civilian had suffered burns and blisters after touching the soil where a shell exploded. According to SPLA intelligence, the NIF had a chemical or biological production plant in Damazin. Then the Commander played his trump card. He claimed the world's number one terrorist Osama bin Laden owned a farm near an airstrip in Kadum. It was a base for *mujahedin* and Islamist terrorists from different countries.[40]

How could such claims be verified? A report produced by the US House of Representatives Task Force on Terrorism and Unconventional Warfare made interesting reading. It claimed Iraq had transferred stockpiles of chemical and biological weapons to Sudan along with the know-how and means of production. Scud missiles and even nuclear material had been shipped out by Iraq for safe keeping. The deal meant Saddam's stockpiles were beyond the reach of UN weapons inspectors, and Sudan would be able to acquire its own weapons of mass destruction to wage war with the South. The report also claimed that Iraq had sent units of Republican Guards to help in the civil war.

The first joint Iraqi-Sudanese project was the chemical weapons munitions plant at Wau exposed by *The Sunday Times*. Iraqi pilots dropped chemical bombs around Kadugli and elsewhere. According to opposition sources 'there was a big change in the colour of the corpses of animals and trees', in line with similar witness accounts from Afghanistan and South East Asia where chemical weapons had been used. Later, Sudan took over the manufacture of mustard gas, which it was to use on the SPLA.

Along with Iraqi-built factories for chemical and biological weapons in Sudan, the report also claimed that a centre for the development of weapons for use by Islamic terrorists, affiliated to Osama bin Laden, was being constructed in Soba, south west of Khartoum.

But if that sounded like an exercise to whip up public opinion in favour of air-strikes, the report's conclusion suggested otherwise. It said allied missile attacks on Iraq would be futile because Saddam's weapons of mass destruction were safely out of the country.[41]

Caroline outlined the key points of the report in the Lords, warning that, 'to focus predominantly, even exclusively, on Iraq may play into Saddam's hands... if the contents of his "treasure chest" of sinister weapons have already been shared with allies capable of carrying out equally ruthless destruction in pursuit of equally ruthless policies... we ignore them at our peril.'[42]

The British government and the White House proclaimed themselves sceptical about the House of Representatives' report, but in August a cruise missile ripped into an alleged chemical weapons factory in Khartoum, with the blessing of Britain – and Caroline Cox. She congratulated the British government 'on their robust position in support of the cruise missile attack by the United States'.

Lord McNair, her old sparring partner, condemned the missile strike against Khartoum as 'an act of unbelievable and cynical cruelty' calculated to divert attention from President Bill Clinton's 'shall we say... more domestic concerns'.[43]

Caroline went on to call for government pressure on Khartoum to scrap its no-go areas and allow access to aid to the war zones of the famine-stricken South. To go along with exclusion zones for aid was, she said, tantamount to condoning the regime's use of the 'politics of hunger'.

By December a government Antonov had carried out six bombing raids on the hospital in Yei. It was in violation of a cease-fire, called because of the famine. Outlawed cluster bombs were used. One cluster bomblet penetrated the leg of a woman patient. She was holding her baby at the time. Mercifully, it didn't explode. A Sudanese bomb disposal engineer managed to remove it, without anaesthetic, and the mother and child survived.

On 5 December, the Roman Catholic Bishop of Torit told the World Council of Churches about the bombing of hospital patients in Yei. He said: 'The suffering people of Sudan hear that great nations have imposed a no-fly zone on the Iraqi Government to protect the Kurds in Northern Iraq. Our people ask: "are we not worth human life to be protected from the Sudanese airforce by the imposition of a no-fly zone?"'

Three days later Caroline called a debate in the Lords and quoted the Bishop. As well as backing the call for an exclusion zone, she demanded further government sanctions against Sudan and support for organizations – like Christian Solidarity – who were prepared to travel to the no-go areas.

Once again she drew a connection between the regimes of Khartoum and Baghdad: 'Both have inflicted incalculable suffering on their own people and continue to do so... until those regimes are brought to account there can be no peace for their own people, except the peace of the dead, and no peace for the rest of the world, except the deluded peace of the ostrich.'

It was a long debate, and demonstrated a growing concern about events in Sudan and the emerging alliance with Iraq. Lord Moynihan demanded to know what action the Government was taking to investigate 'the grave concerns that the NIF is working closely with both Saddam Hussein to develop chemical and biological weapons and with the terrorist Osama bin Laden to launch new terrorist attacks in the future'.

Baroness Williams of Crosby condemned the 'systematic famine and starvation' in Sudan and quoted leading academic lawyer Mary Glendon in the *New York Times* who described Sudan as 'the worst human rights violator in the world today'. Baroness Williams went on to accuse Sudan of manipulating the international relief effort, and of, in effect, 'blackmailing non-governmental organizations with a terrible choice': refusing to work with the NIF and abandoning the people of Sudan, or accepting their imposed no-go zones, and letting others starve. 'I believe this to be one of the most difficult moral questions that anyone has ever had to confront,' she said. She blamed the United States for agreeing to tie-in the NGOs to the NIF-approved Operation Lifeline Sudan. And for good measure she also took a swipe at the arms dealers from the US and Europe who were 'swamping' Sudan with Kalashnikovs.

Baroness Williams went on to pay tribute to Caroline Cox as 'an outstanding example of that famous quotation that it is enough for injustice to triumph that good men remain silent. The noble Baroness is a good woman who does not remain silent, and she encourages others not to remain silent either.'

In response to Caroline's question in the House, the British government agreed to 'press for access to all areas where there is a need for humanitarian assistance'.[44]

As 1999 dawned, the scale of that need seemed as great as ever. UNICEF warned that more than 4 million Sudanese faced the threat of famine.[45] The war had killed one in five in the South and displaced four in every five. The only hope was for both sides to agree to extend their 'cease-fire'.

Both did – for what it was worth. Fighting had been continuing regardless. It was unlikely the renegade Dinka warlord Kerubino Kwanyin Bol would take much notice of cease-fire declarations. The mercurial Kerubino had switched sides three times and returned to the government fold after bungling an assassination attempt against SPLA leader John Garang. Now he was said to be massing a force of up to 13,000 men in Bentiu, the oil-rich region of the South. The government had provided Kerubino with training camps in the largest town in Bahr el-Ghazal, the region worst hit by the famine. That town was Wau, the alleged centre for chemical weapons, and destination of the military train which brings the slave raiders to Nyamlell.[46]

A report by Amnesty International in January added its voice to those condemning modern slavery on the eve of the new millennium. After criticizing both sides for siphoning humanitarian aid intended for famine victims, it confirmed that Government militia had 'abducted thousands of civilians, mostly women and children, and forced them into unpaid labour in the north, in effect turning them into slaves'.[47]

The evidence is compelling that slavery exists in Southern Sudan, that it is raging, and that the perpetrators are Arab militiamen and government soldiers.
Augustine A. Lado, Associate Professor of Cleveland University and President of Pax Sudani, in response to denials from the Sudan Foundation.[48]

NOTES

1. 'Sudan and Regional Concerns: Difficult Neighbours and an Aggressive Superpower', March 1997.
2. *AFRICANS*, 15 February 1997.
3. The peace pact was signed on 21 April, between the government and the South Sudan Independence Movement, Kerubino's Bahr el-Ghazal group, the Equatoria Defence force and the Bor group. Along with two other factions they went on to form the South Sudan Defence Force, under the leadership of Riek Machar. The peace pact was dismissed by John Garang's mainstream SPLA.
4. 'Former guerrilla says Garang has no reason to continue Sudan War', 31 May 1997.
5. Policy Statement of the SPLM/SPLA on the Sudanese Peace Agreement signed in Khartoum on 21 April 1997.
6. Statement of the Umma Party on the Peace Agreement of 21 April 1997.
7. Sirr Anai Keleul-Jang, editor of the *South Sudan Bulletin* observed, 'In Musltaqbal al-Islam fi al-Sudan, Sadiq has proposed five ways to Arabize and Islamize the South... in the view of many Southern Sudanese people, Sadiq's Islamic democracy is as oppressive as the Islamic *jihad* government of al-Bashir and al-Turabi': *South Sudan Bulletin*, vol. 2, no. 3, January 1997.
8. Lyndon H. LaRouche Jr, 'D-Day Looms for the IMF system!', 1 March 1997.
9. *Executive Intelligence Review Talks*, editorial, 6 February 1997.
10. It continued, 'In the face of a collapsing financial system, the policy of the British is to destroy the existence of the modern sovereign nation-state, in Africa and elsewhere, so as to eliminate any opposition to their attempt to re-establish colonial control over the strategic minerals upon which modern life depends.'
11. US State Department noon briefing, 23 January 1997.
12. Reported in *Sudan News and Views*, January 1996.

13. Ghion Hagos, 'Eritrea accuses Sudan of plotting to kill President Afeworki', Panafrican News Agency, 25 June 1997 and 'Great Satan Joins Fray', *Africa Confidential*, 1 August 1997.
14. The US Secretary of State, Madeleine Albright met John Garang and other representatives of the NDA, and described the NDA as 'not only opposing the NIF, but also trying to lay the groundwork for a new Sudan in which people of all faiths and cultures can focus on re-building their country': Africa News Service, 11 December 1997.
15. CSI Sudan Report, 6–11 January 1997.
16. *Release in Action*, no. 3, 1997.
17. 'Disaster "in the Making" in Sudanese Nuba Mountains', Inter Press Service, 6 March 1997.
18. 'Sudanese Govt Forces Liberate Tuloshi Mountains', Panafrican News Agency, 1 June 1997.
19. 'Rights Group Accuses Sudan of Genocide of Nuba People', Associated Press, 5 August 1997.
20. Figure supplied by Association of Christian Resource Organizations Serving Sudan (ACROSS), Nairobi, 1997.
21. Amnesty International's 1997 Country Report on Sudan acknowledged the role played by PDF escorting the military train.
22. CSI Report on Sudan (Northern Bahr el-Ghazal), 11–16 June 1997.
23. CSI Sudan Report, 11–18 March 1997.
24. Caroline reported her findings to the United Nations Commission on Human Rights in Geneva on 9 April. They were refuted the following day by Sudan.
25. 12,000 according to the civil authorities, 40,000 according to the SPLA.
26. *Hansard*, 15 May 1997.
27. Agence France Presse, 1 April 1997.
28. 'Rebel alliance', 25 January 1997.
29. 'The regime of al-Bashir', 29 October 1997.
30. 'Africa's longest war continues', Africa News Service, 5 August 1997.
31. 'World bankers halt loans in crackdown on a web of corruption', *The Times*, 18 August 1997.
32. Africa News Service, 19 November 1997.
33. Attributed to Dr Ghazi Salih el Eddin, the Secretary General of the national ruling congress, Inter Press Service, 11 November 1997.
34. Peter Verney, 'Slavery in Sudan', Sudan Update and Anti-Slavery International, May 1997. The UN Human Rights Committee expressed dismay at the sheer number of reports that pointed to its continuance: 'UN Human Rights Committee Condemns Senegal, Sudan', Pan-African News Agency, 13 November 1997.

Sudan's notoriety extended to Scotland, where, in a landmark legal action, a Sudanese doctor was charged with committing torture in his own country – a case which could open the floodgates to similar actions.
35. 9 May 1997; also Inter Press Service, 21 May 1997.
36. 'The Return', CMS magazine, *Yes*, July 1997.
37. *The Daily Telegraph*, and coverage of Sudan, June 1998.
38. CSW fact-finding visit to Southern Blue Nile Region 7–12 October 1998.
39. Jon Swain, 'Iraq making lethal gas in covert Sudan pact', *The Sunday Times*, 16 November 1997; 'Sudan Has Poison Gas Plant Near Uganda', Africa News Service, 21 November 1997.
40. CSW fact-finding visit to Southern Blue Nile Region, 7–12 October 1998.
41. Task Force on Terrorism and Unconventional Warfare, 'The Iraqi WMD Challenge – Myths and Reality', 10 February 1998.
42. *Hansard*, 17 February 1998.
43. *Hansard*, 26 November 1998.
44. *Hansard*, 8 December 1998.
45. 'Millions of Sudanese may face famine in 1999: UNICEF', Xinhua, 22 December 1998.
46. 'Sudan cease-fire extended', BBC, 15 January 1999.
47. 'Serious risk of human rights abuses after cease-fire ends', Amnesty International, 8 January 1999.
48. 'An Exchange of Correspondence...' September 1997, www.sufo.demon.co.uk/deb003.htm

Appendix

On the Home Front

'Her eyes blaze with conscience –
the very effect is compelling.'

Lord Longford

ONE

An Iron Lady?

Caroline's role in politics, like her involvement in human rights, springs from the same desire to champion the truth as she sees it and to speak up for the underdogs – be they disadvantaged children in Britain's schools or the nation's underpaid and overworked nurses.

But not everyone would describe her contribution in such saintly terms. In Britain, she is still best known for her role in the educational debate. Often controversial and usually criticized, she has been vilified as a rampant right-winger – a charge she denies. She dislikes party politics and sees herself as standing outside them, placing herself where she is most likely to get caught in the crossfire.

Never one to settle for cosy political consensus, her targets have included the core values of the educational establishment. Among them are those aspects of comprehensive schooling, that she believes have failed many children: the wildly varying standards of different local education authorities, and a watered-down and enfeebled religious education. Her other causes include the eradication of political indoctrination in schools.

No-one could accuse her of courting popularity.

A number of her close friends have likened her to Margaret Thatcher, who is both loved and reviled in equal measure. The suggestion makes Caroline wince. Yet there are similarities, however uncomfortable she may find them. Like the iron lady, Caroline has boundless energy and again like Mrs Thatcher, she needs little sleep to replenish it. And once Caroline Cox has made up her mind, like someone else, 'woe betide anyone who gets in her way,' warns her colleague Mervyn Thomas. 'Although she's compassionate, she doesn't suffer fools gladly. Some people who are really not up to it have suffered her tongue.'

Fellow human rights worker Stuart Windsor agrees: 'You shouldn't cross her,' says the big man she gleefully insists on calling Titch, much to his embarrassment. 'If you really cross her on something she cares about, you are in for it. She's a wonderful person but, of all the people I know, I have never met anyone who can cut you down like Caroline. She is very intelligent and very articulate. She can be a killer.'

Right-wing philosopher and colleague, Roger Scruton concurs: 'She's formidable – comparable to Mrs Thatcher, really.'

But is she as indefatigable as the matriarch her friends keep likening her to? 'She doesn't stop,' insists Mervyn Thomas, 'She's always rushing from one meeting to another, and yet she's still got time for people.'

'She works nine days a week,' adds Stuart Windsor. 'To keep up with her, you've got to be up to the job.' And that despite a thyroid disorder, which usually forces sufferers to slow right down.

Caroline's mailbag is a postman's nightmare, but is assiduously dealt with each morning with the help of Jana Pearson, her long-suffering secretary, who has to try to harness the whirlwind.

'It can become frenetic,' says Jana, 'but if she gets too bad, I just say, "Caroline, calm down". But she doesn't take any notice of me. Even when she's driving, she's usually on the mobile phone within five minutes of leaving the office. I don't even try to keep up with her. I just plod on and help as much as I can.'

Their office is a cluster of cramped rooms in a brace of small flats that form Caroline's London *pied-à-terre* in Kingsbury. The walls are lined with books and papers, and filing cabinets encroach upon the floor space. A photocopier and yet more cabinets fill the remaining rooms. Caroline shares the office and the services of her secretary with long-time colleague John Marks: 'You've got to see her working on a speech,' he remarks. 'She is utterly immersed. I can go into the office first thing in the morning and she will already be at the computer, and we won't exchange a word for half an hour, because she's in it – she's concentrating. The intensity is tangible. Then from 9.30 in the morning, the phone goes like a machine-gun but she can switch in and out very effectively. People who know her for one aspect of her work don't realize she is doing about five other things simultaneously at the same level. She has great intellectual ability, and is extraordinarily active. Only very rarely does it become counterproductive. It's a productive hyperactivity.'

Yet she is invariably late. 'Sorry, I'm late – again' was a suggested title for this biography.

Stuart Windsor and others were waiting for a belated Caroline to turn up at a CSI conference in Glasgow. He checked up on her progress on his mobile phone, but forgot to close the call. When he had finished, he turned to his companions and observed: 'She's always late. She's a proper little madam!' 'I'm what?' squawked the handset, more in humour than in outrage.

'She tries to pack in more than one can into every day,' Jana, the keeper of the diary endeavours to explain. 'She gets interrupted, but takes the interruptions because she wants to deal with everyone. She is so kind and charming. I think we've only had one cross word over ten years.'

John Marks concurs. 'She manages to keep that remarkable coolness, charm and sensitivity, even under great pressure.' But from the other end of the phone, Caroline's charm is not always bullet-proof. When she is in a hurry she can subject the caller to a brusque monologue in breathless telegraphese, in a tone that makes it clear that any interjection had better be brief. And she is clearly a woman accustomed to getting her own way.

For a politician, she is refreshingly more interested in action than in words. It is partly a product of upbringing, partly of her Christian concern. She is a woman with a mission: 'She has this feeling that she is given information in order to make constructive use of it,' says John Marks. 'She won't rest until she does. She picks things up, runs with them, and makes them into something constructive which actually makes a difference. She prays a lot about what she is doing to seek guidance, and genuinely tries to infuse her work with her Christian commitment.'

Caroline is adamant she is not a workaholic, but confesses: 'I'm an action-aholic, because there's just so much to do.' 'She simply does not sleep,' says Christopher Besse, of the medical relief organization, MERLIN, a personal friend. 'I will go out to dinner with her or treat her to supper and at 3 a.m. I will hear my letter box go clonk, clonk, and it's a thank you note. She jokes that she dropped it in by hand to save on the postage.'

Without the assistance of sleeping pills, Caroline's 3 a.m. excursions might be more commonplace. 'A lot of the time my mind is whirling round with worries and activities,' she says. And after a trip to Sudan, her thoughts are not always pleasant. 'Anxieties and sadness take over very easily. One could get overwhelmed, especially at night. That's why I make a conscious effort to switch off and think about positive things, or I use that time for prayer.'

She denies keeping busy to justify her existence. What drives her, she says, is neither survivor guilt nor Catholic guilt – although her understanding of her motivation seems to come quite close: 'It's more a Protestant requirement of stewardship – to use one's talents. If we have privilege, freedom and health, there is a certain obligation to use them on behalf of those who do not.'

But how would she cope if ill-health forced her to stop working? She had six months' practice when she had TB. 'I hope I would have the grace to accept the situation,' she says, 'but I don't underestimate it. All the things I look forward to – being out and about with the family, bell-ringing, exercise – are active. These are my recreative mechanisms. It would be very hard.'

'I don't get butterflies, I get eagles'

And with indefatigability the similarities with Mrs Thatcher come to an end. For this is no iron lady. Her nerves before she speaks in the House or elsewhere are legendary, and show no sign of subsiding with experience. 'I don't get butterflies, I get eagles,' she admits. Stuart Windsor has been with her during the run-up to important speeches. 'In the moments beforehand she has panic attacks, when she thinks: "What on earth am I going to say? How am I going to cope? I'm not going to be able to do this."' We were in Australia and she was about to deliver an important speech to parliamentarians and she was in the toilet, praying. If you say something to her she seems to be miles away, she is so completely focused.'

That focus cuts in with an almost audible click the moment she stands up to deliver her speech. The impression in the Chamber is one of cool, measured confidence. There is no tell-tale hint of a flutter about her clothing which would suggest a battle raging to control her nerves. Every speech is scripted and rehearsed, so what could go wrong?

'It could go wrong,' she insists, 'that's what one's always afraid of. Sometimes I stand up and have no idea what I am going to say and my mind is a white-out. If I have a starred question in the Lords, that will hang like a cloud on my horizon for days beforehand and I will rehearse again and again the possible options of my supplementary question.'

'She really does think the next speech is going to be a disaster,' adds John Marks. 'The stage fright is absolutely genuine.'

Even after all these years, Caroline still finds herself in awe of the most accomplished performers in the House: 'I really envy politicians who seem to be able to stand up with such effortless ease and confidence and articulate.' It was that lack of ease – shyness even – that left her uncomfortable as a junior minister. 'It would give me no pleasure to live a politician's life, having to go to formal dinners and make after-dinner speeches. In formal situations I don't have that confidence.' She pauses. 'I'm not always 100 per cent confident in what I'm doing or whether it is the right thing.'

Self-doubt is not something a casual acquaintance would associate with Caroline. But from childhood, it has run like a river within her. 'I have never understood why things have come my way,' she confesses. 'I don't understand why I was made head girl, much to my astonishment. I have never understood why I was made set leader. I barely understood why I was made a peer.'

But her puzzling lack of faith in herself should not be confused with a lack of conviction in her politics. She is a true believer: 'When I feel passionately about something and have thought it through and therefore feel very deeply with conviction, I will fight very hard for that.' Her instinct is to persuade, rather than harangue, though she is certainly prepared to break through the boundaries of politeness, if she feels she has to: 'But I don't enjoy confrontation – I'm much more a consensual person.'

While she believes her friends regard her as outgoing, friendly and fun, she imagines her opponents sum her up as 'opinionated, inflexible and tough'. She does confess to a tendency to see issues in black and white rather than shades of grey. 'Sometimes that conviction could be so single-minded that it might be counter-productive,' she admits. 'I hope I am not intolerant, and that I would have the integrity and openness to adjust my position in the light of new evidence or new situations.'

But having done just that and made the switch from left to right, is this particular lady now for turning? Does she ever change her mind? 'I can't think of a single example at this moment,' she grins. 'But I created the maxim that politicians should have open ears, open eyes and open minds before they have an open mouth. There are lots of dilemmas, and that is probably one of the reasons I hate party politics, because I can usually see both sides of most things. Party politics leads to oversimplification or to polarized approaches which I don't think are always best at producing the most effective solutions to problems.'

What if there were a tussle between head and heart, understanding and emotion; which would win?

'I would have to go back to moral values, of what would concur with the deep values of love, truth, integrity and respect for others. If the head could not justify what the heart had felt, I hope I would look at the emotional response in an analytical way.'

Among her passions she includes England. Caroline describes herself as a patriot, but not a blind one. 'Whenever I've been abroad and the plane comes in over the coastline, my heart gives a leap as I look down and the thought that comes to mind is that this is my own, my native land. There is a lot that is very precious. The stereotype of the British is way off-beam. There is still a very deep love of freedom. People are sincere and kind, and among many British people there is still a great generosity, decency and inherent goodness. Our tradition of voluntary service is one of the most precious in the world. England is a very civil society. We really do have, as Shakespeare said, infinite riches in a little space. I treasure the heritage we've been privileged to receive.'

A whiff of socialism?

Caroline was born into privilege and received from her father the clear understanding that privilege has its responsibilities. Individual freedoms are all well and good, and seeing that freedom crushed behind the Iron Curtain confirmed her in her Conservatism, but there is more than a whiff of socialism about her views on society.

'There are problems in our society,' she says. 'I would like to see reform and improvement, particularly related to poverty and the vulnerable: to those least able to articulate their own needs and assert their own rights. I think the gross inequalities of wealth are unacceptable and some members of the privileged section of our society do show an arrogance, which is a characteristic I find hard to tolerate.'

Another *bête noir* is cynicism which she describes as the eighth deadly sin, much as one would expect from a conviction politician. 'Cynicism is destructive, negativistic, utterly unredemptive and potentially spiritually lethal,' she rails. 'It can poison everything and leave people with an emptiness of life. It's also horribly infectious.' Her hatred of the corrosion of cynicism, so prevalent in the media, is countered in media circles by the suspicion that Caroline is both partisan and naïve in the choice and pursuit of her causes in the field of human rights. 'That dotty baroness...' was how one un-diplomatic editor referred to her.

'I think the media underestimate the thoroughness with which she does her homework,' says John Marks, 'and the way she looks at alternative points of view, weighs the available evidence and evaluates the arguments.'

But both she and John are used to being stereotyped, labelled, discredited and dismissed. In their political careers, both have been caricatured as right-wingers – a view expressed by a good few educationalists and media commentators. But ask a nurse about Caroline Cox and you might get a different answer. In 1988, she marched along Whitehall arm-in-arm with TUC General Secretary Norman Willis to protest at nurses' pay and conditions, 'for which I have never been forgiven by some Tories,' she adds. As a nurse member of Brent Health Authority, she opposed Conservative cutbacks and fought plans for a freeze on manpower. Norman Willis described her as a 'helpful ally in many of our health battles'.[1]

'The best possible medical care should be available free of charge at the point of need,' argues Caroline, like a true radical. 'Costs are unpredictable,' she explains, 'and may be infinite as far as the individual is concerned. You can get a severely malformed baby, or someone who has been in a major road accident, and the state must bear responsibility.'

Roger Scruton shakes his head. 'She's much more a believer in the welfare state than I am,' he says. 'She has this socialist background, but with a religiously inspired moral vision.'

Once a nurse, always a nurse – only today Caroline carries more clout, as a Vice President of the Royal College of Nursing. 'I have yet to see a full-blooded commitment to the health service as a coherent part of Conservative philosophy,' she continues. 'The health reforms we've had have been a mixed bag. The heart of Conservatism at the moment doesn't have that kind of upbeat, coherent, positive, vibrant political philosophy.'

So it came as no surprise to Caroline that Labour defeated the Conservatives in 1997. 'It had to be,' she shrugs. 'There's no way the Tories could have, or should have, got in again. Conservatism was strong on the individual characteristics of choice and responsibility. It was very weak on compassion and support for the vulnerable. On health there was this fatal flaw, because they failed to take up a coherent policy that was related to compassion.'

'Extreme-right menace'

Education was another Tory failure, she believes, though her own campaigning to improve standards for children did much to shape Conservative legislation. 'There should have been more diversity, a greater emphasis on academic standards, accountability, choice – the kind of thing Conservatives stand for. I would have gone to the stake on those. I would also argue for the voucher, which is seen as being to the right of the Conservative Party.'

In 1985, *The Daily Express* mentioned Caroline's name in an article under the headline: 'Tory alarm at the rise of the extreme right menace'. The paper attacked what it described as loony libertarians in favour of drugs and underage sex.

It was to cost the *Express* dearly. 'We would never call ourselves "libertarians" as such,' Caroline and the others protested, indeed 'we do not hold and never have held the views attributed to libertarians in this article.'[2]

The *Express* pinned the blame on inaccurate information published by the Libertarian Alliance. Neither Caroline nor the High Court accepted the paper's apology and damages were awarded.

According to other columnists critical of Caroline, she is a 'Tory moral fundamentalist',[3] 'Ethics Girl', a 'Cassandra of the old Christian right' (along with Mary Whitehouse),[4] a 'right-wing pamphlet junkie' with private access to the then Prime Minister,[5] a 'Johnny-come-lately of the education lobby',[6] and the 'politically correct, narrow-minded [chief of the] fundamentalist thought police'.[7]

If you can tell a person by the company they keep, then many of her friends and associates share a certain outlook. She is or has been a member of the Freedom Association, the Institute of European Defence and Strategic Studies, the Parental Alliance for Choice in Education and the Committee for a Free Britain, which claimed the Thatcher government was losing its cutting edge and urged it to sharpen up its act. She has published on behalf of the right-wing Centre for Policy Studies and mounted a blistering attack on CND and Peace Studies.

'Her association with the kind of people who cannot pronounce the word "egalitarian" without a curl of the lip [gives] the impression of a rather harsh and elitist figure, devoted to the market and the devil take the hindmost,' wrote George Hill in *The Times*, adding: 'The reality is quite different, but the art of personal presentation on a public scale is one of the political arts to which she has not yet troubled to apply herself.'

That was written in 1988, and judging by the critical coverage that has continued to dog her, the same doubts about her personal presentation skills still hold true today. So how does she see herself? 'I am not ashamed of being to the right of centre now,' she says, 'but I don't see myself as being to the right of the Conservative Party. I see myself as uncategorizable. I see this labelling, particularly using words like far and extreme, as a deliberate attempt to put into people's minds a negative mindset. The labels are false. A deep commitment to the National Health Service is more to the centre or left of the political spectrum, and I think it is one of the better products to have come from Fabian Socialism.'

Caroline confesses herself to have been tempted to join the Social Democratic Party when its star was in the ascendant, and is a member of the Movement for Christian Democracy, explaining: 'It shows my political position in the round. I am independent-minded and appreciate the opportunity to meet and work with people from different parts of the political spectrum.'

When all is said and the blizzard of labels subsides, she sees herself as a blend of traditionalist and radical, combining left-wing compassion with a right-wing respect for the freedom of the individual.

'These labels are ridiculous,' said Lord Tonypandy, the former Labour MP, speaker of the House of Commons, and latterly a cross-bencher – a man who managed to shrug off his own stereotypes. 'It's like telling me Winston Churchill was right-wing. What if he was? He saved this country by the way he was able to set other people on fire and inspire us. I have a feeling that the Labour Party and the cross-benches hold her in the same high esteem – she's a remarkable woman making a remarkable contribution.'

Labour peer Lord Longford agrees – and disagrees: 'She is surprisingly Conservative; it's rather extreme in her case, and I ignore those speeches of hers. I've been Conservative; Labour for 60 years; Protestant and Catholic – these things don't really matter. If she happened to be Labour, she would make an excellent Labour peer, but she is above all that sort of thing.'

Smelting house

It is Caroline's combination of political and religious agendas that make her so difficult to pigeonhole. Her religious views were received in childhood, but her political views were forged in the smelting house of the Polytechnic of North London (PNL).

On more than one occasion, students came to her agonizing over the findings of their research projects. If they wrote them up as they stood the work would not fit in to a Marxist framework, therefore they were convinced the project would fail. Yet education, Caroline believed, required the freedom to pursue the truth and the obligation to evaluate new ideas.

She continued to teach according to her values, even when they clashed with the line taken by her department. She quickly found herself challenging parts of the curriculum.[8]

'I was quite prepared to be critical about our own society,' she says, 'after what I had seen in the East End, which had persuaded me to vote Labour. But I also thought it was important to look at the reality of what full-blown Marxist-Leninism was creating in socialist societies. Conditions of life for a lot of people in the Soviet block were worse than for many poorer people in Western societies. But the reading lists were totally biased: totally anti-Western and anti-capitalist.'

At the PNL, International Socialists (IS) dominated the student body, while among the many Marxist members of staff, the IS and the Communist Party were equally represented. Course committees and examiners' meetings became a running battle. Caroline introduced her own, unauthorized, critiques of Soviet society. Invariably, her comparisons drew fire from students on the far-left. Their mildest form of protest was to get out their newspapers, turn their backs and begin to read. At their most vehement they would heckle and shout.

The left-wing foment at the Polytechnic, and the framework she established for understanding it, which she put in place for *Rape of Reason*, swung this Labour voter decisively towards Conservatism: 'The capitalist economy is the best wealth-generating economic system the world has ever known,' she maintains. 'We need that in order to provide health and welfare and education, and to ensure there is a safety-net for the vulnerable and disadvantaged.'

In *Rape of Reason*, Caroline and her co-authors, Keith Jacka and John Marks, found themselves in open conflict with what was happening at the Poly. The kind of thinking they saw taking flesh around them was spelled out in 'Student Power', published by the *New Left Review* and Penguin.[9] Academic freedom was seen as an opportunity to establish a political bridgehead:

The emergent student revolutionaries aim to turn the tables on the system by using its universities and colleges as base areas from which to undermine key institutions of the social order... so long as the universities and colleges provide some sort of space which cannot be permanently policed they can become 'Red bases' for revolutionary agitation and preparation.

The conservative Foundation Endowment recognized parallels with events in American universities, and took an interest in *Rape of Reason*. Caroline was duly invited to go on many lecture tours in the United States.

She was due to speak at Smith College, on the north-east seaboard, where the right-wing politician Jeane Kirkpatrick[10] had been banned from addressing the students. Caroline prepared her speech on the value and importance of freedom and didn't let on she knew about the ban. Her talk was illustrated with graphic examples drawn from her experiences in Poland and behind the Iron Curtain. Then she got round to the issue of freedom of speech on campus.

She explained it was a matter of deep concern that, in some British universities, speakers were being censored, adding: 'The violation of academic freedom is the first step on the road to totalitarianism.' Seeing the faculty members in obvious discomfort, she stopped and threw the floor open to questions. The faculty immediately opened up with a fusillade that she was able to deflect with a well-practised hand. Eventually the staff had to back off and let the students speak. The first, a girl, stood up and promptly burst into tears. Caroline apologized if she had upset her. Between sniffs the student replied: 'No, you haven't upset me at all; it's just that before you came I thought I knew everything I believed in. And now you've spoken, I don't believe it any more.'

NOTES

1. David Moller, 'A baroness goes into battle', *Reader's Digest*, October 1992.
2. 'Lady Cox and the *Express*', 30 May 1985.
3. *The Independent*, 20 December 1995.
4. A.A. Gill in *The Sunday Times*, 16 January 1994.
5. Andrew Marr, *The Independent*, 22 March 1994.
6. *Morning Star*, 30 September 1985; *The Times*, 30 December 1986.
7. Angela Phillips, *The Independent*, 31 January 1994.
8. In Comparative Social Institutions one of her guiding principles was to test theory against practice. It meant examining the social systems that resulted from social, philosophical and political theories.
9. Blackburn and Cockburn, 1969.
10. Kirkpatrick is described as an 'outspoken anti-Marxist', *The Hutchinson Encyclopaedia*.

TWO

'A Clear and Growing Awareness'

From the outset of her parliamentary career Caroline rapidly established herself as a slayer of sacred cows and opponent of what would today be called political correctness. There were times when it resulted in a considerable political backlash and concerted efforts to discredit her.

In 1981 she began to research the shortcomings of the comprehensive education system with John Marks, and their research assistant, Maciej Pomian-Srzednicki. Their book, *Standards in English Schools*, was published on 30 June 1983 by the National Council for Educational Standards. It compared the exam results of grammar, secondary modern and comprehensive schools. What it found was to shake the prevailing political consensus and result in a dirty tricks campaign against its authors.

Their research showed, for the first time, that selective schools were dramatically outperforming the comprehensives. Even some secondary moderns, bereft of the highest achievers, were outclassing many comprehensives, with pupils achieving significantly more O level passes. Exam results varied widely from school to school. Pupils under some local education authorities were attaining three times as many O levels than pupils in others with comparable social class backgrounds. The questions raised by their research continue to fuel debate today.

What their research suggested was that children of below-average ability do best when they have the undivided attention of their teachers. Results were better when teachers were free to pace their work according to their pupils' aptitude and speed of learning. Caroline and John believed the comprehensive system was condemning some children of average or just-below-average ability to educational under-achievement.

'There was an enormous range of performance in our schools,' says John Marks. 'The differences were staggering. And there was a terrible difficulty getting any of this material out into the public domain. You'd have thought it was a matter of national security!'

The architect of the shift towards comprehensivization was Antony Crosland, Secretary of State for Education and Science in Harold Wilson's first Labour government. As Crosland famously put it: 'If it's the last thing I do, I'm going to destroy every f***ing grammar school in England. And Wales. And Northern Ireland.'[1]

In Caroline's view, the shift had been too radical and too quick. Comprehensive education should have been evaluated first, experimentally, before being imposed wholesale. But with both sides of the House backing the ideology, caution was thrown to the wind.

Two factors provoked their consensus-busting research. The first was close to Caroline's heart: she and Murray had chosen to put their children through the comprehensive system. Kingsbury High was, by reputation, one of the best schools in the borough. Besides, they wanted their children to remain close to home. And Brent was a cosmopolitan community, which they believed would be good for them.

Caroline is reticent about matters affecting her children but is prepared to acknowledge, 'a clear and growing awareness that all was not well'. Her daughter Pippa recalls: 'Mum thought the curriculum wasn't being taught and she wouldn't let it pass. She went into the school and asked to speak to the Principal.' At the same time, academic research was pointing to serious shortcomings in the comprehensive system.

A survey by the Institute of Mathematics discovered that one quarter of London's 16-year-olds could not multiply 6 by 79 by the end of their compulsory schooling. 'I wondered what on earth they had been doing for ten years,' said Caroline. It was discovered that British children were two years behind their counterparts in Germany in maths, and questions were being raised about declining standards of literacy. In Caroline's opinion, it amounted to 'a betrayal of many of our children'.

The report went down well with parents, but was damned by the educational establishment. No surprises there. 'What we didn't realize was that people would sink to the depths of leaking misleading reports to the press and sitting back and letting the press destroy the credibility of our research.'

Into the dustbin of history

Early reviews were encouraging. *The Times* the following day took the report at face value, declaring: 'Study marks down comprehensives'.[2] Then, one Sunday morning, Caroline had just returned from taking communion in church when she caught sight of her picture in *The Sunday Times*. The report said the Education Secretary, Sir Keith Joseph, had been advised to discount their claims. With a sinking heart she read on. Their research was described as 'amateurish' and there was pressure to withdraw financial support for any further analysis: 'money should go to bodies untainted by political bias'.[3]

'We were absolutely astounded,' recalls Caroline. There had been no indication anything was amiss. Not a single reporter had approached either her or John for a comment or to get their side of the story.

It turned out a critique had been leaked to the press from the Department of Education and Science (DES). It discredited their report for failing to use a representative sample. Caroline was furious. *Standards in English Schools*[4] was based on the examination results of 2,000 schools with more than 350,000 pupils, spanning urban and rural communities in the north, south, east and west. The aim was to make it as representative as possible. What more could they want?

They tried in vain to get hold of the critique. Then, in desperation on Sunday evening, Caroline rang the Education Secretary, Sir Keith Joseph. All they wanted was the means to defend themselves against unfair criticism. Exasperatingly, Sir Keith refused. Standing on propriety, he insisted the paper was private and confidential to the Department. Caroline argued that as it was all over the Sunday papers, the contents were already in the public domain. But Sir Keith clung to his point of principle and left them to do battle alone.

Worse was to come as more of the press picked up on the story. On a single day, the report was damned in seven different papers. *The Guardian* reported the DES was 'highly critical' of their work, and said their 'credibility... was in question'. 'Fundamentally flawed', was how *The Teacher* described their 'crude, amateurish so-called research,' while the *The Times* described their study as 'discredited'. The National Union of Teachers (NUT) condemned the sample for containing too many selective schools, and the research for making a 'crude and inadequate' allowance for the social background of pupils. It was a public trouncing. 'They were trying to consign us to the dustbin of history,' believes John Marks. 'They hoped that if a sufficient broadside was brought against us, we would go down.'

Mud sticks

Eventually, a journalist took pity on them and handed over a copy of the leaked critique so they could have a chance to reply. It echoed the NUT, claiming the survey was unrepresentative and had failed to make adequate allowance for social class.

Caroline and John reacted to the official document with a mixture of infuriation and relief. Quickly, they realized they could provide a spirited defence against all charges. They drew up an immediate rebuttal. But a denial never has the impact of a juicy allegation. The mud stuck and, despite their best efforts, the damage could not be undone, in the public eye at least. They would have to take the fight through official channels.

On 21 October there was another blow, when Sir Keith refused to consider funding their research. Caroline and John found out about it by reading his letter in the press. It was leaked and published before they could receive it.

Eventually, Sir Keith called a meeting in the House of Commons. John and Caroline were to face it out with the statisticians who had produced the critique. 'It was an extraordinary confrontation,' Caroline recalls. Among the spectators in the oak-panelled room were two ministers and senior officials in the Department of Education, 'all sat around like at a bull-fight'. As Caroline went in she told John: 'We must state our case and demolish the opposition in five minutes.' And in five minutes they had.

The statisticians meekly backed down. It turned out it was the DES whose methods were flawed. The reason their results failed to tally with those of Cox and Marks was because they were based on statistics drawn from different years. The DES had mistakenly taken data from 1981, rather than 1976, which dramatically skewed their version of the results.

The head of the statistics branch admitted the error and distanced himself from the official criticism. Their report had been distorted, he explained, as it was passed from level to level up the Department. Criticisms had been simplified and amplified and caveats had been removed. What was finally presented to the Minister had little bearing on the original. It had become a broad, unrefined, trashing of the research.

Hearing all this, Sir Keith Joseph turned to the officials and demanded, 'Do you mean to say that you have allowed a whole edifice of vilification to be falsely built to damn this report?'

'Yesterday,' reported *The Daily Telegraph*, 'Sir Keith announced that the research was not 'seriously flawed'... indeed, his statisticians now accept that it was they who made a mistake in assuming the sample to be unrepresentative.'[5]

Sir Keith prepared a statement for Parliament which was put in the library of the House, vindicating the Cox and Marks findings and back-tracking on the criticism. But it was too late to change the public perception. Published material acquires an air of authority and is neatly filed in the cuttings library, to be quoted *ad infinitum*.

Many papers continued to give full credence to the now withdrawn critique, and the teachers' union continued to criticize their research.[6] But *The Times* rallied to their defence. It described the whole episode as 'proof that a campaign of leaks and smears can be more effective than honest, open, debate, and that anonymous bureaucrats who resort to such means can effectively silence those who challenge them.'

'Drinking pink champagne'

Caroline and John had slaughtered the sacred cow of comprehensive education. 'It went right against the prevailing orthodoxy – an overriding commitment to comprehensive education in all schools.' Another spur to the smear campaign was given by government reluctance to rock the cosy consensus with the powerful NUT.

In any event, the episode fuelled a further book, *The Insolence of Office*.[7] In it, Cox and Marks attacked the press for double-standards and disregard for the truth. But their most scathing criticism was reserved for Whitehall. They wrote: 'The insolence of office must not be allowed to destroy the accountability which is the safeguard and hallmark of a free society.'

A welcome note of humour was injected by *The Sunday Times*, which lampooned the whole affair with a sketch by Anthony Jay and Jonathan Lynn, authors of the TV comedy series, *Yes Minister*. In it, Whitehall mandarin Sir Humphrey Appleby patiently explains to his fresh-faced junior, Bernard, that the report has to be fixed with a poison label in advance to avoid an unseemly confrontation between the government and the NUT.

Sir Humphrey: 'Bernard, sometimes I despair of you. Those people have compiled a mass of statistics showing that comprehensive schools get unsatisfactory results. If they [Cox and Marks] are not discredited, the Minister may give them public funding. Then they will publish fuller and more damaging reports in future years. So either we show their report is seriously flawed, or we are seriously floored. All right? Next stage: discredit the writers of the report.'

Bernard: 'But they're reputable scholars.'

Sir Humphrey: 'Really? I thought one of them was a baroness.'

Bernard: 'Only since last year. And baronesses can still be – '

Sir Humphrey (interrupting): 'Bernard, we all know about baronesses. They swan around in chauffeur-driven Rolls-Royces drinking pink champagne.'

Bernard: 'It says here she's a director of a research unit at London University, with three children who went to a comprehensive.'

Sir Humphrey: 'Bernard, if she's a baroness, then for the purposes of educational journalists she's an out-of-touch aristocrat, and her children are at Eton. Oh, and by the way, I believe she knows the Secretary of State personally, so if she telephones...'

Bernard: '"The Secretary of State is awfully busy at the moment," Sir Humphrey...'

Sir Humphrey: 'Well done, Bernard. You'll make a true member of the DES yet.'[8]

To circumvent the Sir Humphreys of this world, John Marks and Caroline decided to double-check their research in a further study the following year, which drew on an even bigger sample of 380,000. It came up with a resounding confirmation. 'The findings were startling,' says Caroline. 'The agreement between the two studies exceeded anything we expected.'

Their research also took on the critics who had accused them of failing to consider adequately the social class differences between pupils. The new study found pupils within the same social class were achieving twice as many O levels as others from similar backgrounds in different local education authorities (LEAs). The startling conclusion was that it was the education authority that made the difference. Yet this report failed to make a substantial impact, because of the rubbishing of their previous research.

Radical manifesto

Undaunted by the onslaught over comprehensives, in 1986 Caroline, Roger Scruton, John Marks and others published a 'radical manifesto' to address 'the state of crisis' in Britain's education system. According to Roger Scruton, they had been quietly encouraged by an advisor at Downing Street to create a pressure group which would toughen up party policy. The result was the Hillgate Group and *Whose Schools? A Radical Manifesto*. '[We were told] it would be much easier for the government to have a strong education policy if there was some outside pressure for it,' says Roger Scruton.

Caroline and her co-authors demanded open debate on new types of educational institutions, and made the case for parents to be able to choose their children's schools and move them on to others, as they wished. They argued that 'relevance' and 'child-centred learning' had 'replaced the old educational values, with no discernible benefit to the child', and said schools should be based on 'discipline and order, not free expression and idle play'.

They attacked the newly introduced GCSE examination, where pupils are increasingly assessed by their own teachers, as a 'dangerous and unjustified' departure from good practice.[9]

Significantly, *Whose Schools?* raised a standard for a national curriculum, of which Caroline was a reluctant advocate. 'It was the lesser of two evils,' she explains. 'The only reason I supported it was because we were really falling behind. It's a powerful tool in the wrong hands.'

The wrong hands in question, she believed, belonged to certain LEAs. The Hillgate Group was concerned about the increased politicization of the curriculum and the pushing out of traditional areas of study by trendy new subjects like 'social awareness', which suited the agenda of the left. The example was given of a handbook of lesbian rights by the women's committee of the Greater London Council, which called for 'videos for use in lessons which would... present lesbians in a positive light'.[10]

The Hillgate Group demanded that schools be released from LEA control, claiming: 'The politicized LEAs will be deprived of their major source of power, and of their standing ability to corrupt the minds and souls of the young.'[11]

Unsurprisingly, their radical manifesto was slammed by LEAs, Tory and Labour alike, who feared an attempt to clip their wings after the next election. *Whose Schools?* was damned as 'astounding and offensive' by Bill McNeill, leader of Kent Education Committee, the largest Tory-controlled authority in England and Wales. It was 'grossly insulting' to LEAs, according to David Muffett, of Hereford and Worcester; and 'totally impractical' argued David Hart of the National Association of Head Teachers, who added that it was peppered with exaggerations and inaccuracies.[12]

Even Richard Wilkins, of the Association of Christian Teachers, a natural ally, was ruffled. 'Our impression of Baroness Cox led us to say, "She's all right, it's the people around her who really worry us." They were in a "let's bash the LEAs mode."' But Caroline still maintains the intention was not so much to hit out at the left as to champion the rights of children to a balanced and effective education.

Much of what they proposed subsequently became Tory policy and was later adopted by the incoming Labour government.

'Our success was down to team work,' says Roger Scruton. 'Caroline was a powerful figure in the House of Lords, able to make her mark on Parliamentary debate.'

APPENDIX: ON THE HOME FRONT

NOTES

1. Susan Crosland, *Tony Crosland*, Jonathan Cape, 1982, p. 149. Crosland's circular 10/65 requested all local education authorities to go comprehensive. The Tories threw it out in 1970 and it bounced back in 1974 with the incoming Labour government.

2. 1 July 1983.

3. Peter Wilby (Education Correspondent), 9 October 1983.

4. J. Marks, C. Cox and M. Pomian-Srzednicki, *Standards in English Schools – An Analysis of Examination Results of Secondary Schools in England for 1981*, National Council for Educational Standards, 1983.

5. 'Error in analysis of exam research, but doubts remain', 29 November 1983.

6. The NUT said the researchers did not name individual local authorities in their survey, making it impossible to check the data: *The Daily Telegraph*, 29 November 1983. But Cox and Marks had to promise confidentiality to local authorities and schools before they would give them the data.

7. C. Cox and J. Marks, The Claridge Press, 1988.

8. *The Sunday Times*, 11 December 1983.

9. In 1984, the education study group of the Centre for Policy Studies, chaired by Caroline Cox, warned against plans to scrap O levels and the CSE in favour of a single examination. It described it as an 'ill-conceived attempt… to emasculate the O level… spearheaded by the largest and most socialist of the teachers' trade unions, to gain control for teachers over the examinations and hence the curriculum, in order to subvert quality in the interests of an egalitarian philosophy': 'Think-tank opposes single 16-plus exam', *The Daily Telegraph*, 27 February 1984.

10. Later, during a debate in the House of Lords, she produced a book called *The Milkman's On His Way*, which had been obtained by a schoolgirl from the children's section of Haringey library. The book, recommended by the Inner London Education Authority, gave graphic details of a sexual encounter between a 17-year-old boy and his male adult lover. Caroline said it was so explicit, it should be considered pornographic: *The Times*, 5 February 1987.

11. *The Times*, 5 February 1987, p. 18.

12. 'State schools manifesto derided', *The Times*, 30 December 1986.

THREE

'A Training Ground for Urban Guerrillas'

If Russia could place KGB agents in Central Park, as Caroline had discovered, then Soviet influence, she believed, could extend to British education. She had witnessed the hard left at work at the Polytechnic of North London and the effect they were having on the curriculum, but nowhere could their influence be seen more clearly, in her view, than in the teaching of Peace Studies, a subject memorably described by Lord Beloff as a training ground for urban guerrillas.

Caroline's co-author was once again Roger Scruton. Together they produced an analysis of teaching materials used in Peace Studies drawn from a wide range of publications by local authorities and others.

The attack was hardly a bolt from the blue. In 1985 Caroline had complained in the *Reader's Digest* that in an exercise by Exeter Teachers for Peace, children were asked: 'Which do you prefer: swords or ploughshares, destruction or development, atom bombs or charity?' One Bristol boy came home from school to ask his father: 'Why does President Reagan want to kill us all?' Peace Studies, she argued, was often an exercise in political brainwashing, systematically putting over a one-sided view of defence and deterrence. It was unbalanced and anti-NATO.[1]

'Running through it all was an attack on Western society and its values,' she says. 'You were left with the feeling there was nothing worth defending and nothing that needed to be deterred. What made us challenge it was its intellectual dishonesty. All along it was half-truth.' With Roger Scruton, she called for a balanced curriculum which would look at the realities of Soviet Communism and provide a genuine analysis of Warsaw Pact forces.

As with so many of Caroline's passions, the argument spilled over into the House of Lords, and, as ever, it polarized opinion. Among her allies was the independent peer and former Labour minister, Lord Chalfont, who declared: 'A whole generation of schoolchildren is now beginning to be systematically indoctrinated and brainwashed in a flood of disinformation.'

Its Machiavellian purpose, he continued, was to instil the belief that the word 'peace' was synonymous with unilateral nuclear disarmament, massive reductions in defence spending and withdrawal from all military alliances.

The tune could hardly be expected to play well with Labour's Baroness David, fresh from fund-raising for the leading postgraduate school of Peace Studies in Bradford. Support from Caroline's own benches was also sparse. Government spokesman Baroness Hooper stood shoulder to shoulder with the opposition, pointing out that Peace Studies students included police officers seconded from their forces.[2]

The row set sister publication against sister. *The Times Higher Education Supplement* scolded Cox and Scruton for being 'misleading', while *The Times* denounced the very title 'Peace Studies' as 'an example of the propagandist's art.'[3]

Once again Foundation Endowment took up the theme. Another US lecture tour was arranged, taking in Lake Forest College in Chicago. Caroline was invited by an ally among the governors who was keen to oppose what he saw as the drift to the left.

Lake College boasted two professors of Peace Studies. 'They sat down for my presentation like a couple of dogs about to enjoy a juicy dinner,' recalls Caroline. But she had fought her corner and honed her arguments in the UK and her presentation was meticulous. She prefaced her lecture, as always, by saying, 'I'm in favour of peace and I'm in favour of study, so I'm not against Peace Studies.'

As she warmed to her theme, she noted a drop in the demeanour of the two professors. Then the students demanded to know why they had not heard any of this before. 'One professor looked pretty sheepish,' says Caroline, 'and then replied, "That's why we invited Lady Cox to come and give this presentation."'

She wasn't having that: 'Excuse me,' she retorted, 'I don't think you invited me at all. And, anyway, that doesn't explain why this particular perspective has never featured on the agenda.'

The students, she recalls, were furious with their professors. 'They realized they had been taught an extremely partial, limited and indoctrinatory view of this complex issue.'

Caroline found students on both sides of the Atlantic open-minded and keen to hear her perspectives, which were absent from their curriculum. Her yardstick was as clear as it was simple: 'Students must be given the freedom to explore all facets of a complex question, and the freedom, without pressure, to come to their own conclusions.'

Political correctness

After Peace Studies came World Studies and anti-racism: significant bastions of political correctness. With their claim to the moral high ground, the demonization of anyone with the temerity to oppose them was almost guaranteed. 'If you attack Peace Studies you look like a warmonger. If you attack anti-racism, you immediately look a racist. I abhor racism, but so many of them had moved, in my definition, away from education to indoctrination. One just couldn't let them go unchallenged.'

It was a school book which finally goaded Caroline into action. *How Racism Came to Britain* was written for 11- to 12-year-olds. On the contents page were two black hands holding a banner with the words 'Here to Stay. Here to Fight'. Cartoons mocked colonialism and depicted policemen as racist, prejudiced and brutal. The tone was polemical. 'It was anti-law and order; emotive; totally unbalanced, and I think pernicious.' Curiously, *How Racism Came to Britain* contained a section attacking slavery, a crusade which, ten years later, Caroline was to make her own, exposing and opposing the slave trade on the plains of Southern Sudan.[4]

She denies a sense of humour failure. 'I laugh at the outrageous, and enjoy quick verbal repartee, but I don't like humour which is hurtful of people or which destroys what is precious in our cultural and spiritual heritage.' For Caroline, the book was another example of the 'drip effect': the gradual undermining of British society by the hard-left. Their target – schoolchildren.

Her anxiety was heightened by reports of the elections to the Inner London Teacher's Association, the largest branch of the biggest teaching union, the NUT. The magazine *Education* wrote: 'For the first time in the turbulent history of the union in London, a member of the Trotskyist Socialist Workers' Party is unopposed as treasurer and the choice for the other offices lies between two groups... whose members are composed of either Trotskyists, Maoists, ultra left, hard left or near anarchist... No candidate of more moderate complexion... is standing.'

Capping that came this report in *The Times Educational Supplement*:

Heads agree that there are up to a dozen schools in the city which are virtually in the hands of extremists... there is an atmosphere of daily intimidation, verbal abuse and professional harassment for anyone who does not fall in with the prevailing political line... a staffroom notice was pinned up after strike action saying, 'We feel a great sense of power and excitement at being able to disrupt the school.'[5]

Caroline called for balance in political education. It became an extension of her battle against the hard-left and against prevailing wisdom. It was fought out once again via articles and contributions to books and in the chamber of the House of Lords, where she stood in contention with both government and opposition benches.

On 5 February 1986 she called a debate to de-politicize education. She demanded guaranteed freedom of speech in universities, schools and colleges and an end to the airing of politically controversial issues in primary schools. And where it was necessary to raise controversy in secondary schools, it should be in a balanced way so pupils could make up their minds freely and without pressure.

It was always going to be an uphill struggle. The opposition would attempt to undermine her and the government showed no sign of supporting her. A vote for Caroline was a vote against the NUT at a time when the government was already facing strikes from the teacher's union.

Caroline embarked on a programme of extensive behind-the-scenes lobbying, garnering support from a broad cross-bench coalition. The only remaining obstacle was the little matter of the united front put forward by the government, the opposition and the union.

The smoke of battle

The chamber was well attended and the atmosphere highly charged for what was set to be a battle of ideologies. Caroline rose to her feet in the Tory benches. She positioned herself three rows back and to the right of the leather and gold despatch box, immediately beneath a microphone. Fighting to control her customary nerves – imperceptible to all bar herself – she opened the debate with a warning: 'Those who wish to bring about radical or revolutionary change will try to use education for their ends... I refer to deliberate attempts to undermine and destroy our cultural heritage, our traditional beliefs and our democratic freedoms.'

A number of government ministers had been forcibly prevented from speaking at universities. With these in mind, she cautioned: 'If our academies condone censorship, we are on a road that once led to Nazi Germany and now leads to totalitarianism such as that found behind the Iron Curtain.'

Every word was scripted, in the knowledge that the spoken word would go down as the written word in *Hansard*, and the script was carefully and repeatedly rehearsed, out loud, as are all her speeches to the House.

She rallied to the defence of Ray Honeyford, a former headmaster from

Bradford. He had been hounded out of his post for having the temerity to admit it was difficult to teach when a high proportion of the children at his school could not speak English.

'He was a much-respected head,' continued Caroline, 'held in great affection by pupils and staff. He was subjected to a campaign of hatred and ferocious abuse... to serious death threats and, with his young pupils, to having to run a gauntlet of shouting and jeering crowds on his way to school each day. It is a disturbing portent, when an experienced teacher cannot voice legitimate concerns without being dubbed a racist and is driven from his job.'[6]

Following his suspension after two years of bitter dispute, Mr Honeyford had been invited to 10 Downing Street, along with Caroline and John Marks, for talks on the future of schools and colleges. It had caused a furore. *The Morning Star* described them as arch right-wingers and said: 'The teaching profession will give a horse laugh at the experts she [Mrs Thatcher] has chosen.' The general secretary of the NUT, Fred Jarvis, dismissed them as 'the moaning minnies of the right-wing education lobby.'[7]

Caroline had been undeterred by opposition then, and was expecting worse today.[8] She concluded with a call for a ministerial inquiry: 'Education in a free society should enshrine the principles of freedom of speech, freedom to pursue the truth and freedom to develop views and interests not predetermined by the political commitments of local authorities or of teachers. To deny them this is a betrayal of our birthright... My Lords, I beg to move for papers.'

Caroline took her seat to cries of 'Hear, hear'. It was a long speech, and one that had been listened to, in the main, respectfully. The House of Lords is altogether more respectful than the Other Place – more of a tea garden than a bear garden. But what the noble Lords lack in vehemence they make up for in cunning, and Caroline's opponents were old hands, and would bide their time.

Her ally, Lord Renton, praised her and called for an amendment to the Education Act, 'to ensure that the teaching in schools shall not be used for ramming party political views down children's throats, especially those of young children.'

Support was forthcoming from SDP spokesman Lord Harris of Greenwich. He said the House owed a debt of gratitude to Baroness Cox and warned of 'a determined militant minority in the education profession who are prepared to treat children as political playthings'.

The big gun on parade was former prime minister, Lord Home, who called for an inquiry to be set up, 'soon and with urgency'. 'She could scarcely have selected a topic of more importance to the future of Britain,' he told the House. 'Indoctrination is developing to a point of danger to the nation.'

But even before the smoke had cleared, her opponents began their counterattack. Taking the charge was Labour front-bench spokesman, Lord McIntosh of Haringey. The experience of being ousted from the Greater London Council by a left-wing coup had failed to tarnish his loyalties. He described Caroline as out of step and 'out on a limb'.

Machiavellian motives

Machiavellian motives were attributed to the rebellious Tory backbencher by Labour's Lord Stewart of Fulham. He accused her of trying to divert attention away from the government's 'inept' handling of the teachers' strike, fulminating that her debate had been timed to sabotage the forthcoming elections at the Inner London Education Authority (ILEA).

Joining the frontal attack, Labour's education spokesman quoted correspondence in *The Listener* from William Stubbs, ILEA's chief officer: 'I cannot recall having received one complaint from a parent expressing concern about political education in the curriculum of their child's school. This is an authority which has a school population of over 300,000.'

Next, Her Majesty's Inspectors (HMIs) were invoked to convince the House that Caroline was fighting alone, cut off from the mainstream. For more than 30 years, the HMIs had been calling for greater weight to be given to political literacy in the curriculum.

Battle was rejoined by Lord McIntosh of Haringey, who moved on to another time-honoured debating tactic: muddying the waters. Sliding imperceptibly from the central issue of political indoctrination (bad thing) onto political education (good, necessary and responsible thing), he accused Caroline of not being able to tell one from the other. At worst it would make her appear naïve; at best it would throw the debate sideways. It did both. It gave the impression that she wanted to bar controversy from the classroom in any shape and form.

Caroline's defences were reeling. The might of the NUT was brought into play by Lord Graham of Edmonton, who read out a missive from the union: 'We believe that... teachers are professionals and well able to distinguish fact from opinion, as are their pupils. The so-called evidence suggesting bias in teaching is anecdotal and has not been substantiated.'

The standards of the NUT and the government were mingled in battle, along with those of the ILEA and the HMIs. The crash of precedents could be heard resounding across the chamber, getting ever closer. Baroness Davies (Labour) administered the intended *coup de grâce*, a swift and decisive thrust. The campaign to expose left-wing indoctrination was, she said, orchestrated by a 'handful of the far-right': privateers, isolated within their own party, unwilling to stand beneath the banner of the Education Minister, Sir Keith Joseph. Sir Keith had maintained that controversial issues could be discussed, but pupils and students should be free to come to their own conclusions. It was commendable, responsible, mainstream and, above all, moderate.

The attack from the opposition benches subsided. Now it was the turn of government education spokesman, the Earl of Swinton, to deploy his own, significant forces against those of the turbulent back-bencher. He appeared conciliatory. 'The government stand firmly against any attempt to distort or subvert for partisan political purposes the education of our children,' he said. Politically controversial material should be taught in a fair and balanced way. It should be education and never indoctrination.

Then, unfurling his true colours, he declared his opposition to the motion. Defining bias and indoctrination would be problematic, he said, and enforcement would be difficult: 'These are matters for the professional responsibility of teachers, rather than legislation.' The government was opposing the motion, not on grounds of high principle, but on basic pragmatism.

Government spokesman, Baroness Hooper, moved in for the kill. She acknowledged government concern of 'a creeping politicization... an attempt to influence the minds of students and pupils by biased teaching and distortion of the facts... However... the number of teachers who approach their work in this way is small.'

Then she invited all and sundry to submit any examples of indoctrination to the secretary of state for full and careful investigation. When the smoke had cleared it was hard to tell which side was winning.

The forces regrouped for a second round of battle on 20 May – the Education Bill. A Gallup poll suggested most of the public were broadly behind Caroline and her amendment, which was calling for balance.[9] Once again, *The Times* came out in her favour, on this 'major point of principle', declaring: 'Indoctrination is the opposite of education... a danger to guard against.'[10]

With opposition backing, the government produced their own anodyne and watered-down amendment, designed to strangle the issue at birth. Where 'reasonably practical', it ran, steps should be taken to ensure the teaching of political topics should be 'responsible'. *The Times* described it as simply a devious way of resisting Caroline's arguments.

It failed. Caroline's call to prohibit political indoctrination in primary and secondary schools was carried by a hefty majority of 117 to 87, thanks to her persuasive lobbying. Becoming the ringleader of a substantial back-bench rebellion in the Lords endeared her to neither the whips nor her own front-benches. She shrugs it off: 'It was very sad they had to vote against a Conservative government to get it through, but it was a matter of national concern.'

Freedom of speech

Caroline later initiated amendments to protect freedom of speech on campus. They were sparked off by her experiences at the polytechnic.

In April 1974, the National Union of Students' conference had given its members *carte blanche* to 'take whatever measures are necessary, including disruption of meetings, in order to prevent any members of racialist or fascist organizations from speaking in colleges'. Its broad interpretation was extended to Tory ministers and MPs who were booted off campus, sometimes literally.

And it wasn't just invited speakers who faced a barracking. Earlier, at her old stamping ground, the PNL, a blockade of left-wing students had tried to prevent a member of the National Front from attending philosophy classes. Patrick Harrington had to be given a police escort into the building. Caroline supported his right to education in *The Daily Mail*, while making it clear she deplored the National Front and everything it stood for.[11]

Her call for legislation to protect freedom of speech drew fire from the university vice chancellors. It was declared a gross interference in their autonomy. Parliamentary time ran out before the amendment could be put to the vote, but a head of steam was building and ministers were taking note. The new, reforming, education secretary, Kenneth Baker, introduced his own amendment to ensure invited speakers were given a fair hearing. It later became law.

Roger Scruton is in no doubt about the significance of Caroline's contribution to the debate: 'It was important to put down a marker and say certain things were simply masks for the politicization of the universities and schools. She took a valuable stance at a time when it was necessary for there to be somebody robust and unpopular speaking from a position of influence. I only wish the Tory Party had given more credence to her and put more people like her in a position where they could do that. The Party is notoriously timid in its selection of people to whom to give peerages. But it benefited enormously from having someone who was saying something stronger than it. It was a very significant factor in securing the necessary shift in the climate of opinion.'

NOTES

1. 'Peace study guidelines called for in schools', *The Times*, 25 February 1985.
2. She maintained: 'Allegations that staff are ideologically committed in a way that may be incompatible with academic detachment and impartial teaching have not been substantiated': House of Lords debate concerning educational indoctrination, 5 February 1986.
3. 20 May 1996.
4. She went on to accuse the ILEA of producing literature which incited young black people to violence and a hostile view of the police. It was shortly after the Tottenham riots. The Greater London Council had produced a video called 'Policing London'. Along with it was a wallchart which declared: 'Many police drink heavily. They treat prostitutes as second-class citizens. They treat homosexuals as criminals. They have a cult of masculinity. Racial prejudice is pervasive and fashionable. They over-react routinely': 'ILEA publications inciting young blacks', *The Daily Telegraph*, 9 October 1985. The previous year Caroline, John Marks and Professor Anthony Flew co-authored *Education, Race and Revolution* through the Centre for Policy Studies.
5. Hilary Wilce, 'Ultra left tightens grip on ILEA schools', 10 January 1986.
6. Caroline and John felt strongly enough about Mr Honeyford's plight to resign from the Centre for Policy Studies the previous year when it published a paper criticizing the headmaster for what he had said: 'New Honeyford Row', *The Sunday Telegraph*, 1 December 1985.
7. 'PM invites race-row head to No. 10', 30 September 1985.
8. Earlier, writing in *The Daily Mail*, she had complained about 'politically unacceptable' books being removed from libraries and an English class that had 'recently been encouraged to think about Death to Mrs Thatcher': 'Militants who are getting at your children', 22 April 1985.
9. Legislation was favoured by 77 per cent of Conservative, 81 per cent of Labour and 71 per cent of Liberal voters. Two thirds of men and half of women also backed a change in the law to prevent political indoctrination in schools: *The Daily Mail*, 19 May 1986.
10. 20 May 1986.
11. She claimed the Polytechnic director, Dr David McDowell, had taken early retirement after coming under pressure from ILEA to expel Patrick Harrington from the college. The leader of ILEA, Frances Morrell, denied asking the director to 'behave with any kind of impropriety': 'Graduates in the art of anarchy', 13 December 1984; 'Renewed demands to close Polytechnic', *The Times*, 11 December 1984.

FOUR

An Unholy Row

Another element of education which Caroline believed was sorely in need of reform was teaching on religion. Her controversial campaign for change was to run her headlong into the party whips and stir up an unholy row.

Religious Education (RE) had become part of the compulsory curriculum in 1944, with a freedom of conscience get-out clause. But Caroline believed that, with some honourable exceptions, much of RE was a badly taught mish-mash of various faiths, generating disinterest and confusion in place of enlightenment. 'A lot of young people were leaving school ignorant of the basic tenets of the Christian religion,' she asserts. 'They couldn't even name the four gospels; they didn't know what Good Friday was. One was asked, "Who's Pontius Pilate?" and replied, "Don't know, wouldn't even know how to spell it."'[1]

Britain owed its national identity, culture and heritage to Christianity, whose ethics and principles provided the moral underpinnings of the nation. It was being tossed away and into the vacuum were rushing two elements, both anathema to Caroline. The first, her old *bête noire*, the highly politicized curriculum, with topics like Peace Studies appearing in the guise of RE. The second, the simplistic thematic multi-faith approach, which took out of context and conflated themes like Festivals of Light or Spring Festivals.

Again, the problem was exemplified in the current crop of books for schoolchildren. One, aimed at primary schools, relegated Easter to the last few pages with cosy illustrations of eggs and bunnies. 'There was no way you could understand the significance of Gethsemane, Calvary and Easter in this sort of hotchpotch,' she says.

More worrying was another title, *Beginning Religion*, published by Edward Arnold. 'It was very macabre and heavy,' says Caroline. 'The earlier edition suggested children could go to a seance as part of their homework. There were ouija boards. There was a picture of a human sacrifice, all rather cartoon-like. They dealt with the Lord's Prayer on the same page as shamanism.' The book was widely used in the teaching of RE.

Growing concern was filtering her way about the teaching of the occult in schools. 'We had representations from York that a school had spent the whole summer teaching witchcraft and had visited witches' covens,' she says. A letter was sent round by senior ILEA RE inspectors to all heads, pointing out that parents had complained of children becoming psychologically disturbed by the teaching on the occult.

But her biggest worry was the syncretistic muddle that was passing for multi-faith teaching: the confusion of bits and pieces of different religions under a spurious common theme. Caroline was convinced the approach undermined the integrity of those faiths and, because of its shallowness, did little to enhance any mutual understanding. To cap it all, a lot of schools had simply abandoned RE.

When the 1944 Education Act came up for amendment in 1987 there was much ado about a national curriculum, but scarcely a mention of RE. Throughout that autumn the Religious Education Council campaigned vigorously for more prominence for RE. 'The Department for Education was shy of RE and we could see it fizzling out,' says its then Secretary, Richard Wilkins. But all that was to change when Caroline staged what became known as her midnight ambush in the House of Lords.

When the Education Bill came over from the Commons Caroline took the opportunity to put an amendment that would re-affirm the importance of teaching Christianity as the main spiritual tradition of the land and underscore the 1944 Education Act. RE in all maintained schools would become predominantly Christian, although within the modern context of a multi-cultural society. At the same time the right of other communities to have their faiths taught with integrity would be introduced, giving parents of other faiths the same rights to withdraw their children from religious instruction or worship as Christians, and have their own acts of worship or RE instead.

On Palm Sunday Caroline had a head-to-head with the then Bishop of London, whose particular responsibility was education. 'I don't want you to put this amendment,' he told her. Caroline asked why. He replied: 'Because it would divide the College of Bishops.'

Caroline retorted: 'In that case I'm going to put it, because either the bishops have the gospel to proclaim, so let them proclaim it; or if they haven't, let them say they haven't. It's no reason for not trying to get Christianity back into RE.'

Caroline acknowledged the practical problems. There was a shortage of RE teachers and a hyper-sensitivity to other faith communities. But her amendment would actually give the opportunity for the teaching of their faiths.

Her most vociferous opponents were from the multi-faith lobby, who feared playing up Christianity would marginalize minorities of other faiths and come closer in aim to evangelism than education. Yet the protests of professional academics contrasted strongly with the support she received from leading representatives of different faiths.

During the debate in the Lords, one champion from an unusual quarter was the Chief Rabbi, Lord Jacobovits, who derided the syncretistic approach for creating a cocktail of world faiths. Support was also forthcoming from the Muslim community.

Shortly before the amendment was due to be discussed, Nazar Mustafa, of the Muslim Education Co-ordinating Council, phoned Caroline with some encouraging news. 'He said the Imam in one of London's leading mosques had led between two and three thousand Muslims in prayer that the name of Christ would once again be revered in Britain's schools.' She quoted this in the debate then pointedly looked at the Bishops' bench, and said: 'Would that our bishops could be heard praying the same prayer.'

The whisper of the whips

Behind the scenes, the government seemed to be sitting every bit as uneasily as the Bishops and the religious educators. The whisper came to Caroline that the Chief Whip had been overheard plotting against Lady Cox. He planned to make sure her RE amendments always came on late at night so voting would be out of the question. Tradition in the House has it that voting does not take place when most of the noble Lords ought to be tucked up beneath their duvets.

Sure enough, on 26 February 1988, the debate took place at the midnight hour. A clear consensus was quickly established among those present. It looked set to be a satisfying, if somewhat insignificant, conclusion to an evening's discussion, when the unthinkable happened. Lord Thorneycroft, a senior Tory peer known for his robustness, called out: 'Put the vote. Put it to the vote.'

A frisson went around the House, but at twenty to one in the morning the division was called. 'It caused complete consternation,' recalls Caroline. 'People were caught unawares. Nobody was expecting a vote at that time in the morning. Many didn't know which way to vote, so a lot of people abstained.' Without a full vote, the House was inquorate and immediately had to call a halt to proceedings.

What all this meant was that business would have to be held over to

Monday afternoon: prime-time in the House of Lords. A marginalized debate, consigned to the small hours, had been propelled to centre stage.

That Monday, Caroline arrived to face a blizzard of messages from the Chief Whip. 'I was completely in the dog house. The moment I turned up at the House of Lords, every doorkeeper, every policeman I saw, every yard I walked somebody said, "The Chief Whip wants to see you the moment you arrive."'

Within thirty seconds she was inside the office of the Chief Whip, Lord Denham, who was steaming. He said, 'You do not call divisions at twenty past one in the morning!' Caroline apologized, explaining that a senior member of the party had urged her to put it to the vote and, well, it had seemed the right thing to do. Bertie Denham looked set to explode. He said, 'Do you realize you've upset the parliamentary timetable for the whole of the parliamentary year?' Caroline broke into a grin and replied, 'Rubbish, Bertie.'

The renegade debate went ahead. 'As a nation,' warned Caroline, 'we are in danger of selling our spiritual birthright for a mess of secular pottage.' Her ally, former prime minister Lord Home, described as facile claims by some MPs and churchmen that Britain was no longer a Christian nation. Britain had an established church and Parliamentary proceedings began each day with prayer. 'All that is not a sham,' he concluded. 'It is real, and our young people ought to know the story of Christianity and the commitment of their predecessors to its values. Far too many of them do not know about that today.'

There was further support from representatives of Britain's Muslim and Jewish communities. Viscount Buckmaster, claiming to speak for the nation's Muslims, said they felt strongly that 'Christian education in our schools should be given a more positive image.' Lord Jacobovits, the chief rabbi, added: 'If we consider religious faith and precept as the spiritual lifeblood of the nation... indiscriminate mixing of blood can prove dangerous... If Christianity suffers, so in a curious way, does every other faith.'

Picking up from the chief rabbi, Lord Thorneycroft asked: 'With the West Indians clamouring for it, with the Muslims praying for it, and with the Jews urging it in this House, what case is there for not having Christian education in the schools?'

The Bishop of London finally agreed before the whole House that he would take the issue forward. He would consult all the interested parties and move the amendments. That he duly did, and the 1988 Education Reform Act required teaching in schools to 'reflect the fact that the religious traditions of Great Britain are in the main Christian, while taking account of the teachings of the other principal religions represented in Britain.'

'She could not be ignored'

Hindsight brings forth a mixed response to what Caroline has achieved. She was actively supported in her campaign by the Irish Labour Peer Lord Longford. 'On the whole, it's bad form in England to come out for Christianity,' he says. 'The English have deep inhibitions about speaking about their deepest feelings in public. But occasionally someone is listened to who has the God-given combination of inspiration and the gift of words. The word Christianity was included in the Education Act as a result of that one woman. To come out for Christianity was her special contribution. She could not be ignored.'

But what about the impact at the chalkface? 'She changed RE and made history,' says Richard Wilkins, the General Secretary of the Association of Christian teachers. 'As a result a colossal amount of the Act was devoted to religious education and collective worship clauses. She was able to show that a determined Christian campaign was still capable of putting shivers through the Department of Education and Science, and that anybody who beats the Christian drum might well have widespread support – support which needs to be taken seriously by politicians. Now because head teachers know the inspectors are coming, they make sure the subject is taught appropriately.'

But just how appropriate is the teaching of RE since Caroline's amendments? A change in the law does not always produce a change in practice, especially where it neither reflects a change in heart nor is underpinned by the will to do things differently. In 1993, five years after Caroline first moved to restore the centrality of Christianity to the curriculum, a survey found that 80 per cent of schools were breaking the law by failing to provide RE for all their pupils.[2]

Two years later, half of all secondary schools were still failing to teach the subject properly, if at all, according to the School Curriculum and Assessment Authority. Its chief executive, Dr Nick Tate, said half of 16- to 24-year-olds could not explain the meaning of Good Friday or of Lent. Many sixth formers thought Catholics, Protestants and Christians were three different religious groups. Most schools, he claimed, dismissed religion as unworthy of serious study. Dr Tate told a conference of RE teachers that Britain was 'far advanced in becoming a religiously illiterate society'.[3]

That same year, 1995, inspectors found that more than 40 per cent of secondary schools were ignoring their statutory duty to hold a daily religious assembly. Peter Downes, the president of the Secondary Heads Association, said the law was an ass and that 90 per cent of teachers were unwilling to conduct a formal act of worship.[4]

'It's impossible to get teachers who are essentially cynical atheists to introduce a religious dimension into the curriculum,' says Roger Scruton with characteristic bluntness, 'and if they do, it's done in such a way as to ridicule what they are putting across. Caroline was supporting a position which is the only right one for a Christian to support in difficult circumstances in a society which is increasingly contemptuous of the Christian position. It was very courageous, but idealistic and one couldn't really hope to win.'

Commentators raised other practical concerns. How, exactly, should Christianity be given pride of place in the RE curriculum? Should it be given more time, or treated as a superior truth? The law was vague about its implementation, open to wide and differing interpretation, and was increasingly unworkable.[5]

'The changes that took place in the 1988 Act led to RE being taken more seriously in the years since then,' maintains John Marks. 'The situation might have been worse but for that Act.' When the extent of the non-compliance became obvious, model syllabuses were drawn up for the teaching of RE, which have since been published.

Nevertheless, Caroline was given a roasting by Angela Phillips in *The Independent*: 'I have been waiting now for five years for a tabloid campaign ridiculing you for your political correctness,' she wrote, 'but it hasn't happened. Your beliefs are to be imposed on every single schoolchild of whatever faith, political persuasion or cultural background, as you, in your narrow-minded desire for a world that more perfectly reflected your own, insisted on adding a clause to the 1988 Education Reform Act, to the effect that every pupil must take part in a daily act of collective worship which is "wholly or mainly of a broadly Christian character". Unsurprisingly, many multi-cultural schools have ignored the law. A fact that your fundamentalist thought-police have been quick to note and report.'[6]

But what Angela Phillips might also have taken into consideration was the right of pupils of other faiths to withdraw and have their own RE and worship – a right which Caroline had guaranteed.

In 1997, a report by the left-wing think-tank Demos found that 68 per cent of Britons still professed themselves to be Christians.[7] The Association of Christian Teachers put the UK's active Christian community at 6 million, with adherents to other world faiths at just 4.6 per cent of the population.[8] 'And why should humanism have so much influence in education when the British Humanist Association has such a small membership?' asks Richard Wilkins.[9]

Lord Tonypandy concurred: 'We treat our Lord with a contempt we wouldn't dare show Mohammed, the prophet, and we need someone like Baroness Cox to speak out. She's not afraid. She's aware that her views are not acceptable to everyone. But I share her belief that the schools must fulfil the will of Parliament and give proper instruction in the Christian faith and what it stands for.'

Hate mail

But Caroline' next initiative was to anger many of her natural supporters. She proposed a Bill to allow private schools run by other faith communities to opt-in to the state system, where they would receive government money.

She had become convinced of the rightness of that during a speech-day visit to the Seventh Day Adventist John Loughborough School in north London. What she saw left a deep impression. 'Here were these largely Afro-Caribbean pupils doing extremely well. They were happy, fulfilled, motivated, and going on to get employment and into further education. Many of them might have been among the truants and drop-outs of the local state schools in the same area.'

As the day was drawing to a close, one of the parent governors came up to her and said, with a wide smile: 'We are so thankful for John Loughborough School, because we no longer have to send our kids thousands of miles back to the West Indies to get a good, old-fashioned, traditional British, Christian education. Now we can keep them at home, because they can get that at John Loughborough.'

Caroline took it as a damning indictment of the state system and quoted those words in the Lords, demanding: 'How have we betrayed that community? How have we betrayed a generation?' Parents had set up their own school at great sacrifice and expense, as much out of desperation than any ideal. It and others like it were deserving of state support. How, then, could that support be denied to schools run by different faiths?

It was an argument that won her enemies in the Christian lobby. She began to receive hate-mail. 'Some of it was highly disturbing – almost Nazi. It was really nasty stuff and touched a very raw nerve.'

The problem, as a number of her detractors saw it, was that taxpayers' money would subsidize the indoctrination of children in the tenets of Islam or Hinduism. As a result they would be led away from the one true path,

Christianity. Caroline, they implied, was opening the way to state-sanctioned, state-funded, idolatry.

'It's an issue of social justice and equality,' she retorts, 'According to the European Convention on Human Rights we have a duty to provide education which is compatible with people's deepest religious and philosophical beliefs. We already have Roman Catholic, Anglican and Jewish state-run schools. So other faith communities should have that same right. I don't think one can deny them the freedom that one gives to other schools.'

To refuse them that right, she argues, would be an act of discrimination which would create division and foster grievance. Better to take them on board, require them to teach the national curriculum and bring them into main-line accountability. Besides, there were precedents. A similar system was in operation in the Netherlands.

A Private Member's Bill was proposed to test the water. Despite cross-party support and the backing of leaders of religious minorities, the water turned out to be decidedly chilly. The Bill had a successful second reading, but, as there was no chance of going through the later stages, Caroline withdrew it. Others later ran with the same baton and what she was proposing became the law of the land.

In 1996, as a result of the right that Caroline had secured for them, a significant number of Muslim parents decided to withdraw their children from RE classes. More than 1,500 children were pulled out by parents who feared they could become 'corrupted' by other religions, especially Christianity. There were calls for separate Islamic classes and pupils were removed from RE in 40 schools in West Yorkshire. There was also talk of a nationwide boycott.

In words that echoed Caroline's own, the General Secretary of the Islamic Party of Great Britain, Sahib Blehr, said: 'Anyone of religious commitment of whatever denomination would rather not have this watered-down mish-mash with children fed a spoonful of each religion.'

On 9 January 1998, under a Labour government, two Muslim primary schools in London and Birmingham became the first in the country to be allowed to opt-in and receive state funding. The credit was given to the campaign led by the former pop singer Cat Stevens, who had become a Muslim, but the way was paved by Caroline Cox.

Ground-breaking

For all the changes in the law, religious education is, according to many, in a mess. *The Guardian* described the state of RE as 'One Great Holy Fudge', a cobbled-together compromise to secure agreement from interest groups in and outside parliament leaving a picture that was 'as clear as mud'.

While some would question Caroline's success in reforming RE, many of the radical ideas put forward by herself and her colleagues have become the new orthodoxy. Much of their criticism of the comprehensive system has been received and provision has been made for greater diversity. Modernists point to City Technology Colleges and other specialist schools. Traditionalists welcome the continuing success of the remaining grammar schools. Schools have been encouraged to opt-out and become grant-maintained. Control has devolved to parent/teacher governors. Parental choice has become the buzzword, and leading politicians of both parties have taken advantage of that freedom.[10] The irony is that many of the policies espoused by Caroline and her colleagues, once derided as right-wing, have now been adopted by the Labour Party.

'What we said has been widely accepted,' agrees Roger Scruton, 'though interestingly, it took a Labour government to say it with any real firmness of purpose. We were disappointed the Conservative government always regarded education as very low on its list of priorities and would never confront the socialist establishment. We were hoping to give them the ammunition with which to do that, but it seems easier for Labour politicians than for Conservatives.'

'Many people on the left of party politics are now coming round to supporting the sorts of things we were saying about education 18 years ago,' says John Marks. 'This massive underachievement in primary and secondary schools is now being taken seriously by nearly everybody, and target-setting is what we were suggesting in our first book. If anything, Labour has taken up some of the issues we were concerned about with even more vigour. I welcome it. I am delighted.'

But Caroline would like to go still further. She is a co-director of the Education Research Trust, a former board member of the Teacher Training Agency and a member of its research committee. She wants to see the entire teaching profession become research-based, to step up the pace of improvement. She has been warned it could lead to unrest in the staffrooms – not that rubbing the NUT up the wrong way has ever troubled her. Nor is she one to let sleeping dogma lie.

'I regret the Tory government promoted grammar schools to the exclusion of others,' she says. 'I want to see much more diversity, much more choice. I would have liked to have seen vouchers. Instead, they came up with a half-baked scheme for nursery education which they didn't follow through. Many of our children continue to get a raw deal from our education system, and much of that is due to the inherent pressure coming from within the Department for Education, which is to the left of centre.'

The American magnet schools have fired her imagination. They encourage specialization, aiming to be centres of excellence for music, art and drama, languages or sport. 'Youngsters with a real aptitude for sport, for example, who are less academically inclined, might actually enjoy going to school instead of playing truant,' she says, 'because they would have the opportunity to develop their abilities and enthusiasms.' Admissions policies and catchment areas are more flexible than in the UK, and indications from the US suggest magnet schools increase pupil motivation and boost potential.

Inspiration might also be drawn from Germany, she believes. Technical education there is held in higher esteem than in the UK. 'Germany outperforms Britain consistently,' she says, 'especially in subjects like maths. If the present system is not currently giving our young people the best possible educational opportunities, then we ought to be asking why, and where do we go from here? We ought to be open to all options.'

Yet for all the upheaval that has taken place, radical or otherwise, in 1996 more than 40 per cent of pupils still failed to make the grade in English, maths and science. National curriculum tests revealed more than a third of children entering secondary schools were two or more years behind in their reading. In inner London schools, even after the abolition of the ILEA, inspectors found that one fifth of seven-year-olds were functionally illiterate, and there were still massive discrepancies between the best and worst schools in any given education authority.[11]

Thirteen years after their ground-breaking report on comprehensives, John Marks, who had been elevated to the School Curriculum and Assessment Authority, and helped carry out the research,[12] said the scale of the underachievement still came as a shock. And Caroline found herself calling on the House once again for priority to be given to ensure all schools achieve the highest possible standards for their pupils.[13]

NOTES

1. 'No child should be left in a state of incomprehension or mindless superstition at a wedding,' observed the Association of Christian Teachers ('The vows you are about to take are made in the name of God, who is judge of all and knows the secrets of our hearts') or at a funeral ('Jesus said "I am the resurrection and the life"'): Richard Wilkins, *Time for Christianity: should Christianity be the largest component in the RE syllabus?*, ACT, 1997, pp. 18, 19.

2. *The Independent*, 26 January 1994.

3. 'Schools "biased against religion"', *The Daily Telegraph*, 30 June 1995.

4. The liberal Archbishop of York, Dr John Habgood, agreed it would be hypocritical for non-believers

to lead others in praise, and called for the government to drop the daily assembly, in favour of less worship, but of a better quality: 'Habgood queries school prayers', *The Daily Telegraph*, 6 January 1995. The Association of Teachers and Lecturers extended the concern to the teaching of RE: 'The biggest problem,' said its general secretary, Peter Smith, 'is that 54 per cent of RE teachers have no formal qualification in the subject': *The Independent*, 26 January 1994.

5. Madeleine Bunting, *The Guardian*, 9 April 1996. In the interests of consensus the School Curriculum and Assessment Authority (SCAA) Model Syllabuses had deliberately left it open as to how much time should be spent in the teaching of Christianity and the priority that should be given to Christianity in terms of content. In 1994, the Church of England proposed to the SCAA that 50 per cent should be the minimum time spent on Christianity, while 66 per cent would be normally appropriate and 75 per cent could, in some schools, be appropriate: Richard Wilkins, *Time for Christianity*, p. 18.

6. 31 January 1994.

7. 'Britain still Christian, report finds', REXS, 19 May 1997. 'Christianity is the largest world faith with 1,800 million adherents world-wide. It is the majority faith of four of the five continents [Asia being the exception]. Christianity is, therefore, the religion least vulnerable to racial stereotyping (the typical Anglican is a black African). It is the most multi-cultural of world faiths': Richard Wilkins, *Time for Christianity*, p. 21.

8. Richard Wilkins, *Time for Christianity*.

9. 'Secularism… is largely unchallenged across the whole curriculum,' he wrote in *Time for Christianity*, calling, perhaps tongue in cheek, for secularism to be added to the RE syllabus.

10. Open enrolment was another piece of legislation influenced by the Hillgate Group. Previously, parents were denied the freedom to choose their children's school, even if the school of their choice had surplus capacity. Schools could enrol only up to a prescribed maximum.

11. 'Secondary school intake "two years slow on reading"', *The Daily Telegraph*, 13 May 1996; 'Half of primary pupils failing in basic tests', *The Daily Telegraph*, 26 August 1996; 'Tests at 11 and 14 show pupils' flaws in basics', *The Daily Telegraph*, 18 November 1996.

12. The research published by the Social Market Foundation was based on the results of tests sat by nearly half a million pupils in more than 13,000 primary schools. Dr Marks called on the education secretary to change teaching practices in primary schools and ban calculators from maths lessons.

13. 'Educational Standards', Ofsted Report, *Hansard*, 6 February 1997; 'Half of primary pupils failing in basic tests', *The Daily Telegraph*, 26 August 1996.

FIVE

Backwoods Rebellion

Leaving aside education and human rights, Caroline has been an active campaigner in other spheres of politics, which has sometimes resulted in clashes with her own party. In 1996, she helped stir up a Lords' backwoods rebellion against the Tory government's plans to sell off armed forces' married quarters. There was a good deal at stake. The government intended to raise £1.6 billion from selling the homes of servicemen to private developers and imposed a three-line-whip to quell its restive peers.

The governments' Whips were out for Caroline. Before the debate, at almost every turn in the Palace of Westminster, someone would pass on the message that the Whips wanted to see her – urgently – until she was finally quarried by one of her pursuers:

'You take care...' came the warning, delivered behind teeth parted in a smile.

'Thanks, I always do,' shot back the reply.

'Don't do anything I don't want you to do.'

'Now, would I ever?'

'Please don't...'

'Yes, but I've got to be honest...'

'Otherwise it will be a resignation.'

'It will be nice to be on new benches.'

'No, no. No nonsense.'

'Well, I shall listen to the arguments. I've got to have an open mind and open ears before I have an open mouth.'

Caroline defied the Whip and denounced the scheme as a betrayal of service families. 'They deserve better treatment than this from a government which purports to place defence and family life among its priorities,' she told the House. The cause was defeated by 256 votes to 176, but only thanks to a massive turnout by hereditary peers. It was the first time a three-line-whip was imposed on Tory peers since the Maastricht Bill proposing closer ties with the European Union.[1]

Who cares?

Caroline set herself against the government again that November over an issue even closer to her heart – Care in the Community, the controversial policy of removing from hospitals many mentally ill and mentally handicapped people to be cared for outside.

Care in the Community was coming increasingly under fire after a series of killings by former patients. One discharged schizophrenic stabbed a stranger to death because he thought he was the gangster Ronnie Kray. Another former patient strangled an elderly couple and killed and dismembered his own father as 'practice' for cutting up and eating a younger victim. Warnings about his homicidal tendencies had been ignored by those responsible for his care.[2]

Successive reports were finding that care for the mentally ill was in turmoil.[3] One in 20 patients was being released against medical advice,[4] and a government report confirmed that the mentally ill were responsible for one killing every fortnight.[5] Even the Health Minister himself was finally driven to acknowledge that Care in the Community had failed many mentally ill people.[6]

Caroline led the opposition to her own party in the Lords: 'Large numbers of severely mentally ill patients are being transferred into the community,' she said, 'into hostels, where very often they are cared for by untrained volunteers who are inadequately prepared for the realities of mental illness.'[7] In her mind was 22-year-old Jonathan Newby, a volunteer, who, without training, had been left alone to manage a home for the mentally handicapped in Oxford. He was stabbed to death by a schizophrenic.

Caroline was opposed to a return to the dark old days of asylums. Although she believed there were good examples of Care in the Community, too many mentally ill and handicapped people were being stripped of specialist care and support, sometimes with tragic consequences. Meanwhile, there was a huge shortfall in accommodation, and family carers were ageing and dying out. 'The time-bomb is ticking,' added Lord Pearson, himself the father of a mentally handicapped teenage daughter.

Lord Pearson is the honorary President of ResCare,[8] an organization set up and run by families caring for relatives with a mental handicap, and Caroline is one of ResCare's patrons. Together they produced a report offering a possible alternative to Community Care or institutionalization. [9]

They called for village communities as an option, which would offer a richer and more fulfilling life, with better on-site medical care. The Cox-Pearson plan was to convert disused hospital sites into communities, with gardens and clinics, and a range of facilities including physiotherapy and even swimming pools. It would cost less than £25,000 a year – a third of the cost of Care in the Community. Care-effectiveness would be combined with cost-effectiveness.

'There is one group, and it must be almost unique in the history of pressure groups,' observed *The Daily Telegraph*, 'whose preferred solution to certain painful problems is actually cheaper than present local authority policies... and they are being ignored.'[10]

The Conservative government did promise to research the issue, although they said it could take up to three years. They didn't have three years.

When Labour came into power, being in opposition was not such an unusual experience for Caroline. Business as usual, she rose from the unfamiliar side of the chamber to hammer home the issue of community care once again: 'It has been well said that the extent to which a society is civilized can be judged by the care it provides for its most vulnerable members – the same can be said of governments.'[11]

On 17 January 1998, the new Health Secretary announced the imminent scrapping of Community Care.

Beyond party politics

Could Caroline be in the wrong party? She describes Britain's Labour Prime Minister, Tony Blair, as 'well-meaning and able', though whether robust enough to withstand the pressure from his party's left-wing, remains to be seen. 'The far-left who have been fighting for so long haven't gone away,' she asserts. 'They are waiting in the wings and will make a bid to come back.'

So what about the cross-benches? 'I've often been tempted,' she says. 'People won't tar you with being a Tory and it's less controversial and much more comfortable, in many respects. I've been tempted to resign the Tory whip on issues like their treatment of nurses, and make a political statement. But it is always more effective to be a critic from within a party. And what's held me back is I don't think my resignation would be true to where my political values really are, which is what I think Conservatism should be at its best.'

Now in opposition, Caroline set about New Labour on all of her old themes and some new ones – the care of the mentally handicapped, education, the running down of medical services to the military and, of course, Burma, Karabakh and Sudan.

As for Labour's much-vaunted ethical foreign policy, she says: 'I would like to see more of it in practice – the words are good, but I'm not sure we have seen a fundamental sea-change.'

Caroline accuses Tony Blair of authoritarianism and of setting about reform of the House of Lords in a piecemeal and arrogant way. A life peer, she would have nothing to fear from the end of hereditary peerages, and isn't against it on principle, but she is adamantly opposed to an elected second chamber, which she dismisses as a 'lottery'.

'The characteristics of the House of Lords that I have grown to appreciate are that you can ensure there are experts who can challenge ministers and provide constructive amendments to laws; there is also the political independence to allow you to speak and vote according to conscience.

'At the moment we don't know what is coming down the line. To hack away at something that has been part of our nation's history for a thousand years without putting anything up for consideration, discussion or serious analysis is arrogant.'

Caroline was invited to speak about the Lords at a boys' comprehensive school in Highbury, a run-down area of London. 'If any group of schoolkids didn't have a stake in the system it was them,' she says. Feeling like a fish out of water, she described the way the House of Lords worked and the principles behind it, then asked for questions. A well-built Afro-Caribbean lad put up a muscular arm. Caroline braced herself for the first brickbat. The boy asked: 'What are you so worried about Miss, it works, doesn't it?'

She smiles: 'There's a lot of wisdom in that.'

Her influence, despite being relegated to the opposition benches, appears to be undiminished. According to Bishop Maurice Wood, 'Caroline has become more and more influential and is listened to with greater care than ever before – even though she is not actually in government these days. She is very highly reckoned with.'

And as far as posterity is concerned, it is her values that transcend party politics for which Caroline will be best appreciated: her concern for the oppressed, the repressed and the vulnerable – those least able to articulate their needs and their rights. Caroline Cox strives with a passion to be a voice for the voiceless, whether on the home front in the United Kingdom or abroad, speaking for the forgotten peoples in forgotten lands. In the words of one journalist: 'One hour with her and you wonder what you're doing with your life.'[12]

In 1999 Caroline Cox became a grandmother for the ninth time. The previous year she made more than 20 visits abroad, often to the world's war zones and trouble spots. Her human rights commitments increased after the death of her husband, Murray – 'If God gives you a vacuum, you may as well use it constructively.'

'Everybody in this house admires enormously the work that is done by the noble Baroness, Lady Cox, and particularly her work in Sudan. It has brought to light many of the evils inflicted by the NIF regime on civilians throughout the whole country, not merely the South.'

Lord Avebury, Sudan debate, 2 July 1997

'Her courage in visiting Azerbaijan and Armenia and going to the areas of devastation and suffering, her conversations with the victims of violence and starvation among people of both cultural traditions and her representations on their behalf to all the authorities concerned will one day, I hope, deserve a place in the history books.'

Lord Archer of Sandwell, Unstarred question on Armenia and Nagorno Karabakh, 15 December 1992

'She has the power of conscience. Her eyes blaze with conscience. The very effect is compelling. I don't think I have ever known anyone in the Lords whose conscience was so transparent. To say something different from the majority and be listened to and be effective – that is some person. Like all people who ever achieved anything, she has incredible energy. She also has tremendous inspiration and great goodness. Caroline Cox is an incredible woman. She is the most wonderful person in the House of Lords today. She is a Christian champion.'

Lord Longford

NOTES

1. Alice Thomson, 'Tory peers rally to avert defeat on housing sale', *The Times*; Rachel Sylvester, 'Tory rebels fail to halt sale of Forces' homes', *The Daily Telegraph*, 12 July 1996.
2. *The Daily Telegraph*, 28 March 1996.
3. *The Daily Telegraph*, 26 September 1995. According to a Department of Health survey, one in three health authorities was failing to provide proper standards of care: *The Daily Telegraph*, 6 November 1996.
4. *The Daily Telegraph*, 18 September 1996.
5. *The Daily Telegraph*, 18 September 1996. As many as 40 murders had been committed by Community Care patients in the six years the scheme had been running: *The Times*, 17 January 1998.
6. Stephen Dorrell, cited in *The Daily Telegraph*, 6 November 1996.
7. Care in the Community, 25 November 1996, then Community Care, 27 November 1996.
8. National Society for Mentally Handicapped People in Residential Care.
9. 'Made to Care: The Case for Residential and Village Communities for People with a Mental Handicap', 1995.
10. 9 April 1995.
11. *Hansard*, 21 July 1997.
12. Mary Lean, 'For a Change', November/December 1992.

Index

abandoned children 93, 98-99, 108
Abboud, Lt Gen. Ibrahim 270, 289
Abdel-Halim, Asma 330
Abdellah, Farouk Saleh Mohamed 331
abduction 306, 314, 323, 327, 338
Abid (slave) 313
abolition movement 315, 319-20, 348
Abrahamian, Edik 210
Ad-Da'ein (Sudan) 342
Addis Ababa (Ethiopia) 301, 376
accords 271
Adi, Rev. Ambrose 342
Adler, Katherine 95-97, 103, 106
advocacy 177, 196, 201, 204-206, 253, 329, 332, 412
Afewerki, President Issaias 345, 358, 380
Afghanistan 123, 144, 307, 359, 366
African Commission for Human and People's Rights 342
African Rights 274, 333
Agbulag (Nagorno Karabakh) 117
Aghdam (Azerbaijan) 147, 184
Agro-Action 261, 263
Aguer, Gino 300
Ahmad, Muhammad 268
Ahmed, Issa Mahmoud 364
Ajak, Manut Agoth 295-96
Akol, Joseph Akok 383
Akot, Acai 307-308
Akot, Apin Apin 307-308, 384
Akot, Father Benjamin Madol 291
Akwal, Hannah 331
Alazan rockets 139-40, 145
Alberti, Irina 94-95
Aldrich, Dr Richard 246
Algeria 276, 323, 359
Aliyev, President Geidar 183, 186-87, 203
Allah 243, 279, 286, 356, 363
Allam, Andrew 386
Amaras valley 193
Ambler, Philip 253
American Anti-Slavery Group 259
Amet, Akuac 263, 299, 309
Amnesty International 111, 184, 217, 231, 240, 255, 282, 332, 339, 340, 342, 393
Anei, Tong 351
Anglican(ism) 23, 113, 176, 286, 289, 303, 382, 430
Anglo-Armenian Association 163, 195
Anglo-Burmese War 239
Anglo-Egyptian expeditionary force 269
animism 13, 229, 262, 267, 279, 285, 356, 358
Anna (deported Armenian) 133-35
Annan, Lord 46
Ansar, the 268, 270-71, 355-60
Anti-Fascist People's Freedom League (AFPFL) 224
Anti-Slavery International 10, 331, 386
Anti-Slavery Society 319
Antonov 291-93, 295, 391
Apichella, Michael 170
Arab Lawyer's Union 342
Arabization 274, 292 *see also* Islamization
Arakan State 243
Araks River 182
Ararat, Mt 119, 125
Archbishop of Canterbury 289, 302-304
Archer of Sandwell, Lord 438
Armenia 90, 115, 117-18, 121-24, 126-28, 130-33,

135-42, 145, 149-52, 154-55, 157-61, 165-66, 169-71, 179-80, 182-85, 188-89, 191, 194-97, 201-207, 211, 213, 438
Armenian Apostolic Church 171, 187, 191, 205
Armenian earthquake 122, 141
Armenian Parliament 196
Armour, Corinne 215
arms 160, 236, 240, 252, 275, 288, 323, 345, 392
Article XIX 254
Artsakh 122, 211
Aryoun, William 382
ASEAN 236, 255
Asiaweek 248
Asmara (Eritrea) 321, 345, 358, 361, 370, 372, 374
Asmara Declaration 321, 359
Assemblies of God 113, 167
Association of Christian Teachers 412, 427-28
Association of Women 213
Astsaturian, Vladimir 146
Atkinson, David 101, 182, 213
Atlee, Clement 239
atrocity 93, 157, 197, 203, 351 *see also* ethnic cleansing, massacre
Aung San, General 223-25, 239, 245-46
Aung San Suu Kyi 223-25, 236
Aung Than Lei, President 242
Australia 221-22, 229-30, 243, 250-51, 254, 306
Avebury, Lord 187, 236-37, 249, 255, 276, 322-24, 438
Awiel counties 261-62, 337, 356
Azerbaijan 115, 117-28, 130-31, 133-37, 139-40, 142, 144, 147-48, 151-52, 154-63, 167-68, 170, 174, 178, 182-91, 195-97, 201-204, 206, 212, 438
Azerbaijan government 184, 197, 203
Azerbaijani Communist Party 123, 183
Azeri Motorized Infantry (366th) 158, 197
Babanusa (Sudan) 337
Babayan, Samvel 189
Babikir, Terefi 389
back-bench rebellion 421, 434-436
backlash 324-36, 383, 406
Baden-Powell, Baron Robert 23, 78
Baggara warriors 348
Baghdad 389-90, 392
Baghdad Caliphate 317
Bahr el-Ghazal 285, 289, 291, 296, 306, 322, 342, 377, 388-89, 393
Baku (Azerbaijan) 120-21, 128, 131, 133, 136, 138, 148, 159, 182, 186-87, 189, 197, 201, 203
Balayan, Zori 118, 122, 125, 136-37, 144, 155, 165, 167, 180, 188, 205, 211
Baltimore Sun, The 348, 350, 353
Banatvala, Nick 91
Bangkok Nation 249
Bangkok Post 250
Bany, William Nyon 271-72, 321
Baptist 204, 243
Barka region 362
al-Bashir, Col. Omar Hassan Ahmed 273-74, 287, 326, 359, 377, 386
Bazil, Odette 163
BBC 80, 179-80, 198, 245-46, 306, 312, 316, 330, 372, 385
Bedelian, Maria 162
Beginning Religion 423
Beja Congress 358, 362, 365-66, 368-69, 377
Beja people 358-60, 364-66, 368-69, 372-76
Belgium 55, 267
Beloff, Lord 414